Intellectual Origins of the
English Revolution

Christopher Hill

Intellectual Origins of the English Revolution

CLARENDON PRESS · OXFORD
1980

Oxford University Press, Walton Street, Oxford OX2 6DP

OXFORD LONDON GLASGOW
NEW YORK TORONTO MELBOURNE WELLINGTON
KUALA LUMPUR SINGAPORE JAKARTA HONG KONG TOKYO
DELHI BOMBAY CALCUTTA MADRAS KARACHI
NAIROBI DAR ES SALAAM CAPE TOWN

Published in the United States by
Oxford University Press, New York

© *Oxford University Press 1965*
  First Published 1965
  Reprinted 1966
  Reprinted with corrections as paperback 1980

British Library Cataloguing in Publication Data

Hill, Christopher, *b. 1912*
    Intellectual origins of the English revolution.
    1. England—Civilization—16th century
    2. England—Civilization—17th century
    I. Title
    942.05′5   DA356   65-3182

    ISBN 0-19-822635-7

Printed in Great Britain by
The Camelot Press, Southampton

for T. S. Gregory

And well he therefore does, and well has guessed,
Who in his age has always forward pressed:
And knowing not where Heaven's choice may light,
Girds yet his sword, and ready stands to fight.

A. MARVELL
The First Anniversary of the Government under O. C.

PREFACE

THIS book is an expansion of the Ford Lectures delivered in Oxford in Hilary Term, 1962. My thanks are due in the first place to the Electors for doing me the honour of choosing me for this lectureship; and secondly to the Master and Fellows of Balliol College who gave me a sabbatical term in which to finish the writing. A much abbreviated version of the lectures appeared in *The Listener* between 31 May and 5 July 1962.

The origin of this book in lectures should be borne in mind by the reader. I was advancing a thesis, not attempting to sketch the intellectual history of England in the fifty years before 1640. I therefore picked out evidence which seemed to me to support my case. So, though I hope I have suppressed no facts which make against me, I have often (e.g. in biographical particulars) omitted facts which seemed to me 'neutral'. When I mention the Countess of Carlisle at p. 143 I describe her as Pym's friend, because Pym has occurred in an earlier chapter: I do not add that she was also the friend of the Earl of Strafford, since Strafford has no place in my story. If I had been writing an intellectual history of the period, I should have had to differentiate more sharply than I do between the experimental scientists, the Baconians, and Gresham College professors on the one hand, and on the other the inheritors of the alchemical, astrological, neo-Platonist, and magical traditions. During the revolutionary period the cleavage between the spokesmen of the two attitudes became as sharp as that between Presbyterians and sectaries: indeed the two quarrels often coincided. But I believe that before the civil war men were less conscious of what divided than of what united them, just as 'Puritans' were more aware of their common dislike of Archbishop Laud than of the theoretical differences over which they were soon to disagree. In seeking the intellectual origins of the English Revolution I was more struck by the unexpected connexions which forced themselves upon me than by divisions. Acontius links Thomas Blundeville, the Earl of Leicester, John Goodwin, and John Dury

(p. 175); Prince Henry links the founder of the Lumleian Lectures, Edward Wright, and again John Dury (p. 215). But I am aware that I have dealt inadequately with what separated the experimental scientists from the heirs of Paracelsus. I hope this complicated subject will be tackled by those more competent to deal with it than I.

Secondly, this is not a total account of the origins of the civil war, obviously, nor even of the non-material factors leading up to it. I deal only indirectly with Puritanism; I say nothing about the irrational motives which may have stirred the Parliamentarian rank and file—fear of Catholicism, prophecies, rumours, and so on. It is far from my intention to argue that the intellectual trends which I discuss were the only ones that mattered, or even the most important. I want merely to suggest that they existed, were of some significance, and have been neglected.

One advantage of lectures is that they have no footnotes. In preparing these for publication, I found that I had made some generalizations, with intent to provoke, which could not be substantiated without lengthy digressions or notes. Since my object was not to write a definitive work, but with luck to start a discussion, I have ventured to leave a few such remarks naked of documentation, hoping that readers, and especially my kindly professional colleagues, will give me the benefit of the occasion. I have trespassed into the fields of too many experts not to feel in need of indulgence.

I have drawn a great deal upon the work of others. I am very conscious of my indebtedness to Professors B. Farrington, F. R. Johnson, R. F. Jones, E. G. R. Taylor, L. B. Wright and Commander Waters; and especially to Dr. S. F. Mason. I owe my interest in the history of science mainly to the stimulus of his books and articles, and still more of his conversation during the all-too-brief period when he lectured on the History of Science at Oxford. Articles by Dr. Mason and Mrs. Joan Simon in *The Modern Quarterly*, vol. iv, no. 2 (1949), first made me think about the general theme of this book. I am also grateful to the following for generous help of various kinds: Mr. C. B. L. Barr, Dr. A. C. Crombie, Mr. J. G. Crowther, Professor Mark Curtis, Professor A. H. Dodd, Professor K. H. D. Haley, Mr. and Mrs. G. D. G. Hall, Mr. D. M. Hallowes,

Dr. W. O. Hassall, Mr. Charles Hobday, Dr. H. F. Kearney, Professor J. Le Patourel, Mr. Jack Lindsay, Professor L. Makkai, Mr. Dipak Nandy, Mr. Leo Miller, Mr. R. M. Ogilvie, Mr. Christopher Platt, Mr. Colin Platt, Professor D. B. Quinn, Mr. T. H. H. Rae, Mr. K. V. Thomas, Professor H. R. Trevor-Roper, Mr. Peter Wallis, Dr. C. V. Wedgwood and Mr. F. P. White. The Clarendon Press's reader corrected many careless slips, and helped me to express myself more clearly. Mr. R. S. Roberts very kindly read proofs of part of Chapter II, and Miss Margaret Bamford and Mr. Robin Briggs undertook the labour of reading the whole book in proof. The errors which remain are my own. Above all I am indebted to my wife, without whose encouragement and support the lectures would never have been delivered, let alone published. Professor F. S. Fussner's excellent *The Historical Revolution* unfortunately came out too late for me to make more than occasional reference to it. I should have approached Ralegh rather differently if I had read Professor Fussner first.

Where no reference is given for biographical details, they will be found (I hope) in the *Dictionary of National Biography*, that much maligned and indispensable work.

The dedication acknowledges a thirty-five-year-old debt which can never be repaid. How can one ever be sufficiently grateful to the person who first showed one that all accepted truths, just because they are accepted, tend to become lies?

C. H.

Oxford, June 1963

CONTENTS

ABBREVIATIONS

Add. MSS.	British Museum, Additional Manuscripts.
C.J.	*Commons' Journals.*
C.S.P.D.	*Calendar of State Papers, Domestic.*
C.S.P.Col.,	
Ven.	*Calendar of State Papers, Colonial,* or *Venetian.*
D.N.B.	*Dictionary of National Biography.*
Econ. H.R.	*Economic History Review.*
E.H.R.	*English Historical Review.*
H.L.B.	*Huntington Library Bulletin.*
H.L.Q.	*Huntington Library Quarterly.*
H.M.C.	Historical Manuscripts Commission.
L.J.	*Lords' Journals.*
L.Q.R.	*Law Quarterly Review.*
M.L.N.	*Modern Language Notes.*
N.R.S.	*Commons' Debates, 1621,* ed. W. Notestein, F. H. Relf, and H. Simpson (Yale U.P., 1935).
P.M.L.A.	*Proceedings of the Modern Language Association.*
P. and P.	*Past and Present.*
S.P.	*Studies in Philology.*
T.R.H.S.	*Transactions of the Royal Historical Society.*
U.P.	University Press.
V.C.H.	*Victoria County History.*

Unless otherwise stated, Bacon is quoted from the edition by J. Spedding, R. L. Ellis, and D. D. Heath, 14 volumes, 1862–74. Since there is no standard edition of Ralegh, I have used those which I happen to possess: Ralegh, *History*, refers to *The History of the World*, Edinburgh, 6 volumes, 1820; Ralegh, *Works*, to T. Birch's two-volume edition of 1751. G. Hakewill's *An Apologie or Declaration of the Power and Providence of God* is cited as Hakewill, *Apologie*. I have used the third edition of 1635. It was first published in 1627.

Spelling, capitalization, and punctuation have been modernized in all quotations, but not in titles of books.

I

INTRODUCTION

> When you have considered that ... the vicissitudes of
> things ordained by Providence require a general pre-
> disposition in men's hearts to co-operate with fate toward
> the changes appointed to succeed in the fullness of their
> time, you will think it less strange that Britain, which was
> but yesterday the theatre of war and desolation, should
> today be the school of arts and court of all the Muses. ...
> It hath been the reformation [of the state of learning]
> that drew on the change; not the desire of change which
> pretendeth the reformation.
>
> W. CHARLETON, *The Immortality of the Human Soul* (1657), pp. 49–52

My title is intended to recall that of Daniel Mornet's *Les Origines intellectuelles de la Révolution française*. In this book M. Mornet discussed Montesquieu, Voltaire, Diderot, Rousseau—the intellectual influences which all historians recognize when they try to explain the French Revolution. His title has always seemed to me something of a challenge. It is perhaps not so heretical now as it was thirty years ago to hold that there was more in common between the seventeenth-century English Revolution and the French Revolution of 1789 than traditional English historiography allowed, and that comparisons and contrasts between them can be fruitful and illuminating. But one fact on which there is wide agreement among historians is that the English Revolution had no intellectual origins. It just happened, in the typically British empirical way in which we always like to imagine ourselves muddling through: in a fit of absence of mind. 'There was no Jean-Jacques Rousseau or Karl Marx of the English Revolution.' I might have cited many historians to that effect: in fact the words quoted were my own. And yet, almost by definition, a great revolution cannot take place without ideas. Most men have to believe quite strongly in some ideal before they will kill or be killed. If there was no Rousseau, perhaps

there were Montesquieus, Voltaires, and Diderots of the
English Revolution?

There were. The Bible, especially the Geneva Bible with its
highly political marginal notes, came near to being a revolution-
ists' handbook, not for the last time in history. Mr. Hampden,
we are told, had his vade-mecum in Davila's *History of the Civil
Wars of France*.[1] Sir John Eliot's vade-mecum was Sir Walter
Ralegh's *Prerogative of Parliaments*; Ralegh's *History of the World*
is the only book Oliver Cromwell is known to have recommended. John Lilburne had the Bible in one hand, the writings
of Sir Edward Coke in the other. Levellers and Diggers looked
back to the heretical tradition, to Lollards and Foxe's martyrs.
Milton drew on Knox and Buchanan. The republican Henry
Nevile spoke of 'honest John Calvin' as the originator of the
ideas of him and his like.[2] If we lift our gaze beyond merely
political events, we shall remember that in the seventeenth
century the scientific revolution was completed in England,
a revolution which Professor Butterfield regards as the greatest landmark since the rise of Christianity.[3] In the closely
related Battle of the Books, between the Ancients and the
Moderns, those who believed that it was impossible to improve
on the wisdom of classical antiquity and those who thought that
knowledge was cumulative—in this battle, victory by the end
of the seventeenth century lay with the Moderns. In both fields
the crucial name is that of Francis Bacon: the connexion of
Baconianism with the Parliamentary cause is a subject to which
I shall return later.

A few preliminary cautions. First, I am sceptical about
pedigrees of ideas—A is influenced by B who got his ideas from
C, and that explains action Z. It is always easy to construct
chains of causes once you know what you have to explain.[4]
Nor do ideas evolve in a vacuum. 'The great philosophers',
Mornet wrote in concluding his *Origines intellectuelles*, 'were not
revealing unknown lands: they were. mapping those known. If
the old régime had been threatened only by ideas, the old
régime would have run no risk. The poverty of the people,

[1] Sir Philip Warwick, *Memoirs of the Reign of King Charles I* (1813), p. 265. See
p. 278 below.   [2] See pp. 208–9, 286–7 below.
[3] H. Butterfield, *Origins of Modern Science* (1949), p. 174.
[4] Cf. C. H. and K. George, *The Protestant Mind of the English Reformation, 1570–
1640* (Princeton, 1961), p. 398.

the political *malaise*, were also needed to give the ideas leverage. But the ideas set men in motion.'[1]

Ideas do not advance merely by their own logic. There is clearly a relation between Luther's doctrine of the priesthood of all believers and the practice of lay preaching by many sects in the sixteen-forties, even of preaching by women. Yet a long time intervened between Luther's enunciation of the principle and Mrs. Attaway's tub-thumping practice. The time-lag can be explained by the repressive power of the Church; but another way of putting this is to say that the logical implications of Luther's doctrine could not be realized in practice in England until political circumstances—the collapse of the hierarchy and the central government—were propitious. Ideas were all-important for the individuals whom they impelled into action; but the historian must attach equal importance to the circumstances that gave these ideas their chance. Revolutions are not made without ideas, but they are not made by intellectuals. Steam is essential to driving a railway engine; but neither a locomotive nor a permanent way can be built out of steam. In this book I shall be dealing with the steam.

Yet a sociological approach to intellectual history carries its own risks. Marx himself did not fall into the error of thinking that men's ideas were merely a pale reflection of their economic needs, with no history of their own; but some of his successors, including many who would not call themselves Marxists, have been far more economic-determinist than Marx. It seems to me that any body of thought which plays a major part in history— Luther's, Rousseau's, Marx's own—'takes on' because it meets the needs of significant groups in the society in which it comes into prominence. This is the very opposite of saying that once we have related the ideas of a Luther to his society, then they can be disregarded. There is a danger that historians, trapped in the Namier method, may too lightly assume that the ideas which swayed men and women in the past can be dismissed as hypocrisy, rationalizations, or irrelevancies.

So, although this book will be concerned mainly with intellectual history, I hope I shall make it clear that the thinkers were not isolated from their societies. I shall take as my model

[1] D. Mornet, *Les Origines intellectuelles de la Révolution française* (Paris, 1933), p. 476. I have translated rather freely.

here one of my predecessors in these lectures, Professor Tawney, who was too wise to study religion and the rise of capitalism except in the closest connexion with the agrarian problem of the sixteenth century and with usury; and who associated Harrington's interpretation of his age with the rise of the gentry and with business and politics under James I. But I shall not forget, I hope, that English intellectual history must be related to 'the general crisis of the seventeenth century'.[1] England's intellectual crisis is part of a wider European movement of thought, which itself bears some relation to an economic and social crisis. Since my subject is England, I may seem not to refer as often as I should to this European background. But I shall return to it in my last chapter, and I hope that its presence will be assumed even when it is not specifically mentioned.

Second, the attempt to draw parallels between the English and the French Revolutions has its dangers. The men of 1789 had English experience to draw on, the experience of a successful revolution culminating in 1688, the obverse of subversive anarchy. But seventeenth-century England had very little to look back to. I shall discuss later the influence on England of the Revolt of the Netherlands and of the wars of religion in France:[2] it was considerable. But the Dutch Revolt was directed against an alien and papist king. In France the Huguenots were supporting first the heir to the throne and then the legitimate king. So in each the problems were different from those of seventeenth-century England. Neither stimulated conscious revolutionary thinking about society in the way that English experience, even as summed up by Locke, stimulated it in eighteenth-century France. So we should not expect too much political sophistication in our English revolutionary thinkers. We should indeed recall that even Montesquieu, Diderot, and Voltaire, radical though their criticisms of the old régime were, still hoped for reform, not revolution.

The history of ideas necessarily deals with trends to which there are individual exceptions. I shall argue that on the whole

---

[1] E. Hobsbawm, 'The General Crisis of the European Economy in the 17th century', *P. and P.*, nos. 5 and 6; H. R. Trevor-Roper, 'The General Crisis of the 17th century', ibid., no. 16; and a general discussion, ibid., no. 18.

[2] See pp. 278–87 below.

the ideas of the scientists favoured the Puritan and Parliamentarian cause. I shall not be unduly depressed if it is retorted
that individual Roman Catholics like Nicholas Hill (if he was
one)[1] made important contributions to the new spirit; or that
an individual Parliamentarian like William Prynne attacked
Copernicus;[2] or that Charles I's physician William Harvey
was a royalist during the civil war. Individual Puritans like
Richard Holdsworth,[3] and individual believers in religious
toleration like William Chilingworth, also took the King's side:
yet by and large it remains true that Puritanism and religious
toleration received more encouragement after Parliament's
victory than they had ever done under the old régime.

The problem that I want to discuss is so obvious that we are
apt to overlook it. For as long as history recorded there had
been kings, lords, and bishops in England. The thinking of all
Englishmen had been dominated by the Established Church.
Yet, within less than a decade, successful war was levied against
the King; bishops and the House of Lords were abolished; and
Charles I was executed in the name of his people. How did men
get the nerve to do such unheard-of things? We have come to
regard execution as an occupational risk of kings, but this has
become true only in the last 170 years. Medieval kings in plenty
had been assassinated, not always in the nicest of ways; but the
sanctity that hedged a king had never before been publicly
breached. The execution of Mary Queen of Scots in 1587 came
dangerously near to setting a precedent: Good Queen Bess
would, very naturally, have preferred the old English method
of assassination. The act of 1649 was so uniquely shocking that
on hearing of it, we are told, 'women miscarried, men fell into
melancholy, some with consternations expired'.[4] Men, that is
to say, do not break lightly with the past: if they are to challenge

---

[1] For Hill see pp. 144–5 below.

[2] W. M. Lamont, *Marginal Prynne* (1963), pp. 13–14.

[3] For Harvey see my 'William Harvey and the Idea of Monarchy', *P. and P.*,
no. 27; for Holdsworth see pp. 56, 307–8 below.

[4] W. Sanderson, *A Complete History of the Life and Raigne of King Charles* (1658), p.
1139; cf. *Memoirs of the Life of Mr. Ambrose Barnes* (ed. W. H. D. Longstaffe, Surtees
Soc., 1867), pp. 108–9. Among those alleged to have 'with consternations expired'
were James Gordon, Viscount Aboyne, and John Geree, the Puritan divine
(*D.N.B.*). (I am indebted to Dr. C. V. Wedgwood for the first three references, and
to Mr. K. V. Thomas for Geree.) *Eikon Basilike* (1649) started the fashion of comparing Charles the Martyr with Jesus Christ.

conventionally accepted standards they must have an alternative body of ideas to support them.

Puritanism is the most obvious such body of ideas: you could brave the King of England if you were obeying the orders of the King of Kings. I do not propose to deal directly with Puritanism. There has been a large literature on the subject since Gardiner first invented 'the Puritan Revolution' a century ago. Tawney's *Religion and the Rise of Capitalism*, Haller's *Rise of Puritanism*, and other recent work on the social and economic causes of the civil war, have shown how Puritanism attracted and organized the nameless urban and rural unprivileged classes who supplied most of the volunteers for the Parliamentary armies and who paid for them. Puritanism was perhaps the most important complex of ideas that prepared men's minds for revolution, but it was not the only one. After two decades of economic interpretations of the English civil war, the time, I believe, is ripe for a revival of interest in the ideas that motivated the seventeenth-century revolutionaries.

So, leaving Puritanism aside, I propose to discuss some of the other ideas which seem to me relevant, directing my attention particularly to those which appealed to 'the middling sort', to merchants, artisans, and yeomen. This for two reasons. First, Parliament could never have defeated the King without their enthusiastic backing. 'Freeholders and tradesmen are the support of religion *and civility* in the land', Richard Baxter wrote.[1] Those who cite that passage, including myself, have perhaps neglected the significance of the words which I have italicized. Secondly, it is the expansion of these classes, in numbers and in wealth, which offers the most obviously *new* social fact in England during the century before 1640. Throughout the Middle Ages weavers had been associated with heresy, the urban poor with millenarian revolt. But the heresies and the revolts had been suppressed before the ideas associated with them had attained to the dignity of a system—so far, at least, as we know: the defeated leave little evidence. But in the sixteenth century, thanks to the growing strength of the manufacturing element in society, to its invention of printing, and to the Reformation, new bodies of ideas began to be formulated to challenge those traditionally accepted. This was true of science

[1] R. Baxter, *Reliquiae Baxterianae* (ed. M. Sylvester, 1696), i. 89.

no less than of theology: Paracelsus and Copernicus were contemporaries of Luther, and Paracelsus supported the German peasants in 1525.

Sixteenth-century middle-class Englishmen, encouraged in literacy so as to be able to read the Bible, taught at grammar schools which merchants had founded in order to free education from clerical control, grew up into a confusing world. Traditional ideas were in retreat, but no new synthesis had replaced them. Humanism, with its concern for the education of a ruling class, and with the classics to the exclusion of the vernacular, could not appeal to the 'middling sort'; yet the humanist emphasis on the education of *the individual*, like the Protestant emphasis on the individual conscience, lent itself to more democratic interpretations. The urban way of life, pragmatic, utilitarian, and individualistic, where things mattered more than words, experience more than authority, was in harmony with new trends in Protestant and scientific thought. But nothing was clear-cut. Paracelsan chemistry, with its stress on experiment, was still entangled with alchemy. Some magicians and astrologers accepted the heliocentric system. There is a danger in the history of science of giving marks for being 'right' —e.g. to Copernicus, whose ideas were not scientifically confirmed until the seventeenth century—and of dismissing others as 'wrong'—e.g. astrologers and alchemists, forgetting that the eminent mathematician John Dee was an astrologer and that Robert Boyle was to transmute alchemy into chemistry; forgetting that there were Fellows of the Royal Society who believed in witches; forgetting that both Napier and Newton attached more importance to their researches into the *Apocalypse* than to logarithms or the law of gravitation.[1] For our purposes at least, what subsequent history pronounced to be 'right' is unimportant: Newton's obsession with problems of Biblical chronology was almost certainly a stimulus to his scientific imagination.

The most striking feature, then, of the intellectual life of pre-revolutionary England is its confusion and ferment. 'The

[1] There were twenty-one editions of Napier's *Plaine Discovery of the Whole Revelation of St. John* between 1593 and 1700, the last year to which Napier thought the world could survive. Newton must have seemed far more eccentric at the end of the century than Napier at its beginning. Both were also interested in alchemy.

vision of reality that had supported the rational consciousness
of man for a thousand years was fading.'[1] In retrospect Renaissance and Reformation, the discovery of America and the
new astronomy, had been far more successful in undermining
old assumptions and prejudices than in substituting new truths.
Some of the new ideas—those of Machiavelli and Giordano
Bruno, for instance—must have seemed terribly wicked to
timid traditionalists. (And of course, as the names just quoted
show, this is not merely an English phenomenon: we are in the
age of Montaigne.) There is no need to quote the inevitable
lines from Donne to show that the new philosophy called *all* in
doubt—assumptions about society as well as about the universe
—or that *all* coherence was gone. Long before Donne, Gabriel
Harvey wrote that there were 'every day, fresh-spun new
opinions: heresy in divinity, in philosophy, in humanity, in
manners, grounded much upon hearsay; doctors contemned:
the text known of most, understood of few, magnified of all,
practised of none'.[2] In 1623 Drummond of Hawthornden
echoed Donne to say, 'The element of fire is quite put out, the
air is but water rarefied, the earth is found to move and is no
more the centre of the universe, is turned into a magnet; stars
are not fixed, but swim in the ethereal space, comets are
mounted above the planets; some affirm there is another world
of men and sensitive creatures . . . in the moon; the sun is
lost. . . . Thus sciences, by the diverse motions of this globe of
the brain of man, are become opinions, nay errors, and leave
the imagination in a thousand labyrinths. What is all we know
compared with what we know not?'[3] Drayton, soon after
Donne, said:

> Certainly there's scarce one found that now
> Knows what t'approve, or what to disallow;
> All arsey-varsey, nothing is its own,
> But to our proverb, all turned upside down. . . .
> Where hell is heaven, and heaven is now turned hell.[4]

[1] M. H. Carré, *Phases of Thought in England* (1949), p. 224.
[2] Quoted by H. Haydn, *The Counter-Renaissance* (New York, 1950), p. 13.
[3] W. Drummond, 'A Cypresse Grove', in *Poetical Works* (ed. L. E. Kastner, 1913),
ii. 78.
[4] M. Drayton, 'To my noble friend Master William Browne, of the evil time', in
Works (ed. J. W. Hebel, 1961), iii. 209–11.

'We have seen the best of our time', said Gloucester in *King Lear*, after a similar speech.[1] 'Our age was iron, and rusty too', Donne concluded.[2]

We should not underestimate the depth of this spiritual crisis in which men found themselves. Emphasis on man's 'double heart' is familiar to students of the literature of the time.[3] The despair described in so many autobiographies of the period is too facilely ascribed to Calvinist theology: Calvinists thought it characteristic of the Anabaptists.[4] It was surely as much a sympton as a cause of the melancholy which Robert Burton set himself to anatomize. The great physician William Harvey told a future bishop during the Interregnum that he had met with more diseases generated from the mind than from any other cause. A similar observation was to be made about the French Revolution.[5]

Whilst the intellectuals despaired and anatomized, whilst doctors prescribed elephant tusks as a remedy for melancholy, our merchants and artisans, confident in their ability to handle things, busy, as Professor Jordan has shown us, modernizing the institutions of their society,[6] were in search of an ideology. They looked first and longest, naturally, to the Church: hence the hunger for sermons which is characteristic of the age. But too often they looked in vain. Badly paid parsons were rarely better educated than their urban congregations: Whitgift, Bancroft, and Laud were apt to silence the livelier preachers who tried out unconventional ideas.[7] They looked in vain to the universities, which were still seminaries for training

---

[1] *Lear*, Act I, scene ii.

[2] Donne, 'An Anatomie of the World', in *Complete Poetry and Selected Prose* (1929), p. 208.

[3] W. Perkins, *Workes* (1609–13), ii. 5; R. Sibbes, *The Soules Conflict* (1635), p. 469; Joseph Hall, *Works* (1837–9), viii. 147; Donne, *Complete Poetry and Selected Prose*, p. 285; F. Greville, *Poems and Dramas* (ed. G. Bullough, n.d., ?1939), i. 194–5; R. Burton, *An Anatomy of Melancholy* (Everyman ed.), i. 11–13; Sir F. Beaumont, *Poems* (ed. E. Robinson, 1914), p. 13; A. Marvell, *Poems* (ed. H. M. Margoliouth, 1927), p. 20; A. Cowley, *Poems* (ed. A. R. Waller, 1905), p. 113; J. Bunyan, *Works* (ed. G. Offor, 1860), iii. 253–4. See my *Puritanism and Revolution* (1958), pp. 340–2.

[4] Cartwright spoke in 1609 of 'the Anabaptists' error of desperation' (ed. A. Peel and L. H. Carlson, *Cartwrightiana*, 1951, p. 77). Cf. also Bacon, *Works*, viii. 93.

[5] T. H. Buckle, *Miscellaneous and Posthumous Works* (1872), iii. 631.

[6] W. K. Jordan, *Philanthropy in England, 1480–1660* (1959), *passim*.

[7] See my *Society and Puritanism* (1964), pp. 40, 51.

ministers, and which were becoming finishing schools for the
gentry. There were many, very many, clever young men at
Oxford and Cambridge; but there was little new thought. The
new ideas which I want to consider came from laymen, not
from clerics; and from men not associated with university
teaching.[1]

Against this confusion and failure of nerve among the
traditional intellectuals, we must set the political and artistic
achievements of the new England in which our self-educated
thoughtful artisans and merchants grew up, and which they
were helping to create. The fifty-odd years between the defeat
of the Spanish Armada and 1640 fall into two sharply contrasting periods. The twenty-six years from 1588 to the publication of Ralegh's *History of the World* saw the peaceful union of
the crowns of England and Scotland, the defeat of Spain, the
subjugation of Ireland, the beginnings of the colonization of
America, the foundation of the East India Company. They
also saw the publication of the *Faerie Queene*, of *Arcadia* and Sir
Philip Sidney's poems, most of the poetry of Drayton, Daniel,
Campion, and the beginnings of English verse satire, whilst
Donne's and Ralegh's poems circulated in manuscript; the
tales of Deloney and Nashe; the performance of all Shakespeare's, Marlowe's, Greene's, Chapman's, Tourneur's, Marston's
plays, the best of Jonson's, Middleton's, Dekker's, Beaumont
and Fletcher's, and Webster's; Fulke Greville's plays and *Life
of Sidney* had been written. These years also saw the publication
of the Marprelate Tracts, the works of Perkins and Hooker,
the Authorized Version, Bacon's *Essays*, Coke's *Reports*, the
foundation of the Bodleian Library. Pride in England's
historical achievement was summed up by the full edition of
Sir Thomas Smith's *Common-welth of England* (1589), by Hakluyt's
Principal Navigations, Camden's *Remaines . . . Concerning Britaine*
and *Britannia* (English translation 1610), Speed's *History of
Great Britaine*, Stow's *Survay of London*, Daniel's *Historie of England*,
Ralegh's *History of the World*; and by the many editions of John
Foxe's *Acts and Monuments*, first published in 1563. This was the
heyday of the popular theatre, and historical plays were among
the most popular in its repertoire.[2] The vernacular had arrived

---

[1] See Appendix.
[2] A. Harbage, *Shakespeare and the Rival Traditions* (New York, 1952), pp. 85, 260.

with a vengeance; Puttenham's *Arte of English Poesie* and Sidney's *Defence of Poesie* proclaimed its right to respect.

That rather tedious enumeration was necessary to make the contrast with the next twenty-five years, from whose publications one can pick out only George Herbert's poems (licensed after long arguments with the censor), *Comus*, and *Lycidas*; and a few plays by Jonson, Middleton, Massinger, and Ford: though for completeness we must mention Wither, Quarles, George Sandys, Randolph, and Carew. Apart from Milton and Herrick (whose poems remained mostly unpublished) there was little originality; poets drew on the traditions established by Spenser, Jonson, Donne, and Shakespeare.[1] In prose the typical works were Donne's and Andrewes's *Sermons* and Burton's *Anatomy of Melancholy*; much of the work of Bacon, Ralegh, and Coke remained unpublished until after 1640. The sudden exuberance and national pride of the earlier period gave place to the gloom and introspection of the late Jacobean and Caroline age, in which the confident optimism of Bacon and Hakewill seemed out of place: in which the fussy and self-important Samuel Purchas constituted himself heir to the dedicated patriot Richard Hakluyt. The idea of the progressive decay of nature was more specifically expressed and defended in these years than ever before.[2] This idea, as we shall see, was a main target of Bacon, Hakewill, and the defenders of the Moderns against the Ancients, of science against scholasticism.[3]

National disgrace caused or at least accompanied the change. There were the massacre of Amboyna, unavenged as long as the monarchy lasted, the fiasco of English policy in the Thirty Years War, followed by war with Scotland: colonization of America owed everything to private enterprise and nothing to state support. Royal policy broke the boom which began with the peace of 1604. At court these were the scandalous years. One royal favourite was convicted of poisoning; another was suspected of unnatural vice; a Lord Treasurer and a Lord Chancellor were dismissed after being successively convicted of corruption; Lord Audley was sentenced to death for 'sodomy,

---

[1] I am indebted to Mr. Charles Hobday for this point.

[2] V. Harris, *All Coherence Gone* (Chicago, 1949), pp. 148–9. Mr. Harris dates the appearance of a more optimistic atmosphere from the third edition of Hakewill's *Apologie for the Providence of God* in 1635. All his examples, however, come from after 1640.   [3] See pp. 90, 199–203, 224 below.

unnatural adultery, and incest',[1] and was a papist to boot. At court offices and honours were openly sold, judges dismissed for refusing to give verdicts desired by the government. Economic policy lurched from the disaster of the Cokayne project to the abuse of monopolies. At a time when most Englishmen regarded popery as anti-national, diplomatic relations were restored with the Vatican. Absolutism on the continental model was believed to threaten. Already Fulke Greville's *Life of Sidney*, probably written between 1610 and 1614, sharply contrasts the glories of the later Elizabethan age with the 'decrepit', 'effeminate', and degenerate age into which Sidney's friend had survived.[2] Glorification of Elizabeth was soon to become fashionable among the Puritans. The gloom which followed the death of Prince Henry in 1612 seems exaggerated, important as he had been in many spheres of intellectual life: but men sensed that an epoch had ended.[3]

The contrast between our two periods is particularly striking if we look at the social orientation of literature. From the second period we recall no popular pamphlets and tales like those of Marprelate, Deloney, and Dekker; no popular religious works like Arthur Dent's *Plain Mans Pathway to Heaven* (1601) and Lewis Bayley's *Practice of Piety* (1612 or 1613). There is all the difference in the world between the pastoral of Sidney, Spenser, Wither, Browne (and Milton)—consciously intended to convey a message[4]—and the mere escapism to which dons and some country gentlemen increasingly resorted. Miss Røstvig dates very precisely 'between 1612 and 1616' the first appearance of 'the Stoic theme of the happiness of country life'. 'The high-tide of English neo-Stoicism came in the second quarter of the seventeenth century.'[5] The significance of this for our purposes is that Miss Røstvig identifies her neo-Stoics with the defenders of the Ancients, the opponents of modern

---

[1] I quote from the shocked record of the Puritan E. Burghall, *Providence Improved* (ed. J. Hall, Lancashire and Cheshire Record Soc., 1889), p. 4.

[2] Cf. D. Bush, *English Literature in the Earlier Seventeenth Century* (2nd ed., 1962), pp. 230–1. Rather naturally, the *Life* was not published until after the fall of the monarchy.

[3] See pp. 213–19 below.

[4] Greville makes it clear that the allegorical form of works like *Arcadia* and *The Faerie Queene* 'is an enabling of free-born spirits to the greatest affairs of state' (*Life of Sidney*, ed. N. Smith, 1907, pp. 2–3. First published 1652).

[5] Maren-Sofie Røstvig, *The Happy Man* (Oslo, 1954), pp. 101, 113, 120.

science, and of the Puritans.[1] The Puritan and Parliamentarian George Wither, though he could turn out a poem in praise of rural retreat on occasion, roundly denounced those who withdrew into 'an heremitical solitariness' as 'weak, . . . slothful and unjust', men who 'wrong their country and their friends'.[2]

George Herbert and Nicholas Ferrar abandoned Court and City for God. Shakespeare stopped writing for the stage in his forties, as the cheap popular theatre ceased to exist, and court and stage became more closely identified. 'The courtly and fashionable sections of the London public were thus separating from the rest. . . . The dramatists now tended to identify themselves with the dominant Cavalier section of their public. The age of a national drama was over.'[3] This may have been partly due to the tightening of the censorship in the pre-revolutionary period, and the consequent voluntary abstention of many men from publication. Much of the best writing was anti-court in tone—Massinger, Middleton, Wither, Milton.[4] But by 1613 the light had gone out of English music too.[5] And the age of a national church had also come to an end. The Authorized Version, the product of co-operation between divines of all shades of opinion, was the last great act of a Church to which virtually all Englishmen wanted to belong. Twenty years later Laud was, by Elizabethan standards, as narrow and one-sided as William Prynne. In religion as in literature, causes deeper than government repression were dividing the nation. This is our starting-point.

[1] Ibid., pp. 53–56; cf. my *Puritanism and Revolution*, pp. 349–53.

[2] G. Wither, *Abuses Stript and Whipt* (1622), in *Juvenilia* (Spenser Soc. reprint, n.d.), i. 272.

[3] L. G. Salingar, 'The Social Setting', in *The Age of Shakespeare* (ed. B. Ford, Penguin Books, 1955), p. 45; cf. pp. 110, 429, 440. Cf. Harbage, *Shakespeare and the Rival Traditions, passim*; Glynne Wickham, *Early English Stages*, ii, *1576–1660*, Part 1 (1963), *passim*.

[4] I owe this point to Mr. Hobday. We should add the pamphlets of Thomas Scott (see pp. 206–8 below).

[5] I owe this point to discussions with Dr. H. K. Andrews. Cf. 'a new trend' in English painting from about 1616, caused by the decline of miniature painting (E. Mercer, *English Art, 1553–1625*, 1962, pp. 184–5, 205–10).

II

LONDON SCIENCE AND MEDICINE

> Mechanics and artificers (for whom the true natural
> philosophy should be principally intended).
>
> T. SPRAT, *History of the Royal Society of London* (1667), pp. 117–18.

> And we desire to know the stars in skies
> Ourselves thereby to wished ports to bring.
>
> SIR ARTHUR GORGES, *Poems* (ed. H. E. Sandison, 1953), p. 68.

> We care not for those martial men
> That do our states disdain;
> But we care for the merchant men
> Who do our states maintain.
>
> T. RAVENSCROFT, Song of the Three Poor Mariners,
> in *Deuteromelia* (1609).

I

THERE is a curious academic division of spheres of influence in this country, as a result of which the history of science and the history of ideas have become something quite separate from 'history'. Some 'historians', as we call ourselves, are perhaps dimly aware of another world in which historians of science write the history of science for historians of science, and historians of ideas write the history of ideas for the *Journal of the History of Ideas*. But their work has not been absorbed into our thinking about English history. Yet scholars like Professors R. F. Jones and F. R. Johnson, and (in a different field) Professor E. G. R. Taylor and Commander Waters, have revealed new facts which will transform our understanding even of political history when they have been assimilated. I shall draw heavily on their researches in what follows.

In the past thirty years such scholars have established two apparently contradictory points about Francis Bacon and the early history of science in England. Bacon, they tell us, was a prophet unhonoured in his own country in the reigns of James I and Charles I. Only after 1640 did he acquire the great reputation and influence which he was so long to retain. The second point may be stated in the words of Professor Johnson, who has done so much to establish it: 'Most of the fruitful ideas of science that were popularly associated with the work of Bacon in the seventeenth century were already part of the publicly avowed creed of English scientific workers throughout the latter half of the sixteenth century.'[1] Bacon's task—an important one—was to synthesize and systematize this body of practical thought. So we are left with the paradox that Bacon's ideas, although not novel among scientists, took a long time to win wider acceptance. The reasons for this time-lag, I shall suggest, were social and political.

In the eighty years before 1640 England, from being a backward country in science, became one of the most advanced. English astronomers were making telescopic observations of the heavens long before Galileo's discoveries were announced; they at once tested and confirmed them, and suggested their possible relation to other problems of physical astronomy.[2] In 1639 a twenty-two-year-old Englishman, entirely self-taught in astronomy, was the only man in the world, so far as we know, to observe the transit of Venus.[3] This intellectual revolution, in its initial stages, was virtually ignored by the official intelligentsia. The science of Elizabeth's reign was the work of merchants and craftsmen, not of dons; carried on in London, not in Oxford and Cambridge; in the vernacular, not in Latin. In 1593 Gabriel Harvey, himself the son of a rope-maker, wrote: 'He that remembereth Humphrey Cole, a mathematical mechanician, Matthew Baker, a shipwright, John Shute, an architect, Robert Norman, a navigator, William Bourne, a gunner, John Hester, a chemist, or any like cunning and subtle empiric, is a proud man, if he contemn expert artisans, or any sensible industrious practitioners, howsoever unlectured in schools or unlettered in books.'[4] Bacon assimilated, synthesized, and put before the intellectuals this body of popular thought. Official Oxford and Cambridge still contrived to ignore it.

[1] F. R. Johnson, *Astronomical Thought in Renaissance England* (Baltimore, 1937), p. 296.
[2] Ibid., p. 292; V. Harris, *All Coherence Gone*, p. 94.   [3] See p. 24 below.
[4] Quoted by E. G. R. Taylor, *Tudor Geography, 1485–1583* (1930), p. 161; Taylor, *The Haven-Finding Art* (1956), pp. 196, 201. We shall meet some of these names again.

In sixteenth-century England there was a greedy demand for scientific information. Thus Thomas Langley in 1546 translated Polydore Vergil's *De Inventoribus Rerum* 'to the end that also artificers and others, persons not expert in Latin, might gather knowledge and take pleasure by the reading thereof'. Robert Wyllyams, shepherd 'keeping sheep upon Seynbury Hill' in Gloucestershire, paid 14*d.* for his copy in 1546.[1] Something like an adult education movement, as we shall see, emerged from this desire to 'gather knowledge and take pleasure'. So far as I know, there was nothing similar in Counter-Reformation Italy, Spain, France, or Germany; even in the Netherlands, the only comparable Protestant country, the stimulus of the Revolt was counteracted by the absence of peace and stability, and by the clerical domination, which accompanied it. England seems to have been unique in its vernacular scientific literature, and in its level of popular scientific understanding.

Here are some of the facts:

Over ten per cent. of the books listed in the *Short Title Catalogue* between 1475 and 1640 deal with the natural sciences. Nine out of every ten of these books were in English. With the doubtful exception of Italy, no country has anything like so high a proportion of vernacular scientific books at this date. In William London's *Catalogue of the Most Vendible Books in England* (1657), whose aim was to extend the civilization of London into the four northern counties, one book in every six was scientific. The better vernacular textbooks were superior in scope and quality to those used at the universities, more up to date. They were also relatively cheap. In 1576 Martin Frobisher paid £1 for a ship's Bible; for two scientific handbooks he paid 10*d.*[2] The authors of these textbooks included the ablest scientists of the day, many of them self-educated men who had either never been to a university or held no academic posts there.[3] They consciously aimed at a public of merchants, artisans, mariners, gunners, surveyors. Many of their books ran through a large

[1] D. Hay, *Polydore Vergil* (1952), pp. 67–69. Langley's language is pleasantly reminiscent of that of Tyndale about the Bible.

[2] D. W. Waters, *The Art of Navigation in Elizabethan and Early Stuart Times* (1958), p. 530.

[3] L. B. Wright, *Middle-Class Culture in Elizabethan England* (Chapel Hill, 1935), Chapter XV, *passim*; Johnson, *Astromonical Thought*, pp. 3–13; F. R. Johnson and S. V. Laskey, 'Robert Recorde's Mathematical Teaching and the Anti-Aristotelean Movement', *H.L.B.*, vii. 85–86.

number of editions, some of which have altogether disappeared, perhaps because they were read to pieces. But few of their books are in the libraries of Oxford and Cambridge colleges.

Take Robert Recorde, for instance, 'the founder of the English school of mathematics', who died in 1558. He was a Cambridge graduate, but failing to establish himself in either university he moved to London, where he earned his living as a physician, and gave popular lectures in mathematics. He also depended on the patronage of the Muscovy Company, to which many of his works were dedicated. His writings were all in English, and long remained the standard popular textbooks: his arithmetic (*The Ground of Artes*) had at least twenty-six editions between 1540 and 1662.[1] Countless English scientists of merchant or artisan origin in the century after his death acknowledged him as their tutor. Adam Martindale learnt mathematics from Recorde's books in the early sixteen-forties, though by 1666 he had come to regard him as old-fashioned.[2] Recorde's readers would not only learn mathematics from him: they would also learn that 'it is meet for no man to be believed in all things, without showing of reason'.[3] All statements, including those of Aristotle, should be tested by mathematical reasoning and personal observation.[4]

John Dee (1527–1608), who edited and augmented the twelfth edition of Recorde's *Ground of Artes* in 1582, offers another example. He was an outstanding mathematician, whose work profoundly influenced the next generation. Ramus, who vainly urged Elizabeth to found chairs of mathematics at Oxford and Cambridge, thought that Dee would have been an obvious candidate for one of them.[5] Dee had the greatest mathematical

---

[1] D. E. Smith, *A History of Mathematics* (1923), p. 318. Recorde invented the sign = to denote equality. Johnson and Laskey suggest that it was the excellence of Recorde's textbooks that delayed the translation of Ramus's mathematical writings into English and limited their circulation when they were translated (op. cit., p. 85). But see p. 31 below.

[2] Ed. R. Parkinson, *The Life of Adam Martindale* (Chetham Soc., 1845), pp. 36, 187.

[3] Quoted by Foster Watson, *The Beginning of the Teaching of Modern Subjects in England* (1909), pp. 297–300.

[4] Johnson, *Astronomical Thought*, p. 130; Johnson, 'Thomas Hood's Inaugural Address as Mathematical Lecturer of the City of London (1588)', *J.H.I.* iii. 94; Johnson and Laskey, op. cit., pp. 59, 81–86. Recorde was an active champion of Protestantism at a dangerous time.

[5] E. G. R. Taylor, *The Mathematical Practitioners of Tudor and Stuart England* (1954), p. 170.

and scientific library in England, perhaps in Europe. For thirty years he placed it at the disposal of a wide circle, which included Sir Walter Ralegh, Frobisher, Drake, and Hakluyt at one social extreme, a whole generation of simple pilots and navigators at the other.[1] In 1570 Dee wrote a Preface to and annotated a translation of Euclid made by Henry Billingsley, alderman, later Lord Mayor, of London. The chief reason for making the translation, Dee said, was to help the many 'common artificers', who, thanks to 'their own skill and experience already had, will be able (by these good helps and informations) to find out and devise new works, strange engines and instruments: for sundry purposes in the commonwealth'.[2] This Preface, with its utilitarianism and its vigorous defence of experiment, made a great impact on young men of the middle class, sons of traders and craftsmen. (Dee referred to himself as 'this mechanician'.)[3] Billingsley's *Euclide* was republished in 1651, and Dee's Preface was quoted in 1654 by a chemist who was trying to persuade the universities that mathematics should be taught there as a practical subject of use to merchants, mariners, and mechanics.[4] Dee also produced textbooks of navigation and almanacs for seamen. In 1583 he tried to persuade the government to adopt the Gregorian calendar, but was defeated by the bishops, and England retained a distinct system of dating until the mid-eighteenth century. An intimate friend of Gerard Mercator, Dee was for some thirty years technical adviser to the Muscovy Company, and tutor to their sea-captains. Dee's advice was sought on the subject of the North-West and North-East Passages: Leicester, Sir Philip Sidney, Walsingham, the younger Hawkins, Sir Humphrey and Adrian Gilbert, all came to his house.[5]

[1] Johnson, *Astronomical Thought*, p. 138; 'Gresham College, Precursor of the Royal Society', *J.H.I.* i. 424-5. Dee shared Ralegh's views on sea-power. See pp. 158-9 below.

[2] H. Billingsley, *The Elements of Geometrie of . . . Euclide* (1570), sig. A iiii. Billingsley was later a member of the Society of Antiquaries. See pp. 173-4 below.

[3] Ed. J. Crossley, 'Autobiographical Tracts of Dr. John Dee', in *Chetham Miscellany*, i (1851), 63.

[4] J. Webster, *Academiarum Examen* (1654), pp. 20, 51-52. The Preface was quoted with approval by Samuel Hartlib in 1655 (ed. J. Crossley, *The Diary and Correspondence of Dr. John Worthington*, Chetham Soc., 1847, i. 59). It was sneered at by Samuel Butler in *Hudibras* (ed. A. R. Waller, 1905), p. 157.

[5] G. B. Parks, *Richard Hakluyt and the English Voyages* (American Geographical Soc., 1928), pp. 47-49; C. Fell-Smith, *John Dee* (1909), pp. 37, 67.

Take Dee's pupil and friend, Thomas Digges, another outstanding mathematician and astronomer. He was the son of Leonard Digges, a participant in Wyatt's rebellion against Mary; the father of a leader of Parliamentary opposition under James I and Charles I.[1] Leonard Digges had himself been a popularizing mathematician who believed strongly that artisans should be taught elementary mathematics.[2] The invention of the telescope has been claimed for him, as that of the microscope for his son.[3] Thomas Digges in 1576 was the first Englishman to proclaim Copernicus's as the only possible theory of the universe; and he did so in English. His *Parfit Description of the Celestiall Orbes* had at least seven editions between 1576 and 1605. The year after its publication the Earl of Leicester took Digges under his patronage, a fact to whose significance I shall revert later.[4]

In his discussions of the infinity of the universe—the most intellectually exciting of Copernicus's ideas—Digges went much further than Copernicus himself. His book contained a diagram more daring than anything Copernicus ever produced, showing the stars at varying distances from the sun out to infinity. It was this diagram which became associated in the popular mind with

[1] Sir Dudley Digges was a pupil, friend, and protégé of Archbishop Abbott, the one steady anti-Spanish influence on James I's Privy Council. Sir Dudley was a member of the East India Company, and a pamphleteer on its behalf. He directed the North-Western Company, and helped to finance Hudson's and Baffin's voyages in search of the North-West Passage. He was associated in both these capacities with Sir Thomas Smith and John Wolstenholme, whom we shall often meet again (see pp. 33–34, 47, 62, 70 below). Digges continued his father's and grandfather's scientific interests, taking John Tradescant with him as a naturalist when he was sent on a diplomatic mission to Russia in 1618. He played a large part in winning the Petition of Right. His speech on the impeachment of Buckingham in 1626 was published in 1643 by order of the Long Parliament. A pamphlet attributed to him, *Right and Privileges of the Subject*, had appeared in 1642. A memorandum to Elizabeth on the defences of Dover is variously attributed to Digges or Sir Walter Ralegh (*Harleian Miscellany*, 1744–56, iv. 292–6). See also W. K. Jordan, *Social Institutions in Kent* (*Archaeologia Cantiana*, lxxv), p. 27.

[2] Taylor, *The Haven-Finding Art*, p. 197.

[3] V. Harris, *All Coherence Gone*, p. 94; R. S. Clay and T. H. Court, *The History of the Microscope* (1932), pp. 6–7.

[4] Eleanor Rosenberg, *Leicester, Patron of Letters* (Columbia U.P., 1955), pp. 282–6; and see p. 30 below. Leicester may have been most interested in Digges's application of mathematics to military and navigational problems, as in his *Arithmeticall Militarie Treatise named Stratioticos* (1579). Digges has been called the 'founder of ballistical studies in England'. He was also the first to describe a theodolite, the instrument which rendered surveying an exact art (A. R. Hall, *Ballistics in the 17th Century*, 1952, pp. 34, 43–44, 74).

the new heliocentric theory. Thanks largely to Digges, in
England the idea of an infinite universe came to be taken for
granted: all scientists assumed the need for progressively testing
theories by observation and experiment, and thus the brilliant
metaphysical speculations of a Giordano Bruno were comparatively uninfluential here.[1]

Recorde, Dee, and Digges were scientists of the highest
standing. Their vernacular works were deliberately intended to
help 'mechanicians' to educate themselves.[2] Thus Robert
Norman, mariner for twenty years and compass-maker, whose
discovery of the dip of the magnetic needle greatly influenced
Gilbert, paid tribute to Recorde and to Billingsley and Dee's
Euclide in a book whose Epistle Dedicatory asked the reader to
regard not the words but the matter. Norman rejected 'tedious
conjectures or imaginations', arguing only from 'experience,
reason, and demonstration, which are the grounds of arts'. He
claimed to set down whatever he could find from 'exact trial
and perfect experiments', and defended the experience of
'mechanicians or mariners' against 'the learned in those
[mathematical] sciences . . . in their studies amongst their
books', who 'can imagine great matters and set down their
far-fetched conceits in fair show, and with plausible words: . . .
yet there are in this land divers mechanicians that in their
several faculties and professions have the use of those at their
fingers' ends, and can apply them to their several purposes, as
effectually and more readily than those that would most
condemn them',[3] thanks to the work of translators and

[1] F. R. Johnson, 'The Influence of Thomas Digges on the progress of modern
astronomy in 16th century England', *Osiris*, i, *passim*; Johnson and Laskey, 'Thomas
Digges, the Copernican System, and the Idea of the Infinity of the Universe in
1576', *H.L.B.* v, *passim*: cf. A. Koyré, *From the Closed World to the Infinite Universe*
(Johns Hopkins U.P., 1957), Chapter II, *passim*. Recorde had referred to Copernicus's theory in *The Castle of Knowledge* (1556). The heliocentric theory was accepted
in nearly every important English textbook from that time onwards (Johnson,
Astronomical Thought, p. 291).

[2] Johnson, *Astronomical Thought*, pp. 169–73.

[3] R. Norman, *The Newe Attractive* (1581), sig. A iiiv, B 1–iv. Norman's book was
dedicated to William Borough, Controller of the Navy, the younger brother of the
Muscovy Company's chief pilot. William Borough's *Discourse of the Variation of the
Compasse*, annexed to *The Newe Attractive*, influenced William Gilbert, and was
later used by Gellibrand (see pp. 38, 47 below). Its Preface was directed to 'the
travellers, seamen and mariners of England'. Both Norman and Borough have an
honourable place in A. H. W. Robinson's *The History of Marine Cartography in Britain*
(1962), pp. 27–33.

popularizers. Norman's *Newe Attractive* remained a standard work until the eighteenth century.

What is important for our purposes is the close understanding between the leading scholarly scientists of England and the technicians for whom they wrote, as well as the co-operation between the scientists themselves in this work of adult education. Edward Worsop, 'Londoner', who described himself as 'a simple man among the common people', thought that the books of Recorde and the Diggeses 'cannot be understood of the common sort': so he 'set forth this discourse to their behoof . . . for their easiest understanding', to lay the secrets of geometry 'open unto the understanding of every reasonable man', so that they should not be fooled and cheated by surveyors.[1] Another popularizer was William Bourne, a self-educated man, the first non-university mathematics teacher and writer known to us, who was also the first Englishman to publish a book on the practice of navigation. This was *A Regiment for the Sea*, a manual written in a popular style 'for the simplest sort of seafaring men', which had at least six editions between 1574 and 1596. Bourne's *Treasure for Travellers* (1578) aimed at popularizing the mathematics of Dee's Preface. Bourne also did practical work on lenses.[2]

There was Thomas Hill (died *c*. 1575) who published a vast number of translations and treatises on popular science, many of which went into seven, eight, or nine editions. He, too, signed himself 'Londoner', and was a citizen with no more than a grammar school education. He specialized in expositions in simple English which sold at from 2*d*. to 1*s*., with cheap but serviceable woodcuts. He was himself converted to Copernicanism, and helped to raise the level of popular science above that of the cheap handbooks, mostly translations by incompetent hacks, with which publishers in the first half of the sixteenth century had tried to meet the new demand.[3] The 1600

[1] E. Worsop, *A Discoverie of sundrie errours and faults daily committed by Lande-meeters, ignorant of Arithmetike and Geometrie* (1582), sig. A 2–2v. For the truth of Worsop's assertion that 'the common people for the most part are in great fear when survey is made of their land' (ibid., sig. K 2) see E. G. R. Taylor, 'The Surveyor', *Econ. H.R.* xvii. 130–2.

[2] Taylor, *Mathematical Practitioners*, pp. 33, 332; *The Haven-Finding Art*, p. 201; Waters, op. cit., pp. 15, 130–2, 149. See also pp. 15 above, 49 below.

[3] Johnson, 'Thomas Hill: an Elizabethan Huxley', *H.L.Q.* vii. 329–47; L. B. Wright, *Middle-Class Culture*, pp. 565–71. Hill had close relations with the Paracelsan

edition of Hill's *Arte of Vulgar Arithmetick* contains an eloquent preface establishing mathematics' independence of religion.

II

Economic historians rightly emphasize the importance of the Tudor peace in making possible England's economic advance in the century before 1640. Whilst most continental countries were engaged in dynastic, religious, and civil wars, internal law and order for the most part prevailed in England. The Tudor peace was no less significant for intellectual history. The two are of course intimately connected. As landlords beat their swords into ploughshares, so the professional surveyor began to demand an improved mathematics: Recorde and the Diggeses gave it to him. Gilbert watched foundry-workers and talked to navigators in the preparatory work for his *De Magnete* (1600); pumps used for draining mines and ships supplied Harvey with the idea which proved the circulation of the blood; improvements in glass-making made possible the manufacture of telescopes and microscopes. But to the Tudor peace we should add the Tudor Reformation: for without the Reformation, with its challenge to authority, its stimulus to education and popular literacy, its relatively free discussion (Henry VIII failed to 'abolish diversity in opinions')—without all this the popular contribution to scientific thinking would have been impossible.

The reign of Edward VI, the great age of radical Protestantism, was a period in which the relaxation of the censorship allowed popular science to break through. Northumberland, his son, later the Earl of Leicester, and his son-in-law Sir Henry Sidney, gave enthusiastic support to a deliberate policy of commercial expansion based on improved knowledge of mathematics, navigation, and geography, which derived ultimately from Dee.[1] It is no coincidence that Recorde, both Diggeses, and many others of the early scientists were keen

John Hester, for whom see pp. 29, 79, 145 below, and may have become acquainted with Bruno while the latter was in England (P. H. Kocher, 'Paracelsan Medicine in England (*c.* 1570–1600)', *Journal of the History of Medicine*, ii. 457–8; D. W. Singer, *Giordano Bruno, his Life and Thought*, New York, 1950, p. 39).

[1] Waters, op. cit., pp. 83–87; cf. pp. 98–99; Taylor, *The Haven-Finding Art*, p. 195. For Leicester see pp. 29–30 below. Sir Henry Sidney was father of Sir Philip, for whose significance in our story see pp. 132–8 below. There is an interesting parallel radicalism in the architectural taste of the leading figures of Edward's reign (E. Mercer, *English Art, 1553–1625*, 1962, pp. 60–70). See also p. 270 below.

Protestants.[1] William Turner, 'the true pioneer of natural history in England', an itinerant Protestant preacher under Henry VIII and an exile under Mary, in 1564 was suspended as Dean of Wells for refusing to wear the prescribed vestments. He ordered penance for adultery to be performed in a priest's square cap, thus simultaneously demonstrating his contempt for the sacrament of penance and for popish vestments. He deliberately published his scientific works in English rather than in Latin.[2] The botanist Thomas Penney, 'the first Englishman to anticipate the Baconian insistence upon the collection of data as the essential preliminary to theorizing', was censured by the Archbishop of Canterbury as 'ill-affected towards the establishment', and was a supporter of Thomas Cartwright.[3] Dr. John Halle, at the beginning of Elizabeth's reign, was almost as well known for his anti-popish poems as for his writings on anatomy and surgery and against astrology. William Bullein was at once a medical writer and a Protestant propagandist.[4] Nicholas Udall, a very early advocate of the Reformation at Oxford and another Protestant propagandist, translated one of the most important anatomical treatises of the sixteenth century.[5]

William Fulke, one of the founders of scientific meteorology in England, who by emphasizing secondary as against supernatural causes did much to reduce superstition, was also an outspoken Puritan. He was driven from St. John's College, Cambridge, though as chaplain and protégé of Leicester he later became Master of Pembroke Hall. Fulke was interested in astronomy and optics, and was an opponent of astrology.[6] Reginald

[1] See pp. 17–19 above. Dee was accused of trying to murder Queen Mary, as well as of heresy.

[2] Ed. H. Robinson, *Zürich Letters, 1558–1602* (Parker Soc., 1865), p. 125; C. E. Raven, *English Naturalists from Neckham to Ray* (1947), pp. 93–133; C. Singer, *History of Biology* (2nd ed., 1950), pp. 88–89; A. G. Dickens, *Lollards and Protestants in the Diocese of York, 1509–1558* (1959), pp. 192–4.

[3] Raven, op. cit., pp. 189–90.　　　　　　　　[4] See p. 181 below.

[5] F. R. Johnson, 'Latin *versus* English in the 16th century debate over scientific terminology', *S.P.* xli. 129.

[6] W. Fulke, *A Goodly Gallery to Behold the Naturall Causes of All Kind of Meteores* (1563); *A Defence of the Sincere and True Translations of the Holy Scriptures into the English Tongue* (Parker Soc., 1843), pp. ii–x (first published 1583); P. H. Kocher, *Science and Religion in Elizabethan England* (San Marino, 1953), pp. 154, 163–5, 202–3, 214; S. K. Heninger, Jr., *A Handbook of Renaissance Meteorology* (Duke U.P., 1960), pp. 20–26, 55, 95. For second causes see pp. 181–90 below.

Scot, whose epoch-making *Discoverie of Witchcraft* was published in 1584, distrusted alchemy and astrology, and was a stout opponent of papists and priestcraft. George Gifford, author of a sceptical *Dialogue concerning witches and witchcraft* (1593), was a Puritan lecturer.[1] Napier, the inventor of logarithms, thought the Pope was Antichrist.[2] Jeremiah Horrocks, the young astronomer who observed the transit of Venus in 1639, and who in some respects anticipated Newton's theory of gravitation, came from a Lancashire Puritan family, was an undergraduate at Puritan Emmanuel College and a protégé of the Puritan Gresham professor Samuel Foster. He subsequently became assistant to an extremely Puritan rector in his native county.[3]

Among other leading Puritans favourable to science were Alexander Nowell, George Downham, Richard Greenham, Walter Travers, John Cleaver, William Perkins, and Samuel Ward.[4] There was agreement between scientists like Recorde, Dee, the Diggeses, Thomas Hill, Norman, Bourne, Thomas Hood, William Gilbert, Edward Wright, William Bedwell, John Gerarde, who asserted the perfection of God's universe; and Puritans like Nowell, Perkins, and Preston who used the argument from design to prove the existence of God.[5] John Preston, the Puritan political leader of the sixteen-twenties, had contemplated medicine as a career before he opted for divinity. His sermons show that he retained an interest in astronomy and other sciences.[6]

Sir Thomas Bodley, son of a Marian exile and himself a pupil of Calvin and Beza, founded his Library to forward the struggle against popery. But the Bodleian was a pro-scientific as well as an anti-Catholic influence in Oxford. The frieze in the Upper Reading Room must have shocked conservatives by

[1] K. M. Briggs, *Pale Hecate's Team* (1962), pp. 31–33. Scot also wrote a treatise on hop-gardens.

[2] For Napier see pp. 40–41 below.

[3] W. K. Jordan, *Social Institutions of Lancashire, 1480–1660* (Chetham Soc., 1962), p. 81; see also pp. 15 above, 312 below.

[4] W. Perkins, *Workes* (1609–12), i. 40, 44, 291; ii. 46–47, 287; iii. 506, 607–46, 653–67; Kocher, op. cit., pp. 14–16, 42–43; S. J. Knox, *Walter Travers* (1962), p. 147; H. Baker, *The Wars of Truth* (1952), pp. 22, 168. For Ward see *D.N.B.* and p. 313 below. We might add Bishops Hooper and Ponet to the list.

[5] Perkins, *Workes*, ii. 49–52; Kocher, op. cit., pp. 88–89, 151–5, 202–3.

[6] J. Preston, *The Saints Qualification* (2nd ed., 1634), p. 45; cf. my *Puritanism and Revolution*, pp. 239–40. For Preston see also p. 25 below. He was a protégé of Fulke Greville, for whom see pp. 133–7, 176 below.

including figures so strange to the university as Copernicus, Tycho Brahe, Paracelsus, Vesalius, Mercator, and Ortelius (as well as Guicciardini and Sir Philip Sidney) alongside the great philosophers and theologians.[1] William Hakewill was one of Bodley's executors.[2] Thomas James, the first Librarian of the Bodleian, who was also the radical Protestant son of a Marian exile, used the Roman Index 'that we may know what books and what editions to buy, their prohibition being a good direction to guide us therein'.[3] James himself had a Miltonic dislike of expurgating indexes.[4]

The sharp division in Protestant theology between natural and supernatural knowledge helped to establish the independence of the former. Some (though by no means all) English Protestants denied the association between sin and disease traditionally favoured by the Catholic Church, and became champions of more scientific and hygienic methods.[5] Rejection of the miracle of the mass and of wonder-working images, scepticism of all miracles since the age of the primitive Church, anxiety to minimize the area in which direct divine intervention prevailed and to proclaim the rule of law in the universe—all these Protestant tendencies unwittingly helped to create an atmosphere favourable to science. 'God alters no law of nature', declared Preston, at a time when Popes still practised magic.[6]

Sprat's comparison of the scientific revolution to the Protestant Reformation[7] was thus obvious. Nor was it original. Richard Bostock in 1585 had compared the Copernican revolution in astronomy and the Paracelsan revolution in chemistry

[1] J. N. L. Myres, 'Thomas James and the Painted Frieze', Bodleian Library Record, iii. 87; iv. 37–40, 51. The frieze emphasizes the heretical pre-Protestant tradition, later so dear to the Levellers, by including Wyclif, Hus, and Savonarola.

[2] Ed. N. E. McClure, The Letters of John Chamberlain (American Philosophical Soc., 1939), i. 416. For Hakewill see pp. 177, 199 below.

[3] Myres, op. cit., iv. 44; cf. Richard Dugdale, A Narrative of the wicked Plots carried on by Seignior Gondamore (1679), in Harleian Miscellany (1744–56), iii. 326.

[4] T. James, A Treatise of the Corruptions of the Scriptures, Councils and Fathers (Parker Soc., 1843), pp. 233–68: first published 1612.

[5] Kocher, op. cit., pp. 34–37; W. S. C. Copeman, Doctors and Disease in Tudor Times (1960), pp. 15–17.

[6] J. Preston, The New Covenant (5th ed., 1630), p. 46. Cf. my Society and Puritanism, pp. 245–7; F. A. Yates, Giordano Bruno and the Hermetic Tradition (1964), pp. 375–6, 388–9.

[7] T. Sprat, History of the Royal Society of London (1667), pp. 371–2.

to the Protestant Reformation of which Wyclif had been a precursor: and Bacon claimed Luther as a predecessor.[1] Recent attempts to disprove the well-attested connexion between radical Protestantism and the rise of science have been, in my opinion, unsuccessful.[2] (I stress *connexion*, and suggest no causal relation.) In this book I use the word 'Puritan' to include all those radical Protestants who wanted to reform the Church but (before 1640 at least) did not want to separate from it. The sectaries are 'Puritans' only by extension.[3]

In relation to medicine England's Protestantism put it in an interesting half-way position between Catholic France and the republican Netherlands. Theodore Mayerne, for instance, an advocate of chemical medicine, had been declared by the Paris College of Physicians 'an unlearned, impudent, drunken, mad fellow, . . . unworthy to practise physic in any place', because he opposed Hippocrates and Galen;[4] but he was safe in England with royal patronage, and throve to knighthood. Royalty patronized many Protestant refugee doctors. Mayerne was physician to James I, Theodore Diodati to Princess Elizabeth, Peter Chamberlen the elder to Queens Anne of Denmark and Henrietta Maria. Gideon de Laune was apothecary to Anne of Denmark, Wolfegang Rumler to Charles I.[5] The forceps of the radical Protestant Chamberlens not only brought them the favour of two papist queens; after 1660 they also led the court to overlook the revolutionary radicalism of the younger Peter Chamberlen, who was appointed physician to Charles II.

[1] R[ichard] B[ostock], *The Difference betwene the auncient. . . and the latter Phisick* (1585), Chapter 19; Bacon, *Works*, iii. 282–3.

[2] See, for example, K. Samuelsson, *Religion and Economic Action* (trans. E. G. French, 1961); T. K. Rabb, 'Puritanism and the Rise of Experimental Science in England', *Cahiers d'Histoire Mondiale*, vii. The latter makes his task easier by using a definition of 'Puritan' which would exclude Wilkins, Baxter, and Milton. For the evidence which establishes the connexion, see especially A. de Candolle, *Histoire des sciences et des savants depuis deux siècles* (Geneva, 1873); R. K. Merton, 'Science, Technology and Society in 17th century England', *Osiris*, iv; D. Stimson, 'Puritanism and the New Philosophy', *Bulletin of the Institute of the History of Medicine*, iii; J. Pelseneer, 'L'Origine protestante de la science moderne', *Lychnos* (Uppsala, 1946–7), pp. 246–8; S. F. Mason, 'The Scientific Revolution and the Protestant Reformation', *Annals of Science*, ix. 64–87, 154–75; 'Science and Religion in 17th century England', *P. and P.*, no. 3; R. Hooykaas, 'Science and Reformation', *Cahiers d'Histoire Mondiale*, iii.   [3] See my *Society and Puritanism, passim*.

[4] M. N[edham], *Medela Medicinae* (1665), pp. 22–26; cf. R. Malthauf, 'Medical Chemistry and "the Paracelsans" ', *Bulletin of the History of Medicine*, xxviii. 110.

[5] G. Corfe, *The Apothecary, Ancient and Modern* (1885), p. 21.

In fourteenth- and fifteenth-century Italy merchants and artisans had made contributions to scientific thinking comparable to those of England in the sixteenth and early seventeenth centuries; but this did not survive the shock of Reformation and counter-Reformation in Roman Catholic countries, Venice with its university of Padua only excepted.[1] And even there, though Harvey owed much to Padua, still it was an Englishman and not an Italian who first published the discovery of the circulation of the blood. Some recent historians have written of the persecutors of Galileo with such human understanding of their predicament that we need to remind ourselves that it was Galileo who was forced to recant, and that his ideas could be publicly developed only in Protestant countries. The great anatomist Vesalius was cut off in his prime by the action of the Inquisition.[2] In 1609 the Parlement of Paris ordered chemists to subscribe to the teachings of Aristotle, on pain of death. An inquiring spirit like Lucilio Vanini was burnt at Toulouse in 1619 after having his tongue torn out. Campanella had to endure ghastly tortures, followed by nearly thirty years in Italian dungeons, to reflect on the unwisdom of thinking unorthodox thoughts. Descartes was so worried by Galileo's fate that—even though he retreated to the safety of the Protestant Netherlands—he left much of his work unpublished, and disguised his real beliefs in what he did publish. It did not help. His works were placed on the Index, where they still remained in 1948.[3] Even the Laudian censorship never amounted to anything like the Roman Index, on which all books advocating the Copernican theory remained until the eighteenth century, and which prohibited books like those of Johannes Weyer, who suggested that witches might be psychologically ill.[4]

[1] For Venice and Padua see pp. 276–8 below. For Calvinism and science in Italy see Aldo Stella, 'Ricerche sul socinianesimo: il processo di Cornelio Sozzini e Claudio Textor (Barrière)', *Bolletino dell'Istituto di Storia della Società e dello Stato Veneziano*, iii. 77–120.

[2] Sir William Osler, *The Evolution of Modern Medicine* (Yale U.P., 1921), p. 160. For the effect of the counter-Reformation on the Catholic attitude to science see H. R. Trevor-Roper, 'Religion, the Reformation and Social Change', *Historical Studies*, iv. 44.

[3] A. C. Crombie, *Augustine to Galileo* (1961), ii. 160, 216–18; M. Barjouet, 'Ce qui mourrut et ce qui naissait chez Descartes', *La Pensée*, New Series, no. 32, pp. 25–26.

[4] G. Zilboorg, *The Medical Man and the Witch during the Renaissance* (Baltimore, 1935), *passim*; cf. S. E. Morison, 'The Harvard School of Astronomy in the 17th century', *New England Quarterly*, vii. 5–6.

III

Nevertheless; there was a battle of the books in sixteenth-century England too, as well as in the seventeenth century. Thirty-five years ago Mr. Conley revealed that the first English translators of the classics were a homogeneous group of non-university Protestants and Puritans, mostly young and inspired by an ardent patriotism. A similar group of translators and compilers, recently studied by Miss Rosenberg, occupied themselves in making scientific learning available to all who could read, whether it was in medicine, surgery, geography, mathematics, or astronomy; or in history. Both these groups aimed at 'a mean sort of men', between 'the rascal multitude and the learned sages', and regarded the creation of an enlightened lay public opinion as a bulwark of true religion and national independence at a time when both protestantism and England's existence as an independent state seemed to be threatened by Spain.[1]

These were braver enterprises than one might think. Again and again the early popularizers, from Sir Thomas Elyot onwards, like the early translators of the Bible, had to defend themselves against the charge that they were debasing the value of the originals, or making learning too common. They show constant fear of the greedy conservatism of the vested interests whose secrets they were revealing—the universities, the College of Physicians.[2] Even in the seventeenth century the view that 'the Moderns exceed the Ancients' seemed to Bishop Goodman 'an opinion most prejudicial to the professors of all

---

[1] C. H. Conley, *The First English Translators of the Classics* (Yale U.P., 1927), *passim*; E. Rosenberg, *Leicester, Patron of Letters*, *passim*; and 'Giacopo Castelvetro, Italian publisher in Elizabethan London and his patrons', *H.L.Q.* vi, *passim*. The quotation is from John Dolman, translator of Cicero's *Tusculan Discourses* (1651), cited by R. P. Stearns, 'The Scientific Spirit in England', *Isis*, xxxiv. 297. H. B. Lathrop, *Translations from the Classics into English from Caxton to Chapman* (Madison, 1933), argues against Conley's thesis (pp. 230–3), on the grounds that in other countries too translators were young, dedicated their works to those in power, opposed rebellion, dealt with the art of war and were anti-medieval; and that Elizabeth's government anyway did not want to spread liberal principles through a critical study of history. These criticisms ignore Conley's central point, that Elizabeth's government was not monolithic, and that Leicester and his followers were by no means certain to survive, still less to triumph.

[2] P. H. Kocher, 'Paracelsan Medicine in England (*c*. 1570–1600)', *Journal of the History of Medicine*, ii. 463, 471–3; cf. C. Goodall, *The Royal College of Physicians* (1684), pp. 289–472. See pp. 75–77, 81–83 below.

sciences, to universities, colleges, libraries, and all ancient foundations; . . . and is therefore of dangerous consequence'.[1] 'The Papists and the College of Physicians', declared Nicholas Culpeper in 1649, 'will not suffer divinity and physic to be printed in our mother tongue, both upon one and the same ground.'[2] 'Vile men would, prelate-like, have knowledge hid', sang John Collop ironically six years later.[3]

Thomas Gale, whose *Certaine Workes of Chirurgie*, published in 1563, is 'a landmark in British surgery', sought the protection of the Earl of Leicester in a dedication which reveals, quite simply, that he was afraid. His translation of Galen, completed in 1566, was not published until twenty years later, despite Gale's high patrons.[4] In 1570 John Dee had to argue that the translation of Euclid did not diminish the honour and estimation of the universities or hinder their studies.[5] Robert Norman in 1581 defended translation on patriotic grounds, and attacked learned mathematicians who wish 'that all mechanicians were such as for want of utterance should be forced to deliver unto them their knowledge and conceit, that they might flourish upon them, and supply them at their pleasures'.[6] In 1585 Richard Bostock, defending Paracelsan medicine, savagely attacked the Galenists who (in the College of Physicians) 'shroud themselves under the wings and protection of princes, privileges, and charters', and prevent the development of true experimental chemistry.[7] William Clowes's *A Prooved Practice for All Young Chirurgians* (1588) suggested that the old guard did not want to see any medical books published at all.[8]

[1] Hakewill, *An Apologie*, ii. 129.
[2] Nicholas Culpeper, *A Physicall Directory, or A translation of the London Dispensatory* (1649), sig. A 2v. This translation was itself made in defiance of the College.
[3] Ed. C. Hilberry, *The Poems of John Collop* (Wisconsin U.P., 1962), p. 94.
[4] Rosenberg, *Leicester*, pp. 30–35.
[5] Dee's Mathematicall Preface to Billingsley's *Euclide*, sig. A iii–iiii.
[6] R. Norman, *The Newe Attractive*, Epistle Dedicatorie to William Borough and Preface to the Reader. See pp. 20–21 above.
[7] R[ichard] B[ostock], *The Difference betwene the auncient . . . and the latter Physick*, Chapter 19. Observe that Bostock did not sign his full name. The only one of the early Paracelsans who had the courage to do so was John Hester (P. H. Kocher, 'John Hester, Paracelsan', *Joseph Quincy Adams Memorial Studies*, Folger Library, 1948, p. 622). See pp. 79, 145 below. Paracelsus also had used the vernacular. For difficulties of translators see also L. Einstein, *The Italian Renaissance in England* (Columbia U.P., 1902), pp. 355–6.
[8] Cf. *Selected Writings of William Clowes* (ed. F. N. L. Poynter, 1948), pp. 161–7.

These fears and suspicions were not idle. The spreading of popular knowledge had democratic implications and was for this reason opposed by political and religious conservatives, papists in high places, and advocates of a Spanish alliance.[1] The translators and popularizers continually found it necessary to appeal against persecution to their patrons, who fortunately included Cecil and Leicester. For our purposes Leicester's patronage of Clowes and William Cunningham is worth noting. Cunningham's *Cosmographicall Glasse* (1559) 'did for cosmography, and to some extent for navigation, what Robert Recorde's books had done for mathematics; it brought the subject from the recesses of the scholar's closet to the shelves of the gentry and the desks of the merchants'.[2] Leicester's patronage of Thomas Blundeville, whom we shall meet again as a popularizer of William Gilbert, is also of interest.[3]

It is easy for us, who know the end of the story, to assume that the victory of this group of Elizabeth's councillors was always inevitable, and to discount the popularizers' shrill cries for help. But this would be a mistake. Leicester's policy of encouraging popular enlightenment, for whatever reasons he adopted it, was by no means certain of success. Had Mary Queen of Scots or some other papist succeeded Elizabeth—as always seemed possible down to 1588—the consequences might have been very unpleasant for him and for the group of scientists and translators which he protected. Leicester might after all have taken warning from the fate of his father, the Duke of Northumberland, from whom he seems to have inherited an interest in overseas expansion as well as a readiness to gamble on the victory of radical Protestantism. Leicester and his protégés performed an important service to their country, whose significance is only just beginning to be appreciated, thanks to the work of Miss Rosenberg.[4]

---

[1] Conley, op. cit., pp. 84–101 and *passim*.

[2] Waters, op. cit., pp. 98–99, 104; Taylor, *The Haven-Finding Art*, p. 199.

[3] Rosenberg, *Leicester, Patron of Letters*, pp. 30, 46–62. See pp. 38, 175 below. Cf. also p. 19 above for Leicester's patronage of Thomas Digges.

[4] Rosenberg, *Leicester, passim*, esp. pp. xvi–xix, 30–38, 153–4, 180–3, 196–7; cf. Taylor, *The Haven-Finding Art*, p. 195. Miss Rosenberg's emphasis on the genuineness of Leicester's 'Puritanism', if we abandon the nonconformist overtones of that abused word, is strikingly confirmed from an entirely different angle by P. Collinson, *Letters of Thomas Wood, Puritan, 1556–1577* (Bulletin of the Institute of Historical Research, Special Supplement no. 5, 1960). Wood's son was later in Bacon's

It is formally true to say, then, as Professor Kocher does, that 'neither the Church nor any other organized body in Elizabethan England ever persecuted a single scientist or imposed upon a single scientific book the kind of censorship which obtained in some continental countries'.[1] But the negative pressures of Church and conservative opinion, still socially powerful, may well have been more oppressive than Professor Kocher's statement implies. George Gascoigne, whom Ralegh admired, was a victim of persecution for his activities as a translator.[2] In 1577 the third part of Dee's *General and Rare Memorials Pertaining to the Perfect Arte of Navigation* was banned as politically dangerous. Recorde and Hill were cautious and ambiguous in their references to the Copernican theory. Professor Jones believed that this theory 'was more widely accepted in private than is apparent from published opinions'.[3] Some translators of Ramus were reluctant to put their names on the title-page. Dudley Fenner's 1584 translation of Ramus's *Dialecticae Libri Duo* was published at Middelburg, where he was serving as chaplain to the English merchants after being expelled from Cambridge for Puritanism. Fenner defended himself against those who opposed the popularization of academic subjects, and warned them against keeping learning rare and dear 'lest the people curse them'.[4] The first translator of Ramus into English had also felt it necessary to rebuke those who 'would have all things kept close either in the Hebrew, Greek or Latin tongues'.[5] One translation of Ramus was suppressed, and the translator expected 'storms of reproach and ingnominy' when he tried again as late as 1632.[6]

household (ibid., p. iii). The link between radical Protestantism, popular enlightenment, and science—and an anti-Spanish foreign policy—was no personal quirk of Leicester's. We shall often meet it again. See pp. 153–65 below.

[1] P. H. Kocher, 'The Old Cosmos: a Study in Elizabethan Science and Religion', *H.L.Q.* xv. 107–8.

[2] Conley, op. cit., pp. 97–99. See p. 137 below.

[3] R. F. Jones, *The Ancients and the Moderns* (Washington University Studies, New Series, Language and Literature, no. 6, 1936), pp. 11, 288, 291.

[4] D. Fenner, *The Artes of Logike and Rethorike* (Middelburg, 1584), sig. A 2–2v, quoted in W. S. Howell, *Logic and Rhetoric in England* (Princeton, 1956), pp. 219–20. This rationing of knowledge by the purse might be worth investigating.

[5] R. MacIlmaine, *The Logike of the moste Excellent Philosopher P. Ramus, Martyr* (1574), p. 15, quoted in Howell, op. cit., p. 185.

[6] Howell, op. cit., p. 232; R[obert] F[age], *Peter Ramus, his Logick* (1632), sig. A 2–A 3v. The objection to Ramus's logic was akin to the objection to translating the

In other spheres—drama, history—we know something of the working of the censorship.[1] Elizabethan and Jacobean governments refused to license the printing of Machiavelli's *Il Principe* and *Discorsi*, either in the original or in translation.[2] Together with hints like those noted in the preceding paragraph, all this leads me to suspect, though I cannot prove, that there was a silent censorship, usually self-imposed, which made Gilbert leave so much of his work unpublished, and may mislead us into supposing that Bacon, Hakewill, and Harvey were relatively uninfluential in their own country before 1640, and then suddenly leap into prominence.[3] It seems to me more probable that this is an optical illusion: that it was the breakdown of the old régime and its censorship after the meeting of the Long Parliament which allowed men to speak and write more freely: though this freer atmosphere would also allow new ideas to circulate faster and more widely.

We might have expected things to improve after the defeat of the Armada had made Protestantism and English independence secure; but this did not happen. The external danger had forced radicals to remain loyal to Elizabeth for fear of a worse alternative: the removal of this unifying factor roused the Queen and the conservatives to a flurry of repressive activity. With Leicester and Walsingham dead and Ralegh in disgrace in the fifteen-nineties, the bishops began a determined drive against Puritanism and free thought. This was not checked by the accession of James I, as the Hampton Court Conference shows. Under James the two leading patrons of science after Leicester, Ralegh and the Earl of Northumberland, both found themselves in the Tower. It was in 1608 that Ralegh's friend the great mathematician Thomas Hariot wrote to Kepler: 'Things with us are in such a condition that I still cannot philosophize

classics: thanks to Ramus, Aristoteleans thought, 'every cobbler can cog a syllogism, every carter crack of propositions. Hereby is logic profaned' (A. Fraunce, *The Lawiers Logicke*, 1588, Preface). See p. 292 below.

[1] See my *Century of Revolution* (1961), p. 98; F. S. Fussner, *The Historical Revolution* (1962), pp. 38–39; and pp. 177–8, 203 below.

[2] Pirated Italian editions and manuscript translations circulated; but the *Discorsi* were not translated until 1636, *Il Principe* not till 1640 (F. Raab, *The English Face of Machiavelli*, 1964, pp. 52–53, 96, 274–5).

[3] For Harvey see my 'William Harvey and the Idea of Monarchy', *P. and P.*, no. 27, pp. 58–61; for Bacon and Hakewill see pp. 116–19, 199–202 below.

freely. We are still stuck in the mud. I hope almighty God will soon put an end to it.'[1]

IV

In 1594 the great navigator John Davis, who himself kept fully abreast of the new mathematics, declared proudly, 'our country is not inferior to any for men of rare knowledge, singular explication, and exquisite execution of the arts mathematical; for what stranger may be compared with M. Thomas Digges, Esq., our countryman, the great master of archemastry? and for theoretic speculations and most cunning calculation, M. Dee and M. Thomas Hariot are hardly to be matched'.[2] Among the scientific popularizers who helped to pass the new mathematics down was Thomas Hood (c. 1556–soon after 1611), son of a merchant tailor of London. He was the author of a series of textbooks on mathematics, astronomy, and navigation, and wrote a treatise on the use of globes 'for the mariners', as well as translating part of Ramus's *Scholae Mathematicae*. He also practised physic. In 1589 Hood was, with Hakluyt, one of the subscribers to Ralegh's Virginia Company.[3] Hood invented a sector, ancestor of the slide-rule and the calculating machine, in 1598, the same year as Galileo.[4] In the fifteen-eighties he was lecturing privately in the Staplers' Chapel, Leadenhall, on mathematics, geography, and navigation. This lecture was financed by a group of Londoners, headed by Thomas Smith, later first Governor of the East India Company, Governor of the Muscovy Company, and Treasurer of the Virginia Company.

In 1588, with the approval of the Privy Council, a public lecture in mathematics was endowed at the initiative of the

[1] J. Jacquot, 'Thomas Hariot's Reputation for Impiety', *Notes and Records of the Royal Society*, ix. 167. Cf. the quotation from Chapman on p. 141 below.

[2] John Davis, *The Seamans Secrets* (1594), quoted as epigraph to J. O. Halliwell's *Collection of Letters Illustrative of the Progress of Science in England* (1841). Davis was a Puritan, very conscious of England's historical mission. For Hariot see pp. 139–42 below.

[3] R. B. Parks, *Richard Hakluyt and the English Voyages* (American Geographical Soc., 1928), pp. 135, 172; ed. D. B. Quinn, *The Roanoke Voyages* (Hakluyt Soc., 1955), ii. 570.

[4] Waters, op. cit., p. 357. Sir Arthur Throckmorton engaged Hood to teach him geometry in 1595–6, and bought a globe from him (A. L. Rowse, *Ralegh and the Throckmortons*, 1962, pp. 61, 197). Throckmorton also knew Hariot. For globes see pp. 42–43 below.

same sponsors; it was intended primarily for captains of trained bands, but was also open to the general public; and Hood was the lecturer. Richard Hakluyt had been trying for years to get such a public lecture endowed, with special reference to navigation: and Drake had promised to contribute £20 a year towards it.[1] But it needed the panic of the Armada year to get it started: now it was 'earnestly requested by the whole City'.[2] Once the invasion scare was over, however, the emphasis of Hood's lectures shifted from the mathematical basis of military tactics and fortifications to problems of navigation, of greater interest to the seamen who formed the bulk of his audience. This experiment in adult education came to an end when it was replaced by the more grandiose project of Gresham College.[3]

Sir Thomas Gresham (1518–79), merchant and financier, the son and nephew of Lord Mayors of London, built the Royal Exchange and left the revenue from shops there jointly to the City of London and the Mercers' Company to endow a college. Despite pleas from Cambridge that the money might more appropriately be left to the university, Gresham followed the example set by many merchants who endowed grammar schools in the sixteenth century, and was careful to put control of his college in the hands not of clerics but of merchants like himself. He endowed seven professorships: in Divinity, Law, Rhetoric, Music, Physic, Geometry, and Astronomy, with higher stipends than Henry VIII had given the Regius Professors of Divinity at Oxford and Cambridge. Gresham College, like the Bodleian Library, was founded to combat popery. The Professor of Divinity was naturally the senior professor: he was to employ his time in sound handling of controversies, 'especially against the common adversary of the Church of Rome'.[4]

The Gresham professors were instructed to lecture, free of

[1] Ed. E. G. R. Taylor, *The Original Writings and Correspondence of the two Richard Hakluyts* (Hakluyt Soc., 1935), pp. 179–80, 208–9, 429–32. Alderman Barnes, Governor of the Muscovy Company, and John Wolstenholme (for whom see pp. 47, 70 below) also lent their support.

[2] Hood to Burghley, in Halliwell's *Collection of Letters Illustrative of the Progress of Science in England*, p. 31.

[3] Johnson, 'Thomas Hood's Inaugural Address', pp. 94–98; *Astronomical Thought*, pp. 198–9.

[4] *An Exact Copy of the Last Will and Testament of Sir Thomas Gresham* (1724), p. 36.

charge, in Latin for the benefit of foreigners, and in English because the founder had 'a special respect of the citizens, of whom few or none understand the Latin tongue', and did not want the lectures to be for the learned only.[1] For the first ten years the music lectures were delivered in English only, because John Bull could speak no Latin. The instructions for the lectures, drafted by City merchants, were astonishingly forward-looking. The professors were set free from the university practice of merely commenting on a set text. The astronomy lecturer was to demonstrate the use of nautical instruments 'for the capacity of mariners', and to apply this to practical purposes by teaching them geography and navigation. The geometry professor was to lecture on arithmetic and both theoretical and practical geometry. 'Forasmuch as the greatest part of the auditory is like to be of such citizens and others as have small knowledge, or none at all, in the Latin tongue, and for that every man for his health's sake will desire to have some knowledge in the art of physic', the physic professor was told to deal with modern theories of physiology, pathology, and therapeutics. His lectures were to follow the method of Fernelius 'rather than be disjointed and delivered out of order by exposition of some part of Galen or Hippocrates'. The law lectures were not to be delivered after the manner of the universities, by commenting on texts, but 'in the most perspicuous method', by selecting topics such as 'are more usual in common practice, . . . to the good liking and capacity of the said auditory'. The handling was to be analytical, after the order of Wesenbekius and certain others.[2]

These two models, Fernelius and Wesenbekius, call for a word of comment. Jean Fernel (1497–1558) was a French physician who revolted against scholasticism and proclaimed that 'it seems good for philosophers to move to fresh ways and systems'. He was a resolute partisan of the Moderns: 'There is nothing for which our age need envy its predecessors.' Although

[1] Ibid., p. 42.
[2] Ibid., pp. 37–38. Cf. J. Ward, *Lives of the Professors of Gresham College* (1740), British Museum copy with Ward's manuscript annotations, pp. iii–viii, 29–30, Appendix, pp. 21, 30. See also Johnson, 'Gresham College', *passim*, and J. S. Burgon, *Life and Times of Sir Thomas Gresham* (1839), ii. 517. The first occurrence of the word 'pathology' recorded by the *Oxford English Dictionary* is in 1597, in a translation from the French.

he had not mastered the experimental method, he believed in observation, and had no servile veneration for Aristotle and Galen. He was the first man of modern times to measure a degree of the meridian. He was a skilled anatomist, and wrote the earliest systematic treatises on physiology and pathology, inventing the modern usage of both terms. His works were used as textbooks in all European countries until the end of the seventeenth century. There had been thirty-four editions of his *Opera* by 1681. Fernel's great merit lay in his hitherto unequalled analytic method, and in his rejection of a mass of medieval superstitions, as well as of astrology and alchemy. Within half a century after Gresham College had adopted him Fernel's system was outmoded by the discoveries of Harvey and Descartes: but in 1598 he was a good model.[1]

Wesenbekius, Mathaius Wesenbeck (1531–86), was a Fleming who migrated to Saxony because of his Protestantism.[2] His commentary on the Digest, published 1565–82, dominated juristic literature on the Continent for the century after his death, and his method was the ruling one until the eighteenth century. The essence of this method was Wesenbeck's emphasis on practice, on matters of daily use, and dislike of logical subtleties, scholasticism, excessive citation of authorities.[3] The attraction which this approach to the law would have for citizens is obvious. The Gresham professor was instructed to deal with subjects like wills, trusts, usury, contracts, sale and purchase, ships, seamen and navigation, monopolies, trade and merchants, pirates, &c., which would be of direct interest to his audience.[4] Lectures were followed by discussion.

[1] L. Figard, *Un médecin Philosophe au XVIe Siècle: étude sur la psychologie de Jean Fernel* (Paris, 1903), pp. 65–68, 363–4; Sir Charles Sherrington, *The Endeavour of Jean Fernel* (1946), p. 17 and *passim*; J. D. Bernal, *Science in History* (1954), pp. 277–8; G. Sarton, *Six Wings: Men of Science of the Renaissance* (1957), pp. 191–6; Copeman, *Doctors and Disease in Tudor Times*, pp. 73–76. In 1575 William Clowes translated part of Fernel's *Pathologia*. Gilbert referred to Fernel in the *De Magnete* (1600), p. 4. Pp. 25–62 of the anonymous *Two Treatises Concerning the Preservation of Eie-sight* (1616) draw on Fernel's work. The egregious Alexander Ross, who attacked every significant thinker of his time, managed to oppose *both* Fernel *and* Harvey! (A. R[oss], *Arcana Microcosmi*, 2nd ed., 1652, pp. 224–6.) For Ross see pp. 204, 212 below.

[2] A relation of his wrote a eulogy of the Waldenses and Albigensians (Petri Wesenbecii, *Oratio de Waldensibus et Albigensibus Christianis*, Jena, 1585).

[3] R. Stintzing, *Geschichte der Deutscher Rechtswissenschaft* (1880), i. 352–66; ii. 250; *Allgemeine Deutsche Biographie*.

[4] *The Last Will . . . of Sir Thomas Gresham*, pp. 37–38.

This system of free adult education was consciously designed to supply the teaching in modern subjects which the universities were conspicuously failing to give. At Oxford and Cambridge lecturers on medicine had to proceed by way of commentary on Hippocrates and Galen, astronomy lecturers by commenting on Ptolemy, cosmography lecturers on Pliny, Strabo, and Plato. In 1574 a Ramist at Cambridge was ordered to defend Aristotle against all other philosophers.[1] In 1586 questions 'disagreeing with the ancient and true philosophy' (i.e. Aristotle's) were forbidden even to be discussed in the Oxford schools.[2] In 1583 Matthew Gwinne, future Gresham Professor, was permitted by the University of Oxford to discontinue his lecture on music because 'suitable books were difficult to procure, and the practice of that science was thought to be disregarded (inusitata) if not useless'.[3] There was no chair of mathematics at Cambridge until 1663.

V

Gresham College was primarily a teaching rather than a research institution. But it also gave scientists what they had hitherto lacked, a central meeting-place and clearing-house for ideas. The first Gresham Professor of Geometry, until his resignation in 1620, was Henry Briggs. He was a man of the first importance in the intellectual history of his age, who still awaits a full-scale modern biographer.[4] He was born in 1561 near Halifax, turbulent centre of economic activity and radical Protestantism, and lived until 1631. Under him Gresham at once became a centre of scientific studies. He introduced there the modern method of teaching long division, and popularized the use of decimals.[5] He published many books on arithmetic, geometry, and trigonometry, as well as tables for navigation: his Commentaries on Ramus's *Geometry* were

---

[1] M. Curtis, *Oxford and Cambridge in Transition, 1558–1642* (1959), p. 250.

[2] P. Allen, 'Medical Education in 17th century England', *Journal of the History of Medicine*, i. 118–22; C. R. Thompson, *Universities in Tudor England* (Folger Library, 1959), p. 20; M. H. Carré, *Phases of Thought in England* (1949), pp. 202–3, 212–13.

[3] Ed. A. Clark, *Register of the University of Oxford*, ii (*1571–1622*), Part i (Oxford Historical Soc., 1887), p. 100.

[4] There is an excellent brief study by D. M. Hallowes, 'Henry Briggs, Mathematician', in the *Transactions of the Halifax Antiquarian Soc.* (1962), pp. 79–92.

[5] R. T. Gunther, *Early Science in Cambridge* (1937), p. 34; Hallowes, op. cit., pp. 86–87.

not published. But, significant though Briggs was as a mathematician in his own right, his greatest importance was as contact and public relations man.

He was a member of William Gilbert's circle at Wingfield House, one of the less plausible of the many claimants for the honour of being the original nucleus from which the Royal Society developed.[1] In his productive years Gilbert (1540–1603) was living in London and actively collaborating with scientists there. His De Magnete, 'the first physical treatise . . . based entirely upon experiment',[2] so important for the science of navigation, was in many respects a co-operative work. Gilbert drew on the earlier research of craftsmen like Robert Norman and William Borough.[3] Briggs was at the centre of Gilbert's group. At Gilbert's request he calculated a table of magnetic dip and variation. Their mutual friend Edward Wright recorded and tabulated much of the information which Gilbert used, and helped in the production of the De Magnete.[4] Thomas Blundeville, another member of Briggs's group, and—like Gilbert—a former protégé of the Earl of Leicester, popularized Gilbert's discoveries in The Theoriques of the Seven Planets (1602), a book in which Briggs and Wright again collaborated.[5] Blundeville, Wright, and William Barlow (another member of Briggs's circle) constructed the instruments which would render Gilbert's work accessible to mariners; Gresham College popularized them.[6] So the great work of 'the father of electrical science', which Galileo admired, and which gave such impetus to the scientific imagination and prepared for Newton's theory of

[1] Rufus Suter, 'A Biographical Sketch of Dr. William Gilbert of Colchester', Osiris, x. 377–80; contrast D. H. D. Roller, The De Magnete of William Gilbert (Amsterdam, 1959), p. 91.

[2] M. Ornstein, The Role of Scientific Societies in the 17th century (1938), p. 22.

[3] See pp. 20–21 above.

[4] S. P. Thompson, William Gilbert and Terrestrial Magnetism in the Time of Queen Elizabeth (n.d., ?1903), pp. 1, 6–7, 13; Taylor, Mathematical Practitioners, p. 49.

[5] Blundeville's Exercises (1594), a treatise on the mathematics and astronomy necessary for navigation, went through eight editions in forty-four years. It popularized, among other things, the nautical instruments invented by John Blagrave of Reading, a non-university man who also invented instruments of use for artillery and surveying (Waters, op. cit., pp. 212–15, 165–6; R. T. Gunther, 'The Uranical Astrolabe and other Instruments of John Blagrave of Reading', Archaeologia, cxxix. 56–72). Blundeville himself invented many instruments, including the protractor. See p. 175 below.

[6] Waters, op. cit., pp. 217–19, 246–7. For Barlow see pp. 65–66 below. His The Navigators Supply (1597) was dedicated to the Earl of Essex.

gravitation, derived from the work of unlearned craftsmen and was closely connected in origin and publicization with the Gresham group. Christopher Wren, in his inaugural lecture as Professor of Astronomy at Gresham in 1657, lauded Gilbert as 'the father of the new philosophy, Cartesius being but a builder on his experiments'; and added that Gilbert's work was 'augmented' by the Gresham professors.[1]

We should note in passing the extent and variety of Gilbert's scientific interests. In addition to those already discussed, he was President of the College of Physicians, and physician-in-ordinary to Elizabeth; and, like his friend Richard Hakluyt, he was keenly and expertly interested in chemistry and botany.[2] Gilbert was also attracted by Bruno's astronomical views.[3] Hakluyt, who like Gilbert was on the fringe of the Gresham circle, was another polymath, who studied biology and anthropology, and was 'no less excellent in the chiefest secrets of the mathematics'. His brother was a doctor.[4] A full study of the intellectual origins of the English Revolution would have to take account of the wide-ranging scientific interests of key figures like Gilbert and Hakluyt, who helped to link the many spheres in which original work was being done.[5] Knowledge was shared by men working in what would now be regarded as unrelated fields. Matthew Gwinne was Professor of Physic at Gresham College after being lecturer in music at Oxford; Thomas Clayton, Professor of Music at Gresham from 1607 to 1610, was later reader of the anatomy lecture at Oxford.[6] Professor Quinn has pointed out that each of the significant figures in natural history in sixteenth-century England (William Turner, Thomas Penney, Thomas Moffet, John Gerarde, and others) collected information from pioneers of overseas enterprise like Drake, Cavendish, Frobisher, and John White.[7]

Edward Wright (1558–1615), who co-operated with Briggs

---

[1] Christopher Wren, *Parentalia* (1750), pp. 205–6.
[2] Roller, op. cit., p. 87; J. M. Oppenheim, 'William Gilbert: Plant Grafting and the Grand Analogy', *Journal of the History of Medicine*, viii. 167–82; Taylor, *Writings of . . . the two Richard Hakluyts*, i. 45–46.
[3] Singer, *Giordano Bruno*, p. 67; Roller, op. cit., p. 70. Cf. pp. 134–5 below.
[4] Roller, op. cit., p. 90; Parks, *Richard Hakluyt and the English Voyages*, pp. 167–8, 58.
[5] Cf. pp. 173–4 below, where I discuss the links between science and history.
[6] Ward, *Lives of the Gresham Professors*, pp. 208–11. Petty too combined anatomy and music—and much else besides. See p. 124 below.
[7] Ed. D. B. Quinn, *The Roanoke Voyages* (Hakluyt Soc., 1955), i. 48.

and Gilbert, is a man whose work has been underrated because of the way in which he shared it with the members of the Gresham circle. Wright was a former Fellow of Caius, who went to sea with the Earl of Cumberland in 1589. He explained theoretically the method of constructing maps upon Mercator's projection, and made it practically useful for mariners. The Wright–Mercator projection was 'probably the greatest advance ever made in marine cartography'. Wright's discovery was made known to the world, with his permission, by Blundeville and Barlow. In 1598 Wright published *Certaine Errours in Navigation detected*, a work which revolutionized the science and 'set the seal on the supremacy of the English in the theory and practice of the art of navigation'. To this work Briggs contributed a number of tables, later improved by another Gresham professor, Edmund Gunter; Gellibrand, a third Gresham professor, added an appendix to a later edition.[1] Wright was also a skilled instrument-maker and a surveyor, who was employed by Sir Hugh Myddelton in his New River scheme for bringing water to London.[2]

Briggs seems to have been the first person to appreciate the significance of Napier's invention of logarithms—another great advance which owed nothing to the universities. As soon as Briggs heard of it he rushed off to Edinburgh; and from his interview with Napier onwards Briggs used all Gresham College's resources to popularize this discovery. Briggs himself made a significant contribution to the development of logarithms in a work which was 'never superseded by any subsequent calculations'.[3] Logarithms were at once introduced into the teaching at Gresham. In 1617 Briggs published a table of logarithms 'for the sake of his friends and hearers at Gresham College';[4] two years later he edited one of Napier's works.[5] Briggs's friend

[1] Waters, op. cit., pp. 121–2, 211–29, 367, 393; Taylor, *Mathematical Practitioners*, pp. 45–49; J. H. Parry, *The Age of Reconnaissance* (1963), p. 113. For Gunter and Gellibrand see pp. 46–47 below.

[2] D. Chilton, 'Land Measurement in the 16th century', *Transactions of the Newcomen Soc.*, xxxi. 127.

[3] W. Lilly, *History of His Life and Times* (1715), pp. 105–6; F. Cajori, *A History of Mathematics* (1894), pp. 164–5; Hallowes, op. cit., pp. 82–83. It has recently been claimed that in calculating his logarithms Briggs used results equivalent to the Binomial Expansion, whose discovery is normally attributed to Newton (T. D. Whiteside, in *The Mathematical Gazette*, xlv. 9–12, quoted by Hallowes, op. cit., p. 86).

[4] H. Briggs, *Logarithmorum Chilias Prima* (1617).

[5] Waters, op. cit., pp. 407–8.

Edward Wright translated Napier into English as *A Description of the Admirable Table of Logarithmes*, but died before it was published in 1616. The inevitable Briggs saw it through the press, for the benefit of 'those who . . . cannot come to hear me' at Gresham, added a preface and completed a table. The work was dedicated to the East India Company, which had encouraged Wright to make the translation.[1] Through *A Description* logarithms were first brought into popular use, originally for navigators and surveyors, though their commercial importance was soon realized. In 1619 John Speidall, a self-educated mathematics teacher and a member of Briggs's circle, published *New Logarithmes*, of which six impressions appeared in five years.[2] The rapid adoption of logarithms all over Europe in the early seventeenth century owed much to the enthusiasm of Briggs and later Gresham professors.[3] Logarithms even reached the stage by 1632.[4]

Another friend of Briggs's who was influenced by the new teaching at Gresham was Aaron Rathborne, who advocated the use of logarithms for surveying within a few years of their invention. His *Surveyor* (1616) was an orderly and formal textbook teaching the elements of geometry and trigonometry, a great advance on the chatty Elizabethan dialogues. It looks forward to Leybourne's classic *Compleat Surveyor* of 1653. The surveyors were among the first to use the slide rule.[5] The College

---

[1] See p. 62 below for Wright's lectures for the East India Company.

[2] Taylor, *Mathematical Practitioners*, pp. 58, 195, 352; Waters, op. cit., p. 403. Speidall (*fl.* 1600–34) was later appointed Professor of Mathematics at Sir Francis Kynaston's Academy, for which see p. 62 below. He christened his son Euclid.

[3] Napier himself was interested in improving industrial processes. He designed a hydraulic screw for pumping water out of mines, and introduced the use of salt as a fertilizer (J. G. Crowther, *Founders of British Science*, 1960, p. 6). He also invented a burning mirror for the destruction of ships, and an armoured chariot, 'profitable and necessary in these days for the defence of this island and withstanding of [Spanish] enemies of God's truth and religion' (quoted in W. T. Sedgwick and H. W. Tyler, *A Short History of Science*, New York, 1929, p. 242).

[4] Compass: [Sir Moth Interest] 'has reduced his thrift
            To certain principles, and in that method
            As he will tell you instantly, by logarithms,
            The utmost profit of a stock employed
                 (*The Magnetic Lady*, in Ben Jonson, *Plays*, Everyman ed., ii. 516.)

[5] Taylor, 'The Surveyor', *Econ. H.R.* xvii. 124, 132; *Mathematical Practitioners*, pp. 59, 343, 87, 184. Leybourne too has connexions with Gresham: he edited some of the posthumous works of Samuel Foster (see p. 48 below).

brought together many groups of scientists. Raphe Handson, a pupil of Briggs's, was persuaded by Hakluyt in 1600 to publish the first English textbook on *Trigonometrie*, a translation with additions of his own. It greatly simplified the calculations necessary for mathematical navigation. It was dedicated to the two Governors of the East India Company who had founded Wright's lecture on navigation, and in the book Handson makes clear his debt to Briggs.[1]

The indefatigable activities of Briggs extended into many other spheres. He acted as link between Gresham College and a group of master shipwrights and others interested in navigation which centred round the mathematician John Wells, Keeper of Naval Stores at Deptford. Briggs was one of the referees in a dispute about a new design for ships. The connexion continued after Briggs's resignation, and brought Gresham into direct contact with practical navigational problems.[2] The publication of Wells's *Sciographia* (1634) had been earnestly solicited by Briggs and Gunter, and Gellibrand wrote a preface to it.[3] Another friend of Briggs and later Gresham professors was John Man (*fl.* 1614–47), compass- and dial-maker successively to James I and Charles I.[4]

Briggs knew and admired the mathematical genius of Thomas Hariot, and so had at least some connexion with Sir Walter Ralegh's circle of scientists which I shall be discussing later.[5] Another member of Ralegh's circle, Robert Hues, is also associated with Gresham College in one seventeenth-century account.[6] The cheap globe which Emery Molyneux made,

[1] Taylor, *Mathematical Practitioners*, pp. 50–54, 203; Waters, op. cit., pp. 393–401, 590. See p. 70 below. Handson probably also owed something to Wright, Hariot, and Gellibrand, for whom see p. 47 below.

[2] Edward Wright dedicated one of his works to Richard Polter, Master of Trinity House, Deptford (*The Haven-Finding Art*, 1599). Among the Deptford group associated with the Gresham professors we find Henry Goddard, whose son Jonathan was to be Cromwell's physician and Fellow of the Royal Society.

[3] Aubrey, *Brief Lives*, ii. 295.

[4] Taylor, *Mathematical Practitioners*, p. 203.

[5] G. Hakewill, *An Apologie*, p. 302. First published in 1627. Cf. Taylor, 'The Doctrine of Nautical Triangles', *Journal of the Institute of Navigation*, vi. 137. Hariot had read some of Gilbert's manuscripts (H. Stevens, *Thomas Hariot*, 1900, pp. 178–80). For Hariot and Ralegh's circle see pp. 139–42 below.

[6] Sir Edward Sherburne, *The Sphere of Marcus Manilius made an English Poem* (1675), Appendix, p. 86; cf. Add. MS. 6197, f. 110. Sherburne had been one of Bacon's secretaries (*Letters of John Chamberlain*, ii. 355).

with help from Ralegh, John Davis, and Hakluyt, was popularized by Hues; globes were used for teaching at Gresham.[1]
Hues pointed out that Molyneux's globes were smaller and
cheaper than their predecessors, so that 'the meaner students
might herein also be provided for'.[2] Briggs was an active
member of the Virginia Company, serving on its committees
and acting as auditor. He was a great friend of its secretary,
Nicholas Ferrar, who at Briggs's instance was offered the
Gresham chair when Briggs moved to Oxford.[3] Briggs wrote a
Treatise on the North-West Passage which was published in a
volume of Virginia Company propaganda put out by the
Company's secretary, and was later reprinted by Briggs's friend
Samuel Purchas, together with a map also attributed to Briggs.[4]

Another member of Briggs's circle was Mark Ridley (1560–
1624), a protagonist of the Copernican hypothesis and one of
the earliest English writers to recommend the carrying out of
popular scientific experiments. He had been physician to
English merchants in Russia.[5] There was also William Bedwell
(1561 or 1562–1632), a distinguished Arabic scholar, translator
of the Authorized Version and of Ramus's *Geometry* (1636), who
wrote popular science manuals for the use of carpenters and
produced almanacs.[6] Bedwell is said to have been a friend and
admirer of Thomas Hood.[7] So close was Bedwell's association

[1] Waters, op. cit., p. 456.

[2] R. Hues, *Treatise on Globes* (Hakluyt Soc., 1889), p. 16: first published 1594.
See also p. 142 below. Thomas Hood's earlier treatise on *The Use of both the globes*
(1592) was written 'for the mariners'. Sir Christopher Hatton's copy of Hues's
Tractatus was in Sir Edward Coke's library (ed. W. O. Hassall, *A Catalogue of the
Library of Sir Edward Coke*, Yale Law Library Publications, no. 12, 1950, p. 80).

[3] Add. MS. 6209, f. 89; Hallowes, op. cit., p. 88.

[4] Ward, *Lives of the Gresham Professors*, p. 337; ed. M. Christy, *The Voyages of
Captain Luke Foxe of Hull, and Captain Thomas James of Bristol* (Hakluyt Soc., 1893),
i. lxi. The *Treatise* first appeared annexed to the second edition of Edward Water-
house's *Declaration of the State of the Colony and Affaires in Virginiia* (1622). See also
Purchas His Pilgrimes (1625), iii. 177–8, 825. The *Treatise* is reprinted in *The Voyages
of William Baffin* (ed. C. R. Markham, Hakluyt Soc., 1880), pp. 169–73. In it Briggs
stressed the importance of bringing Christianity to the American Indians (ibid.,
p. 170; cf. pp. 155–6, 162 below).

[5] Waters, op. cit., p. 335; Taylor, *Mathematical Practitioners*, p. 403.

[6] Waters, op. cit., p. 356; Taylor, *Mathematical Practitioners*, pp. 194, 356; Howell,
Logic and Rhetoric in England, p. 246. See pp. 48–51 below for the importance of
almanacs.

[7] So *D.N.B.*, but there may be some confusion between William Bedwell and his
uncle Thomas, also a mathematician and instrument-maker.

with the Gresham group that Aubrey thought he had been a professor at the College.[1] Bedwell, who dabbled in astrology, forms another link with Ralegh's circle, since he helped with the chronology of the *History of the World*.[2] Briggs was also interested in the new astronomy, though 'the most satirical man' against astrology 'that hath ever been known', the astrologer Lilly tells us.[3] When Briggs's friend George Hakewill published his manifesto of the partisans of the Moderns against the Ancients, Briggs contributed a paper on modern inventions in mathematics, and went out of his way to write to Hakewill emphasizing his agreement with his thesis.[4]

The youthful mathematical prodigy John Pell (1611–85) was discovered by Briggs, and later worked with another Gresham professor, Gellibrand. Pell was subsequently associated with the Comenian group in England, of which I shall shortly say more.[5] In 1643, none of the few jobs for mathematicians in England being vacant, Pell accepted a mathematics chair in the Netherlands. He returned only in 1652, when the Commonwealth's Council of State promised him £200 a year, a house, and a mathematics lectureship. The latter did not materialize, and Pell became instead the republic's diplomatic representative at Zurich. In 1658 he was meeting with the group which later formed the Royal Society, and was one of its original Fellows.[6] In 1628 Briggs was active in trying to raise funds for the relief of Calvinist academics who had fled from the Palatinate —enthusiastic support for whom was the shibboleth which divided Puritans from Arminians. Briggs was a great friend of

---

[1] Aubrey, *Brief Lives*, i. 96.

[2] Ward, *Lives of the Gresham Professors*, pp. 120–9. Bedwell recommended the study of Arabic, among other reasons, because of the importance of Arabic science (J. B. Mullinger, *The University of Cambridge from . . . 1626 to the decline of the Platonist Movement*, 1911, pp. 93–94). Cf. Lilly, *History of His Life and Times*, p. 23, though Lilly confuses Bedwell with William Bedell, for whom see p. 277 below. For Bedwell see also pp. 50, 64 below.

[3] Ed. T. Birch, *The Court and Times of James I* (1848), ii. 110; Lilly, op. cit., p. 106. Lilly, a Puritan by origin, used to attend the divinity lectures of Richard Holdsworth (see pp. 56, 58, 307–8 below) as well as those of William Gouge (ibid., pp. 4, 20). He was a friend of William Oughtred (see p. 53 below).

[4] Hakewill, op. cit., pp. 301–2.

[5] See pp. 100–9 below.

[6] Taylor, *Mathematical Practitioners*, pp. 203, 215–16; R. Vaughan, *The Protectorate of Oliver Cromwell* (2 vols., 1839), *passim*; R. R. Barnett, *Theodore Haak, F.R.S.* (The Hague, 1962), pp. 30, 46, 53, 97–98, 121, 127.

the Calvinist Archbishop of Armagh, James Ussher, himself a
keen mathematician and one of Comenius's patrons.[1] Theodore
Haak, a refugee from the Palatinate to whom Briggs lent
manuscripts, and who also knew John Greaves, Gresham
Professor of Geometry, was later a central figure both in the
Comenian group and in the group which formed the nucleus of
the Royal Society. It was at Haak's instance that the famous
meetings of this latter group started at Gresham College in
1645.[2]

Under Briggs, then, Gresham College was a centre of advanced science as well as of adult education. In 1601 Richard
More, a master carpenter, told his fellow artisans to read
Billingsley's *Euclide* and to attend Briggs's lectures every
Thursday if they wanted to learn modern methods of mensura-
tion and quantity surveying based on geometry. Richard
Delamain, a joiner who acted on this advice, acquired enough
mathematics from lectures and discussions at Gresham to
become a teacher of the subject himself, and to invent a slide
rule. Another who educated himself at Gresham was Edmund
Wingate (1596–1656), a lawyer who in 1630 published a
textbook of arithmetic with a commercial emphasis, which
went through many editions.[3] We hear of such cases only by
accident: not many of those whom Briggs helped recorded
their gratitude as eloquently as the sea-captain who named
some north-western islands 'Brigges his Mathematickes'.[4] (In
view of Briggs's interest in the North-West Passage, the
compliment was appropriate.) But there can be no doubt
that Gresham College helped greatly to raise the level of

---

[1] Thomas Smith, *Vitae Quorundam eruditissimorum et illustrium virorum* (1707), Vita
Henrici Briggs, p. 3. Letters from Briggs to Ussher are printed in Richard Parr's
Life of . . . Usher (1686). They deal with mathematics and astronomy among other
things. Cf. Hallowes, op. cit., pp. 88–89.

[2] P. R. Barnett, 'Theodore Haak and the Early Years of the Royal Society',
Annals of Science, xiii. 210.

[3] Taylor, *Mathematical Practitioners*, pp. 50, 201, 205; D. E. Smith, *History of
Mathematics*, p. 414; Waters, op. cit., pp. 295–6, 477–9. Wingate retained his connexion with Gresham, publishing two posthumous volumes from the papers of his
old friend Samuel Foster, Professor of Astronomy, who died in 1652. (For Foster
and Wingate see pp. 48, 72 below.) Wingate, whose mathematical writings
appeared in French as well as in English, also published books on law.

[4] This was Luke Foxe, a fellow Yorkshireman, whose earliest patron was Briggs,
and whom Briggs helped in many ways with the preparations for his voyage of 1631
(*The Voyages of Captain Luke Foxe*, i. lxii–iii).

mathematics teaching in this period, as well as to increase the number of teachers.[1]

Briggs left his chair for Oxford in 1620, but his tradition was continued by Edmund Gunter and Henry Gellibrand, who held the chair of Astronomy from 1619 to 1636. Gunter (1581–1626) was a close friend of Briggs's, and may have obtained the chair on Briggs's recommendation. Gunter was a notable mathematician who continued Briggs's work on logarithms. He took very seriously the instruction to Gresham mathematics professors 'to explain the use of common instruments for the capacity of mariners'. The publication of his Gresham lectures made him with Edward Wright the most important English writer on mathematical navigation of his period. His books, written with great clarity and with easily comprehended mathematics, ran to many editions. 'Before,' wrote Aubrey with some exaggeration, 'the mathematical sciences were locked up in the Greek and Latin tongues and so lay untouched, kept safe in some libraries. After Mr. Gunter published his book ["of the quadrant, sector, and cross-staff"], these sciences sprang up amain, more and more, to that height it is at now (1690).'[2] With John Wells and Phineas Pett Gunter devised a more accurate method of calculating ships' tonnage.[3] Gunter also invented a number of instruments to simplify calculations—Gunter's line of numbers, Gunter's Scale (a slide rule), Gunter's Quadrant, Gunter's Chain, this last remaining in use until the mid-nineteenth century. He gave the first clear explanation of the use of the log-line to assess distances travelled at sea, and so to calculate position: Gunter may even have invented it. When Captain Thomas James went to look for the North-West Passage in 1630, his instruments were Gunter's, and Gunter's textbook was his principal guide to practice. Before he sailed he made a special journey to discuss his voyage with Briggs, now in Oxford.[4]

[1] Taylor, op. cit., pp. 50, 57–58.   [2] Aubrey, Brief Lives, i. 276.
[3] S. F. Mason. A History of the Sciences (1953), p. 201. Pett was another skilled non-university mathematician.
[4] The Voyages of Captain Luke Foxe, i. xli, ii. 604–6; Taylor, Mathematical Practitioners, p. 69; The Haven-Finding Art, pp. 228–9; Waters, op. cit., pp. 358–92, 416–39, 499, 572–3. Gunter invented the words cosine and cotangent. A John Gunter was an officer in the Parliamentary army, who was later said to be a great favourite of Oliver Cromwell's (E. Peacock, The Army Lists of the Roundheads and Cavaliers, 1874, p. 49; B. Dale, Yorkshire Puritanism and Early Nonconformity, n.d., ?1909, pp. 63–64;

I suggested earlier that we should not despise the beliefs of the early scientists just because we know that they turned out to be unfounded: they might for all that be fruitful. The existence of the North-West Passage is such a belief. Its historical importance is that it led to scientific, nautical, and commercial enterprises, which linked John Dee with Sir Humphrey Gilbert and George Gascoigne,[1] Gresham College (Briggs, Gunter) with practical explorers like Foxe and James, with Hakluyt, with the Virginia Company, with big City financiers like Sir Thomas Smith and Sir John Wolstenholme, and with Parliamentarians like Sir Dudley Digges. The discovery of a North-West Passage, John Davis argued in 1595, by offering the speediest route for the import of Indian commodities, would make England 'the storehouse of Europe'.[2]

Gellibrand (1597–1637), another friend and protégé of Briggs's, completed his master's work on logarithmic trigonometry tables; wrote on navigation; and demonstrated the secular variation of magnetic declination.[3] His work was known to Mersenne.[4] When we recall the close connexion between Gresham and the technical experts of the Royal Navy and Trinity House throughout the forty years covered by the professorships of Briggs, Gunter, and Gellibrand, we get some idea of the College's ramifications.

In 1633 the thirty-year-old virtuoso Kenelm Digby, desolated

W. C. Abbott, *Writings and Speeches of Oliver Cromwell*, Harvard U.P., 1937–47, iii. 682–8; iv. 799). There were later many nonconformist ministers called Gunter (ed. A. G. Matthews, *Calamy Revised*, 1934, pp. 239–40).

[1] Ed. D. B. Quinn, *The Voyages and Colonising Enterprises of Sir Humphrey Gilbert* (Hakluyt Soc., 1940), i. 96; ii. 483–8.

[2] J. Davis, *The Worldes Hydrographicall Description* (1595), Dedication to the Privy Council, printed in the 1600 edition of Hakluyt's *Principall Navigations*. Cf. p. 70 below. For Smith's Puritan connexions see H. C. Porter, *Reformation and Reaction in Tudor Cambridge* (1958), pp. 132–5.

[3] The original edition of Gellibrand's *Epitome of Navigation*, probably published some time in the sixteen-thirties, has not survived, nor has the first edition of Henry Bond's *Discovery of the true and infallible way of finding the long hidden secret of longitude*. The fact that we know of the existence of these editions, and of many other books, only by accident should teach us caution in bibliographical matters relating to books of this period designed for use (Taylor, *Mathematical Practitioners*, pp. 71, 74, 319, 338, 349–50; Waters, op. cit., pp. 15, 127, 191; G. H. Turnbull, 'Samuel Hartlib's Influence on the Early History of the Royal Society', *Notes and Records of the Royal Society*, x. 108).

[4] Harcourt Brown, *Scientific Organizations in 17th century France* (Baltimore, 1934), pp. 50–51.

by the death of his Venetia, came to settle at Gresham College. For two years he had a laboratory under Richard Holdsworth's room, in which he conducted experiments in botany, embryology, magnetics, and optics. Digby was also closely associated with the Deptford circle, and was later a friend of William Harvey. He made significant contributions to embryology, and as a foundation Fellow of the Royal Society illustrates the connexion between that body and Gresham College.[1]

Samuel Foster, Gellibrand's successor, continued Briggs's tradition. He had been an usher at Coventry Grammar School between going down from Emmanuel and his appointment to his chair. Foster helped Jeremiah Horrocks, improved Gunter's Quadrant, and published popular treatises on *The Use of the Quadrant* and *The Art of Dialling*. So it was no accident, but the natural result of half a century of history, that it was in Foster's chambers at Gresham, after his weekly astronomy lecture, that the group which later formed the Royal Society first began to meet, in the year of Naseby.[2] In 1648–9 the leading figures of this group—Wilkins, Wallis, Goddard—were imported to Oxford by the Parliamentary commissioners, though they still retained close connexions with Gresham. So the higher scientific achievements of London and Gresham were brought to a reluctant Oxford.[3]

Gresham College rendered another service to popular education through its association with almanacs. Almanacs often included pages on astronomy, cosmography, and the tides, as well as on astrology; and at 1*d.* were cheap enough to have a very wide circulation among the lower classes. With the Bible they might often be the only literature in a small household. An almanac might be the first stimulus to an interest in mathematics: teachers of the subject thought it worth while to advertise their services in almanacs. Many almanacs were used especially by

---

[1] Aubrey, *Brief Lives*, i. 226–7; J. Needham, *History of Embryology* (2nd ed., 1959), p. 123; R. T. Petersson, *Sir Kenelm Digby* (1956), pp. 107–9, 195–6, 278. Digby quoted Gellibrand (ibid., p. 341). Digby reverted to Catholicism soon after he had left Gresham College in 1635. For Holdsworth see pp. 56, 58, 307–8 below.

[2] J. Wallis, *A Defence of the Royal Society* (1678), pp. 7–8; Taylor, *Mathematical Practitioners*, pp. 77–79, 206.

[3] At Wadham—Wilkins's College, and the centre of the scientific group—even the manciple was an instrument-maker in 1651, a son-in-law of Briggs's friend William Oughtred. He had probably served at sea for the Parliament under Captain William Baddiley (Taylor, op. cit., pp. 85, 234). For Oughtred see p. 53 below.

seamen, whom the almanac-makers deliberately aimed at educating in mathematics and astronomy.[1]

Since the mid-sixteenth century many leading mathematicians, doctors, and scientists had contributed to this form of popular education. Andrew Boorde is the first Englishman known to have issued a printed almanac and prognostication.[2] John Field, who taught in London, printed an almanac in 1556 (with a preface by Dee) which included one of the earliest English references to Copernicus.[3] Richard Forster (President of the College of Physicians and mathematician, protégé of Leicester), William Cunningham, Dee, Leonard and Thomas Digges, William Bourne (whose almanacs were intended especially for mariners), Richard Grafton (the chronicler), and Thomas Hill all published almanacs under Elizabeth. Thomas Digges's *Prognostication Everlasting*, which was regularly republished until 1635, did much to popularize the Copernican system.[4] Knowledge of the heliocentric theory was extended in the seventeenth century by the almanacs of Edward Gresham and Arthur Hopton.[5] In 1601 John Tapp, a self-educated mathematics teacher, started *The Seamans Kalendar*, prototype of the *Nautical Almanack*. This was written in a very simple popular style. Tapp 'ranks high amongst the men who . . . went far towards transforming the art of navigation into a science by bringing into use the methods of arithmetical navigation'. In 1613 he dedicated his *Path-Way to Knowledge* to Sir Thomas Smith.[6]

In all this Gresham had its share. Tapp probably knew Gunter and had access to his papers. Thomas Bretnor, who published *A Newe Almanake and Prognostication* from 1605 to 1630, was also a friend of Gunter's. Bretnor was the most

---

[1] E. F. Bosanquet, *English Printed Almanacks and Prognostications to 1600* (1917), p. 10; Bosanquet, 'English 17th century almanacs', *The Library*, 4th Series, x. 378–9; C. Camden, 'English Almanacs and Prognostications', ibid., 4th Series, xii. 84–85; Taylor, *Mathematical Practitioners*, pp. 57–58; Waters, op. cit., p. 239.

[2] Bosanquet, *English Printed Almanacks*, p. 5. See pp. 76, 296 below.

[3] Waters, op. cit., p. 128.

[4] Bosanquet, *English Printed Almanacks*, p. 67; Camden, op. cit., pp. 92–99; Taylor, *Mathematical Practitioners*, p. 176; Waters, op. cit., pp. 96, 127, 143–4, 162. For Grafton see p. 178 below.

[5] Johnson, *Astronomical Thought*, pp. 250–1; Waters, op. cit., p. 318.

[6] Taylor, *Mathematical Practitioners*, pp. 55–56, 337; *The Haven-Finding Art*, p. 226; Waters, op. cit., pp. 320, 401.

advanced Copernican among the almanac-makers, and referred to Ptolemaic astronomy as 'the old dotage'.[1] William Bedwell, Briggs's friend, produced an almanac in 1614, *The Travellers Companion*, the Preface of which speaks favourably of Bretnor and Hopton.[2] George Gilder, who produced an almanac in 1616, was another friend of Gunter's.[3] After Tapp's death in 1631, Henry Bond (*c.* 1600–78) edited *The Seamans Kalendar* for the next twenty years. He was a humble man who taught himself mathematics from Briggs's textbooks, and became 'Reader of Navigation to the Mariners' in the Royal Dockyards, Chatham. He remained closely associated with the Gresham circle, and was influenced by Gellibrand to put forward a new method of discovering longitude in which the Royal Society was later interested. Bond was a friend of Samuel Foster and edited his posthumous works, as well as those of Gunter.[4] Gellibrand got into trouble with Laud for helping to produce an almanac.[5]

The prophetical element in almanacs had always worried governments and conservatives. One lucky prognosticator came perilously near to forecasting the date of Queen Elizabeth's death in 1603, and Nashe associated almanac-makers with rebels.[6] In 1635, a correspondent told John Winthrop two years later, almanac-makers had been 'blasted ... with Jupiter's thunderbolt for being too curious in their predictions', and had abandoned prophecy in consequence.[7] The breakdown of the censorship after 1640 naturally benefited almanac-makers, who at once became more polemical and propagandist, and

---

[1] Johnson, 'The Influence of Thomas Digges on the progress of modern astronomy in 16th century England', *Osiris*, i. 404; M. Nicolson, 'English Almanacs and the "New Astronomy"', *Annals of Science*, iv. 14; Taylor, *Mathematical Practitioners*, p. 197.

[2] Johnson, *Astronomical Thought*, pp. 250–1. For Bedwell see p. 44 above.

[3] See p. 63 below.

[4] R. C. Winthrop, 'Correspondence of Hartlib, Haak, Oldenbourg and others of the Founders of the Royal Society with Governor Winthrop, 1661–72', *Proceedings of the Massachusetts Hist. Soc.*, 1878, p. 40; Taylor, *Mathematical Practitioners*, pp. 65, 207, 352; *The Haven-Finding Art*, pp. 232, 247.

[5] See p. 57 below.

[6] The sneers at almanac-makers of Greene, Ben Jonson, Middleton, and Sir Thomas Overbury, as well as Nashe, contrast with the co-operation of doctors, mathematicians, and Gresham professors (Camden, op. cit., pp. 87–89).

[7] Reyce to Winthrop, 1 March 1636–7, *Massachusetts Historical Soc. Collections*, 4th Series, vi. 410.

appealed to a wider public. They also became more universally Copernican and Baconian.[1] It was highly appropriate that when in June 1643 Parliament set up its own censorship, the licenser for books on mathematics, almanacs, and prognostications was the Reader of Gresham College for the time being, or Master John Booker.[2]

But in pursuing the tradition started by Briggs we have run on too far. There were other traditions at Gresham College. Matthew Gwinne, first Professor of Physic (1596–1607), was a former associate of the Sidney group and an acquaintance of Giordano Bruno.[3] In 1592 he had defended the Moderns against the Ancients in a disputation at Oxford before Queen Elizabeth. He was apparently so alarmingly successful that the Proctors cut him off after a quarter of an hour. He returned to the same theme in his Inaugural Lecture at Gresham, preferring London to Athens or Rome.[4] Gwinne also lectured on anatomy at Barber-Surgeons' Hall.[5]

Edward Brerewood, first Professor of Astronomy (1596–1613), wrote on logic, linguistics, geography, optics, and the weights and measures of the ancient world, as well as on his own subject: he was a member of the Society of Antiquaries. His *Enquiries touching the Diversities of Languages and Religions* (1614) was translated into French and was much admired by Mersenne.[6] Brerewood was an advocate of Protestant unity on lines which anticipate those later associated with the name of John Dury.[7] Brerewood also wrote a most remarkable treatise on Sabbatarianism. His nephew, apprenticed to a City merchant, suffered a *crise de conscience* in consequence of his master ordering him to perform household duties on Sunday. The prentice had heard

---

[1] Nicolson, op. cit., pp. 7–8, 14–17.

[2] *Acts and Ordinances of the Interregnum* (ed. C. H. Firth and R. S. Rait, 1911), i. 187. Samuel Foster, Professor of Astronomy, must have been intended, since the Professor of Geometry, John Greaves, was politically unsound, and anyway out of England (see p. 59 below). Booker (1603–67), originally apprenticed to a haberdasher, was himself an almanac-maker.

[3] J. Buxton, *Sir Philip Sidney and the English Renaissance* (1954), p. 161. Gwinne encouraged Greville to write Sidney's life and helped him to edit the 1590 *Arcadia* (ibid., p. 176). He was a friend of Sir William Paddy the physician and of John Florio the translator, who in his turn was a friend of Richard Hakluyt.

[4] Ward, *Lives of the Gresham Professors*, pp. 90–105.

[5] A. T. Young, *The Annals of the Barber-Surgeons of London* (1890), p. 334.

[6] Harcourt Brown, *Scientific Organizations in 17th century France*, p. 52.

[7] For Dury see pp. 102–3 below.

from Nicholas Byfield, a minister in Chester, that servants should refuse to obey such orders. Edward Brerewood was himself liable to suffer if his nephew's indentures of apprenticeship were broken, since he had gone surety for him. So the uncle refuted Byfield's thesis in a powerful argument which must have delighted the hearts of City employers. The law of nations, he argued, binds servants to obey their masters; and the law of God did not dissolve the law of nations. The commandment to observe the Sabbath was given to masters: it was not given, was not fit to be given, to servants, who 'do not need to be commanded to take their ease on the Sabbath'. Servants are not *homines juris sui*, nor *operum suorum domini*: they are but their masters' living instruments.[1] If the master gave wrongful commands, the sin was his, not the apprentice's: the latter's duty was to obey without question. In any case the commandment to obey the Sabbath had been in part revoked by the teaching of Jesus; 'the Apostles knew full well that to tell servants to disobey their masters was not the way to propagate the Gospel'. Mr. Byfield's doctrine could lead to 'nothing but disturbance and sedition both in church and commonwealth'.[2] No one penetrated so deeply into the social issues involved in the Sabbatarian controversy.

VI

When Gresham College was started, great care was taken not to offend Oxford and Cambridge. Lectures in English were defended (possibly rather disingenuously) on the grounds that they would be 'less offensive and damageable to the universities'.[3] Oxford and Cambridge were asked to make recommendations for filling the first chairs, and six of the seven went to their nominees. But rivalry inevitably remained. Heywood's

---

[1] Cf. C. B. Macpherson, *The Political Theory of Possessive Individualism* (1962), Chapter III.

[2] E. Brerewood, *A Learned Treatise of the Sabbath* (1630) and *A Second Treatise of the Sabbath* (1632), *passim*. See my *Society and Puritanism*, pp. 176–9. A tract of Brerewood's, reprinted in 1641 as propaganda for episcopacy, was wrongly so used (*Certain Briefe Treatises . . . wherein . . . the Primitive Institution of Episcopacie is Maintained*, 1641, pp. 96–119). Brerewood's tract argues merely that the Church in England from Constantine onwards was not subject to Rome but had its own bishops.

[3] Ward, *Lives of the Gresham Professors* (British Museum annotated edition), p. iii, Appendix, p. 21.

play, *If You Know Not Me You Know Nobody* (1606-9) shows us the popular image of Gresham. He has Puritan sympathies: his son tries to play up to these by promising to attend morning lectures at St. Antholin's! Gresham, the richest commoner in England, cries 'Tut in thy teeth, although thou art a knight!' to the papist Sir Thomas Ramsay.[1]

The whole method of teaching at Gresham was an implied criticism of Oxford and Cambridge, where for the first twenty years of Gresham's existence geometry and astronomy were either not taught, or taught very badly. At most grammar schools mathematics was taught only to 'dull' boys unfitted for a university education. The many excellent Elizabethan scientists and doctors of university origin learnt their subjects after they had gone down. Medical men went abroad, to Padua or Leiden, to complete their training.[2] None of the most famous scientists and mathematicians of the early seventeenth century—Gilbert, Harvey, Bacon, Napier, Hariot, Wright, Oughtred—held university posts. In the sixteen-thirties men like Wallis and Seth Ward who wanted to study mathematics had to leave the university and stay near London with the greatest mathematician of his day, William Oughtred (1575-1660), a parson for whom the universities had found no place, but who was a member of Briggs's circle.[3] It was difficult for a scientist to earn a living without a patron (Hariot, Hues), unless he sold instruments (Norman, Wright) or became a doctor (Recorde, Hood).[4] 'Alas!' said Bishop Williams to the mathematician John Pell: 'what a sad case it is that in this great and opulent kingdom there is no public encouragement for the excelling in any profession but that of the law and divinity. Were I in place as once I was, I would never give over praying

---

[1] Ed. J. P. Collier, *Thomas Heywood's Two Historical Plays of the Life and Reign of Queen Elizabeth* (1851), pp. 73, 83. Gresham's cousin Edmond was a Puritan, the founder of a lectureship in Essex (W. K. Jordan, *The Charities of Rural England, 1480-1660*, 1961, p. 181). See also p. 178 below.

[2] P. Allen, 'Medical Education', pp. 125, 131. See p. 83 below.

[3] Oughtred left evidence about the meetings of Briggs's group in his rooms at Gresham. Oughtred perfected Gunter's slide rule. His private pupils included several later Gresham professors, Samuel Foster among them, and Fellows of the Royal Society. Foster remained Oughtred's friend, and translated some of his writings into English (W. O[ughtred], *An Apologeticall Epistle*, sig. B 3v-B 4, in *The Circles of Proportion*, 1632; F. Cajori, *William Oughtred*, 1916, p. 71).

[4] Kocher, *Science and Religion in Elizabethan England*, p. 115.

and pressing his Majesty till a noble stock and fund might be raised for so fundamental, universally useful and eminent [a] science as mathematics.'[1]

From 1619 an effort was made to 'Greshamize' Oxford. The Savilian chairs of Geometry and Astronomy, the Sedleian chair of Natural Philosophy, the Tomlins Lecture in Anatomy were established.[2] Geometry is almost totally unknown and abandoned in England, said Sir Henry Savile in the preamble to the deed of foundation of his chairs.[3] The first two Savilian Professors of Geometry and the second Professor of Astronomy were all ex-Gresham professors. When Briggs came to the chair of Geometry in 1620, followed by Degory Wheare to the newly established Camden readership in ancient history in 1622, the battle for modern subjects in Oxford might seem to be won.[4] In 1622 the University Press reprinted a book entitled *Philosophia Libera*, originally published abroad, which attacked the Aristotelean system of philosophy.[5]

But the university has always been skilful at resisting reform and absorbing reformers. The Savilian professors were instructed to lecture in the traditional way, by commenting on the familiar classical authorities, Plato and Aristotle, Euclid and Archimedes; Copernicus was the sole modern mentioned. The Sedleian Lectures on Natural Philosophy, endowed in 1622, were to be on Aristotle. Even the Tomlins lecturer did not himself dissect, still less his students.[6] Aubrey's story of Gunter's interview when being considered for the geometry chair may be apocryphal, but it illustrates the difference between the

[1] Aubrey, *Brief Lives*, ii. 129–30. There was a proposal in 1604 to found a College at Ripon with some scientific teaching, but it came to nothing (F. Peck, *Desiderata Curiosa*, 1779, pp. 284–9).

[2] Bacon had hoped to establish lectureships in natural philosophy, with 'the science in general thereunto belonging', but did not leave enough money (Mullinger, op. cit., pp. 65–66); cf. pp. 176–7, 309 below.

[3] Savile, like Briggs, was a Halifax man, and the two were friends.

[4] For Wheare see pp. 176–7 below.

[5] By Nathanael Carpenter, for whom see p. 305 below. There were further editions at Oxford in 1636 and 1637.

[6] Curtis, op. cit., pp. 153–4, 163. Richard Tomlins of Westminster had founded his lectureship in anatomy in 1622 because 'down to the present day, in neither of the universities of this kingdom . . . hath there been any anatomy lecture founded or instituted', and there were no dissections. The Regius Professor took his money and gave the lectures, but did not dissect (Allen, 'Medical Education', p. 118). Petty was later Tomlins lecturer (see p. 124 below).

Oxford and the Gresham conceptions of lecturing, and the Oxford attitude towards handicrafts. Gunter 'came and brought with him his sector and quadrant, and fell to resolving of triangles and doing a great many fine things. Said [Sir Henry Savile] "Do you call this reading of geometry? This is showing of tricks, man!" and so dismissed him with scorn.'[1] Briggs's successor in this chair was not Gunter but a supporter of the Ptolemaic astronomy, who had to be purged by the Parliamentary commissioners in 1648. In 1636 the Laudian Statutes insisted that the holder of the Tomlins anatomy lectureship should lecture 'in Hippocrates or Galen', and proclaimed that the authority of Aristotle was paramount.

When Briggs moved to Oxford, he did not enter as a conqueror: he expressed a timid hope that 'Oxford will go further', and that Cambridge would follow apace.[2] He was right to be cautious. Looking back in 1656, after the Parliamentarian purge, Osborn tells us that 'not a few of our then foolish gentry' used to keep their sons away from Oxford, 'lest they should be smutted with the black art' of mathematics: slender though the university's proficiency in that subject had then been, to its shame.[3] Since the universities were becoming so dependent on sons of the gentry, this was a serious matter. Even Seth Ward, even in 1654, when Oxford really had been 'Greshamized', thought the full Baconian programme of 'abandoning disputations and public lectures for agriculture, mechanic chemistry and the like' would not be very suitable 'for the nobles and gentlemen who send their sons here'. Hobbes, whom Ward quoted, said that the universities themselves had only just stopped thinking geometry was an 'art diabolical'.[4] That Hobbes and Osborn did not exaggerate can be seen by a glance at Thomas Hall's hysterical *Vindiciae Literarum* (1655).[5]

Meanwhile Gresham College itself had been the object of conservative attention. The most obviously dangerous chair

---

[1] Aubrey, *Brief Lives*, ii. 215. It was Sir Henry Savile who refused a fellowship at Merton to Robert Blake, the future admiral, because he was not tall enough. Yet Savile was one of the *avant garde* at Oxford, with a taste for paradox. In 1572–3 he had defended the rotation of the earth, and democracy as the best form of political constitution (J. R. L. Highfield, 'An Autograph Manuscript of Sir Henry Savile', *The Bodleian Library Record*, vii. 78).

[2] Curtis, op. cit., p. 118.

[3] F. Osborn, *Advice to a Son* (1656), in *Miscellaneous Tracts* (1722), i. 5.

[4] [Seth Ward], *Vindiciae Academiarum*, pp. 40–58.   [5] See Appendix.

was that of divinity, about which anxiety had been expressed from the beginning, lest it should stir up controversy.[1] The first professor, Anthony Wotton, chaplain to the Earl of Essex,[2] was a Modernist and Ramist. In 1604, after he had left Gresham—presumably to marry—Wotton was in trouble with Bancroft because as lecturer at All Hallows he was alleged to have prayed 'God to open the eyes of the King, that he may be resolved in the truth, without respect of antiquity'. Wotton defended William Perkins; attacked Richard Montague's *Appello Caesarem*; translated Ramus's *Art of Logick* (1626); was accused of Socinianism, and was defended by no less a person than his friend the Puritan Thomas Gataker: a good radical career.[3] So it is hardly surprising that, after the resignations of Wotton and his successor, James in 1604 ordered the electors to choose a harmless Cambridge don who was needed in London to translate the Bible, 'for that the place is of importance to be well supplied, being in our chiefest city of this kingdom', and the lectures being delivered to the common people. James again intervened in 1606 to order the election of George Mountayne, later to have a decorous episcopal career.[4] Samuel Brooke, who followed Mountayne in 1612, was an Arminian in 1618, if not earlier.[5] Not until 1629 was a London preacher popular with the Puritans appointed as divinity professor—Richard Holdsworth, who succeeded John Preston as Master of Cambridge's most Puritan college and was one of the few patrons of modern educational methods in either university. He started his Gresham lectures by referring to Jesus Christ as 'the good merchant'.[6] But meanwhile in 1607, when the

[1] Ward, *Lives of the Gresham Professors* (British Museum annotated copy), Appendix, pp. 22–24.   [2] Add. MS. 6209, f. 10.

[3] Ward, op. cit., pp. 40–41. Wotton's preaching was greatly admired by Nicholas Ferrar as a boy (Add. MS 6209, f. 89). For Ferrar's connexion with Gresham College see p. 43 above.

[4] Ward, *Lives of the Gresham Professors*, pp. v, 45–49. Another consideration to which James referred in 1606 was 'the confluence of numbers of persons of quality, who are commonly of the best sort repairing to that lecture'.

[5] Cambridge University Library MS. Add. 44(16); Trinity College MS. 349. I owe these references to Mr. N. Tyacke. Brooke had been chaplain to Prince Henry, who recommended him for the Gresham chair.

[6] R. Holdsworth, *Praelectiones Theologicae habitae in Collegio Greshamensi* (1661), p. 1; Ward, op. cit., p. 57; Curtis, op. cit., pp. 108–13, 131–4; see also pp. 307–8 below. The next holder of the chair, Thomas Horton, was a Presbyterian (Ward, op. cit., pp. 65–69).

sinister Dr. Cowell was a candidate for the Chair of Law, he was passed over in favour of Clement Corbet, uncle of one of the Five Knights of 1627, and of the regicide Miles Corbet.[1]

Briggs was 'a severe Presbyterian', who associated mainly with 'persons of that judgement', Lilly tells us.[2] He co-operated actively with the Puritan party in Cambridge before his election to the Gresham chair. In 1589 he had even supported the campaign in favour of the imprisoned Francis Johnson, soon to emigrate to the Netherlands as a separatist. Six years later Briggs was one of those who protested against William Barrett's attack on Calvin; he campaigned actively on the Puritan side in a disputed election to the mastership of St. John's. So he was a known Puritan when the Gresham electors appointed him. He plotted with Ussher and William Crashawe about the printing of books which they expected the bishops to dislike.[3]

Under Laud, Gresham College had more trouble with the ecclesiastical authorities. Gellibrand had to appear before the High Commission for approving the publication of an almanac which annoyed Henrietta Maria by omitting many of the traditional saints and replacing them by Marian martyrs.[4] Though Gellibrand was acquitted when he showed that similar almanacs had been printed earlier, Laud threatened him with further prosecution since 'I hear you keep conventicles at Gresham College after your lectures there'. Prynne alleged that Gellibrand died of a fever fit as a result.[5] In 1636 Samuel Foster was ejected from his Gresham chair for refusing to kneel at the Communion table: he was restored in 1641.[6] His will

---

[1] Ward, op. cit., pp. 238–9. For Cowell see p. 228 below.

[2] Lilly, *History of His Life and Times*, p. 106.

[3] Hallowes, op. cit., pp. 89–91; Parr, *Life of Usher*, ii. 11–36. Crashawe, like Briggs, was a member of and propagandist for the Virginia Company.

[4] Laud, *Works* (1847–60), iv. 261–6; Prynne, *Canterburies Doome*, pp. 182–3, 513.

[5] Prynne, op. cit., p. 182. Gellibrand's father, Henry, had a living in Kent, where he also practised as a physician (J. H. Raach, *A Directory of English Country Physicians (1603–43)*, 1962, p. 47). It may be only a coincidence that Edward Gellibrand of Kent had been a leader of the classis movement in Oxford in the fifteen-eighties and was later minister of the English church at Middelburg, where he died in 1601 (R. G. Usher, *The Presbyterian Movement in the Reign of Elizabeth*, Camden Soc., 1905, p. xli; R. Bancroft, *Dangerous Positions*, 1593, pp. 74–75). His daughter married the Puritan Julines Hering. The professor's brother, Major Thomas Gellibrand of Bread St., gave evidence against Laud at his trial. A Samuel Gellibrand was a Presbyterian printer in the sixteen-forties.

[6] I take the reason for his deprivation on the authority of M. Ornstein, *The Role of Scientific Societies in the Seventeenth Century*, p. 94: she gives no reference.

shows him to have been a zealous Puritan. Richard Holdsworth, though he took the King's side in the civil war, had
protested in the Convocation of 1640 against the fourth canon,
which prescribed the kneeling position for refusing which
Foster had been deprived; and he objected to Convocation
sitting after Parliament had been dissolved. He defended the
Petition of Right even in 1642.[1] Laud thus silenced some
scientists and drove others into exile (like the self-taught
ex-seaman, Richard Norwood),[2] just as he silenced some
Puritans and drove others into exile. The two were united in Sir
Kenelm Digby's friend, the younger John Winthrop, clamour-
ing from New England for the latest scientific books and instruments.[3]

Meanwhile many Gresham scientists assisted the Professors
of Divinity to carry out the founder's instructions to combat 'the
common adversary of the Church of Rome'.[4] Hungarian
Calvinists had contacts with Gresham College in the sixteen-
thirties. Sir Kenelm Digby had the assistance of a Hungarian
chemist, Hans Hunneades (Bánffyhunyadi), in his laboratory
at Gresham.[5] When Lord Clarendon described the regicide

[1] Ward, *Lives of the Gresham Professors*, British Museum annotated copy, p. 58;
J. B. Mullinger, *The University of Cambridge from . . . 1626 to the decline of the Platonist
Movement* (1911), p. 145; R. Holdsworth, *The Valley of Vision* (1651), p. 13. For
Holdsworth see Appendix.

[2] Richard Norwood, who ran away to sea from his apprenticeship to a fish-
monger, taught himself mathematics by reading Recorde's *Arithmetic*. For twenty
years he taught mathematics in London, publishing a *Trigonometrie* (1631), which
owed much to Gunter, Gellibrand, Handson, and Wright, and *The Seamans Practice*
in 1637. But he ran into trouble with Archbishop Laud and emigrated to the Ber-
mudas, which he had surveyed for the Bermuda Company twenty years earlier.
From there he corresponded with the Royal Society (Taylor, *Mathematical Practitioners*, pp. 202, 347; Waters, op. cit., pp. 342–5, 432, 480–91).

[3] Thirty-five out of 1,000 books which Winthrop brought to Massachusetts in
1631 were scientific, including works by Paracelsus, Dee, Norwood. Letters to him
in 1634 and 1640 mention Robert Norton's *The Gunners Dialogue* (1628), Wingate's
Logarithms (1626 or 1630), Bedwell's *Mesolabium Architectonum* (1631), Wilkins's
Discovery of a New World in the Moon (1640), and books by Robert Fludd. Winthrop
corresponded with Comenius and probably tried to make him the President of
Harvard College. Winthrop later became a Fellow of the Royal Society (S. E.
Morison, *Builders of the Bay Colony*, n.d., ?1930, p. 272; *Collections of the Massa-
chusetts Historical Soc.*, 4th Series, vi. 497, 509–12; cf. pp. 456–7).

[4] See p. 34 above.

[5] L. Makkai, 'The Hungarian Protestants and the English Revolution', *Acta
Historica* (Budapest), v. 22; R. T. Petersson, *Sir Kenelm Digby*, p. 108. See p. 101
below for other connexions between Transylvanian Calvinists and English Baconians and Puritans. Bánffyhunyadi died soon after his return to Hungary.

Isaac Dorislaus as a former Gresham professor, he was wrong; but the mistake is significant of Gresham's reputation.[1]

What is not clear, and will not be until we have a full modern history of the College, is how far royal intervention and closer relations with Oxford and Cambridge counteracted the original character of Gresham College as an institution of popular adult education. There is even some doubt as to how far professors carried out their obligation to reside at the College. This is a difficult question, for some professors were anxious in the later seventeenth century to prove that their predecessors had not resided: so some of the evidence is tainted.[2] Brerewood and Holdsworth at least seem to have resided: John Greaves did so in the period immediately following his election as Professor of Geometry in 1630,[3] but subsequently spent most of his time abroad, until he was deprived for negligence in 1643. He can have contributed little to adult education in London. But Greaves was a respectable scholar. He wrote a useful book on astronomy and geography, and when in 1637-8 he went to examine the Pyramids he made careful measurements and drawings which he afterwards published. He also printed studies in the history of astronomy.[4] But he was a supporter of the Ptolemaic astronomy, and was purged from Oxford by the Parliamentary commissioners in 1648.

Greaves seems to have owed his election at Gresham College to his predecessor, Peter Turner: both Turner and Greaves held fellowships at Merton together with their Gresham professorships: both were royalists in the civil war. Peter Turner was a Laudian, although the grandson of William Turner, Marian exile, embattled Puritan controversialist, and father of scientific biology in English. Peter Turner's father was Sir Walter Ralegh's doctor, who in 1603 wrote against the use

[1] Clarendon, *History of the Rebellion* (ed. W. D. Macray, 1888), v. 24; Ward, *Lives of the Gresham Professors*, p. xix. See p. 176 below.

[2] e.g. *An Exact Copy of the Last Will . . . of Sir Thomas Gresham*, pp. 68-69.

[3] Add. MSS. 6203, ff. 4, 28. For Holdsworth see Appendix.

[4] Taylor, *Late Tudor and Early Stuart Geography*, pp. 134, 156, 293-6; cf. A. R. Hall, *Ballistics in the 17th century* (1952), p. 65. Greaves was a friend of William Harvey, whose appointment as Warden of Merton Greaves is said to have recommended to Charles I in 1645 (W. Harvey, *Works*, translated with *Life* by Robert Willis, 1847, p. xxxi; G. Rolleston, *The Harveian Oration*, 1873, p. 81). Greaves was also a friend of Archbishop Ussher (Parr, *Life of . . . Usher*, ii. 509-10).

of amulets against the plague.[1] Peter's brother, Samuel, was the M.P. who in 1625 charged the Duke of Buckingham as the author of all the state's misfortunes. Samuel had failed to be elected to the Gresham chair of Astronomy in 1613; his brother apparently drew the appropriate conclusions.[2] Mungo Murray, a renegade Scot in Anglican orders, was made Professor of Astronomy on Charles I's recommendation in 1636. He published nothing. The chair of Rhetoric was held by a dynasty of the legal family of Croke from 1613 to 1638. But the Crokes had opposition associations, and Edward Williamson, who married a Croke and succeeded a Croke as Rhetoric Professor, was to be a member of the Westminster Assembly of Divines.

An interesting tract of 1633 gives a full account of the Gresham science and mathematics lectures, which suggests that they were still highly utilitarian in content and expressed in a popular way.[3] There were complaints that the less scientifically minded seamen failed to attend; but the repeated demand for the lectures to be given out of as well as in term suggests that they were popular both with London citizens and with gentlemen and others who found themselves too occupied during the law terms.[4] But—apart from Gunter and Gellibrand—too many of the later professors seem to have published, if at all, in Latin.[5]

We may perhaps provisionally conclude then that the institutionalization of adult education by Gresham College was a mixed blessing, since it gave the chance of control from above. Nevertheless, the contribution of the College to the history of science in England has been persistently under-

[1] H. Craig, *The Enchanted Glass* (2nd ed., 1950), p. 104.

[2] Ward, *Lives of the Gresham Professors*, pp. 129–35. Samuel Turner was a friend of the mathematician Thomas Hariot, for whom see pp. 139–42 below (ed. J. O. Halliwell, *A Collection of Letters Illustrative of the Progress of Science in England*, 1841, p. 46).

[3] 'Philopolites' (Thomas Nash), *Quaternio or a Fourefoll Way to a Happie Life* (1633), quoted by L. B. Wright, *Middle-Class Culture*, pp. 600–1.

[4] J. Tapp. *The Pathway to Knowledge* (1613), quoted by Waters, op. cit., p. 320; Allen, 'Medical Education', p. 134.

[5] Their connexions, so far as we know them, were with intellectuals like Selden, Twysden, Harbottle Grimston, Bulstrode Whitelocke, mostly Parliamentarian in sympathy. But Thomas Eden, Law Professor from 1613 to 1640, Master of Trinity Hall, Cambridge, Chancellor to Bishop Wren of Ely, and four times M.P. for Cambridge University, was just a career civil lawyer, who survived to take the Covenant in 1643.

estimated by historians who fix their eyes on Oxford and Cambridge. Contemporaries made no such mistake. Wren, in his inaugural lecture at Gresham in 1657, mentioned the names of Gunter, Brerewood, Gellibrand, Foster as 'perhaps in the mouths of all mathematicians'. 'I must congratulate this City', he continued, 'that I find in it so general a relish of mathematics and the *libera philosophia*, in such a measure as is hardly to be found in the academies themselves.'[1] Sprat, the historian of the Royal Society, said that although at Gresham the choice of professors was 'wholly in the disposal of citizens', nevertheless those appointed were 'of the most learned men of the nation'.[2]

John Woodward, Gresham Professor of Physic, 1693–1728, writing probably in the late seventeen-twenties, was even more lyrical about his College: 'The fame of it went over the whole world. The most important discoveries of those times took their rise from Gresham College. . . . There's hardly any part of useful knowledge that has not received great accessions from thence; and some of the most considerable discoveries in philosophy, physic, anatomy, in all the parts of mathematics, in geometry, in astronomy, in navigation, came forth of Gresham College. . . . We feel them in our persons, in our health, in the enlargement of our minds, in our strength by sea and land, as well as in our power and interest abroad. This everybody must assent to that is not wholly a stranger to the history of learning; or does not know that Dr. Gwinne, Mr. Gunter, Mr. Foster, Mr. Bainbridge, Mr. Briggs, Mr. Gellibrand, Mr. Greaves, Mr. Brerewood, Dr. Winston, Dr. Holdsworth . . . were all professors there. . . . Their instructions have been happily extended to mechanics, and even the meanest artificers: to trade and all the manufactures of the nation.'[3]

VII

Gresham College was not the only place where scientific lectures were given in London. There were lectures at Surgeon's

[1] Wren, *Parentalia*, pp. 205–6. By 1657 'the academies' had been substantially modernized.   [2] T. Sprat, *History of the Royal Society*, p. 93.
[3] Add. MSS. 6209, ff. 337–9. For Winston, Professor of Physic 1615–42, 1652–5, see p. 162 below. I cannot place Bainbridge at Gresham.

Hall, the College of Physicians, and the Society of Apothecaries.[1] Gentlemen and lawyers at the Inns of Court took advantage of these facilities. Matthew Hale left Oxford innocent of science; but whilst at Lincoln's Inn he became well versed in medicine, anatomy, surgery, and mathematics.[2] As early as 1581 William Borough had said there was enough arithmetic and geometry taught in England for all seamen to learn them.[3] After Hood's lectureship lapsed,[4] the same sponsors paid for a lecture on navigation in Sir Thomas Smith's house 'for the better instruction of our mariners'.[5] The financing of this lecture was subsequently taken over by the East India Company itself: Edward Wright held it at a salary of £50 a year until his death in 1615. In the early sixteen-thirties there was a mathematical lecture for mariners at Chatham, given by Henry Bond.[6] Mathematics, together with medicine, astronomy, navigation, and cosmography, held an important place in the curriculum of the Musaeum Minervae which Sir Francis Kynaston founded about 1634 to give the modern education which the universities failed to provide. Only the armigerous were to be admitted, but Kynaston nevertheless felt that he had to defend himself against those who 'made some doubts and objections, that the institution of our academy here in London would be a prejudice' to the 'honour and flourishing estate of Oxford and Cambridge'.[7]

William Harrison in 1587 and Sir George Buc in 1612 spoke of the capital as 'the third university of England'. Though Buc's main emphasis was on law and theology, he listed among the subjects taught in London—in addition to Gresham's astronomy, geometry, and physic—arithmetic, surgery, mathematics, hydrography, geography, navigation, languages, cosmography,

---

[1] See pp. 74–79 below. In 1636 the Barber-Surgeons' Company decided to commission Inigo Jones to build them a lecture theatre (Young, *The Annals of the Barber-Surgeons of London*, pp. 129, 132, 363–5, 368, 405; cf. J. J. Keevil, *Medicine and the Navy, 1200–1900*, i. 1957, p. 215).

[2] Wood, *Athenae Oxonienses* (ed. P. Bliss, 1813–20), iii. 1060–1. Hale later wrote on the vacuum, the magnet, and other scientific topics. He was a friend of Wilkins as well as of Selden.

[3] W. Borough, *A Discourse of the Variation of the Compasse* (1581), sig. iiiv.

[4] See pp. 33–34 above.

[5] Taylor, *The Original Writings . . . of the two Richard Hakluyts*, ii. 510.

[6] Waters, op. cit., p. 569. For Bond see p. 50 above.

[7] Sir F. Kynaston, *The Constitutions of the Musaeum Minervae* (1636), sig. ¶¶, p. 4. For John Speidall, Kynaston's Professor of Mathematics, see p. 41 above.

artillery.[1] Four years later George Gilder—a teacher of mathematics and a friend of Gunter's—wrote 'Never were there better or nearer helps to attain [a knowledge of mathematics] than at present in this City'. He referred to the teaching and textbooks of Briggs, Gunter, and Speidall; and there were many other teachers in London, especially around Tower Hill.[2] Sprat said of Gresham College 'if it were beyond sea, it might well pass for a university.'[3] The Royal Society, the title of Sprat's book reminds us, was the Royal Society *of London*.

If we want to find a nursery of science in early seventeenth century England, we might do better to look for it not at Oxford or Cambridge but in London—not only at Gresham College and in the halls of City companies but also in the schools founded and supervised by merchant companies. Take Merchant Taylors', for instance. It was founded in 1561 by a radical Protestant, Richard Hilles. Its great headmaster, Richard Mulcaster, was a friend of Dee, Hakluyt, and Camden, a correspondent of Ortelius. The old boys of the school include Matthew Gwinne, Nicholas Hill, Thomas Hood, Robert Jacob (physician to Elizabeth), Sir William Paddy (physician to James I), Peter Chamberlen, Sir Edwin Sandys, Edmund Spenser, William Croome (an original Fellow of the Royal Society), Thomas Heath (astronomer), Richard Andrews (physician), and William Howe (botanist), along with many men distinguished in other fields.[4]

In 1599 Dekker, addressing Elizabeth, spoke of God as 'a great mathematician'.[5] Governments had to encourage mathematics, since similar mathematical principles were involved in navigation and gunnery. William Bourne wrote a treatise on

---

[1] Holinshed, *Chronicles* (1587), p. 151; Sir George Buc, *The Third University of England*, appended to the 1631 edition of Stow's *Chronicle*. Buc dedicated his essay to Sir Edward Coke, who in 1602 had referred to the legal inns in London as 'the most famous university . . . that is in the world' (*3 Reports*, sig. D. iv–v). For Buc see M. Eccles, 'Sir George Buc, Master of the Revels', in *Thomas Lodge and Other Elizabethans* (ed. C. J. Sisson, 1933), pp. 457–506: and p. 173 below.

[2] Taylor, *Mathematical Practitioners*, pp. 58, 203. There were also mathematics teachers, who had mastered Gresham's modern methods, at Bristol, Hull, Birmingham, Deal, and Dover before 1640; and local almanacs for the first three towns. The Birmingham mathematics lecturer was a master gunner for Parliament during the interregnum (ibid., pp. 77–80). [3] Sprat, *History of the Royal Society*, p. 93.

[4] F. W. M. Draper, *Four Centuries of Merchant Taylors' School, 1561–1961* (1962), pp. 5–6, 25–26, 31–35, 57–60.

[5] T. Dekker, *Old Fortunatus*, Epilogue.

each.[1] Robert Norton, a gunner at the Tower of London, said that geometry was 'the sinews of artillery', and expected a gunner to be able to use trigonometrical and logarithmical tables.[2] The idea of fighting by geometry was sufficiently familar to raise a laugh on the London stage in the sixteen-twenties and thirties.[3]

> The grace and disgrace of . . .
> Arithmetic, geometry, astronomy,
> Rests in the artisans' industry or vein.[4]

Fulke Greville's rather snob comment was confirmed by the title-page of a translation of Ramus by William Bedwell published in 1636. Geometry, it said, was 'necessary and useful for astronomers, geographers, land-meeters, seamen, engineers, architects, painters, carvers, etc.'[5] It was of the decade before the civil war that John Wallis in 1697 made his famous remark: 'Mathematics . . . were scarce looked upon as academical studies, but rather mechanical; as the business of traders, merchants, seamen, carpenters, surveyors of lands, or the like; and perhaps some almanac-makers in London. . . . For the study of mathematics was at that time more cultivated in London than in the universities.'[6] Wallis never heard of 'the new experimental philosophy' until years after he had left Cambridge.[7] The accuracy of Wallis's list of professions interested in mathematics in the sixteen-thirties enhances our confidence in the accuracy of his recollection sixty years later: it has sometimes been impugned.[8] We may compare John

[1] J. H. Parry, *The Age of Reconnaissance* (1963), p. 123.

[2] R. Norton, *The Gunner* (1628), quoted by A. R. Hall, *Ballistics in the 17th century*, p. 34. The opinion had indeed already been expressed that English gunners were too reliant on theory (ibid., pp. 44–45).

[3] B. Jonson, *The New Inn* (1629), Act ii, scene iii: Shakerley Marmion, *Hollands Leaguer* (1632), in *Dramatic Works* (1875), p. 91. Cf. Jonson's *Every Man Out of His Humour* (acted 1599), for a character who 'makes congies to his wife in geometrical proportions' (Act i, scene i).

[4] F. Greville, *Poems and Dramas* (ed. G. Bullough, n.d., ?1939), i. 183.

[5] W. Bedwell, *Via Regia ad Geometriam*; the Way to Geometry (1636). For Bedwell see p. 44 above.

[6] Appendix to the Preface to T. Hearne's edition of Peter Langtoft's *Chronicle* (1725), p. cxlvii. Wallis, having had the benefit of Richard Holdsworth's encouragement at Emmanuel, made his way to the home of William Oughtred and learned mathematics there.

[7] Ward, *Lives of the Gresham Professors*, p. x. Cf. p. 306 below.

[8] See p. 128 below.

Graunt's reference to 'the mathematics of . . . shop-arithmetic' underlying his pioneer work on statistics.[1]

In London it seems clear that any 'mechanician' had access to a scientific education as good as any in Europe, and much better than that given in English universities and most grammar schools. Popular scientific treatises had long circulated which taught him to suspect the authority of Aristotle or anyone else so long as such authority was not confirmed by his own experience. Anyone interested in science would have to come to London: Recorde, Dee, Gwinne, Gunter, and Fludd were all of Welsh descent, but all made their way to the capital.

For our purposes the importance of these facts lies less in their effect on the organization of science in England than on intellectual development. In 1614 a Scot, who had lived many years in England, in describing the national characteristics of the various European countries, *singled out* the English for their opposition to the Aristotelean cosmology and their support for Copernicus: 'In philosophy and the mathematics, in geography and astronomy, there is no opinion so prodigious and strange, but in that island was either invented, or has found followers and subtile instancers.'[2] Among these prodigious and strange opinions was a growing lack of respect for the authority of classical antiquity and a new critical freedom towards sacred texts. Gilbert, whilst paying due honour to the Ancients, pointed out that far more information was available to the Moderns, who therefore might 'philosophize freely'. He criticized only those who 'stubbornly ground their opinions on the sentiment of the Ancients', and 'adopted as theirs, from books only, without magnetical experiments, certain inferences, based on vain opinions'. He dedicated his great work to those 'who look for knowledge not in books but in things themselves', and praised craftsmen like Robert Norman.[3]

Edward Wright, in his book on navigation, completely ignored the Ancients, because they knew neither the compass nor the science of magnetism.[4] In 1618 Archdeacon William Barlow,

---

[1] J. Graunt, *Natural and Political Observations . . . upon the Bills of Mortality* (1662), Epistle Dedicatory to the President of the Royal Society. Cf. p. 272 below.

[2] John Barclay, *Icon Animorum* (1614). I quote from *The Mirrour of Mindes*, Englished by T. M[ay], 1631, p. 117. May was later the historian of the Long Parliament. See also p. 150 below.

[3] W. Gilbert, *De Magnete*, Preface.

[4] R. F. Jones, *Ancients and Moderns*, pp. 17–19. 'Before 1600—I should say by

son and brother-in-law to six bishops, noted with regret that mechanics were inclined to prefer reason and experiment before the literal words of Scripture. He took umbrage at the Laudatory Address prefixed to Gilbert's *De Magnete* by Edward Wright, which refused to reject the theory of the earth's diurnal motion on Scriptural evidence alone. Moses and the prophets, Wright argued in a way that was to become very familiar among Christian apologists later, adapted themselves 'to the understanding of the common people and to the current fashions of speech, as nurses do in dealing with babes; they do not attend to immaterial minutiae'.[1] Barlow consoled himself by reflecting that though arguments in favour of the earth's rotation 'may go current in a mechanical tradesman's shop, yet [they] are very insufficient to be allowed for good by men of learning and Christians by profession'.[2] The contrast between 'mechanical tradesmen' who favoured the new science and 'men of learning' who despised it, could hardly have been made more sharply or more contemptuously. But alas: barely twenty years later John Wilkins abandoned even Wright's argument that the Holy Ghost accommodated himself to his hearers: the 'penmen of Scriptures', said this future bishop, might be grossly ignorant.[3]

VIII

At the beginning of Elizabeth's reign England had been backward both in mathematics and in the art of navigation. By the end of Gresham College's second decade of existence,

---

1570—the scientific spirit ... had become a point of view 'popular with middle-class amateurs' (Stearns, 'The Scientific Spirit in England', *Isis*, xxxiv. 299). Cf. Robert Hues, p. 142 below.

[1] Gilbert, *De Magnete*, p. xli. The argument, Calvin's, was used by Ralegh in his *History of the World* (1820), i. 63; by Nathanael Carpenter in his *Geographie* (1625), p. 96 (for Carpenter see p. 305 below); and by John Wilkins in *A Discourse Concerning a New Planet* (1640). For Barlow see T. Fuller, *Worthies* (1840), iii. 249.

[2] W. Barlow, *A Briefe Discovery of the Idle Animadversions of Marke Ridley, Doctor of Physicke*, quoted by Johnson, 'The Influence of Thomas Digges on the Progress of Modern Astronomy in 16th century England', *Osiris*, i. 403. Cf. Cudworth's later reference to 'mechanic atheism', of which he thought 'an undiscerned tang' hung about the Cartesians (R. Cudworth, *The True Intellectual System of the Universe*, 1678, quoted by J. Tulloch, *Rational Theology and Christian Philosophy in England in the 17th century*, 1874, ii. 248–9). 'Mechanic atheism' was the philosophy of rude mechanicals.

[3] J. Wilkins, *A Discourse concerning a New Planet* (1640), pp. 10–14, quoted by G. McColley, 'The Ross–Wilkins Controversy', *Annals of Science*, ii. 159.

Commander Waters tells us, a revolution in nautical thinking had been completed in England which ended the empirical phase and introduced mathematical navigation, thanks very largely to the instruction in the use of scientific instruments and logarithms given at Gresham.[1] English mathematicians like Hariot and Wright proved better at solving the problem of 'Mercator's projection' than Mercator himself.[2] Well might Hakewill devote a chapter to 'The Art of Navigation, brought to perfection in this latter age'.[3]

As early as 1577 Richard Willis noted that geography had ousted grammar, poetry, logic, astrology, and Greek in popular approbation.[4] A common seaman of humble origins, Will Adams, after being apprenticed to a shipbuilder in 1576, learnt enough mathematics to teach the subject to the Shogun of Japan.[5] England's new proficiency in mathematics and navigation was recognized abroad. By 1618 Hues's *Treatise on Globes* had been translated into French. Edmund Wingate started his literary career in 1624 by popularizing Gunter's mathematical discoveries in French. Mersenne and Descartes followed the progress of mathematics in England.[6] This revolution in navigation made possible the defeat of the Armada[7] and the colonization of North America. It also led very soon to conflicts between gentlemen captains, many of whom lost interest in the sea after the peace of 1604 had diminished the chances of loot, and the tarpaulins who stayed on to master the new scientific navigation.[8] But an amateur interest in

---

[1] Waters, op. cit., pp. 196, 247–51, 319, 328, 341–2, 353, 416, 432–5, 496–500. The commercial sale of telescopes dates from after 1609. Waters notes 1614 as an important turning-point in this revolution (ibid., pp. 298–9, 341). Cf. Taylor, *The Haven-Finding Art*, pp. 195–201.

[2] M. Boas, *The Scientific Renaissance, 1540–1630* (1962), pp. 206–8; cf. A. H. W. Robinson, *Marine Cartography in Britain* (1962), pp. 27–33.

[3] Hakewill, *Apologie*, pp. 306–12. In 1640 a London clothworker hoped that a school he was endowing in Norfolk would teach navigation (W. K. Jordan, *The Rural Charities of England, 1480–1660*, 1961, p. 164).

[4] Richard Willis, Preface to Richard Eden's *History of Travel* (1577), quoted by C. S. Lewis, *English Literature in the 16th century* (1954), p. 308.

[5] P. G. Rogers, *The First Englishman in Japan* (1956), pp. 1–2, 32.

[6] See pp. 45, 47, 140. Cf. Harcourt Brown, *Scientific Organizations in 17th century France, passim.*   [7] M. Lewis, *Armada Guns* (1961), p. 204.

[8] Waters, op. cit., pp. 463–5, 499.

    Some by the school, some by the laws do mount,
    Some by the sword, and some by navigation:

so Sir Francis Hubert made Edward II reflect (ed. B. Mellor, *The Poems of Sir*

mathematics and allied subjects remained fashionable. Many fathers anticipated Oliver Cromwell's advice to his son Richard to 'study mathematics and cosmography; . . . these fit for public services for which a man is born'.[1] Lord Herbert of Cherbury similarly prescribed for a gentleman the serious study of geography, medicine, anatomy, and botany; Francis Osborn mathematics and medicine.[2]

More important for our present purposes, the revolution in mathematics and astronomy had philosophical implications. It was apropos the comet of 1618 that Richard Corbett wrote:

> Physicians, lawyers, glovers on the stall,
> The shop-keepers speak mathematics all. . . .
> The mason's rule, the tailor's yard alike
> Take altitudes.

By removing comets beyond the moon, the new astronomy made it less easy for rational men to treat them as portents foreshadowing future events on earth; by breaking the hard walls of the universe and suggesting the possible existence of infinite worlds, astronomers began to create a climate of opinion in which it seemed less likely that God would intervene in the day-to-day affairs of mankind. Simultaneously the science of meteorology, by explaining cloud-formations, diminished the probability of educated men seeing armies fighting in the sky.[3] In all spheres the miraculous was being ruled out of nature. Already men were seeing God as a geometer—Recorde, Dee, William Cunningham, Thomas Hill, Bedwell.[4] And the scientific revolution spread into more spheres than I can now discuss. Thus in England there was a controversy over astrology similar to that which was raging on the Continent in the late

---

Francis Hubert, Hong Kong, 1961, p. 45); but the thought was more appropriate to 1629, when Sir Francis published, than to the fourteenth century.

[1] Abbott, *Writings and Speeches of Oliver Cromwell*, i. 26 n. Cf. pp. 209–10 below for Cromwell's recommendation of history to his son.

[2] D. Bush, *English Literature in the Earlier Seventeenth Century*, p. 18; cf. *The Letter Books of Sir Samuel Luke* (ed. H. G. Tibbutt, 1963), p. 20; the Duke of Manchester, *Court and Society from Elizabeth to Anne* (1864), i. 375.

[3] Ed. J. A. W. Bennett and H. R. Trevor-Roper, *The Poems of Richard Corbett* (1955), p. 64; P. H. Kocher, 'The Old Cosmos: A Study in Elizabethan Science and Religion', *H.L.Q.* xv. 117–21. See pp. 19–20 above for Englishmen's unique readiness to entertain the idea of an infinity of worlds.

[4] Kocher, *Science and Religion in Elizabethan England*, pp. 151–5, 178–9.

sixteenth and early seventeenth centuries. But in England, unlike continental countries, this controversy was conducted in the vernacular, and so was not confined to academics.[1] In 1650 John Jones of Neath, refuting the slander that tradesmen and artisans were illiterate, claimed that many merchant adventurers in London were well-versed in arithmetic, geometry, astronomy, and physic: they had mastered 'the very encyclopaedia and summary of all good and necessary arts and learning'.[2]

Thus before Bacon began to write an intellectual revolution was under way. The utilitarian value of science as a means for the relief of man's estate on earth was being glorified; some men accepted the idea of progress through science, and of cooperation between the humblest craftsman and the scientist. 'That which is now hidden, with time will come to light', wrote Robert Ashley in 1594, 'and our successors will wonder that we were ignorant of them.'[3] *Plus ultra* was not Bacon's device only.[4] In 1601 Nicholas Hill, in the first modern work to preach atomic theories, said that new concepts demand new terms in writing, not in order to display the writer's style, but in order to convey his ideas. To arrive at truth, we must begin by clearing our own minds.[5] It was still true, as Bacon wrote in the *Novum Organum*, that 'Men have been kept back as by a kind of enchantment from progress in the sciences by reverence for antiquity'.[6] But the more intelligent merchants and craftsmen

[1] D. C. Allen, *The Star-Crossed Renaissance* (Duke U.P., 1941), p. 143. I have said nothing about the vast flood of vernacular books on popular medicine or popular psychology, from Timothy Bright's *Treatise of Melancholie* (1586: three editions by 1613) to Burton's *Anatomy*. Scientific literature for 'men simple and plain', 'the sailor and husbandman', 'the poorer sort', 'the wealth of unlearned persons', 'the meanest capacity', 'men that are simple and unlearned', is carefully studied in Professor Wright's invaluable *Middle-Class Culture in Elizabethan England*, Chapter XV, *passim*. For Bright see pp. 75, 133, 311-12 below.

[2] J. Jones, *The Jurors Judges of Law and Fact* (1650), pp. 75-76. Jones was arguing that artisan jurors had as much right and ability to try cases as upper-class judges. See p. 261 below.

[3] Louis Leroy, *Of the Interchangeable Course, or Variety of Things in the Whole World* (translated by R[obert] A[shley], 1594), Introduction, quoted by Johnson, *Astronomical Thought*, p. 296.

[4] Cf. the opening of Book II of *The Faerie Queene*, where we are led from the geographical and astronomical discoveries to contemplate the possible existence of worlds in the moon and stars.

[5] G. McColley, 'Nicholas Hill and the *Philosophia Epicurea*', *Annals of Science*, iv. 390-2, 403-4.

[6] Bacon, *Works*, iv. 81-82.

had already discovered that they needed an up-to-date astronomy and mathematics if they were to navigate ships, drain mines, and measure lands accurately.

From the mid-sixteenth century, when first Recorde and then Dee was adviser to the Muscovy Company, and the Company authorized the translation by Richard Eden, one of Dee's pupils, of a Spanish work on navigation, through the careers of the two Hakluyts, we can see an intimate connexion between merchants and science. The lectures of Hood and Wright were sponsored by Sir Thomas Smith and John Wolstenholme of the East India and Virginia Companies. The same two together with Sir Dudley Digges ran the North-West Passage Company, and sponsored the voyages of Hudson (1610), Button (1612), Bylot and Baffin (1615), Hawkridge (1619), Foxe (1631).[1] William Sanderson, a wealthy merchant connected with Ralegh, commissioned the mathematician Emery Molyneux to construct terrestrial and celestial globes for the use of seamen and students.[2] In 1614 the East India Company appointed John Woodall, an eminent surgeon, their Surgeon-General. Three years later he published the first serious treatise on medicine, surgery, and hygiene at sea—*The Surgions Mate*. In 1633 the Vintners' Company asked William Oughtred to design an instrument for the more accurate gauging of wine vessels.[3]

Governments gave far less encouragement to science than did merchant companies. There was a partial break-through in Elizabeth's reign, thanks to the patronage of men like Leicester, Gresham, and Ralegh, and to the need to rally support in the hour of England's danger. William Gilbert had a royal pension, and in 1588 he was asked to help with the health of the navy.[4] But despite agitation by Hakluyt with Drake's backing, it was only in the same year that the Privy Council gave its blessing to the scheme for Hood's public mathematics lecture, sponsored by leading City figures. Once the panic was over, no

---

[1] See pp. 34, 47 above. Smith and Wolstenholme were the patrons of Raphe Handson, who dedicated his *Trigonometrie* to them (see p. 42 above).

[2] Waters, op. cit., pp. 190, 197. See pp. 166–7 below. These were the globes to which Robert Hues referred in his *Tractatus de Globis* of 1592 (see pp. 42–43 above, 142 below).

[3] Taylor, *Mathematical Practitioners*, pp. 64–65; cf. p. 172; Johnson, 'Preparation and Innovation in the Progress of Science', *J.H.I.* iv. 57. See p. 76 below.

[4] Roller, *The* De Magnete *of William Gilbert*, p. 79.

further official interest was taken, despite pleas for a public mathematics lecture put forward (for instance) by William Barlow in 1597, by Hakluyt in 1598, by Wright in 1599, by John Tapp in 1613, by Admiral Sir William Monson some time before 1624, and by George Hakewill in 1627.[1] In James's reign court patronage was less easy to come by. Archbishop Abbott, who himself wrote a popular geographical textbook and was interested in mathematics, was not unfriendly: he was a member of the Virginia Company, and his brother was one of London's leading merchants.[2] But after Prince Henry's death in 1612, there was so far as I am aware no patron of science of social eminence comparable to Leicester. Ralegh and the Earl of Northumberland were in the Tower; Abbott was too anti-Spanish to retain much influence, and was in disgrace from 1621. Courtiers and the King himself might interest themselves in a speculative scientific or technological project if profits were anticipated;[3] and some government favour was shown to the armaments industry, for obvious reasons. But there was no considered policy of supporting even those aspects of science which were of immediate use. The Royal Navy's medical standards lagged far behind those set by men like Woodall and Ralegh. Organized agitation in the sixteen-twenties to get a reasonable allowance for medical supplies and equipment in the Navy failed. There was some improvement in the next decade, but only after Parliament had taken over control of the Navy was the medical situation radically altered.[4]

It might be argued that support for science was no part of the business of seventeenth-century governments. But the first four decades of the century were a period of greater paternal-istic government activity in all spheres than any before in English history. Not only did the demand for mathematics

---

[1] Waters op. cit., pp. 242-3, 320, 549; ed. M. Oppenheim, *The Naval Tracts of Sir William Monson*, iv (Naval Records Series, XLV), 391-6; Hakewill, *Apologie*, pp. 311-12.

[2] P. A. Welsby, *George Abbott, the unwanted Archbishop* (1962), pp. 7-9, 146. For Abbott see also p. 19 above.

[3] Simon Sturtevant, for instance, promised James I and his courtiers eighteen of thirty-three shares in the estimated profits of his scheme for smelting iron with coal (Bernal, *Science in History*, pp. 285-6; cf. p. 218 below). Cf. also p. 77 below for royal favour to some doctors.

[4] J. J. Keevil, *Medicine and the Navy*, i. *1200-1649* (1957), pp. 181-224; ii, *1649-1714* (1958), pp. v, 1-75.

lectures come from an ex-admiral, but the idea of government patronage for science received its strongest backing from
James I's Lord Chancellor, Francis Bacon.

IX

My object of course is not to suggest a direct relationship
between London science and the Parliamentary cause. It is
interesting that Parliament was believed to have more support
from doctors and so its troops got better medical treatment than
the King's.[1] The New Model Army had a regular medical
establishment. Its doctors were mostly apothecaries or surgeons, not physicians.[2] Thomas Sydenham and his four
brothers fought for Parliament; Nicholas Culpeper was
wounded at Newbury; Paul Hobson, barber-surgeon, was a
preaching colonel. Thomas Streete, who emigrated from Ireland to London, where he first attended lectures at Gresham
College and then taught mathematics, made astronomical
observations as an ensign in the Parliamentary army. Edmund
Wingate, who also taught himself mathematics by attending
Gresham lectures as a young man, and himself published very
popular books on the subject, opposed the King in the civil
war, and became a friend of Oliver Cromwell and a member
of Parliament in 1654.[3] The Robartes family neatly illustrates
the links between science, Puritanism, and the Parliamentary
cause. Richard, first Lord Robartes, who made a fortune in
wool and tin sufficient to purchase a peerage, had an excellent
library. This was looked after by his chaplain, Hannibal
Gammon (c. 1582–c. 1650), a Puritan divine interested in medicine, a correspondent of Degory Wheare, and a member
designate of the Westminster Assembly of Divines. The second
Lord Robartes led the Parliamentarian cause in Cornwall
during the civil war, and was a Fellow of the Royal Society.[4]

Such examples are of some interest, but they prove nothing
in themselves, and facts can be found which point the other way.

[1] See p. 76 below.

[2] C. H. Firth, *Cromwell's Army* (1902), pp. 255–6.

[3] Taylor, *Mathematical Practitioners*, pp. 89–90, 225–6, 205; W. T. Whitley, 'The
Rev. Paul Hobson', *Baptist Quarterly*, New Series, ix. 307–10. See p. 45 above.

[4] A. Wood, *Athenae Oxonienses* (ed. P. Bliss, 1813–20), iii. 103. I am indebted to
Miss Irene Cassidy for drawing my attention to Robartes and Gammon.

The relationship is less direct. Perhaps the most important scientific developments in England during the three generations before the civil war took place in mathematics, astronomy, and the related science of optics. I have suggested some economic applications of these sciences. But the advances were made possible only by an extraordinarily high level of skill and crafts-manship in instrument-making. These were the decades in which the English school of clock-making was established, which in the later seventeenth century was to be famous throughout Europe.[1]

Instrument-makers had to be mathematicians to do their job properly. But the theoreticians of the new science had to go beyond mathematics. All Gilbert's instruments were nautical instruments, and he obtained much of his information from practical navigators like Borough, Drake, Cavendish, Robert Norman. But he also closely studied the techniques of metal-lurgy, which were being revolutionized in sixteenth-century England by the rule-of-thumb practices of craftsmen. 'True philosophers', he declared, 'look for knowledge not in books only but in things themselves.'[2]

So far our emphasis has been mainly on mathematics and astronomy, of value to surveyors, navigators, merchants, and on medicine. But there was also the alchemical tradition of the craftsmen, which from the time of Paracelsus had begun to influence medicine and to interest the scientists. Dee was in this tradition, and Gilbert was not uninfluenced by it. This helps to explain Bacon's emphasis on the study of the crafts. 'The vexations of art are certainly as the bonds and handcuffs of Proteus, which betray the ultimate struggles and efforts of matter.'[3] The nearest that sixteenth- and early seventeenth-century scientists could get to a laboratory, it has been well said, was in the workshops of metal-workers, glass-makers, paper-makers, dyers, brewers, sugar-refiners—new industries, or industries in which new processes had been introduced. William Petty was the son of a clothier, who 'did dye his own cloths'; his greatest delight as a boy 'was to be looking on the

[1] R. W. Symonds, *Thomas Tompion, His Life and Work* (1951), pp. 6–8, 244.
[2] S. P. Thompson, *William Gilbert and Terrestrial Magnetism*, pp. 6–7; E. Zilsel, 'The Origins of William Gilbert's Scientific Method', *J.H.I.* ii. 2–32.
[3] Bacon, *Works*, iv. 257.

artificers—e.g. smiths, the watchmaker, carpenters, joiners.'[1]

Bacon's intention was to compile a History of Trades in which scientific reports would be made of the successful experiments carried on in these workshops. It would then be the job of the philosopher to analyse, clarify, and co-ordinate this information, with a view to 'a connection and transferring of the observations of one art to the use of another'.[2] Harvey's comparison of the heart to a water bellows or pump is a good example of the stimulus which Bacon had in mind.[3] Harvey, we recall, learnt from sow-gelders and game-keepers. Bacon's object was to bring about 'the true and lawful marriage of the empirical and rational faculties, the unkind and ill-starred separation of which has thrown into confusion all the affairs of the human family'. 'For where philosophy is severed from its roots in experience, whence it first sprouted and grew, it becomes a dead thing.'[4] In Bacon's *New Atlantis* scientific research was state-supported and state-controlled. Philosophers there, 'looking into the experiments of their fellows, . . . cast about how to draw out of them things of use and practice for man's life and knowledge, as well for works as for plain demonstration of causes'.[5] So, by studying and theorizing upon the achievements of the craftsmen, Bacon broadened and enriched the general philosophy towards which the mathematicians and astronomers had been working their way.

X

But before we turn to Bacon, let us pause for a moment to look at the organization of the medical profession. There was the College of Physicians, a self-selected body open only to university graduates, which had the right to license all medical practitioners within seven miles of London, and to fine and imprison the recalcitrant. There was the Company of Barber-Surgeons, an independent City Company since 1540, membership

---

[1] Aubrey, *Brief Lives*, ii. 139–40; W. E. Houghton, 'The History of Trades: its relation to 17th century Thought', *J.H.I.* ii. 35–36.

[2] Houghton, loc. cit., pp. 35–38. The History of Trades, Mr. Houghton sapiently observed, became superfluous in the later seventeenth century as laboratories replaced workshops as the main sources of scientific information (ibid., p. 60). Petty, under Hartlib's encouragement, planned a History of Trades. A great many of Boyle's works were called 'histories' (Ornstein, *The Role of Scientific Societies*, p. 42).   [3] Mason, *A History of the Sciences*, p. 177.

[4] Bacon, *Works*, iv. 19.   [5] Ibid., iii. 165.

of which involved a seven-year apprenticeship. Finally there were the Apothecaries, who were given freedom to prescribe for the poor by an Act of 1543, and were incorporated as a City Company together with the Grocers in 1606. In 1617 the Society of Apothecaries obtained separate incorporation—on the recommendation of Sir Theodore Mayerne and thanks to the intervention of Bacon; Sir Edward Coke, the Grocers' Company, and the Lord Mayor and Aldermen objected.[1]

Between these three groups there was considerable rivalry. Surgery, said 32 Henry VIII, cap. 40, was part of physic, and any physician could practise it; but the converse was not also true. Surgeons were not allowed to administer internal medicines. The College of Physicians was hostile to all 'empirics', especially to Paracelsans, and disliked knowledge being made available in English.[2] The College was denounced as an oligarchical monopoly, jealous of any new tendencies in medicine. In 1559 a doctor was threatened with imprisonment unless he withdrew a suggestion that Galen might have erred. Since the College could prevent him earning his living, he submitted.[3] There are many examples of surgeons, apothecaries and other craftsmen, and clergymen, some holding radical political and religious views, being fined and imprisoned for practising in London without a licence. Charles Goodall's *The Royal College of Physicians of London* (1684) gives 'an historical account of the College's proceedings against empirics and unlicensed practisers', including the elder Chamberlen and Alexander Leighton. The latter was deprived of the possibility of earning a living by the College, just as Laud prevented him earning it as a minister.[4] Many of those whom the College thus persecuted were

[1] N.R.S. vii. 80–85, 326; W. S. C. Copeman, *Doctors and Disease in Tudor Times* (1960), p. 45.

[2] [Anon.], *The Copy of a Letter written by E. D. Doctour of Physicke to a Gentleman* (1606), Part II, pp. 15–50. This argues that experience without classical learning is useless; books in English are dangerous for those who have not studied Latin grammar and rhetoric; the fact that empirics do many cures is irrelevant. See pp. 28–31 above, and cf. Kocher, 'Paracelsan Medicine', pp. 471–4. In Lacy's play, *The Dumb Lady* (1669, printed 1672) it is assumed that an apothecary will be a Paracelsan, and that doctors will oppose chemistry (J. Lacy, *Dramatic Works*, 1875, pp. 92, 98).

[3] C. E. Raven, *Synthetic Philosophy in the 17th century* (1945), p. 15.

[4] Goodall, op. cit., pp. 367, 376, 384–8, 401, 413–20; cf. my *Society and Puritanism*, p. 105. In 1587 Timothy Bright (for whom see pp. 133, 311–12 below) was summoned to appear before the College authorities: but he had powerful patrons and evaded punishment (W. J. Carlton, *Timothe Bright*, 1911, pp. 69, 111).

unqualified quacks: but its activities must also have alienated some more respectable medical men.

Thomas Vicary, who took the initiative in founding the Barber-Surgeons' Company, wrote the first textbook of surgery in English. Andrew Boorde, who wrote vernacular best-sellers— *The Brevyary of Health* (1541), *The Dietary of Health* (1542)— appears never to have been a member of the College of Physicians. Thomas Gale (1507–87), surgeon to Henry VIII's army and Elizabeth's navy, who made many innovations in surgical practice, wrote in English and incorporated his own experience. So did John Halle, a surgeon who attacked the old guard who 'think that only to physic belongeth theory or speculation, and that to surgery belongeth only practice'. 'Whereas theory and practice go not together,' he added, 'whether ye call it physic or surgery, I dare boldly affirm that there is in them no manner of perfection worthy commendation.'[1] Other vernacular writers were John Bannister (1533–1610), author of *The Historie of Man* (1578), which long remained the standard textbook of surgical anatomy; William Clowes (1540–1604), who translated part of Fernel's *Pathologie*; and John Woodall (1569–1643), author of the first practical manual of surgery and probable discoverer of fruit-juice as a remedy against scurvy.[2] Their writings enormously raised the prestige of surgery in the sixteenth century and helped scientists to appreciate that they had much to learn from non-university practitioners. But only the more intelligent physicians grasped the point.

The structure of the medical profession in London, and the behaviour of its members during the civil war, may be compared with the structure and behaviour of the merchant community of the City.[3] A contemporary noted that among the 'great advantages the Parliament hath had of his Majesty' was their much greater choice 'both of sea and land-chirurgeons', and consequently the far more successful medical treatment of the Parliamentarian wounded.[4] But as with the privileged ruling

---

[1] John Halle, *An Historiall Expostulation Against the beastlye Abusers, bothe of Chyrurgerie, and Physike in our tyme* (Percy Soc., 1844), p. 42; cf. pp. xiv, 38–39, 44. First published 1565.　　[2] Copeman, op. cit., pp. 9, 39, 41–43, 75–77, 154.

[3] For the City see V. Pearl, *The City of London and the Outbreak of the Puritan Revolution* (1961).

[4] Ed. G. Bernard, *Life of Sir John Digby, 1605–45* (Camden Miscellany, xii, 1910), pp. 111–12. Shortage of doctors in the royalist armies is confirmed by I. Roy, *The Royalist Army in the First Civil War* (Oxford D.Phil. Thesis, 1963), pp. 61, 169–70.

oligarchy in the City government, so the monopoly ruling group of the College of Physicians was dependent on the royal court for maintenance of its privileges. Just as some merchants— monopolists, customs farmers—provided services indispensable to the government, so the royal family had need of good doctors. A man like William Harvey was so intimately associated with the court that he had little choice but to accompany the King when civil war broke out. But he took care to get Parliament's permission to do so.[1] In Dr. Bonham's Case (1608–10) the common-law judges stopped the College extending its jurisdiction, and called its right to fine and imprison in question.[2] In 1612 the Lord Mayor of London helped to get the Barber-Surgeon Peter Chamberlen released from imprisonment by the Censors of the College.[3] The Barber-Surgeons often petitioned Parliament for permission to prescribe internal medicines, describing the Physicians' patent as 'very prejudicial to all His Majesty's subjects'. In 1621 Parliament threatened to bring the patent before its Committee of Grievances. The Barber-Surgeons' Company seems during the civil war to have been more solidly in favour of Parliament than the College.[4]

In the sixteen-thirties the College took a tougher line with its rivals: apothecaries appealed to Magna Carta.[5] The apothecaries, those independent craftsmen of the medical profession, looked to the Crown before 1640 for protection against the College of Physicians and the Company of Barber-Surgeons. Their charter of 1617 contained clauses restraining the privileges of the Barber-Surgeons: the latter appealed to Parliament against it.[6] But after 1640 many of the apothecaries supported Parliament and were very radical politically. Again

[1] Goodall, *The College of Physicians Vindicated* (1676), p. 11. See my 'William Harvey and the Idea of Monarchy', *P. and P.*, no. 27. [2] See p. 236 below.
[3] J. H. Aveling, *The Chamberlens* (1882), pp. 5–6; cf. p. 19.
[4] Goodall, *The Royal College of Physicians of London*, pp. 359–61; Young, *Annals of the Barber-Surgeons of London*, p. 138; [Anon.], *An Historical Account of Proceedings between the College of Physicians and Surgeons* (n.d., ? late seventeenth century), pp. 4–6; F. N. L. Poynter, 'The Influence of Government Legislation', in *The Evolution of Medical Practice in Britian* (ed. Poynter, 1961), p. 10.
[5] C. Wall, H. C. Cameron, and E. A. Underwood, *A History of the Worshipful Society of Apothecaries of London*, i (1963), 283, 287, 302.
[6] Young, op. cit., p. 126. In 1624 the Commons denounced the Charter as a grievance. For William Harvey's insistence on the necessity of subordinating apothecaries see Roberts, 'The Personnel and Practice of Medicine in Tudor England', *Medical History*, vi. 378.

this is parallel to the behaviour of the independent artisans in many City companies, who first looked to the Crown to help them to win separate organization, and who later turned to the Levellers.[1] We may also note attempts to organize the midwives made by members of the Chamberlen family in 1616 and 1634 and again during the revolution; and observe that the younger Peter Chamberlen became an Anabaptist.[2]

But though the medical profession thus falls into three distinct groups organizationally, ideas could not be prevented from passing freely backwards and forwards between them. Distinguished medical men like John Caius, President of the College of Physicians, William Cunningham, William Paddy, Matthew Gwinne, and Peter Chamberlen lectured on anatomy at the Company of Barber-Surgeons, in order to emphasize the necessity for linking medicine and surgery.[3] In 1583 the Lumleian lectures on anatomy were established at the College of Physicians: William Harvey announced his discovery of the circulation of the blood when he was Lumleian lecturer.[4] These lectures were intended to direct the attention of physicians to the more practical aspects of their profession, hitherto largely left to Barber-Surgeons. After the Lumleian lectures had been delivered in Latin, a summary was given in English, so 'as whether he be learned or unlearned that shall become an auditor', he might still profit.[5] In 1632 the Gulstonian lecture in pathology was added, soon to be delivered wholly in English.[6]

[1] G. Unwin, *Industrial Organization in the Sixteenth and Seventeenth Centuries* (1904); M. James, *Social Policy during the Puritan Revolution* (1930), Chapter V.

[2] Aveling, *The Chamberlens*, pp. 34–49. The motives of the Chamberlens may not have been entirely disinterested: it was alleged that by incorporating midwives they wished to establish a monopoly for the use of their family forceps. But Bacon perhaps sympathized with the scheme (ibid., pp. 21–24, 49–50); and cf. the concern for midwives shown by the very radical Nicholas Culpeper in his *Directory for Midwives* (1651). Cf. also Goodall, *The Royal College of Physicians of London*, pp. 463–6; P. Chamberlen, *A Voice in Rhama* (1647), *passim*.

[3] Copeman, op. cit., p. 27; P. Allen, 'Medical Education', p. 139; Gunther, *Early Science in Cambridge*, p. 149. Cf. B. Farrington, 'Vesalius on the Ruin of Ancient Medicine', *The Modern Quarterly*, i (1938), 23–25.

[4] Lumley had been one of the sponsors of Hood's mathematical lecture at Leadenhall (Waters, op. cit., p. 185; see p. 34 above and p. 215 below.)

[5] R. Holinshed, *Chronicles* iii (1587), p. 1349, quoted in W. Harvey, *Lectures on the Whole of Anatomy and Surgery* (ed. C. D. O'Malley, F. N. L. Poynter, and K. F. Russell, University of California, 1961), pp. 3–4.

[6] Allen, op. cit., p. 138; Rosenblum, *Leicester, Patron of Letters*, p. 36; R. P. Stearns, op. cit., p. 298; J. J. Keevil, *The Stranger's Son* (1953), p. 111.

Hakewill thought the science of anatomy belc nged exclusively to modern times;[1] and the fashionableness of the word (cf. *The Anatomy of Abuses, of the World, of Melancholy, of Wit*) is significant. The Paracelsan chemist John Hester, who sold chemical medicines and drugs, had a long fight with the Barber-Surgeons in the fifteen-seventies and eighties; but after 1590 he became more friendly to the Company, praising the books of some of its members like Clowes and Gale; and Clowes returned the compliment. Thanks to the efforts of courageous freelances like Hester, Paracelsan medicine was becoming intellectually respectable.[2] Simultaneously the *Herbals* of John Gerarde (surgeon) and John Parkinson (apothecary) established British botany as almost the best in Europe. In 1585 the College of Physicians laid out a physic garden round their Hall, and appointed John Gerarde as curator.[3] Sir Theodore Mayerne, himself an experimenter and inventor, is supposed to have persuaded the College of Physicians to adopt chemical remedies in their *Pharmacoepia Londinensis* of 1618.[4]

Yet as late as 1665 Marchamont Nedham asserted that 'till of late years' Aristoteleans and Galenists had stirred up princes and magistrates against the chemists. The College of Physicians, devoted to Hippocrates and Galen, tried to keep down the new 'laborious sect of philosophers'. But ultimately their great achievements had opened the eyes of governors, and even the common people came to see that the College of Physicians was a selfish monopoly. Even Charles Goodall admitted that in Mayerne's time 'the physicians' education and practice had too much prejudiced them against the noble art of chemistry'; but he claimed that this prejudice did not last long.[5]

The controversies among medical men also helped to advance scepticism. The Paracelsans (Richard Bostock, for instance)

---

[1] G. Hakewill, *An Apologie*, pp. 271–5. None of the anatomists whom Hakewill cites are English, and he goes out of his way to criticize Oxford's backwardness, until very recently, in this and other sciences.

[2] P. H. Kocher, 'John Hester, Paracelsan (*fl.* 1576–93)', in *Joseph Quincy Adams Memorial Studies* (Folger Library, 1948), pp. 621–38.

[3] Copeman, op. cit., pp. 46–47, 97. Gerarde is also credited with discovering watercress as a remedy against scurvy (ibid., p. 133).

[4] R. Malthauf, 'Medical Chemistry and "the Paracelsans"', *Bulletin of the History of Medicine*, xxviii. 110, 124.

[5] M. N[edham], *Medela Medicine* (1665), pp. 7–8; Goodall, *The College of Physicians Vindicated*, pp. 13–17. For confirmation see Keevil, *The Stranger's Son*, p. 138.

accused the Galenists of atheism, of studying second causes only. Many medical men threw doubts on witchcraft.[1] The Paracelsans themselves were accused of witchcraft and astrology.[2] 'The best way is to join Galen and Paracelsus', Hakewill thought, with a new openness of mind.[3] It was not for nothing that Nicholas Culpeper invoked Doctors Reason and Experience against Dr. Tradition.[4]

Outside London, where there was no effective machinery of repression, there was both greater freedom and greater demand for apothecaries and surgeons to practise as physicians. As the East India trade in the seventeenth century began to bring new drugs into England, so the significance of the special knowledge of apothecaries (and to a lesser extent surgeons) rose. By the second half of the sixteenth century some gentlemen were apprenticing their sons to apothecaries; by the sixteen-thirties apothecaries were being licensed to practise as physicians in increasing numbers. The common lawyers seem to have assisted this development. In a test case of 1607 Sir Edward Coke imposed a severe sentence on a physician who had libelled an apothecary who was ousting him from his practice. In consequence of this *cause célèbre*, says Mr. Roberts, 'the apothecaries of the West . . . won the right to practise'.[5]

In large part the rivalry was economic. 'The physician, as a great commander, has as subordinate to him the cooks for diet, the surgeons for manual operation, the apothecaries for confecting and preparing medicines.'[6] But as their practice expanded, surgeons and apothecaries rejected this inferior

---

[1] e.g. John Cotta, *A Short Discoverie of the Unobserved Dangers of severall sorts of ignorant and inconsiderate Practisers of Physick in England* (1612), pp. 49–71. Cotta was a doctor of physic at Northampton. He quoted Fernel (ibid., p. 23). Cf. Kocher, *Science and Religion in Elizabethan England*, Chapter VI, *passim*; and my 'William Harvey and the Idea of Monarchy', p. 65.

[2] Kocher, op. cit., pp. 70, 251–4.

[3] Hakewill, *Apologie*, ii. 135. Goodman, naturally, had attacked Paracelsus, whom Hakewill defended (ibid., ii. 134).

[4] Matthew Mackaile, *Moffet-Well* (1664), p. 178.

[5] This paragraph derives from Mr. R. S. Roberts's excellent article, 'The Personnel and Practice of Medicine in Tudor and Stuart England', *Medical History*, vi. 363–82, *passim*. I have also benefited by discussions with Mr. Roberts. For Coke see pp. 236–7 below.

[6] J. H. Raach, 'English Medical Learning in the early 17th century', *Yale Journal of Biology and Medicine*, xvi. 285–6, quoting F. H[ering]'s translation of Johann Oberndoerffer's *The Anatomyes of the True Physician* (1602).

status. 'Pray, Sir, how came the apothecaries to be your servants?' a pamphleteer was to ask in 1670.[1] Apothecaries were the doctors of the poor and middling sort. 'If none should be suffered to use [physic and surgery] but the learned', said an itinerant herb-doctor in Kent in 1564, 'a great many poor people should perish for lack of help.'[2] In the seventeenth century some provincial apothecaries were beginning to have a fashionable clientele,[3] but in London they remained the doctors of the poor. 'Surgeons and apothecaries are sought unto, the physicians seldom but in a desperate case are consulted with', said a London physician in 1684.[4] Apothecaries were often poor themselves. We recall Shakespeare's in *Romeo and Juliet*, 'in tattered weeds; . . .

> Sharp misery had worn him to the bones. . . .
> About his shelves
> A beggarly account of empty boxes.'

'Famine is in thy cheeks', Romeo said to him;

> Need and oppression starveth in thy eyes. . . .
> The world is not thy friend, nor the world's law.[5]

During the revolutionary decades the apothecary and zealous Puritan Nicholas Culpeper (1616–54) conducted a passionate campaign against the College of Physicians' monopoly on precisely the ground that it put medical treatment beyond the reach of the poor. In 1649 he published *A Physicall Directory, or A translation of the London Dispensatory made by the College of Physicians in London. Being that book by which all Apothecaries are strictly commanded to make all their Physicke*. It was a translation of the *Pharmacoepia Londinensis* of 1618, which the Physicians preferred to keep in Latin. Thanks to its most useful index, Culpeper's translation proved extremely popular. The third edition appeared in 1651, and it was reprinted at least fourteen times before 1718. An enemy said in 1664 that 'in this age . . . Mr. Culpeper hath been, by the ignorant, more highly esteemed

---

[1] [Anon.], *Lex Talionis* (1670), p. 13: attributed to Henry Stubbe, for whom see p. 127 below.
[2] J. Halle, *An Historiall Expostulation*, p. 23.
[3] Roberts, op. cit., *passim*.
[4] Goodall, *The Royal College of Physicians of London*, p. 444.
[5] Shakespeare, *Romeo and Juliet*, Act v, scene i.

than both Hippocrates and Galen'.[1] In a series of hard-hitting
Prefaces, Culpeper denounced the College as 'a company of
proud, insulting, domineering doctors, whose wits were born
above 500 years before themselves', and who will not attend to
those who cannot pay their fees. His translation of the *Dispensatory* was made out of 'pure pity to the commonalty of England,
. . . many of whom to my knowledge have perished either for
want of money to fee a physician or want of knowledge of a
remedy happily growing in their garden'. He added physicians
to the traditional monopolist enemies of the radicals, priests and
lawyers.[2] Culpeper was attacked by the royalist *Mercurius
Pragmaticus* as a disciple of John Goodwin, as a seeker and atheist.[3]

Persecution of apothecaries by the College was brought to
an end in 1640. Under Cromwell, 'who could scarcely have
affection for a society of men established by royal power, of
whom several had expressed so great loyalty to their sovereign',
Chief Justice St. John, to the accompaniment of loud applause
in Guildhall, refused to recognize the validity of the College of
Physicians' patent because it had not been established by Act
of Parliament.[4] In 1647 a statute of the College envisaged the
possibility of apothecaries and surgeons being admitted to their
body if they withdrew from their own companies. Four years
later a partial licence was granted to an oculist by the College.
But such concessions failed to survive the Restoration.[5] Even
after 1660, however, the Physicians still failed to get confirmation of their powers and privileges by Act of Parliament.[6] In

[1] Matthew Mackaile, *Moffet-Well*, sig. A 2v. Culpeper himself translated
Galen's *Art of Physicke*, published posthumously in 1657.

[2] N. Culpeper, *A Physicall Directory* (1649), sig. A–Av, pp. 344–5; cf. 1651 ed.,
sig. A 2–A 2v. Robert Burton for this reason proposed to nationalize medicine in
his Utopia (*Anatomy of Melancholy*, Everyman ed. i. 103). Peter Chamberlen used to
charge lower fees to the poor (*Diary of the Rev. John Ward*, ed. C. Severn, 1839, p. 107).

[3] *Mercurius Pragmaticus*, September 1649, quoted by F. N. L. Poynter, 'Nicholas
Culpeper and his Books', *Journal of the History of Medicine*, xvii. 155–9.

[4] A. Huyberts, *A Corner-Stone Laid towards the Building of a New Colledge (that is to
say, a new Body of Physicians) in London* (1675), pp. 4–7; Goodall, *The College of
Physicians Vindicated*, p. 11. See also Keevil, *The Stranger's Son*, pp. 74–76.

[5] J. M. Good, *The History of Medicine, so far as it relates to the Profession of the
Apothecary* (1795), pp. 129–36; Keevil, op. cit., pp. 140–1.

[6] Huyberts, op. cit., p. 14. Huyberts, an apothecary himself, proposed that the
apothecaries of London should be taken under the City's government, as the best
way of training 'apothecaries indeed, such as may practise with real knowledge,
not fill the world with cobwebs of idle speculations and notions, as men of the old
way of education are wont to do' (ibid., pp. 27–28, 33).

1669 it was argued that the Physicians' monopoly must be preserved if gentlemen were to be bred up to the profession: 'nowadays want of learning and degrees are adjudged as needful a qualification for the exercise of physic as formerly 'twas for preaching, and the shops fit to supply both'.[1] The radicalism of apothecaries was emphasized in Goodall's history of the Royal College of Physicians. Noah Biggs had accused the Galenists of the College of 'antipathy' to the Commonwealth.[2]

Outside London any medical or surgical practitioner who had not graduated from or been licensed by Oxford or Cambridge had to obtain a licence from an archbishop or the bishop of his diocese. Midwives too had to have episcopal licences.[3] Unlicensed practitioners were presented to and punished by the church courts. Laud in 1635 used his metropolitan visitation to restrict medical practice to those with degrees. This in some cases involved repudiating licences granted by his own officers.[4] It was to Laud and the Bishop of London that the 1634 petition for incorporating midwives was referred by the Privy Council.[5] Outside London perhaps two-thirds of the members of the medical profession were licensed by the ecclesiastical authorities, one-third by the universities.[6] The Regius Professor of Physic at Cambridge admitted in 1635 that serving-men and apothecaries might be licensed to practise physic 'without

[1] Christopher Merrett, *A Short View of the Frauds and Abuses committed by the Apothecaries* (1669), p. 42; cf. J. Goddard, *A Discourse Setting forth the Unhappy Condition of the Practice of Physick in London* (1670), pp. 11–12.
[2] Goodall, *The Royal College of Physicians of London*, sig. A 4 ('A few men not of academical but mechanic education, who being either actually engaged in the late rebellion, or bred up in some mean and contemptible trades, were never taught the duty they owe to God or their sovereign'); cf. *The College of Physicians Vindicated*, sig. A 4v–A 5v, pp. 22–23 ('state-fanatics'); N. Biggs, *The Vanity of the Craft of Physick* (1651), sig. b 1, p. 3.
[3] J. H. Aveling, *English Midwives—their History and Prospects* (1872), p. 89.
[4] Lambeth Palace Library, Diocese of Canterbury, Comperta 1634–6, ff. 111–260 d. I owe this reference to the kindness of Mr. R. S. Roberts.
[5] Aveling, *The Chamberlens* (1882), pp. 34–49.
[6] J. H. Raach, 'English Medical Licensing in the early 17th century', *Yale Journal of Biology and Medicine*, xvi. 273–8; Phyllis Allen, 'Medical Education in 17th century England', p. 142. Miss Allen caustically remarks that Lambeth medical degrees issued in conjunction with theological studies may have produced men no worse fitted to practise than those who had taken a degree in medicine at Oxford or Cambridge. For the backwardness of medical education in these universities, which drove serious medical students to go abroad, to Leiden or Padua if they could, see also D. C. Dorian, *The English Diodatis* (Rutgers U.P., 1950), pp. 64–70, and Curtis, op. cit., pp. 153–4, 163.

giving any public testimony of their learning and skill in the profession'.[1] But none could be admitted to a doctorate without subscribing to the three Articles prescribed in Canon 36 of 1604. It could be argued that the apprenticeship which surgeons and apothecaries served gave them a better vocational training than the purely academic education of physicians.

The bishops' right of licensing brought them into conflict with the Barber-Surgeons' Company in London.[2] From the reign of James I, and no doubt earlier, religious orthodoxy seems to have been as important as medical skill in procuring an episcopal licence.[3] Many ministers deprived for Puritanism were prevented by the ecclesiastical authorities from practising physic. A number of 'poor country vicars, for want of other means', were driven 'to turn mountebanks, quacksalves, empirics': they might have no qualifications at all.[4] During the Interregnum, when the bishops' licensing broke down, there was a quarrel between the College of Physicians and the Company of Barber-Surgeons over the right to license midwives. It was finally agreed that they should be licensed at Surgeons' Hall, after three examinations taken before six midwives and surgeons. The 1662 Act of Uniformity sent them back to the ecclesiastical authorities, 'where they had to pay their money', take an oath which it was impossible for them to keep, 'and return home as skilful as they went thither'.[5]

So there were many good reasons why all but the ruling oligarchy of the medical profession might look sympathetically upon the cause of Parliament. 'Thou hast a rotten stinking heart within thee', cried a Grantham apothecary in June 1642 to a man who said he would support the King against Parliament. But this apothecary went too far for the Commons when he proposed that Charles should be deposed.[6]

[1] Goodall, *The Royal College of Physicians of London*, pp. 443–5.

[2] J. H. K. Bloom and R. R. James, *Medical Practitioners in the Diocese of London* (1935), pp. 6, 9–11.

[3] Ibid., pp. 7, 27, 43, 69, 72, 81–82; cf. *C.J.* ii. 26, 137.

[4] R. Burton, *Anatomy of Melancholy* (Everyman ed.), i. 36; cf. John Cotta, *A Short Discoverie of the Unobserved Dangers of severall sorts of ignorant and unconsiderate Practisers of Physick in England* (1612), pp. 86–94.

[5] Aveling, *English Midwives*, p. 89. This is given only on the not very reliable authority of Mrs. Cellier in 1687: but she was writing of events within living memory, and does not seem to have been contradicted.

[6] Harleian MSS. 163 f. 623 a. I owe this reference to the kindness of Mr. Robin Clifton.

III

FRANCIS BACON AND THE
PARLIAMENTARIANS

Our best and most divine knowledge is intended for
action; and those may justly be accounted barren studies
which do not conduce to practice as their proper end.

JOHN WILKINS, *Mathematicall Magick* (1648), p. 2.

What art or science soever doth not advantage mankind,
either to bring him nearer unto God in his soul, or to free
him from the bondage of corruption in his body, is not at
all to be entertained; because at the best it is but a
diversion of the mind.

A Seasonable Discourse written by Mr. John Dury (1649), pp. 10–11.

I

FRANCIS BACON lived from 1561 to 1627. He climbed
slowly in Elizabeth's reign, despite his flying start as the
son of a Lord Keeper. But he was always near the centre
of power, and under James I he rose to be Lord Chancellor.
He was a leading figure in the government until in 1621 he was
disgraced on a charge of taking bribes. He had hoped to use
his influence at court to get his scientific schemes adopted: it
may only have had the effect of delaying their recognition by
the Parliamentarians.[1]

But we are concerned with Bacon the thinker, whom we can
now perhaps get into historical perspective. He was doubly
related to Sir Thomas Gresham. Bacon's father married
Gresham's wife's sister (though she was not Francis's mother),
and Francis's half-brother married Gresham's daughter. Bacon's
intellectual relation to Gresham College was very similar: closely
connected but not directly descended. Bacon was not an original
scientific thinker; he underestimated the achievements of some

---

[1] See p. 117 below.

of his contemporaries, notably Gilbert. Much of what Bacon said in criticism of Aristotle and the Schoolmen, and in favour of co-operation between scientists, his utilitarian assumptions, his belief in state-supported programmes for the relief of man's estate—much of this had been proclaimed before him by the popular scientific writers whose importance in England we have been considering. Gilbert, in addition to his brilliance as an experimenter, had also criticized scholasticism and speculated about 'a new style of philosophizing', for men 'who look for knowledge not in books only, but in things themselves'. But though Gilbert combined experiment with generalization, he had not yet fused them into a single all-embracing system.[1]

So there are difficulties in assessing Bacon's influence. Rather similar difficulties beset those seventeenth-century theologians who worried about the bodily resurrection of a missionary who had had the misfortune to be eaten by cannibals. Bacon incorporated his predecessors as the cannibals incorporated the missionary: it may be unfair that we speak of his influence when we mean the influence of a whole generation: but this sort of historical cannibalism is, I suppose, inevitable.[2]

Bacon was a social as well as a scientific thinker. With his powerful historical sense, he saw that something *new* was happening, in society as well as in science: he defined what this was, and showed how it could be consciously utilized for the relief of man's estate. 'The industry of artificers maketh some small improvement of things invented: and chance sometimes in experimenting maketh us to stumble upon somewhat which is new: but all the disputation of the learned men never brought to light one effect of nature before unknown.' Printing, gunpowder, the compass, the three great inventions of modern craftsmen, had been 'stumbled upon and lighted upon by chance': yet they had transformed the world. If all this could be done by the 'blind and stupid' method of uncoordinated experiment, more like 'a kind of hunting by scent than a science',

[1] W. Gilbert, *De Magnete*, Preface. A reaction has recently set in against attempts to discount Bacon's original contribution to scientific thinking. See J. R. Partington, 'Chemistry as Rationalized Alchemy', *Bulletin of the British Society for the History of Science*, i. 131–2; *History of Chemistry*, ii (1961), 389–414.

[2] Cf. H. P. Bayon, 'William Gilbert (1544–1603), Robert Fludd (1576–1637) and William Harvey (1578–1657) as Medical Exponents of Baconian Doctrine', *Proceedings of the Royal Society of Medicine*, xxxii. 39.

how much greater the advance would be if experiments were planned and directed, not haphazard as even Gilbert's had been. When 'experience has learned to read and write', a purposeful philosophy of knowledge for action could enable men to escape from the necessities of nature.[1]

This philosophy was 'the offspring of time rather than of wit'. It was part of God's plan that 'the opening of the world by navigation and commerce, and the further discovering of knowledge, should meet in one time'.[2] Thus Bacon gave a co-operative programme and sense of purpose to merchants, artisans, and philosophers, each of whom hitherto had seen only in part. This was his first great achievement. Secondly, he settled accounts with religion, and established that scientific investigation not only did not conflict with divinity but was positively virtuous.[3] This was very important in winning the support of Puritan Parliamentarians, without whose backing the victory of science in England would have been much longer delayed. Thirdly, whereas previous scientific thinking had been inextricably confused with alchemy and magic in a man like Dee, had been humdrum and practical and middle-class at Gresham College, with Bacon it attained both social dignity and philosophic grasp. It was not unimportant that he wrote philosophy like a Lord Chancellor. Bacon elevated to a coherent intellectual system what had hitherto been the only partially spoken assumptions of practical men. That is what Bacon meant when he claimed to be no more than the articulate spokesman of the inarticulate forces of his age.

'The true and lawful goal of the sciences is none other than this, that human life be endowed with new inventions and powers. But of this the great majority have no feeling, but are merely hireling and professorial. Only occasionally it happens that some artisan of unusual wit and covetous of honour applies himself to a new invention, which he mostly does at the expense of his fortunes.' But in order to make the scientific progress which is now possible for humanity, we must expand our minds

---

[1] Bacon, *In Praise of Knowledge*, in *Works* (1826), ii. 118–21. On the inadequacy of medieval academic science because of its divorce from technology, see A. C. Crombie, 'Quantification in Mediaeval Physics', *Isis*, lii. 154, 159–60.

[2] Bacon, *Works*, iv. 11, 77; iii. 221.

[3] See pp. 91–94 below.

to an understanding of the whole universe: for this purpose the philosopher must co-operate with the craftsman.[1]

'The destiny of the human race will supply the issue [of my work], and that issue will perhaps be such as men in the present state of their understandings cannot easily grasp or measure. For what is at stake is not merely a contemplative happiness but the very reality of man's well-being and all man's powers of action. Man is the helper and interpreter of Nature. He can only act and understand in so far as by working upon her or observing her he has come to perceive her order. . . . Nature cannot be conquered but by obeying her. Accordingly, these twin goods, human knowledge and human power, come in the end to one. To be ignorant of causes is to be frustrated in action.'[2]

Closer contact between scientists and craftsmen had been established in London. Men like Recorde, Dee, Digges, Hood, Gilbert, Briggs had practised new methods and glimpsed some of their possibilities. But Bacon gave men a noble and all-embracing programme of co-operative action, in which the humblest craftsman had a part to play. 'My way of discovering sciences goes far to level men's wits; and leaves but little to individual excellence, because it performs everything by the surest rules and demonstrations.'[3] We can grasp at something of the difference which Bacon made if we compare Dee's hope in 1570 that 'common artificers' might be able to 'devise new works, strange engines and instruments' with Milton's vision of London in 1644 as 'a city of refuge, the mansion-house of liberty', where men were 'reading, trying all things, assenting to the force of reason and convincement'.[4] John Hall five years later saw 'the highest spirits, pregnant with great matters, and in despite of these tumults and troubles which environ them on every side, labouring with somewhat the greatness of which they themselves cannot tell, and with a wonderful deal of courage attempting the discovery of a new world of knowledge'. Dee wanted craftsmen to have the opportunity of inventing useful gadgets: Milton and Hall thought that the whole community was advancing in knowledge, wisdom, power, and virtue,

[1] Bacon, *Works*, iv. 79. Here and elsewhere I have sometimes made use of the translation of Professor B. Farrington (*Francis Bacon, Philosopher of Industrial Science*, 1951, p. 91).

[2] Bacon, *Works*, iv. 32.   [3] Ibid. iii. 221.

[4] Milton, *Complete Prose Works* (Yale ed.), ii. 553-4.

'chasing away . . . shadows before the break of the great day'.[1] Bacon (and the Revolution) had come in between to give this wider audacity, this readiness to test everything, this confidence.

The most astonishing aspiration of Bacon's was that his scientific method would in certain respects liberate mankind from the consequences of the Fall. He hoped for 'a restitution and reinvigorating (in great part) of man to the sovereignty and power . . . which he had in his first state of creation'.[2] The object of *The Great Instauration* was to *restore* the commerce of the mind with things to its original perfection, or to something like it. 'For man by the Fall fell at the same time from his state of innocency and from his dominion over created things. Both these losses can even in this life be partially repaired; the former by religion and faith, the latter by arts and sciences.' The Fall had entailed that 'In the sweat of thy face shalt thou eat bread': labour was at once the curse and the salvation of man. For 'by various labours (not certainly by *disputations* or idle magical ceremonies, but by various *labours*)' nature could be 'at length and in some measure subdued to the . . . uses of human life'. But for the future, Bacon hopes, 'we may hand over to men their fortunes, the understanding having been emancipated— having come, so to speak, of age'. Hence 'there must necessarily ensue an improvement in man's estate, and an increase of his power over nature'.[3]

This breath-taking Utopian vision picks up ideas which long had haunted the Paracelsans and the alchemists.[4] But Bacon's programme was based not on the philosopher's stone but on the facts of industrial production. He proposed to reverse the whole course of human history as previously understood. When Karl Marx held forth hopes of an egalitarian classless society to the exploited, the idea of progress had already become a commonplace. But Bacon spoke to men for whom, for centuries, the dogma of the helplessness of fallen humanity

---

[1] J. Hall, *An Humble Motion to the Parliament of England concerning the Advancement of Learning and the Reformation of the Universities* (ed. A. K. Croston), 1953, p. 21. First published 1649.

[2] *Valerius Terminus, passim*, in *Works*, iii. 217–52.

[3] *Works*, iv. 21, 247–8.

[4] Haydn, *The Counter-Renaissance*, pp. 191, 250–1, 516–19. See also G. H. Williams, *The Radical Reformation* (Philadelphia, 1962), pp. 375–7, 857, for 'restitutionism' in Anabaptist thought. See pp. 95–96, 298 below.

had been axiomatic. Practice naturally had conflicted with theory. The craftsmen whom we have been considering, and the scientists who wrote for them, were optimists in practice. But Bacon gave them a theory which united a coherent optimism for humanity with a critique of Aristotle and the Schoolmen on grounds not only of their uselessness but also of their wickedness. 'Such teachings, if they be justly appraised, will be found to tend to nothing less than a wicked effort to curtail human power over nature and to produce a deliberate and artificial despair. This despair in its turn confounds the promptings of hope, cuts the springs and sinews of industry, and makes men unwilling to put anything to the hazard of trial.'[1]

That went far beyond the criticisms of Aristotle and the scholastic philosophy which had become almost common form among radical Protestants: it turned the tables on the theological opponents of the new science; and yet Bacon rightly claimed only to be giving voice to opinions which were the product of time, not of wit. He wanted to draw up 'a record of the highest mental and physical attainments of humanity, to balance the miseries of man copiously set forth by philosophers and theologians'.[2] So Bacon unfurled the philosophic banner of the Moderns, not only against the Ancients and their defenders in the universities, but also against the theologians. Hakewill followed up Bacon in assuming that 'the apprehension of [natural] truth helps to repair . . . the Fall', and that 'the first steps to enable a man to the achieving of great designs is to be persuaded that by endeavour he is able to achieve it'. To Goodman's argument that if we disparage the Ancients 'the country boors may rise in sedition', Hakewill replied that sedition was more likely if country people 'be once persuaded that nothing can be improved by industry'.[3] And Milton, who spoke up for the right of carpenters, smiths, and weavers to have a voice in the election of ministers, also thought that 'the end . . . of learning' was 'to repair the ruins of our first parents'.[4]

[1] Bacon, *Works*, iii. 592–4; cf. iv. 90; v. 317–18.

[2] Ibid. iv. 11, 77, 314–35.

[3] Hakewill, *Apologie*, p. 17, sig. a 3, ii. 132; cf. pp. 20–23, ii. 319. The view sometimes expressed, that Hakewill owes little to Bacon, will not bear examination, I think. Direct quotations are relatively few (e.g. pp. 42, 221, 261, 302); but as in the above passages, the Baconian spirit is everywhere.

[4] Milton, *Complete Prose Works* (Yale ed.), i. 934; ii. 366–7.

II

Bacon inherited from his pious parents, and imbibed from the world around him, Calvinist assumptions about the priority of faith over reason (the reason of the Schools—Bacon saw Aristotle as Antichrist)[1] as well as about the necessity for strenuous effort. 'All knowledge is to be limited by religion, and to be referred to use and action.'[2] Speculative knowledge is a contradiction. Calvin elevated the power of God, whilst discouraging excessive speculation about his nature and attributes, which are unknowable and on which the authority of the Bible is final. God is law.[3] But the power of God is manifested in his creation. For Bacon 'the works of God . . . show his omnipotency and wisdom, but do not partake of the image of the Maker', and so science can teach us nothing about the divine mysteries.[4] 'If any man shall think, by view and inquiry into these sensible and material things, to attain to any light for the revealing of the nature or will of God; he shall dangerously abuse himself. Approaching and intruding into God's secrets and mysteries' was the cause of the Fall. 'The contemplation of the creatures of God hath for end, . . . as to the nature of God, no knowledge, but wonder.'[5] 'Let us never . . . think or maintain that a man can search too far or be too well studied in the book of God's word or in the book of God's works.' But —and theologically this was a very big but indeed—'let men beware that they apply both [study of the Bible and study of nature] to charity, and not to swelling; to use, and not to ostentation; and again, that they do not unwisely mingle or confound these learnings together'.[6] 'The prejudice hath been infinite, that both divine and human knowledge hath received by the intermingling of the one with the other.' 'In aspiring to the throne of power, the angels transgressed and fell; in

[1] Bacon, *Works*, iii. 567. See p. 122 below. [2] Ibid. iii. 218.

[3] J. Calvin, *Institutes of the Christian Religion* (trans. H. Beveridge, 1949), i. 57, 235–7; ii. 227, 577. Cf. Luther: 'A theologian is born by living, nay dying and being damned; not by thinking, reading or speculating' (M. Luther, *Werke*, Weimar, 1883, v. 163, quoted by E. H. Erikson, *Young Man Luther*, 1959, p. 245; cf. p. 222).

[4] F. H. Anderson, *The Philosophy of Francis Bacon* (Chicago U.P., 1948), pp. 153, 212, and references there cited.

[5] Bacon, *Works*, iii. 218.

[6] Anderson, op. cit., pp. 54–55, and references there cited.

presuming to come within the oracle of knowledge, man transgressed and fell; but in pursuit . . . of . . . love . . . neither man nor spirit ever hath transgressed.'[1] To endow the condition and life of man with new powers and works was a religious duty.[2]

This subsumes a long trend in Protestant thought, from Luther onwards, which equated charity with works done with intent to benefit the commonwealth or mankind:[3] and so Bacon's separation of science from religion, so vital for the future advance of science, was in the best Protestant tradition.[4] This helped to free the scientists from not unfounded suspicions of witchcraft, alchemy, astrology, and atheism. When Sir Walter Ralegh said, 'We have principles in our mathematics', and wanted to apply them to a discussion of the human soul and the existence of God, he very naturally came under suspicion of atheism.[5] Bacon turned the tables and created the mental climate in which John Wilkins could say, 'Astronomy proves God and a Providence', and confirms the truth of the Scriptures.[6] It is thanks to Bacon that the father of the Royal Society 'may be termed the English godfather of natural or moral religion'.[7] It was not long before Sir William Petty could call an anatomy theatre '(without metaphor) a temple of God'.[8]

So Bacon gave the scientists' activities a moral sanction more socially acceptable than mere utilitarianism. Although, as we have seen, there were links between Puritanism and the scientific spirit,[9] their ways had diverged. Bacon justified this separation, and showed to the satisfaction of the next generation that

---

[1] Bacon, Works, iii. 217.   [2] Ibid. iii. 298; iv. 24, 104, 114.

[3] See my 'Protestantism and the Rise of Capitalism', in Essays in the Social and Economic History of Tudor and Early Stuart England, presented to R. H. Tawney (1961), pp. 15–39.

[4] It was not peculiar to Bacon. Nicholas Hill in his Philosophia Epicurea (1601)was convinced that organized religion was unfriendly to scientific investigation. Men should 'accept angelic revelation, but spit back ecclesiastical traditions' (quoted by G. McColley, 'Nicholas Hill and the Philosophia Epicurea', Annals of Science, iv. 400). This is one of the many passages that make one doubtful of Hill's alleged Roman Catholicism. See p. 145 below.

[5] Ed. G. B. Harrison, Willobie His Avisa (1594) (1926), p. 267. Cf. pp. 170–1 below.

[6] J. Wilkins, A Discourse concerning a New Planet (1640), pp. 237–40, quoted by G. McColley, 'The Ross–Wilkins Controversy', Annals of Science, iii. 161. As we saw above (p. 66), Wilkins was less sure of the literal truth of the Bible.

[7] McColley, op. cit., pp. 155, 186. Wilkins became a bishop, and his posthumous Of the Principles and Duties of Natural Religion was published in 1675 by the future Archbishop Tillotson. It ran to six editions in thirty-five years.

[8] Ed. Lansdowne, Petty Papers (1927), ii. 172.   [9] See pp. 22–27 above.

so far from there being any reason to fear science, the scientists glorified God in their calling no less than ministers in theirs. Religion, therefore, instead of opposing science, 'should dearly protect all increase of natural knowledge'. Only unenlightened superstition or fanatical enthusiasm—popery or anabaptistry— could oppose scientific inquiry.[1] Was Boyle writing as a radical Protestant or as a scientist when he called the members of the Invisible College 'persons that endeavour to put narrow-minded-ness out of countenance, by the practice of so extensive a charity that it reaches unto everything called man, and nothing less than a universal good will can content it. And indeed they are so apprehensive of the want of good employment that they take the whole body of mankind for their care'?[2] Puritans and scientists had long had enemies in common. Now they shared a cause and an idealism. It is no accident that Bacon always advocated moderation towards the Puritans, and in 1624 urged Buckingham not 'to withdraw your favour from such as are honest and religious men' simply because papists called them 'Puritans'. 'For of this kind is the greatest body of the subjects.'[3]

It is important to realize that this religious element in early Baconianism was genuine, though it lent itself so easily to later secularist developments. Bacon was not separating religion and science because he was a secret atheist who wished to be free to discuss science without interference from ignorant priests. The separation sprang from his Protestant beliefs, and was an inseparable consequence of his whole philosophy. Calvin him-self assumed the importance of final and formal causes, and gave unusual significance to material and efficient causes. This was also the starting-point of Ramus's logic, of which Bacon was well aware.[4] What Bacon opposed was 'controversies of religion', which, he believed, 'must hinder the advancement of science'.[5]

Bacon professed no such narrow utilitarianism as later went under his name. In this respect he was as little a Baconian as

[1] Anderson, op. cit., p. 95.
[2] R. Boyle, letter of 1647, in *Works* (1744), i. 20.
[3] Bacon, *Works*, xiv. 448-9.
[4] For an early example of the religious uses of Baconianism, see a letter from Dr. William Gilbert to Archbishop Ussher (1638), in Parr, *Life of . . . Ussher*, ii. 493-4.
[5] Letter of 10 October 1609 to Tobie Mathew, in *Works*, xi. 138.

Karl Marx was a Marxist. In attacking academic separation of theory and practice he emphasized that 'in natural philosophy practical results are not only the means to improve human well-being. They are also the guarantee of truth. . . . Science too must be known by its works. It is by the witness of works, rather than by logic or even observation, that truth is revealed and established. It follows from this that the improvement of man's lot and the improvement of man's mind are one and the same thing.' Practice, said Bacon over and over again, is the sole test of truth; 'whether knowledge is possible or not must be settled not by argument, but by trying'.[1] But 'works themselves are of greater value as pledges of truth than as contributing to the comforts of life'. All knowledge is corrupt that is not mixed with love. Bacon distinguished between the 'vulgar and degenerate' ambition of those who seek only their own power; the more dignified 'though not less covetous' ambition of those who laboured to extend the power and dominion of their own country; and on the other hand his own endeavour 'to establish and extend the power and dominion of the human race itself over the universe'.[2] Knowledge should not be sought as 'a couch, whereupon to rest a searching and restless spirit; or a terrace, for a wandering and variable mind to walk up and down with a fair prospect; or a tower of state for a proud mind to raise itself upon; or a fort or commanding ground, for strife and contention; or a shop for profit and sale'. It should rather be 'a rich storehouse, for the glory of the Creator, and the relief of man's estate'. 'I do not mean, when I speak of use and action . . . the applying of knowledge to lucre.' Men should seek knowledge 'for the benefit and use of life; and . . . perfect and govern it in charity'.[3] We have not yet caught up with Bacon.

[1] Farrington, op. cit., pp. 68, 97–98.   [2] Ibid., pp. 45, 148, 7.

[3] Anderson, op. cit., p. 96, and references there cited. In this *religious* utilitarianism Bacon recalls Fulke Greville, who wrote:

Use therefore must stand higher than delight,
The active hate a fruitless instrument:
So must the world those busie idle fools
That serve no other market than the Schools . . .
I wish all curious sciences let blood.

(F. Greville, *A Treatie of Humane Learning*,
in *Poems and Dramas*, ed. G. Bullough, i. 170.)

Cf. G. Bullough, 'Bacon and the Defence of Learning', in *17th Century Studies presented to Sir Herbert Grierson* (1938): '*Musophilus* worthily anticipates *The Advancement of Learning*' (p. 13). For Greville see pp. 133–7, 176 below.

In my first chapter, when I tried to visualize the world into which our self-taught, eager, self-confident artisans and merchants grew up, I distinguished between two generations: that before about 1614 and that after. The date was no doubt arbitrary: but there does seem to me to be a real difference between the turbulent achievement of the generation after the Armada, when Englishmen suddenly realized that they were citizens of a nation equal to any other; the period in which virtually all that we call Elizabethan literature was written; and the second period of economic recession, of national humiliation in politics, of doubt and self-searching in literature. This failure of nerve of the traditional intellectuals was reinforced by the increasingly rigorous censorship, 'this impertinent yoke of prelaty, under whose inquisitorious and tyrannical duncery no free and splendid wit can flourish'.[1] I suggested that in these decades the confident optimism of Bacon (and Hakewill) seemed strangely out of tune with the dominant mood. With the dominant mood of the intellectuals, the wits, the Inns of Court poets, the universities, true: but not, we can now see, with the mood of our inquiring artisans and merchants, so sure of their ability to expand their nation's wealth, to remould its institutions, to extend its trade to unknown realms—if only the government would not hinder them. It was precisely this confidence in the expansive power of science and industry that Bacon expressed, a confidence which broke forth in ebullient speculation and discussion as soon as the prelatical censorship was overthrown.

So now perhaps we can in some sort resolve the paradox from which we started.[2] Before Bacon began to write there had been a great development of mathematics and astronomy in England, centred in London, especially around Gresham College. There had been a similar development of alchemy, traditionally associated with the craftsmen, into Paracelsan medicine, stimulated by the new industries and the use of new drugs in medicine. Both of these scientific trends had been expressed in a popular scientific literature which was anti-Aristotelean, utilitarian, and optimistic. There was also a powerful Puritan tradition, which was equally anti-authoritarian, opposed to Aristotle and the Schoolmen, inclined to separate

[1] Milton, *Complete Prose Works* (Yale ed.), i. 820.   [2] See pp. 14–15 above.

reason and faith. The two scientific traditions and the Puritan tradition seem to have appealed to merchants and artisans, especially in London. What Bacon did was to join the three traditions, and to make of them an intellectual system. By so doing he immeasurably strengthened the scientific movement.

But what he strengthened was a body of ideas which had pushed its way up from below. This applies particularly to the ideas of the Paracelsans. The universities were still the preserve of Aristoteleanism. Bacon spoke cautiously but plainly when 'in men of a devout policy' he noted 'an inclination to have the people depend upon God the more, when they are less acquainted with second causes; and to have no stirring in philosophy, lest it may lead to an innovation in divinity, or else should discover matter of further contradiction to divinity'. These opinions are 'the most effectual hindrance to natural philosophy and invention'.[1] Here Bacon was hitting back at those political conservatives and vested interests which were the main opponents of popular science. Oxford and Cambridge, those clerical strongholds, had little use for Bacon until they had been purged. An occasional young radical like Milton might defend Baconianism in the sixteen-twenties; a former Gresham professor like Richard Holdsworth may have recommended some of Bacon's works to his Cambridge pupils.[2] But significant outward evidence of Bacon's influence dates from after 1640. We still do not know how far this time-lag was the direct result of clerical censorship, how far it was due to the discouraging intellectual climate of the Laudian era.

III

So far I have said nothing of Bacon's political career, though much might be said. For Gardiner he was the Turgot of the English Revolution, the one man who might have averted it, a man whose political thinking was not inferior to his scientific thinking.[3] In many respects Bacon's ideas are closer to those of the Parliamentarians than to those of the kings whom he served. He shared the desire for war with Spain at sea, which

[1] Bacon, *Works*, iii. 500. See p. 185 below.
[2] Milton, the second and third *Prolusions*; Curtis, *Oxford and Cambridge in Transition*, p. 133. See Appendix.
[3] *D.N.B.*, Bacon.

many members of Parliament, Ralegh, and Coke expressed: since he was in favour of 'free trade into all parts of both East and West Indies'.[1] 'The wealth of both Indies', he observed in the Essay 'Of the True Greatness of Kingdoms and Estates', 'seems in great part but an accessory to the command of the seas.'[2] For this reason Bacon shared Ralegh's ambivalent attitude to the Netherlands: 'We could not abandon them for our safety, nor keep them for our profit.'[3] Nevertheless, like Ralegh, he expressed great admiration for their political and economic organization.[4] Especially he approved of the fact that in the Netherlands 'wealth was dispersed in many hands'; and those the hands 'where there is likest to be the greatest sparing and increase, and not in those hands, wherein there useth to be greatest expense and consumption'. For 'those states are least able to aid and defray great charge for wars, or other public disbursements, whose wealth resteth chiefly in the hands of the nobility and gentlemen'. Bacon wanted an England where wealth 'resteth in the hands of the merchants, burghers, tradesmen, freeholders, farmers in the country, and the like'.[5]

With Bacon's uncompromising statement of the priority of *bourgeois* interests went an advocacy of economic liberalism—at least when Bacon was not acting as government spokesman.[6] High corn prices, he said in 1592, would be a better inducement to convert land from pasture to tillage than all the penal laws that could be passed.[7] He disliked the Cokayne Project, and urged its abandonment insistently.[8] His remark to James that 'trading in companies is most agreeable to the English nature' as opposed to 'free or loose trade' must be taken in its context. Bacon was contrasting England with 'that same general vein of a republic, which runneth in the Dutch, and *serveth to them*

---

[1] Bacon, *Works*, xiv. 22–28, 446, 460–5, 469–505. For Ralegh and Coke see pp. 153–65, 233–5 below.

[2] Ibid. vi. 451. Cf. Ralegh, quoted on pp. 167–8 below.

[3] Ibid. vii. 177. See p. 161 below.

[4] Ibid. vi, p. 405, 410. See pp. 160–1, 167, 280 below.

[5] Ibid. vii. 60–61; vi. 406, 446–7; viii. 172–4. Cf. the well-known passage in *The History of King Henry VII* on the yeomanry with Ralegh's views on the subject (pp. 195–6 below). 'And yet', Bacon observed, 'where men of great wealth do stoop to husbandry, it multiplieth riches exceedingly' (Bacon, *Works*, vi. 461).

[6] Contrast Bacon, *Works*, xi. 97–104, with x. 308, 346–61.

[7] W. H. R. Curtler, *Enclosure and Redistribution of Our Land* (1929), p. 123.

[8] Bacon, *Works*, xii. 171–2, 236–8, 256–9; xiii. 171.

instead of a company'.[1] The implication is that a republic would be better for trade. In view of this liberalism it is ironical that the campaign which led to Bacon's fall started with an attack on monopolies, and then moved on to an onslaught by Cranfield and Coke on Chancery's protection of insolvent debtors.[2] Bacon did not 'altogether mislike banks', but he knew that they were regarded as incompatible with a monarchy: 'they will hardly be brooked in regard of certain suspicions'.[3] 'Mechanical arts and merchandise' flourish 'in the declining age of a state', Bacon thought; and he quoted without comment the view that Elizabeth's reign saw 'the declination of a monarchy'.[4] His explanations of and remedies for sedition were almost all economic.[5]

His own policies aimed at economic self-sufficiency. He wanted the wilds of Scotland to be colonized, Ireland to be civilized, the Netherlands and their empire to be annexed.[6] He shared Hakluyt's view that England's over-population was only relative: a resolute policy of fen drainage, cultivation of the wastes and commons, colonization of Ireland, expansion of the fishing industry, overseas trade, and the carrying trade would soon show that the problem was 'rather of scarceness, than of press of people'.[7] This view did not become common in England until the late seventeenth century; but in the *New Atlantis* the growth of population was looked on with favour.[8]

Bacon's defence of the Commons' privileges in 1593, and his refusal to recant, impeded his career under Elizabeth. He told James in 1612 that, though 'a perfect and peremptory royalist', he believed he 'was never one hour out of credit with the lower house'.[9] When in 1614 the Commons decided that no attorney-general should sit in the House, they made an exception for Bacon. Even in 1617 Bacon was 'ever for a Parliament'.[10] In his *Proposition touching . . . amendment of the common law*

---

[1] Bacon, *Works*, xii. 259. My italics.
[2] R. C. Johnson, 'Francis Bacon and Lionel Cranfield', *H.L.Q.* xxiii. 311–12.
[3] Bacon, *Works*, vi. 476.
[4] Ibid. vi. 517.   [5] Ibid. vi. 409–10, 430.
[6] Ibid. iii. 144; xi. 74. The Rump did its best to carry out this programme.
[7] Ibid. x. 312–13. See pp. 154–5, 299 below.
[8] Ibid. iii. 149. See M. Campbell, 'Of People either too few or too many', in *Conflict in Stuart England: Essays in honour of Wallace Notestein* (ed. W. A. Aiken and B. D. Henning, 1960), pp. 169–202.
[9] Bacon, *Works*, xi. 280.   [10] Ibid. xii. 31–33; xiii. 233.

(1616) he recommended that this reform should be entrusted to a commission named by Parliament, not to the one already appointed by James.[1] So Bacon was right to think of himself as a good House of Commons man. Yet at an early date he had forebodings of 'civil wars which seem to me about to spread through many countries—*because of certain ways of life not long since introduced*'.[2] He hoped the advancement of learning might damp down religious passions and so prevent social upheaval.

Bacon worked desperately to win royal favour for his scientific schemes, which, he told James without (in this case) flattery, 'may be to this work [the *Novum Organum*] as much as an hundred years in time; for I am persuaded the work will gain upon men's minds in ages, but your gracing it may make it take hold more swiftly'.[3] But James, well-trained scholastic intellectual that he was, had no use for Bacon's book: 'It is like the peace of God, that passeth all understanding.'[4] When in 1608 Bacon drew up a list of probable supporters, they included no one of the highest political standing—Sir Thomas Chaloner, Governor of Prince Henry's household, through whom the Prince might be interested; Sir Walter Ralegh and the Earl of Northumberland, even then in the Tower, of whom Ralegh was executed in 1618; Thomas Hariot, their protégé; Lancelot Andrewes (d. 1626), and Archbishop Abbot, disgraced in 1627.[5] And when James failed him, what could a Charles I, a Buckingham, a Laud, make of Bacon's plans, if indeed they ever tried to read them? (That we are dealing here not with some personal accident affecting Bacon, but with social causes, is suggested by the similar fate of Harvey's discovery of the circulation of the blood. Harvey, the royal physician, was an impeccable King's man; but his discovery, announced in 1616, published in 1628, was little regarded in England—at least so far as the printed record goes—before 1640. During the interregnum, ironically enough, it was widely acclaimed.)

The Baconians were Bishop Williams, Bacon's literary executor, who was disgraced in 1625; opposition peers like Lord Brooke, who quoted Copernicus, Kepler, and Galileo as well

---

[1] Ibid. xiii. 61 ff.
[2] Anderson, op. cit., p. 11. My italics.   [3] Bacon, *Works*, xiv. 120.
[4] Ed. N. E. McClure, *Letters of John Chamberlain*, ii. 339.
[5] Bacon, *Works*, xi. 23. For Chaloner, Northumberland, and Hariot see pp. 214, 139–45 below.

as Bacon;[1] Sir John Eliot in the Tower. When in the sixteen-thirties Hartlib, Dury, and Comenius tried to give effect to Bacon's plans, their most enthusiastic supporter was John Pym; backed by the Earls of Bedford, Essex, Leicester, Pembroke, Salisbury, and Warwick, by Lord Brooke, Lord Mandeville, Lord Wharton, Sir Thomas Roe, Sir Benjamin Rudyerd, Sir Thomas Barrington, Sir Nathaniel Rich, Sir William Waller, Sir Arthur Annesley, Sir John Clotworthy, John Selden, Oliver St. John. It is very nearly a list of members of the Providence Island Company. It is a list of the leaders of the opposition in the Long Parliament.[2]

IV

We must pause for a moment over the Comenian group. Hartlib and Haak were connected with the scheme sponsored by four leading Puritan divines, Thomas Taylor, Richard Sibbes, John Davenport, and William Gouge, asking for financial help for Calvinist refugees from the Palatinate: Briggs seems to have acted as their agent in Oxford. The four divines were reprimanded by the Privy Council.[3] George Harwood, merchant and Feoffee for Impropriations, John Bastwick the Independent martyr, and John White the Patriarch of Dorchester were also supporters of Dury and Hartlib.[4] In 1634, when Dury went to Sweden in pursuit of Protestant unity, he had the support of a group of thirty-eight outstanding Puritan divines, including Richard Holdsworth,[5] who is said to have recommended Comenius's writings to his pupils.[6] Hartlib was later in touch with Alexander Henderson, the Scottish Commissioner in London.[7] In May 1639 Hartlib was arrested and

[1] Bush, *English Literature in the Earlier Seventeenth Century* (2nd ed., 1962), p. 358.

[2] R. F. Young, *Comenius in England* (1932), pp. 6, 41–46, 59–60; cf. Young, *Comenius and the Indians of New England* (1929), pp. 6–10, 23; G. H. Turnbull, *Hartlib, Dury and Comenius* (1947), *passim*. Dury married a connexion of Sir John Clotworthy's. Leicester was Sir Philip Sidney's nephew.

[3] Turnbull, *Samuel Hartlib* (1920), p. 34; cf. pp. 77, 128, for Hartlib's links with Puritan ministers; J. M. Batten, *John Dury* (Chicago U.P., 1944), p. 52, for Dury's.

[4] Turnbull, *Hartlib, Dury and Comenius*, pp. 20, 128, 187; F. Rose-Troup, *John White, the Patriarch of Dorchester* (New York, 1930), p. 47.

[5] G. Westin, *Negotiations about Church Unity, 1628–34* (Uppsala Universitets Årsskrift, 1932, Band I), p. 207; cf. *Massachusetts Hist. Soc. Collections*, vii. 504.

[6] Curtis, op. cit., p. 132; see p. 308 below.

[7] D. Masson, *Life of John Milton* (1859–94), iii. 219–20.

questioned in connexion with measures for 'examining Puritan rogues, searching for their seditious papers and discovering their plots and villainies'.[1] When the Long Parliament met the roles were reversed, and Hartlib was a witness against Laud in his trial for high treason.[2] Hartlib was a friend of John Stoughton, a stalwart Puritan from Emmanuel College, who referred to Bacon as one of the principal pioneers of the new age, and was also a supporter of Comenius.[3] Stoughton was under government surveillance in 1634 because suspected of sedition. He left £25 to Hartlib in his will, the contingent remainder to Emmanuel. He was also a supporter of Dury.[4]

Hartlib, who originally came to England as a merchant, had useful connexions by marriage in the City, and with gentlemen. His associations seem to have been mainly with the Independents. In 1644 he stimulated a reply to Thomas Edwards's attack on the five Independent divines.[5] In the revolutionary period he had a vigorous career as propagandist and pamphleteer, for which he was rewarded by the Commons with grants totalling £400 and a recommendation that he should be given a post in the University of Oxford in recognition of the gratitude owed to him not only by Parliament but by all 'that are wellwishers for the advancement of learning'.[6] Throughout

---

[1] Turnbull, *Samuel Hartlib*, p. 16.

[2] Prynne, *Canterburies Doome*, pp. 539-42.

[3] J. Stoughton, *Felicitas Ultimi Saeculi* (1640), p. 34 and *passim*, a letter to Tolnai, published after Stoughton's death by Hartlib, with dedication to George Rakosi. See p. 58 above.

[4] J. C. Whitebrook, 'Dr. John Stoughton the Elder', *Trans. Congregational Hist. Soc.*, vi. 96, 105-7, 182-5. Stoughton was also associated with John White of Dorchester in handling funds for suppressed ministers, including those in New England. Stoughton's brother emigrated to New England, returned in 1643 and served as a lieutenant-colonel in the Parliamentary army. Stoughton himself was the stepfather of Ralph Cudworth, and took great pains with his education. Another stepson of Stoughton's, James Cudworth, emigrated to Massachusetts in 1632 (ibid., pp. 92-99, 179-84). Ralph Cudworth, a marked Puritan under Charles I, preached before the House of Commons in 1647 and remained closely associated with Cromwell and Thurloe in the sixteen-fifties. He was keenly interested in science and became a Fellow of the Royal Society. Like the other Cambridge Platonists he aspired to create a philosophy which could accept the findings of modern science. He had links with Locke and Newton (Tulloch, op. cit., ii. 203-10; J. A. Passmore, *Ralph Cudworth*, 1951, pp. 2, 79). For Hartlib's relations with Cudworth and More see also *The Diary and Correspondence of Dr. John Worthington*, ed. J. Crossley, i (Chetham Soc., 1847), *passim*; Tulloch, op. cit., ii. 90, 427.

[5] Masson, *Life of Milton*, iii. 193, 230-1.

[6] *C.J.* iv. 588; v. 131. Hartlib was appointed to no position in Oxford.

his life Hartlib was passionately interested in mathematics and science. His friend Hezekiah Woodward issued a number of Baconian and Comenian pamphlets in 1640–1. Hartlib knew Samuel Foster, probably as early as 1639,[1] and was also a friend of Sir Kenelm Digby, Robert Boyle, Seth Ward, and John Wallis; an admirer of Dee's Preface to Billingsley's *Euclide*, and of Jeremiah Horrocks's work in astronomy.[2] In 1649 Hartlib touted for Sir Balthazar Gerbier's Academy, which included 'experimental natural philosophy' in its curriculum.[3]

John Dury was an hereditary rebel, whose Scottish father had been pastor at Leiden to the Presbyterian congregation of English and Scottish refugees. Dury was himself educated at Leiden University.[4] He had early associations with Gresham College, to which in 1639 he was urging a learned Swede to leave his books and manuscripts.[5] In 1642 he suggested that chairs of practical divinity should be established at the two universities, and in London at either Sion or Gresham College; and that there should be a popular lectureship in London 'to teach the common people' how to make use of Scripture.[6] Parliament appointed him tutor of the King's younger children, who were under the care of the tenth Earl of Northumberland, the son of Ralegh's associate.[7] In 1648 Dury was snubbed by the Assembly of Divines (of which he was a member) for co-operating with the radical John Goodwin in the publication of Acontius's *Satans Stratagems*, favouring religious toleration.[8] After the execution of Charles I, Dury acted as propagandist on behalf of the Commonwealth, to which he urged submission. He translated Milton's *Eikonoklastes* into French. Dury was appointed to take charge of what had been Prince Henry's library.[9] He 'practically started the first agitation in favour of' admitting the Jews to

[1] Turnbull, 'Samuel Hartlib's Influence on the early history of the Royal Society', *Notes and Records of the Royal Society*, x. 108.

[2] R. T. Petersson, *Sir Kenelm Digby*, p. 259; Worthington, *Diary*, i. 59–60, 124–5, 130–1; ii. 226; Bush, op. cit., pp. 18–20. The early Fellows of the Royal Society shared Hartlib's interest in Horrocks (Add. MSS. 6193, ff. 114–15). Horrocks's posthumous works were published by Wallis in 1673.

[3] H. R. Williamson, *Four Stuart Portraits* (1949), p. 52.

[4] Batten, *John Dury*, pp. 12–14.

[5] Turnbull, *Hartlib, Dury and Comenius*, p. 196.

[6] Dury, *A Motion Tending to the Publick Good of This Age and of Posteritie* (published by S. Hartlib, 1642), sig. C 3–3v.

[7] Batten, op. cit., p. 113. See p. 143 below.

[8] Ibid., pp. 110–11. See p. 175 below.   [9] See p. 215 below.

England.[1] He corresponded on the subject with Menasseh ben Israel, an old friend of Robert Boyle (Dury's uncle by marriage) who later became a friend of Henry Oldenburg (Dury's son-in-law).[2] In 1653 Dury accompanied Whitelocke to Sweden. He had considerable influence on Cromwell's foreign policy, and acted as unofficial diplomatic agent for the Protector in Sweden, Switzerland, Germany, and the Netherlands.[3] He thought that foreign missions should accompany merchants as they expanded the frontiers of English trade.[4] Dury's emphasis on practical divinity, on morals, and ethics to the exclusion of theological controversy makes him with John Wilkins a forerunner of the latitudinarian thought of the later seventeenth and eighteenth centuries.[5]

The programme on which Comenius, Dury, and Hartlib had been working throughout the thirties fused religious and Baconian aims. Dury in 1631 announced that the purposes of his travels included the observation of 'all inventions and feats of practice in all sciences, . . . such as may be profitable to the health of the body, to the preservation and increase of wealth by trades and mechanical industries . . .'; and of all 'arts and sciences philosophical, chemical and mechanical; whereby not only the secrets of disciplines are harmonically and compendiously delivered, but also the secrets of nature are thought to be unfolded'.[6] He hoped to find out the 'best experiments of industrial practices in husbandry and manufactures, and in other inventions . . . tending to the good of this nation'. Comenius thought Bacon's Instauratio Magna 'the most instructive philosophical work of the century now beginning'. To Bacon 'we owe the first suggestion and opportunity for common counsels with regard to the universal reform of the sciences'.[7] The Comenians advocated a system of universal education, though

---

[1] L. Wolf, Menasseh ben Israel's Mission to Oliver Cromwell (Jewish Historical Soc., 1901), pp. xxii–xxviii, xliii; Harleian Miscellany (1744–56), vii. 240–4—a letter from Dury to Hartlib.

[2] Batten, op. cit., pp. 140–1; C. Roth, The Resettlement of the Jews in England in 1656 (Jewish Historical Soc., 1960, pp. 12, 23). In 1659 Dury and the Baptist Henry Jacie were working together to collect money for Jews endangered by the war between Sweden and Poland (Anon., The Life and Death of Mr. Henry Jessey, 1671, pp. 75–77).

[3] Batten, op. cit., Chapters VII–VIII, passim.   [4] Ibid., p. 139.

[5] Ibid., pp. 92, 132. See p. 92 above for Wilkins.

[6] Turnbull, Samuel Hartlib, pp. 10–13.

[7] S. S. Laurie, John Amos Comenius (1899), pp. 69, 92; R. H. Syfret, 'The Origins of the Royal Society', Notes and Records of the Royal Society, v. 103–4, 112–13.

socially graded, together with a revolution in educational methods which would shift the emphasis from words to things, from learning by rote to the use of experiment, observation, and practice in the teaching of languages and science.[1] Dury called for the establishment of an agency for the advancement of universal learning, which should be at once an institute of educational research with its own printing press, a ministry of education which would oversee all schools and schoolmasters, and an international correspondence centre 'for the beating out of matters not yet elaborated in sciences'.[2]

In a sermon preached to the House of Commons in the first month of the Long Parliament's existence, John Gauden, chaplain to the Earl of Warwick, urged that Dury and Comenius should be invited to England. Eight months later, in July 1641, the invitation was issued, under the patronage of Williams, now Archbishop of York; of Ussher, Archbishop of Armagh, soon to be invited to join the Westminster Assembly of Divines;[3] of Lord Brooke, John Selden, and John Pym, now leader of the House of Commons. Dury and Comenius were to reform English education. Already religious tests had been abolished at the universities. On 15 June 1641 the Commons resolved that all the lands confiscated from deans and chapters should be devoted to the 'advancement of learning and piety'.[4] The Baconian phrase speaks for itself: so does the Baconian conception of state intervention to promote education. Comenius himself believed that Parliament would finance 'the plan of the great Verulam respecting the opening somewhere of a universal college wholly devoted to the advancement of the sciences'.[5] *Macaria*, by Hartlib's protégé Gabriel Plattes, was dedicated to Parliament in October 1641, in the hope that that 'honourable court will lay the cornerstone of the world's happiness'. Among other Baconian schemes, *Macaria* advocated medical research.

[1] Dury, *A Seasonable Discourse* (1649), p. 8; Batten, op. cit., pp. 92–93, 112–13, 136–7.

[2] Dury, *The Reformed Library Keeper* (ed. R. S. Granniss, Boston, 1906), p. 49 (first published 1650); *A Seasonable Discourse*, sig. D–D 4v.

[3] For Ussher's interest in the Comenians' schemes see Parr, *Life of Usher*, ii. 546, 557, 623–4. For the 'Puritan' bishops, including Bedell, who supported them, see *C.S.P.D., 1640*, pp. 568–70; Turnbull, 'Letters written by John Dury in Sweden, 1636–38,' *Kyrkohistorisk Årsskrift*, 1949, pp. 225 ff.

[4] *C.J.* ii. 176. There were several other resolutions to the same effect.

[5] Young, *Comenius in England*, pp. 53–55.

Comenius was given the plans and inventories of several colleges to look over, with a view to one being assigned to him and his collaborators as the universal college which would make England the centre of European learning. Chelsea College was the favourite choice, the building in fact given to the Royal Society by Charles II in 1667. In a pamphlet dedicated to the Royal Society in 1668 Comenius referred to this when he said 'the territory offered to us for the search for light has passed into your keeping, according to the great Word of Christ (applicable in its proper sense on this occasion),"Others have laboured and you have entered into their labours" '. The pamphlet which this dedication introduced, the *Via Lucis*, had been written in England in 1641–2 for private circulation: when Comenius published it he thought that the Royal Society's work would be 'the fairest part of those forecasts' made in the *Via Lucis*.[1] Hartlib similarly claimed in December 1660 that the Royal Society then in process of formation was a realization of 'the grand design' for which he had so often pleaded.[2]

So we may accept the claim that the Comenian group in 1641 sowed the seeds from which the Royal Society was ultimately to grow. It was Hartlib's protégé, Theodore Haak, friend of Briggs,[3] Greaves and other Gresham professors, as well as of Hunneades, Oughtred and Thomas Allen, who took the initiative in 1645 in calling together a scientific group deriving from the Gresham circle. Wallis, Wilkins, and many other later Fellows of the Royal Society participated in this group, which met in the rooms of Hartlib's friend Samuel Foster at Gresham College. It was distinct both from Boyle's Invisible College and from the many other interlocking groups discussing science and social reform in the mid-forties to which Hartlib was, in Boyle's words, 'midwife and nurse'. But Haak almost certainly saw his initiative as part of his Comenian activities.[4]

[1] Syfret, op. cit., pp. 116–17, I have drawn heavily on this admirable article for this and the four following paragraphs.

[2] Worthington, *Diary*, i. 248–9; cf. p. 342.

[3] Briggs's MSS. commentaries on Ramus's *Geometry* were in Haak's possession (Barnett, *Theodore Haak*, The Hague, 1962, p. 79).

[4] Turnbull, 'Samuel Hartlib's Influence', *passim*; Syfret, op. cit., pp. 120–37; Barnett, 'Theodore Haak and the early years of the Royal Society', *Annals of Science*, xiii. 212; Johnson, 'Gresham College', *J.H.I.* i, *passim*; Batten, op. cit., p. 134; Harcourt Brown, *Scientific Organizations in 17th century France*, p. 274.

Haak had been a member of the Comenian group since at least 1638: in 1639–40 he corresponded on scientific and other subjects, on behalf of this group, with Mersenne. In the later sixteen-forties he acted as corresponding secretary for the Gresham group. In 1643–4 Haak was Parliament's emissary to Denmark, anxious, as he said, to 'do what I can in so good a cause as the Parliament's'. He had a pension from the Long Parliament 'for the advancement of arts and learning', and—like Dury's—his allegiance did not weaken after the execution of Charles I. Haak gave paid service as correspondent and translator to both the Commonwealth and the Protectorate.[1] In 1645 the Westminster Assembly of Divines (whose assistant clerk was John Wallis, also a member of the Gresham group and later Fellow of the Royal Society) asked Haak to translate the Dutch Bible and its marginal notes into English: this was ultimately published in 1655.[2] Haak too became a Fellow of the Royal Society. At every stage his career illustrates the connexion between Puritanism, Parliamentarianism, and science.[3] Correspondence with foreign scientists, to which Bacon and the Comenians had attached such importance, was taken over for the Royal Society by Henry Oldenburg, 'the direct heir of the Comenius–Hartlib tradition in England'. Oldenburg was another German Protestant, who came to England in the sixteen-forties. He was associated with Hartlib then, with Petty and Boyle in Oxford in 1654–6. He became Dury's secretary, later his son-in-law.[4] Further evidence of Comenius's influence on the founders of the Royal Society and their associates is to be found in the

[1] P. R. Barnett, *Theodore Haak, passim*, esp. pp. 52–53, 65, 91–93, 107–11. In the early stages of the Revolution indeed, before Parliament developed its own civil service, it was greatly dependent on foreigners. Haak in Denmark reported back to his friend the German poet Weckherlin, Secretary to the Committee of Both Kingdoms and Latin Secretary—a post in which he preceded and succeeded Milton. Weckherlin was also a friend of Hartlib's. See p. 176 below for another example—Dorislaus. This international aspect of the English Revolution might repay further investigation.

[2] Haak had translated English religious works into German before the civil war; he also translated at least the first three books of *Paradise Lost* into the same language (Barnett, op. cit., pp. 13, 71–12, 115, Chapters XIII–XV *passim*).

[3] Cf. also Syfret, op. cit., pp. 89, 129; Turnbull, *Samuel Hartlib*, pp. 48–51; 'Samuel Hartlib's influence', p. 105.

[4] Harcourt Brown, op. cit., p. 96; Syfret, op. cit., pp. 129–37; Barnett, *Annals of Science*, xiii. 213.

interest of Wilkins, Ward, Petty, Hartlib, Haak, Pell, Webster, and others in Comenius's scheme for a 'real character'. The Royal Society was later to support similar projects.[1]

Given this significance of the Comenian group in the origins of the Royal Society, the relations of its members with Gresham College on the one hand, and with Pym and the Parliamentary opposition on the other, acquire new importance. It is too often assumed that the appeal of Comenius's plans for the Parliamentary leaders was primarily religious, but this will hardly bear investigation. The religious and scientific aspects of the programme of the Comenians were closely linked; and Hartlib himself, in one of his many unpublished papers showing preoccupation with Gresham College, called for abolition of the lectures in divinity, law, and rhetoric there and the substitution of lectures on technology.[2] Neither of the standard biographies of Pym, nor the books of A. P. Newton or Professor Hexter, mention Pym's interest in science or even his connexion with the Comenian group. Indeed his full correspondence with Hartlib still remains to be published. But since 1947 enough has been in print to show that reconsideration of this aspect of Pym's career is called for. Pym subscribed money to Dury's scheme for Protestant union (together with the Eastland and Mercers' Companies); he also contributed generously to the support of Hartlib, his 'intimate and familiar acquaintance'.[3] Pym told Hartlib in 1636 that he would be glad to be 'an instrument of any encouragement to that worthy man Comenius in those works and designs which he hath for the public good. As soon as it shall please God to restore to us liberty of commerce and intercourse, I shall be very desirous to consult with you how it may be done.' Only his anxiety about the possibility of his letter being intercepted prevented Pym being more specific. He was 'so affected' to Comenius's 'undertakings', he assured Hartlib two years later, 'that if I were able I would support

[1] B. DeMott, 'Comenius and the Real Character in England', *P.M.L.A.* lxx. 1074–8; Carré, *Phases of Thought in England*, p. 278; Barnett, *Theodore Haak*, pp. 108–9, 138. At least for Webster, this interest was linked with magical theories about Egyptian hieroglyphics (*Academiarum Examen*, 1654, p. 24).

[2] Turnbull, *Samuel Hartlib*, p. 49. Hartlib tried in 1649 to get Petty appointed to advance experimental and mechanical knowledge at Gresham College.

[3] Turnbull, *Hartlib, Dury and Comenius*, pp. 20, 27. The words are Dury's. For Hartlib's papers see ibid., pp. v–vii.

them alone, and I pray God to stir up those to be as forward who can do it with ease'.[1]

Pym's interest was in the scientific and educational as well as the religious aspects of Comenius's work. Pym was a great admirer of Bacon, especially of the *Novum Organum*.[2] In 1637 he endowed a school for the parish of Brill, Buckinghamshire.[3] In 1638–9 he was corresponding eagerly with Hartlib about a scheme for draining coal mines.[4] The day before Comenius finally left England in June 1642, Pym found time, at the height of military and financial preparations for civil war, to write to Hartlib asking him 'to consult with Mr. Comenius if he be not gone, as I hope he is not' about the astronomical discoveries of Captain Marmaduke Nielson and his design to make a small model of the solar system 'without all those chimaeras of epicycles and eccentrics by which the minds of young students are rather terrified than taught'.[5] If we see the Comenians, together with Gresham College, as active agents in bringing together the group which later formed the Royal Society, as I think we must, then we should also see John Pym as one of the founding foster-fathers of the Royal Society.

Comenius left England only when the threat of civil war had clearly postponed realization of the hopes of the Baconians. In 1641 the Commons resolved to appoint a Committee for the Advancement of Learning, but none seems in fact to have existed until 1653, when Jonathan Goddard was one of its members.[6] In 1643 the Westminster Assembly, of which Dury was a member and Wallis the assistant clerk, supported the idea of a university in London. Anthony Burges, formerly Wallis's tutor at Emmanuel, added the hope that 'some collops might be cut out of deaneries and chapters for the cherishing

[1] Hartlib's *Ephemerides*, of which Professor Trevor-Roper was so kind as to give me a transcript, quoted by permission of Lord Delamere. Printed in part in Turnbull, *Hartlib, Dury and Comenius*, pp. 187, 342, 346.

[2] *Ephemerides*.

[3] Jordan, *The Rural Charities of England*, p. 57.

[4] *Ephemerides*, Pym to Hartlib, 14 and 22 November 1639.

[5] Turnbull, *Hartlib, Dury and Comenius*, p. 365. The last words are from a petition which Nielson submitted to Parliament through Pym. Nielson claimed to have discovered a method of finding longitude at sea. An earlier petition of 1636 had been referred to a commission including Selden, Gellibrand, and Oughtred, but nothing seems to have come of it.

[6] *C.J.* vii. 287.

of young scholars'.[1] In 1641 the citizens of Manchester, with Fairfax's support, had petitioned for a university, 'many ripe and hopeful wits being utterly lost for want of education'. There were similar petitions from York, in 1641 and 1648. Universities were also proposed for Wales, Norwich, and Durham. Only at Durham was a College 'for all the sciences and literature' established, with Hartlib on its committee. It lasted from 1657 to 1660.[2] In 1658 there was a renewal of the project for an institution of learning or philosophical college, in which Hartlib, Dury, Boyle, and 'our special friend' Benjamin Worsley were involved, and towards which Richard Cromwell was said to be favourable.[3] Next year a college was proposed for Westminster, which would teach (*inter alia*) optics, mechanics, physic, anatomy, chemistry, and the philosophies of Descartes and Gassendi.[4] But the Restoration put a stop to all that.

V

Bacon had hoped to 'ring the bell which called the wits together'. Books could be and are written on his influence: we have already indicated some of it. But a few points may be drawn together in order to justify associating his influence with the English Revolution. Bacon's emphasis on secondary causes and his relegation of direct divine intervention to a long-past historical epoch—this fortified and gave deeper signi-

[1] Quoted by W. H. G. Armytage, 'Prejudice and Promise, 1600–60', *The Universities Review*, xxiii. 114.

[2] Ed. G. W. Johnson, *Fairfax Correspondence* (1848), ii. 271–80; M. James, *Social Policy during the Puritan Revolution* (1930), pp. 324–5; *V.C.H., York*, p. 199; Turnbull, *Samuel Hartlib*, p. 63; Abbott, *Writings and Speeches of Oliver Cromwell*, ii. 397.

[3] R. F. Jones, *Ancients and Moderns*, pp. 171–2, 317–18. Benjamin Worsley, possible author of the 1651 Navigation Act, Surveyor of Ireland, and Secretary to Cromwell's and to Charles II's Councils of Trade, was a friend of Hartlib and of John Hall. In 1661 he 'hath much the ear of the Lord Chancellor'. Hartlib told John Winthrop that Worsley was in favour of 'any public good, just liberty of conscience, and any sort of ingenious kind of improvements'. If his scheme to get himself sent over as 'agent or resident of all the plantations' had come off after the Restoration, 'great numbers of honest people' would have emigrated (R. C. Winthrop, *Correspondence of Hartlib, Haak, Oldenbourg and others of the Founders of the Royal Society with Governor Winthrop, 1661–72*, Proceedings of the Massachusetts Historical Soc., 1878, pp. 12–13; Turnbull, *Hartlib, Dury and Comenius, passim*; 'John Hall's Letters to Samuel Hartlib', *Review of English Studies*, New Series, iv. 228–9; G. L. Beer, *The Old Colonial System, 1660–88*, New York, 1912, i. 244, 248).

[4] G. B. Tatham, *The Puritans in Power* (1913), pp. 190–1.

ficance to the Parliamentarian preference for the rule of law as against arbitrariness. Bacon himself attempted to evolve a universal science of jurisprudence. A similar emphasis on the law-abiding nature of the universe can be seen in the dominant school of Puritan theologians under Charles I, Preston and Ames.

The new science, moreover, combined respect for law with a willingness to innovate that must have helped the radicals to shake off the dead weight of tradition and precedent which hamstrung early Parliamentarian political thinking. Robert Norman's *The Newe Attractive*, Gilbert's (unpublished) *Physiologia Nova*, and Bacon's *Novum Organum* were only three examples of an emphasis on novelty from many that might be given.[1] In his *Discovery of a World in the Moon* (1638) John Wilkins said it was the Devil who had persuaded mankind to believe that novelty was a sign of error.[2] The association of Wilkins's book with political radicalism is made clear by Heath's lines,

> Nothing but fair Utopian worlds i' the moon
> Must be new form'd by revolution.[3]

Bacon's scientific method is the trial and error of the craftsmen raised to a principle. His theories suggested that reality could be changed by human effort. He drew men's attention to the real world in which they lived, made them sceptical of armchair theorizing. Mere intellectual activity divorced from practice is a form of laziness and escapism: 'to spend too much time in studies is sloth'.[4] Here again the parallel with the Puritan effort to realize God's kingdom on earth is valid.

The Baconian attitude of mind would be hostile to all mere authority which would not submit to the test of use and experience. Bacon, like Nicholas Hill, insisted that men should re-examine the things that they took for granted, the apparently obvious and self-evident: with minds cleared of all prepossessions. A man steeped in Baconianism would, if he applied the

---

[1] See Lynn Thorndike, 'Newness in 17th century Science', *J.H.I.* xi. 585–98, for many other examples. The fact that the *Novum Organum* was part of the *Instauratio Magna* shows how Bacon combined the backward and the forward look. 'Froward retention of custom is as turbulent a thing as innovation', he said in his Essay *On Innovations* (Works, vi. 433). [2] Op. cit. (3rd impression, 1640), p. 2.

[3] Robert Heath, *Clarastella*, 1650, quoted by Marjorie Nicolson, 'English Almanacs and the "New Astronomy" ', *Annals of Science*, iv. 21.

[4] Bacon, *Works*, vi. 497.

method to politics at all, not be an unquestioning supporter
of the *status quo*. He would be sceptical of most things except
the test of practice—by their works ye shall know them. 'I am
certain of my way but not certain of my position', Bacon said;
as Cromwell was to say that he could tell what he would not
have, though he could not what he would.[1] Bacon's principles
would supply no political dogmas, but they might offer
a guide to action. Even his errors had an historical significance.
He grossly underestimated the complexity of the tasks he was
setting humanity. 'The invention of all causes and sciences
would be the labour of but a few years.'[2] Marx made a similar
mistake in thinking that world revolution was just round the
corner, Lenin in thinking that the classless society could be
be realized in the lifetime of men who made the Russian
Revolution: but in all three cases the apocalyptic vision acted
as a stimulant to action which was its own justification.

If Professor Butterfield is right to regard the emergence of
a new scientific civilization in the later seventeenth century as
the greatest landmark since the rise of Christianity,[3] then so
far as England is concerned Bacon is clearly the decisive figure,
and was recognized to be so in the seventeenth century (as he
was for France in the eighteenth century).[4] His ideas became
widely influential during what used to be called the Puritan
Revolution; yet their ultimate tendency was towards 'a colossal
secularization of thought in every possible realm of ideas'.[5] The
paradox is more apparent than real. I have already tried to
suggest the congruence of some of Bacon's central ideas with
the Protestant orthodoxy in which he grew up. The obverse of
this would be to point out that the body of ideas which we call
'Puritan' was in fact far more complex and far more concerned
with this-worldly matters than it has been usual to suppose.[6]

---

[1] Ibid. v. 559; Sir Philip Warwick, *Memoirs of the Reign of King Charles the First*
(1813), p. 194.
[2] Quoted in H. Butterfield, *The Origins of Modern Science* (1949), p. 90.
[3] Ibid., p. 174. Professor Butterfield is careful to point out that this
was a social as well as an intellectual revolution: 'the changes which took place in
the history of thought in this period . . . are not more remarkable than the changes
in life and society' (ibid., p. 169). Cf. Ornstein, *The Role of Scientific Societies in the
17th century*, pp. 3–20.
[4] J. G. Crowther, *Francis Bacon* (1960), p. 4.
[5] Butterfield, op. cit., p. 166.
[6] I argue this point at length in my *Society and Puritanism*.

We must think not of scientists who happen to be Puritans (or for that matter, though much more rarely, Catholics), nor of Puritans whose theology 'looks forward to deism', as we helplessly say: we must become aware of a single society in which Bacon *really* believed that science 'is a singular help and preservative against unbelief and error'.[1] An ardent Baconian of the sixteen-fifties, the Rev. John Webster, thought that divinity should not be taught in schools, for religious truths came only through the spirit of God.[2]

Copernicus's theory had 'democratized the universe' by shattering the hierarchical structure of the heavens; Harvey 'democratized' the human body by dethroning the heart.[3] In the social sphere, Bacon's method went 'far to level men's wits, and leaves but little to individual excellence'.[4] (It is of interest that Nicholas Hill approved of 'government by assemblies'.)[5] The new experimental philosophy, of Robert Norman no less than of Bacon, made all men equal, as Hobbes was soon to proclaim. One researcher was as good as another, and better than any mere speculative scholar. Every man could be his own expert. In just the same way the radicals used the Protestant doctrine of the priesthood of all believers to justify preaching by laymen, and not merely by university-trained specialists. Bacon was in favour of careers open to the talents, recommending to the youthful Sir George Villiers 'that which I think was never done since I was born, . . . which is that you countenance and encourage and advance able men, in all kinds, degrees, and professions'.[6] It was a lesson which the Duke of Buckingham never learnt; but Oliver Cromwell did.

Bacon's method is based on personal observation, personal experience, as against the authority of books or learned men. 'We have experience for our infallible and uncontrollable tutor', wrote Captain Saltonstall in 1636, 'which did not dwell all his days within the confines of a quiet closet.'[7] 'By your opinion',

[1] Bacon, *Works*, iii. 221.

[2] Webster, *Academiarum Examen* (1654).

[3] See my 'William Harvey and the Idea of Monarchy', *passim*. Harvey was aware of a parallel between astronomical and anatomical discoveries.

[4] Bacon, *Works*, iii. 221.

[5] McColley, 'Nicholas Hill and the *Philosophia Epicurea*', *Annals of Science*, iv. 403–4.

[6] *Cabala* (1654), ii. 71.

[7] C. Saltonstall, *The Navigator* (1636), quoted by Taylor, *Mathematical Practitioners*, p. 77.

Bishop Goodman exploded to Hakewill, 'a man's own experience is the best part of learning.'[1] This is highly individualistic doctrine, and compares strictly with the Puritan demand for first-hand religious experience against the traditions of men. University divines preached 'a dead doctrine', said William Dell, 'which other men have spoken, but themselves have no experience of'.[2] 'Men must speak their own experienced words, and must not speak thoughts', Winstanley agreed.[3] 'Everyone who speaks of any herb, plant, art, or nature of mankind is required to speak nothing by imagination, but what he hath found out by his own industry and observation in trial.'[4]

Science, like religion, is a co-operative activity: the test of the truth of experiment is social, in the sectarian congregations no less than in the community of scientists. 'Faithfulness to experiment is not so different a discipline from faithfulness to experience', said a professor of chemistry recently.[5] Consider the following passage, written in 1582:

All their logic is in names and words, without any use. . . . But translate them into English, and you need not go to Cambridge to learn them. . . . You take away their wisdom if you speak so plain English. O ye merchants, strengthen your hands unto merchandise by this logic. . . . This is deep cookery, not to know how to dress and make ready all meats, but to know . . . what is a species and what is genus. . . . Their logic hath held them so long in learning what they should do that they have done little or nothing at all.

That is not by a scientist; it is by Robert Browne, the father of Congregationalism.[6] Such passages remind us of what Walwyn was to write in 1644: 'The party who are now in arms to make us slaves consists . . . chiefly of such as have had esteem for the most learned arts men in the kingdom.'[7]

---

[1] Hakewill, *Apologie*, ii. 129.

[2] W. Dell, *Several Sermons and Discourses* (1709), p. 640. First published 1652.

[3] G. Winstanley, *Truth Lifting up its Head above Scandals* (1649), in G. H. Sabine, *The Works of Gerrard Winstanley* (Cornell U.P., 1941), p. 125.

[4] Ibid., p. 564; cf. pp. 579–80. The instructions are for Sunday lecturers on the sciences in Winstanley's ideal commonwealth: see p. 121 below.

[5] H. C. Longuet-Higgins, in *The Times Literary Supplement*, 25 October 1963.

[6] Ed. A. Peel and L. H. Carlson, *The Writings of Robert Harrison and Robert Browne* (1953), pp. 177, 18. Cf. the deposition of John Gray, arrested in connexion with the first English conventicle in 1550: 'All errors were brought in by learned men' (C. Burrage, *The Early English Dissenters*, 1912, ii. 2).

[7] W. Walwyn, *The Compassionate Samaritan* (1644), p. 35, in W. Haller, *Tracts on Liberty in the Puritan Revolution*, iii. 82.

Consider again the advice given in 1604 by the Puritan Hugh Broughton to James I about translating the Bible:

> It was very needful that many others (mechanics and artificers) should be likewise at such a work; . . . geometricians, carpenters, masons, [should help for terms] about the temple of Solomon, . . . gardeners, for all the boughs and branches of Ezekiel's tree.

Lectures should be given at Gresham College 'upon the places of difficulty, . . . to be judged of all men'.[1] Rather naturally, James did not accept the advice. John Robinson, pastor to the Pilgrim Fathers in Holland, said that ministers should not in anything 'be obeyed for the authority of the commander, but for the reason of the commandment'.[2] This reminds us of Harvey's *dictum*, 'I propose both to learn and to teach anatomy not from books but from dissections, not from the positions of philosophers but from the fabric of nature.'[3] 'True knowledge of Christ', wrote Thomas Taylor, 'is experimental.' It is acquired 'not . . . by reading, not out of books or relations, as the physician knows the virtue of books by reading; but by experience of himself'.[4] 'Knowledge without practice is no knowledge', wrote the author of the marginal headings to Greenham's *Workes*.[5] To the converted, said Thomas Hooker, 'things appear as they be. . . . Such judge not by outward appearance, as is the guise of men of corrupt minds, but upon experience, that which they have found and felt in their own hearts.'[6] It should not surprise us that in New England 'the Puritan clergy . . . were the chief patrons and promoters of the new astronomy, and of other scientific discoveries'.[7]

Here is a scientist again, John Wilkins: 'It would be much better for the commonwealth of learning if we would ground

[1] J. Strype, *Life of Whitgift* (1822), ii. 529. For Broughton see p. 170 below.

[2] Quoted in P. Miller, *Errand into the Wilderness* (Harvard U.P. 1956), p. 21; cf. Bunyan's first Baptist pastor, holy Mr. Gifford, who urged him to take no truth on trust, but to await personal conviction from the Holy Spirit speaking through the Scriptures (*Grace Abounding*, in *Works*, 1860, i. 20).

[3] W. Harvey, *Works* (1847), p. 7.

[4] T. Taylor, *Works* (1653), p. 411.

[5] R. Greenham, *Workes* (1612), p. 196; cf. p. 343.

[6] T. Hooker, *The Application of Redemption* (1657), p. 557, quoted in P. Miller and T. H. Johnson, *The Puritans* (New York, 1938), pp. 39–40.

[7] S. E. Morison, 'Astronomy at Colonial Harvard', *New England Quarterly*, vii. 13.

our principles rather upon the frequent experience of our own than the bare authority of others.'[1] This is from a religious politician, George Wither:

> Nor unto this assurance am I come
> By any apophthegms gathered from
> Our old and much-admired philosophers.
> My sayings are mine own as well as theirs:
> For whatsoe'er account of them is made,
> I have as good experience of them had.[2]

And here again is a religious merchant, Nicholas Ferrar, with the tone of disapproval to be expected after his conversion to a religion of ceremonies: 'Our age verily hath taken it for a main principle of wisdom to give no credit to anything which is . . . without the compass of personal experience.'[3] Finally, Gerrard Winstanley the Digger, most radical of political and religious thinkers: 'All that I have writ concerning the matter of digging, I never read it in any book, nor received it from any mouth . . . before I saw the light of it rise up within myself.'[4] When Milton in a noble passage of *Areopagitica* denounced the wealthy man who resolves 'to find himself out some factor, to whose care and credit he may commit the whole managing of his religious affairs' and resign 'the whole warehouse of his religion', he was echoing Bacon, whether consciously or not. 'When men have once made over their judgement to others' keeping', Bacon had written, 'and . . . have agreed to support some one person's opinion, from that time they make no enlargement of the sciences themselves, but fall to the servile office of embellishing certain individual authors and increasing their retinue.'[5]

We can trace the influence of Bacon (or of the scientific spirit which Bacon summed up) on such influential thinkers as George

[1] Quoted by J. G. Crowther, *Founders of British Science* (1960), p. 27.
[2] Wither, *Juvenilia* (Spenser Soc.), i. 444.
[3] Ed. B. Blackstone, *Ferrar Papers* (1938), p. 191.
[4] G. Winstanley, *Religious Works* (1649), Introduction, dated 20 December 1649, p. 4. The introduction to this volume, not printed by Sabine, may be found in *The Law of Freedom and Other Writings* (Pelican Classic, 1973).
[5] Milton, *Complete Prose Works* (Yale ed.), ii. 544; Bacon, *Works*, iv. 14. Milton had in fact quoted Bacon a page or two earlier. It is no doubt a coincidence that Milton's metaphor is as flatly *bourgeois* as Bacon's is feudal.

Hakewill,[1] John Robinson,[2] William Ames,[3] Henry Jacie,[4] Hugh Peter,[5] William Dell,[6] Thomas Goodwin,[7] Samuel Gott,[8] Richard Baxter,[9] as well as on more obviously political figures like Sir Walter Ralegh,[10] George Wither,[11] Sir John Eliot,[12] Lord Brooke,[13] John Milton,[14] William Walwyn,[15] Richard Overton,[16] Gerrard Winstanley,[17] John Saltmarsh,[18] Anthony Burges,[19] William Petty,[20] James Harrington.[21] Even more significant perhaps are the Baconian assumptions which pervade the writings of popular Interregnum journalists like Marchamont Nedham and of essayists like Francis Osborn.

In the popularization of Baconian and scientific ideas in England the forties and fifties seem to have been the decisive decades. More of Bacon's works were published in England in 1640–1 than in all the 14 years since his death.[22] Most of them

[1] See pp. 199–203 below.

[2] A. Barker, *Milton and the Puritan Dilemma* (Toronto U.P., 1942), pp. 86, 358.

[3] See passages quoted by P. Miller, *The New England Mind: from Colony to Province* (Harvard U.P., 1953), pp. 12–13.

[4] *Collections of the Massachusetts Historical Soc.*, vi. 456–7: Jacie's interest in astronomy.

[5] H. Peter, *Good Work for a Good Magistrate* (1651), *passim*; and see p. 119 below.

[6] See pp. 120, 123–4 below.

[7] T. Goodwin, *Works* (1861–3), iv. 541: 'that great and excellently learned man, Sir Francis Bacon'.

[8] [S. Gott], *Nova Solyma* (trans. W. Begley, 1902), i. 162–73, and *passim*. Published 1648.

[9] Quoted by R. K. Merton, 'Science, Technology and Society in 17th century England', *Osiris*, iv. 435, 453.   [10] See pp. 145–9, 223–4 below.

[11] G. Wither, *Juvenilia* (Spenser Soc.), i. 252–3: knowledge to reverse the effects of the Fall.

[12] Sir J. Eliot, *The Monarchie of Man* (ed. A. B. Grosart, 1879), ii. 224–7.

[13] Lord Brooke, *The Nature of Truth* (1640), pp. 28–29, 125–7, 142–3; *A Discourse . . . of . . . Episcopacie* (1641), pp. 1–2.

[14] Milton, *Third, Fifth and Seventh Prolusions*.

[15] W. Walwyn, *A Whisper in the Eare of Mr. Thomas Edwards* (1646), p. 6; and see pp. 121, 125 below.   [16] See p. 121 below.

[17] Ed. Sabine, *Works of Gerrard Winstanley*, pp. 563–8, 580.

[18] J. Saltmarsh, *Examinations, or a Discovery of some Dangerous Positions* (1643).

[19] A. Burges, *The Doctrine of Original Sin* (1659), p. 201.

[20] Sir W. Petty, *Economic Writings* (ed. Hull), i. lxiii–lxiv.

[21] J. Harrington, *The Art of Lawgiving* (1659), in *The Oceana and other Works* (1737), pp. 429–34; cf. p. 120 below. Bacon, Grotius, and Machiavelli are the three names that occur most often in the writings of Harrington (R. W. Gibson, *Supplement to a Bacon Bibliography*, 1959, p. 9). I found S. B. L. Penrose, *The Reputation and Influence of Francis Bacon in the 17th Century* (New York, 1934), of little use for my present purposes.

[22] H. R. Trevor-Roper, 'Francis Bacon', *Encounter*, No. 101, p. 76. The following dates of publication are relevant:

   1640 *Certain Considerations touching the Church* (reprinted 1642).
      The Advancement of Learning (English translation, two issues).

were on political and religious rather than on scientific subjects, but their tone would help to establish Bacon's bona fides with the Parliamentarians. Hitherto his political record and his close association with the court must have cut him off from those who were to be his natural audience. The *Essays*, of which there had been seventeen editions by 1639, would not alter the picture of a cynical, worldly man. Bacon's name frequently appears in almanacs after 1640; rarely before. This was at a time when almanacs themselves were beginning to appeal to a wider public, and to take up a more decidedly political attitude. Wilkins seems to have been the man who did most to popularize Bacon (and Galileo too).[1] By 1649 Dury was able to say that 'the advancement of learning hath been oftener, *and in a more public way*, at least mentioned in this nation of late than in former times, partly by the publication of those excellent works of the Lord Verulam'.[2] Sir William Temple, at some date between 1690 and 1696, said that 'the new philosophy had gotten ground in these parts of the world' in the past fifty or sixty years.[3] It was only after 1650 that Thomas Bushell, former servant, friend, and disciple of Bacon, thought it to his advantage to claim that his master had instructed him in 'the theory of the mineral profession'. But the claim henceforth loomed large in his self-advertisement.[4] In his *Britannia Baconica* (1661)

1641   *A Discourse concerning Church Affairs* (two issues).
      Advertisement concerning the Controversies of the Church of England.
      The History of Henry VII.
      Three Speeches concerning Union with Scotland.
      Cases of Treason.
      Confession of Faith (three editions 1641–2).
1642   *The Office of Constable.*
      Reading on the Statute of Uses.
1643   *Nova Atlantis* (English translation 1659).

It was especially to those of Bacon's works published after 1640 that Milton referred in his pamphlets—*Certain Considerations, Advertisement, New Atlantis.*

[1] M. Nicolson, 'English Almanacs and the "New Astronomy" ', *Annals of Science*, iv. 7–8, 16–17, 32–33.   [2] Dury, *A Seasonable Discourse*, sig. D–D 2. My italics.

[3] Temple, 'Some Thoughts upon Reviewing the Essay of Ancient and Modern Learning', in *Five Miscellaneous Essays* (ed. S. H. Monk, Michigan U.P., 1963), p. 72.

[4] J. W. Gough, *The Superlative Prodigall: a Life of Thomas Bushell* (1932), pp. 87–88; cf. pp. 117–21. Cf. Farrington, *Francis Bacon*, pp. 10–12, who takes Bushell's claims more seriously. Whether true or not, they were worth making after the civil war. Bushell had supported the King, as he could scarcely avoid doing, since he farmed lead mines in Cavalier-occupied Wales. But he was Puritan in outlook (see his *The Miners Contemplative Prayers*), and made no difficulty about accepting the Commonwealth and Protectorate. Cromwell renewed his lease.

John Childrey confessed that '(*Secundum Deum*) he owes all this new knowledge to the Lord Bacon'.[1]

Few popular almanac writers before 1640 cared to commit themselves to the Copernican system;[2] but the collapse of the censorship gave them a new confidence and willingness to speculate. By the sixteen-fifties the Ptolemaic system was dead. Henceforth the only question was whether Copernicus or Tycho Brahe was to succeed. Both Aubrey and Sir William Temple dated the end of belief in 'fairies, sprites, witchcraft and enchantments' to the revolutionary decades.[3] 'Till about the year 1649', Aubrey tell us precisely, ' 'twas held a strange presumption for a man to attempt an innovation in learning.' Civil wars, he added, 'do not only extinguish religion and laws, but superstition'.[4] In 1651 Harvey first clearly challenged the traditional belief in spontaneous generation (which even Bacon had stressed) with his *omnia ex ovo*.[5]

The Epicurean Walter Charleton, later Fellow of the Royal Society, spoke in 1657 of 'those heroical wits among our countrymen, who have addicted themselves to the reformation and augmentation of arts and sciences, and made a greater progress in that glorious design than many ages before them could aspire to'. Great advances in natural philosophy, medicine, optics, astronomy, geometry, and chemistry had been made 'by the ingeny and labours of men now living in England and as yet in the prime of their strength and years'.[6] There had also been a change in intellectual habits. 'Our late wars and schisms

---

[1] J. Childrey, *Britannia Baconica: or The Natural Rarities of England, Scotland and Wales* (1661), sig. B 7.

[2] Nicolson, 'English Almanacs', esp. pp. 16–17, 20–23, 32–33; cf. G. McColley, 'The Ross–Wilkins Controversy', *Annals of Science*, iii. 183.

[3] Temple's essay 'Of Poetry', written at some period between 1681 and its publication in the second part of his *Miscellanea* (1690, p. 285), dates it thirty or forty years earlier; Aubrey, *Brief Lives*, ii. 318. Charles Edwards, of Jesus College and Llanrhaiadr, attributed the silencing of elves and ghosts to the arrival of newer knowledge (T. Richards, *Religious Developments in Wales (1654–62)*, 1923, p. 297).

[4] J. Aubrey, *Natural History of Wiltshire* (1847), p. 5; *Remaines of Gentilisme and Judaisme* (1881), p. 21.

[5] Harvey, *Works* (1847), pp. 454–66; frontispiece to *De Generatione Animalium* (1651).

[6] W. Charleton, *The Immortality of the Human Soul* (1657), pp. 32–46. Charleton was a pupil of Wilkins at Magdalen Hall, but seems to have been a neutral with royalist sympathies during the civil war. His dialogue is set among English royalist *émigrés* in Paris. Charleton himself speaks through the character Athanasius, who wishes to convince the exiles of the advances made by revolutionary England. He refers especially to scientists in Oxford.

having almost wholly discouraged men from the study of theology, and brought the civil law into contempt, the major part
of young scholars in our universities addict themselves to physic.'[1]
Marchamont Nedham agreed that more progress had been
made in the profession of medicine since Bacon's *Advancement
of Learning* 'than ever was done in the world before', when
men just commented on the Greek and Arab doctors. 'Look but
twenty years back'—this is 1665—'and you will say, never had
any other science or art in the world such an advance and
alteration in so short a time.'[2]

1642 was 'the year of discoveries'.[3] Just as the sectaries came
up from underground and met publicly as soon as the hierarchy collapsed: so, as soon as the Laudian censorship broke
down, the works of Bacon, Coke, Ralegh, and many more were
freely published, discussed and commented on. London citizens
and the 'middling sort' who formed the backbone of the
Parliamentary armies had for nearly a century been discussing
the new scientific ideas as well as claiming the right to elect
ministers. They had learnt to reject the authority of Aristotle
as well as of bishops, to rely on religious and scientific experiment,
the test of their own independent critical senses. 'They believe
nothing except what they see', said Dury of the Independents.[4]
It was the Duchess of Newcastle, wife of the *beau idéal* Cavalier,
who preferred 'rational arguments' to 'deluding experiments'.[5]

VI

We might indeed suggest very tentatively a link between
kinds of interest in science and degrees of political and religious
radicalism. One of the earliest Baconians was John Robinson,
pastor in the Netherlands to the Pilgrim Fathers.[6] Hugh Peter,
chaplain in Cromwell's army, in 1646 told Parliament that the
state should further 'the new experimental philosophy'.[7] Webster,

---

[1] Ibid., p. 49.
[2] M. N[edham], *Medela Medicinae*, p. 215; cf. Keevil, *The Stranger's Son*, p. 138.
[3] Harleian Miscellany (1744–56), vi. 119.
[4] Quoted by Merton, 'Science, Technology and Society in 17th century England',
Osiris, iv. 453. 'Knowing is seeing', Locke was soon to say.
[5] Carré, *Phases of Thought in England*, p. 231.　　　[6] See p. 116 above.
[7] H. Peter, *Gods Doings and Mans Duty*, a sermon preached before both Houses of
Parliament, the Westminster Assembly, and the Lord Mayor and Aldermen of
London, 2 April 1646; cf. *Good Work for a Good Magistrate* (1651), esp. pp. 74–78.

who in the sixteen-fifties urged the introduction of chemistry into the universities, was also an army chaplain and advocate of religious toleration: other adherents of iatromechanism were Dell and James Harrington.[1] Culpeper was as radical in politics as in medicine. He hoped in 1649 that English liberty would 'within a few years' be grasped at by 'all the nations in Europe'. 'Do you think times of knowledge will not come?' he thundered at the College of Physicians.[2] The regicide John Cook suggested free medical treatment for the poor, the Baptist Samuel Hering a state-salaried free medical service.[3] Chamberlen, another medical radical, observed that 'rich men are none of the greatest enemies to monarchy', and called for public works to relieve unemployment.[4] It is perhaps no accident that the three men whom Margaret James singled out as really anxious to improve the lot of the poor during the Revolution—Hartlib, Chamberlen, and Gerbier—all have a place in our story.[5]

The Commonwealth's Council of State said in September 1650 that it was ready to receive, and give all possible furtherance to, propositions for the reforming of schools.[6] The Barebones Parliament had its Committee for the Advancement of Learning. The Independent army tried to stop the Scottish Kirk persecuting witches, and Cromwellian rule led to increased revenues for Scottish universities and to the setting up of a College of Physicians in Edinburgh. The salaries of Professors of Astronomy and Physic at Oxford were augmented.[7] The first article on flying to appear in an English newspaper was in the Leveller *Moderate*. The story (from Warsaw) of a proposed flying

[1] J. Harrington, *The Mechanics of Nature*, in *Oceana and Other Works* (1737), pp. xlii–xliv. I am indebted to Mr. D. Nandy for drawing my attention to this.

[2] *A Physicall Directory, or A translation of the London Dispensatory* (translated by N. Culpeper, 1649), sig. A.; 3rd ed., 1651, sig. A–Av.

[3] J. Cook, *Unum Necessarium* (1648), *passim*; ed. J. Nickolls, *Original Letters . . . addressed to Oliver Cromwell* (1743), p. 101.

[4] P. Chamberlen, *The Poore Mans Advocate* (1649), p. 21.

[5] M. James, *Social Policy during the Puritan Revolution* (1930), pp. 279–81. A fourth name might perhaps be added—Peter Cornelius Plockhoy, whom Hartlib patronized (L. and M. Harder, *Plockhoy from Zurik-Zee*, Mennonite Historical Series, No. 2, Newton, Kansas, 1952, pp. 37–41).

[6] W. A. L. Vincent, *The State and School Education, 1640–60, in England and Wales* (1950), p. 80, and *passim*.

[7] J. Simon, 'Educational Policies and Programmes', *The Modern Quarterly*, iv (1949), 165. H. R. Trevor-Roper, 'Scotland and the Puritan Revolution', in *Historical Essays, 1600–1750, presented to David Ogg* (ed. H, E. Bell and R. L. Ollard, 1963), pp. 107–8, 127, 114–15; *C.S.P.D., 1658–9*, pp. 66, 243, 263–4.

machine was presented seriously as 'a matter of delight and pleasure', especially to those who 'have studied the mathematics'. The conclusion was appropriately Baconian, when we recall that the *Moderate*'s readers would be mainly London artisans: 'Experience daily shows us that nothing is impossible unto man, but that through labour and industry the most difficult things at length may be obtained.'[1]

The Leveller Richard Overton, who had read Copernicus, Tycho Brahe, and Ambrose Paré, suggested (not very seriously) an experiment to test the immortality of the soul.[2] The Leveller William Walwyn explained religious experience in psychophysical terms: excessive fasting might lead to visions and ecstasies.[3] The Quakers Edward Burrough and George Fox called for a laboratory analysis to see whether bread and wine really could be transformed into body and blood.[4] The troops who guarded Charles I called him 'Stroker', 'in relation to that gift which God had given him in curing the [King's] evil'.[5] Winstanley, the most radical of all politically, wanted Gresham-type lectures on natural science to replace the Sunday sermon in all parishes.[6] If we recall the analogy which has been drawn between the sermons of seventeenth-century lecturers and an adult education course today,[7] we can see Winstanley's idea as a logical development of radical puritanism.

Under the Commonwealth the 'mechanicians' saw with delight the purge of royalists and drones from the universities; the former bastion of clericalism and royalist stronghold, Oxford, became for a few years a centre of Baconian science. We can under-

[1] *The Moderate*, 12–19 December 1648, pp. 207 ff., quoted in J. Frank, *The Beginnings of the English Newspaper 1620–60* (Harvard U.P., 1961), pp. 158–60.
[2] R. Overton, *Mans Mortalitie* (Amsterdam, 1643), pp. 11–13, 18, 33.
[3] W. Walwyn, *The Vanitie of the present Churches* (1649), in W. Haller and G. Davies, *The Leveller Tracts, 1647–53* (Columbia U.P., 1944), p. 259. Cf. p. 116 above. Gilbert Burnet, later Bishop of Salisbury, arrived at similar conclusions in the sixteen-sixties (ed. H. C. Foxcroft, *A Supplement to Burnet's History of My Own Time*, 1902, p. 474).
[4] W. and T. Evans, *Edward Burrough* (1851), pp. 251–2; G. Fox, *Gospel Truth Demonstrated* (1706), p. 1088. Fox was much interested in natural science, and left property in Philadelphia to be used as a botanical garden. Penn spoke of him as 'a divine and a naturalist' (R. B. Schlatter, *Social Ideas of Religious Leaders, 1660–88*, 1940, p. 241). The most famous watchmakers of the later seventeenth century were Quakers (A. Raistrick, *Quakers in Science and Industry*, 1950, pp. 223–41).
[5] *Mercurius Elencticus*, 7 February 1649.   [6] Sabine, op. cit., pp. 564–6.
[7] G. R. Cragg, *Puritanism in the Period of the Great Persecution* (1957), pp. 210, 165; cf. my *Society and Puritanism*, pp. 86–87.

stand the deep historical roots of the contempt which many radicals felt for Oxford and Cambridge. The dons tried to pretend that this was mere levelling, the hostility of the ignorant vulgar towards learning as such; but it was rather hostility to the maintenance of vested interests which opposed new ideas, and to the emphasis on formal education, rather than experience, in training ministers. Nor was it dictated merely by religious fanaticism: it drew much more on the Paracelsan and utilitarian traditions of popular London science. 'Who are our jailors?' Nicholas Culpeper asked in 1651. 'I say scholars.'[1]

Similar considerations apply to Bacon's apparent distrust of reason in devising theories, and his insistence on the primacy of experiment and direct observation of material things. 'Reason' had become so inextricably associated with scholasticism that the distinction was as natural and necessary as it had been in the Reformation.[2] Bacon would no doubt have agreed with Milton's 'Down Reason then, at least vain reasonings down'. Much of the denigration of the interregnum Baconians by the defenders of the universities stemmed from this. Historians have accepted too easily the contention that men like Hartlib and his friend John Hall, George Snell, John Webster, Noah Biggs, William Dell, Nicholas Culpeper, John Saltmarsh, George Stanley, William Sprigge, Hugh Peter, William Walwyn, and Gerrard Winstanley were mere religious fanatics.

Yet there are distinctions to be drawn, which I suggested when I associated mathematics and astronomy with London merchants and Gresham College, chemistry with artisans and religious radicals.[3] There was no chair of chemistry at Gresham. On the contrary: John Argent, Gresham Professor of Physic from 1615 to 1655, was also President of the College of Physicians. The Parliamentarian scientists who 'Greshamized' Oxford had no thought of introducing chemistry there. Ward thought 'agriculture, mechanic chemistry, and the like' unsuitable for the sons of the nobility and gentry.[4] The supercilious Sir William Temple 'always looked upon alchemy in natural philosophy

---

[1] N. Culpeper, *A Directory for Mid-wives* (1651), Epistle to the Reader.

[2] For similar difficulties with 'reason' and law see pp. 250–6 below.

[3] For connexions between radical Protestantism and alchemy, see A. Stella, 'Ricerche sul socinianesimo', *Bolletino dell' Istituto di Storia Veneziano*, iii. 77–120. Cf. M. West, 'Notes on the Importance of Alchemy to Medical Science in the Writings of Francis Bacon and Robert Boyle', *Ambix*, ix. 102–14.   [4] See p. 55 above.

to be like enthusiasm in divinity, and to have troubled the world much to the same purpose'.[1] Chemistry, excluded from the universities, did not succeed in shaking off either its lower-class subversive aura, or its alchemical and magical fancies.[2]

Many of the critics of the universities were moderate men. John Hall was a friend of Hobbes as well as of Hartlib. The title of his *An Humble Motion to the Parliament of England concerning the Advancement of Learning and Reformation of the Universities* (1649) demonstrates his Baconian approach. Hall wanted new chairs in chemistry and anatomy, and the endowment of research, especially in mathematics, science, and medicine.[3] (The bishops had opposed research in the universities,[4] and even Bacon had thought of Solomon's House as a separate research institute.) Hall was also critical of the universities' neglect of history, and himself wrote *Of the Advantageous reading of History* (1657).[5] He opposed censorship, and wanted England to imitate the Dutch by importing learned foreigners. He was an admirer of Samuel Ward and other Cambridge Puritans.[6] Hall acted as contact man between Hartlib and the Cambridge Platonists.[7] He himself translated some of Comenius's works. Under the Commonwealth he was an official government pamphleteer, at a salary of £100 a year. In 1649 he employed the astrologer William Lilly to run the government paper *Mercurius Rusticus*.[8]

Webster quoted Dee's Preface to Billingsley's *Euclide*, and praised Briggs, Napier, Gilbert, Harvey, and Hobbes, as well as Bacon and Comenius.[9] He wanted universities to provide 'laboratories as well as libraries, and work in the fire as well as building castles in the air'. Later he defended the Royal Society and attacked belief in witches.[10] Dell hoped to see

[1] Temple, *Five Miscellaneous Essays*, p. 87.
[2] See p. 298 below.
[3] J. Hall, *An Humble Motion* (ed. A. K. Croston, 1953), pp. 27, 29, 39–43.
[4] See p. 311 below.
[5] Cf. Turnbull, *Hartlib, Dury and Comenius*, p. 74.
[6] See his poems to them in G. Saintsbury, *Caroline Poets* (1905–21), ii. 203, 209. For Ward's interest in mathematics see p. 313 below.
[7] G. H. Turnbull, 'John Hall's Letters to Samuel Hartlib', *Review of English Studies*, New Series, iv. 221–30.
[8] Hall, *An Humble Motion*, p. vii. For Lilly see p. 44 above.
[9] Webster, *Academiarum Examen*, pp. 20, 41, 44, 51–52, 74, 99. Cf. Noah Biggs, *The Vanity of the Craft of Physick* (1651), sig. b, pp. 230–1.
[10] Webster, op. cit., pp. 106–8; *The Display of Supposed Witchcraft* (1677), pp. 4, 14, and *passim*.

universal education, with new state-maintained universities in London, York, Bristol, Exeter, Norwich, and the like. At these universities intellectual should be combined with manual labour.[1] His main concern was, and was recognized by his enemies to be, the provision of better educational opportunities for 'townsmen's children'.[2] In 1648 Petty, who later became Commonwealth Surveyor of Ireland and Professor of Anatomy in purged Oxford, proposed (to Hartlib) a university in London. He also recommended 'literary workhouses' for poor children and 'colleges of tradesmen', where able mechanicians should be subsidized whilst performing experiments. He wanted more vocational training.[3] Hartlib in his turn hoped Petty would be seconded to Gresham College to advance experimental science there. He became Gresham Professor of Music in 1650.

When Bacon attacked theologians who dwelt on the irresistible power of sin, he had been interested primarily in clearing the decks for scientific and industrial advance. He drew no political conclusions. But his successors did, when in the freer atmosphere of the revolutionary decades sin became the great deterrent of conservative preachers. 'It is reserved only for God and angels to be lookers-on', Bacon wrote in criticism of Aristotle's emphasis on contemplation. Milton no doubt recalled the passage when at the height of the civil war he refused to praise a fugitive and cloistered virtue that held men back from political struggle.[4] To look for a first cause beyond the chain of natural causes is to abandon the principle of causation, Bacon had thought, and to fly from solid knowledge into a realm of fantasy.[5] Winstanley carried the idea rather further:

To reach God beyond the Creation, or to know what He will be to a man after the man is dead, if any otherwise than to scatter him into his essences of fire, water, earth, and air of which he is compounded, is a knowledge beyond the line or capacity of man to attain to while he lives in his compounded body.[6]

---

[1] Dell, *Several Sermons and Discourses* (1709), pp. 645–8. See p. 109 above.
[2] [Seth Ward], *Vindiciae Academiarum*, pp. 62–64.
[3] *The Advice of William Petty to Samuel Hartlib* (1648), *passim*.
[4] Bacon, *Works*, v. 8. Milton may not have been echoing Bacon: his is an application to politics of the sense of athletic purpose which Calvinist Puritanism gave to its adherents. Bacon is ultimately drawing on the same attitude in his critique of a contemplative non-active philosophy. Here we are at the roots of Protestantism's contribution to science, as well as to the Parliamentarian cause.
[5] Anderson, *The Philosophy of Francis Bacon*, p. 291.   [6] Sabine, op. cit., p. 565.

Bacon's Utopian vision of undoing the consequences of the Fall was restricted to scientific activity. But Winstanley asked 'Why may not we have our heaven here (that is, a comfortable livelihood in the earth) and heaven hereafter too?'[1]

VII

It was only natural that when the scientists were ejected from Oxford in 1660 they should regroup round Gresham College, and that four of the twelve founding members of the Royal Society should be Gresham professors. The Society's meetings were symbolically held in the building 'once the mansion-house of one of the greatest merchants that ever was in England'.[2] Natural philosophy, Hobbes observed, is 'removed from Oxford and Cambridge to Gresham College in London, and to be learned out of their gazettes'.[3] Samuel Butler referred to Sprat as 'the historian of Gresham College', and many others spoke of Gresham College when they meant the Royal Society.[4] Once Gresham College had given birth to the Royal Society it decayed as an independent institution—as though its task was completed.

So the radicals were defeated, but science survived. 'All before 1650 is ancient', the historian of technology declares, 'all after modern.'[5] Charles II, wiser than his father and grandfather, became the patron of science. So far from bishops continuing to oppose the onward march of science, the leading scientists—Cromwell's brother-in-law included—now became bishops: 'to get his former errors forgot', said Burnet, explaining Seth Ward's 'high-flown notions of a severe conformity' after 1660; 'for prevention of those panic causeless terrors', said Joseph Glanvill, thinking of the need to reassure old-fashioned men that

[1] Ibid., p. 409. Walwyn too thought the Fall could be retrieved on earth (W. Haller, Tracts on Liberty in the Puritan Revolution, Columbia U.P., 1934, i. 40, 62).
[2] Sprat, History of the Royal Society, p. 93.
[3] T. Hobbes, Behemoth (1679), in Works (ed. Molesworth), vi. 348.
[4] S. Butler, Characters and Passages from Notebooks (ed. A. R. Waller, 1908), pp. 406, 424. Cf. Henry Power, Experimental Philosophy (1664), pp. 83, 149 ('the Royal Society at Gresham'); ed. Lansdowne, The Petty–Southwell Correspondence 1676–87 (1928), pp. 11, 26, 87; Sir W. Temple, Five Miscellaneous Essays, p. 73.
[5] C. Singer, Technology and History (L. T. Hobhouse Memorial Trust Lecture, 1952), p. 16.

science was now respectable.[1] In 1663 a bishop could still reject the Copernican hypothesis;[2] but by the end of the century the Archbishop of Canterbury was a Baconian.[3] Robert Boyle told gentlemen scientists that they must 'converse with tradesmen in their workhouses and shops'. It was 'childish and . . . unworthy of a philosopher' to refuse to learn from craftsmen.[4] 'By the beginning of the third quarter of the century' Bacon 'was not unjustly dubbed by his opponents a "dictator" of philosophy.' With Locke, 'Bacon's most considerable philosophical disciple', Baconianism bore down all its rivals.[5] John Ray, who had been born in 1627, said in 1690 that it was within his lifetime that vain and empty scholasticism had been replaced by a new and solid philosophy based on experiment.[6]

Intellectual life in England was freer after and because of the Revolution than it had been before. Take the Marquis of Halifax as a witness:

The liberty of the late times gave men so much light, and diffused it so universally among the people, that they are not now to be dealt with as they might have been in an age of less inquiry. . . . Understandings . . . are grown less humble than they were in former times, when the men in black had made learning such a sin for the laity, that for fear of offending they made a conscience of being able to read. But now the world is grown saucy, and expecteth reasons, and good ones too, before they give up their own op: ions to other men's dictates, though never so magisterially delivered to them.[7]

And yet—not all of Baconianism had triumphed. The Royal Society was a private body: Bacon's House of Solomon had controlled the economy and the whole social order.[8] The educational enthusiasm of the Baconians achieved great things during

[1] G. Burnet, *History of his own Time* (ed. O. Airy, 1897), Part I, i. 343; J. Glanville, *Plus Ultra* (1668), Preface.
[2] W. Lucy, *Observations, Censures and Confutations of . . . Mr. Hobbes* (1663), p. 49, quoted by S. I. Mintz, *The Hunting of Leviathan* (1962), p. 65.
[3] T[homas] T[enison], *Baconiana* (1679), pp. 3–5.
[4] Quoted by Crowther, *Founders of British Science*, pp. 54–55.
[5] Anderson, *The Philosophy of Francis Bacon*, pp. 293, 299, 302–3.
[6] J. Ray, *Synopsis Methodica Stirpium Britannicarum* (1690), Praefatio, sig. A 4v; cf. Jones, *Ancients and Moderns*, pp. 48–49, 65 122.
[7] H. C. Foxcroft, *The Life and Letters of Sir George Savile, Bart., First Marquess of Halifax* (1898), ii. 308; cf. Aubrey, *Remaines of Gentilisme and Judaisme*, pp. 67–68.
[8] Crowther, *Francis Bacon*, p. 3.

the Revolution, though not as much as they had hoped. Hartlib by 1650 had come to despair of changing the mental attitude of adult Englishmen, and to put all his hope in educating the younger generation.[1] But at the Restoration all the Parliamentarian reforms in this sphere were swept away, and the Royal Society had little to say about their master's educational programme. After 1660 it falls into the background.[2] Oxford and Cambridge survived virtually unchanged, and freed themselves from the scientists. Scientific radicals like Webster were driven into the nonconformist underworld. The Hon. Robert Boyle dropped Hartlib at the Restoration because of his radical associations, and neither Hartlib nor Dury became Fellows of the Royal Society.[3] A vigorous attack was mounted against the scientists, specifically because of their Parliamentarian connexions. Their opponents were apt to attribute to the revolt from traditional thought all the religious and political manifestations of revolution. Bacon, said the renegade Henry Stubbe, created 'in the breasts of Englishmen such a desire of novelty as rose up to a contempt of the ancient ecclesiastical and civil jurisdiction and the old government, as well as the governors of the realm; and the root of all our present distractions was planted by his hand'.[4] Robert South, former panegyrist of Oliver Cromwell, used the occasion of the dedication of the Sheldonian Theatre at Oxford (built by a F.R.S.) for satirical invectives 'against Cromwell, fanatics, the Royal Society, and new philosophy'.[5] 'Plebeians and mechanics', said Bishop Parker, 'have philosophized themselves into principles of impiety, and read their lectures of atheism in the streets and highways.'[6]

Royal, aristocratic, and episcopal patronage were necessary

---

[1] Hartlib, Preface to Dury's *The Reformed School* (1650).

[2] Apart from occasional remarks by Petty, e.g. in *Economic Writings* (ed. Hull), i. 20. Cf. Irene Parker, *Dissenting Academies in England* (1914): 'Probably no event in English history has had so far-reaching and disastrous an effect upon education as the Restoration' (p. 43).

[3] Jones, *Ancients and Moderns*, pp. 181, 322.

[4] H. Stubbe, *The Lord Bacon's Relation of the Sweating-sickness examined* (1671), Preface. Stubbe was said to have been paid by a leading member of the College of Physicians to attack the Royal Society (Keevil, *The Stranger's Son*, pp. 138–9, 178–80).

[5] Wallis to Boyle, 17 July 1669, in Boyle, *Works* (1744), v. 514.

[6] S. Parker, *A Demonstration of the Divine Authority of the Law of Nature and of the Christian Religion* (1681), pp. iii–iv. (I owe this reference to Mr. D. Nandy.) Parker was Andrew Marvell's rival and butt.

before the Society's position was secure: the propaganda of
Sprat's *History*, playing down the Greshamite and Parliamentarian origins of the Society, was a necessary part of the
campaign, bewildering though historians have found the dis-
crepancies between it and other accounts, either less official or
published when the danger was over.[1] But the price paid was a
high one. Sprat had to emphasize that experimental science
embodied no threat to the Church of England, to the nobility
and gentry; he hushed up the educational aspirations of the
Baconians during the Revolution, and even argued that the
scientists saved Oxford from Puritan destruction.[2] The gentry
were lured into the Royal Society, which needed them for
financial as well as social reasons. Anyone of the rank of baron
was automatically accepted if he wished to honour the Society
by becoming a Fellow. Some of the Fellows—Sir John Berkenhead for instance—would seem more conspicious for their
opposition to than for their interest in science.[3]

The Society became more utilitarian than Bacon would have
wished, pushing to its extreme the attitude implied in Boyle's
remark about his Comenian associates: 'Our College values no
knowledge but as it hath a tendency to use.'[4] But at the same
time the Royal Society became more dilettante too. The
narrowly patriotic note which is struck in Sprat's *History* contrasts oddly with Bacon's theory (if not his practice) and with
Comenius's internationalist and anti-imperialist *Angelus Pacis*,
published in the same year 1667.[5] And as the century advanced,

---

[1] For this reason the lateness of Wallis's testimony, often urged against accepting it when it appears to conflict with Sprat, may in fact be a reason for giving
it greater weight. Cf. *The Diary of the Rev. John Ward*, p. 116.

[2] Sprat, *History of the Royal Society*, p. 54.

[3] P. W. Thomas, *Sir John Berkenhead, 1617–1679* (Oxford U.P., 1969), pp. 233–4.
Cf. Sprat, op cit., pp. 72–73.

[4] Quoted by Taylor, *Mathematical Practitioners*, p. 84. Cf. the dedication to
Charles II of Robert Hooke's *Micrographia* (1662), with its blatant emphasis on the
profit motive. See M. 'Espinasse, 'The Decline and Fall of Restoration Science',
P. and P., no. 14, pp. 71–89.

[5] Comenius in this pamphlet called for an end to all war, on economic grounds
('Is it worth while to catch fish with a golden hook?') and on moral grounds, hoping
'that in the entire human race there will finally be one voice on all matters, that
there will be agreement in desires, and that there will be accord in efforts made for
the common weal'. He was sure that 'these voyages of Europeans to foreign lands
have brought evil to Europeans no less than to those peoples from which we obtain
worldly goods' (J. A. Comenius, *Angelus Pacis*, Prague, 1926, pp. 132–49). 'We are
all fellow citizens of one world, all of one blood, all of us human beings. Who shall

so—perhaps in reaction to the utilitarianism and dilettantism of the amateurs—the science of the professionals became increasingly dominated by abstract mathematics. This too was a very different emphasis from that of Bacon, with its unified vision of science working for the glory of God and the relief of man's estate. The Royal Society brought together some great scientists in the later seventeenth century, with benefit to all of them: but it did not establish the Utopia of which Bacon, Milton, and Comenius had dreamed, still less that of Winstanley. It was the dissenting academies rather than the Royal Society that carried the radical Baconian tradition on to the Industrial Revolution which Bacon had in part foreseen.

But one aspect of the pre-Baconian scientific inheritance the Royal Society did take over more effectively than Bacon himself. Sprat defined the Society's ideal of prose as 'mathematical plainness . . ., the language of artisans, countrymen, and merchants.'[1] This hardly describes Bacon's terse but pregnant style —though Sprat spoke of it with approval. But it is a literal description of the prose of the popular scientists, who wrote plainly and straightforwardly because they were writing for 'men that are simple and unlearned'.[2] It describes too some of the best prose assembled by Richard Hakluyt in his epic, prose written again by plain merchants and navigators for their fellows. The connexion between science and the new prose was noted by Earle as early as 1628. His 'self-conceited man' 'prefers Ramus before Aristotle and Paracelsus before Galen, and Lipsius his hopping style before either Tully or Quintilian'.[3]

The Puritan divines, and later the sectarian, Leveller, and Digger pamphleteers, similarly had to master the style of merchants and artisans, because it was for them that they wrote.

---

prevent us from uniting in one republic? Before our eyes there is only one aim: the good of humanity, and we will put aside all considerations of self, of nationality, of sectarianism' (Comenius, Panegersia, quoted in The Teacher of Nations, ed. J. Needham, 1941, p. 6).

[1] Sprat, History of the Royal Society, p. 113.

[2] Cf. R. K. Merton, 'Science, Technology and Society', Osiris, iv. 378–9; Johnson, Astronomical Thought, pp. 292–3. Gilbert in De Magnete (1600) had attacked the use of learned jargon by academic philosophers (pp. 47–49). He said he had not 'brought into this work any graces of rhetoric, any verbal ornateness': he used only 'such terms as are needed to make what is said clearly intelligible' (Preface). Even though he wrote in Latin, these are similar views of the function of prose.

[3] J. Earle, Microcosmographie, 'A Self-conceited Man'.

Richard Holdsworth, who taught his pupils a 'plain, easy, and familiar style' stands at the junction of the Puritan and Gresham trends towards a simpler prose. Wilkins similarly personifies the fusion of Puritan and scientific influences. His *Ecclesiastes* (1646) was a popular handbook to plain preaching; and his scientific treatises set an example which many followed.[1] Professor Bush remarked that it might be taken as allegorical that this father of the Royal Society was father-in-law of Tillotson.[2] The allegory is the more complete if we reflect that Wilkins was also the grandson of the great Puritan preacher and pamphleteer Decalogue Dod, great-grandson of the Sabbatarian Nicholas Bownde—and Oliver Cromwell's brother-in-law as well. Here too the triumph of science saw the triumph of the standards of the common man over those of his social superiors; and English became a language in which Bunyan, Defoe, and Swift could write.

[1] Sir E. Gosse, *History of 18th century Literature* (1889), pp. 75–76, was one of the first to stress Wilkins's share in pioneering the new prose. Cf. W. T. Costello, *The Scholastic Curriculum at early 17th century Cambridge* (Harvard U.P., 1958), p. 57; Howell, *Logic and Rhetoric in England, 1500–1700*, pp. 117–18, 385–91. Professor Howell notes the influence of Ramus in simplifying prose. Webster also advocated plain prose (*Academiarius Examen*, p. 88).

[2] Bush, *English Literature in the Earlier Seventeenth Century* (second ed., 1962), p. 329. Tillotson, like Briggs and Sir Henry Savile, was a Halifax man.

Additional Note. Cowley's *Ode to the Royal Society* is remarkable for the way in which the royalist poet stresses Bacon's revolutionary role: all the more remarkable if the metaphors are unconscious:

> Some few exalted spirits this latter age has shown
> That labour'd to assert the liberty . . .
> Of . . . captiv'd Philosophy;
> But 'twas rebellion call'd to fight
> For such a long-oppressed right.
> Bacon at last, a mighty man, arose . . .
> Authority . . . he chas'd out of our sight, . . .
> Bacon has broke that scare-crow deity

and restored humanity to the pre-lapsarian state. No longer would men try to see good and evil 'without the senses' aid within ourselves'. For Bacon has directed our study 'the mechanic way', to things not words. In the Preface to his *Poems* (1656) Cowley said that the royalists must dismantle their cause 'of all the works and fortifications of wit and reason by which we defended it' (*Poems*, ed. A. R. Waller, 1905, pp. 448–50, 455). His *Propositions for the Advancement of Experimental Philosophy* (1661) are pure Baconianism; in his *Essay of Agriculture* he praised the industry and public spirit of Hartlib. John Houghton similarly attributed agricultural improvement in England to 'the industry and indefatigable pains of Mr. Hartlib and some others' (*Husbandry and Trade Improv'd*, 1728, iv. 56, 85).

IV

RALEGH—SCIENCE, HISTORY, AND POLITICS

Raleigh . . . was gradually transformed, by their common misfortunes, into the idol of earnest, conventional, parsimonious, provincial, puritan, inland squires. . . . When in the Great Rebellion they rose at last and swept away . . . the last Renaissance court in Europe, they did it in the name of the greatest of all courtiers and virtuosi, Sir Walter Raleigh.

H. R. TREVOR-ROPER, *Historical Eassys* (1957), p. 107.

I

SIR WALTER RALEGH was born in 1554,[1] so he was not fifty when Elizabeth died and his career as a royal favourite came to an end. But Ralegh had been no mere courtier. He founded the first English colony in America, in Virginia, though it failed to survive. He wrote *The Discovery of Guiana*, a first-rate travel book as well as a classic of empire. But within a year of James I's accession the great proponent of anti-Spanish policies was condemned to death on a highly dubious charge of conspiring with Spain. He was imprisoned in the Tower, where he wrote the *History of the World*. In 1616 he was released to sail to Guiana, whence he promised to bring back gold for the King without fighting the Spaniards. He brought no gold, and he did fight the Spaniards: in 1618 he was executed, at the demand of the Spanish ambassador, Gondomar.

At first sight Ralegh would seem an unsuitable Parliamentarian and Puritan hero: the unpopular favourite at Queen Elizabeth's court,[2] with the reputation of an atheist; the man who was made to blush in the Parliament of 1601 when

[1] A. M. C. Latham, 'A Birth-date for Sir Walter Ralegh', *Études Anglaises*, 1956, pp. 243–5.
[2] In May 1587 Ralegh was described by Sir Anthony Bagot as 'the best-hated man of the world, in Court, City, and country' (E. Thompson, *Sir Walter Ralegh*, 1935, p. 31).

his monopoly of playing cards was attacked, and whose 'sharp speech' in defence of his office as Lord Warden of the Stannaries caused a 'great silence' in the House.[1] But 'the country hath constantly a blessing for those for whom the court hath a curse';[2] to be publicly tried and executed for treason was a sure way to popularity under the old monarchy, a posthumous popularity that the Earl of Essex[3] shared with Ralegh. And his two trials dramatized Ralegh's anti-Spanish position.

There are many other reasons why Ralegh's name carried weight with the seventeenth-century revolutionaries. If we ask ourselves what were the main changes which the political revolutions of the century brought about, I suppose we should say (i) a decline in the power of the crown *vis-à-vis* Parliament; (ii) the adoption of an aggressive imperialist foreign policy; (iii) an extension of economic liberalism; (iv) the redistribution of taxation; (v) the beginnings of religious toleration; and I should like to add (vi) the triumph of modern science. To all these changes Ralegh contributed significantly. Let us look at each of them in turn, starting with science.

In her work, *Leicester, Patron of Letters*, Miss Rosenberg has established Ralegh as the heir of Leicester's patronage. After what she modestly described as a fairly thorough survey of the field, she concluded that 'the writers and scientists associated with the patriotic cause of establishing England's empire in the western world dedicated their works by common consent to its acknowledged leader Sir Walter Ralegh and to those openly associated with his plans for exploring and colonizing America'. I shall return to this 'clearly defined propaganda campaign' later.[4] At the moment I wish only to draw attention to Ralegh's inheritance of Leicester's influence. Ralegh, we are told, hired Thomas Churchyard to write a play in the cause of Leicester's foreign policy.[5]

Ralegh was in many ways the heir of Sir Philip Sidney and his group, as well as of Sidney's uncle Leicester—not least in

---

[1] H. Townshend, *Historical Collections* (1680), pp. 232, 235.

[2] T. Fuller, *The Church History of Britain* (1842), iii. 350.   [3] *D.N.B.*

[4] Rosenberg, *Leicester, Patron of Letters*, p. xix. Leicester himself was heir to the patronage of science and especially navigation exercised by the Duke of Northumberland (ibid., p. 31). See pp. 153–65 below.

[5] E. G. Clarke, *Ralegh and Marlowe* (New York, 1941), p. 390. Cf. *Harleian Miscellany* (1744–56), iii. 249–55 for Ralegh's patronage of Churchyard.

his patronage of science. Sidney and his friend Sir Edward Dyer (Leicester's secretary) at one time took lessons in chemistry from John Dee.[1] Before and after Sidney's death Dyer acted as patron to Dee, as well as to, Thomas Digges, Humphrey Cole the instrument-maker, and John Frampton, the merchant who had been racked in the Spanish Inquisition and who was a translator of scientific books and a propagandist for overseas expansion.[2] The younger Hakluyt had been a protégé of Dyer and the Sidney group: his *Divers Voyages* of 1582 was dedicated to Sidney. Michael Lok dedicated to Sidney his map designed to show English priority in the exploration of North America.[3] Timothy Bright, the inventor of shorthand, dedicated more than one of his books to Sidney, with whom in 1572 he had taken refuge from the Massacre of St. Bartholomew in the English Embassy. Bright was the author of a popular treatise on melancholy in which he compared the human mind to a clock or a windmill: Shakespeare and Robert Burton both probably studied this treatise. Bright was also a supporter of chemical medicine, and published an abridgement of Foxe's *Acts and Monuments*, dedicated to Sir Francis Walsingham.[4]

Bright was an enthusiastic Ramist, as were most members of the Sidney group. De Banos's life of his master was dedicated to Sidney in 1576 because of Ramus's affection and respect for him. Sidney's tutor, Nathaniel Baxter, was a supporter of Cartwright, a translator of Calvin, and commentator on Ramus, whom he venerated. His commentary on Ramus's *Dialectics* contained a foreword to Fulke Greville.[5] Sidney paid for the

---

[1] J. Buxton, *Sir Philip Sidney and the English Renaissance* (1954), p. 87. Sidney had studied astronomy and geometry during his stay at Padua.

[2] Johnson, *Astronomical Thought*, p. 169. For Cole see p. 15 above.

[3] Buxton, op. cit., p. 143. Leicester had been a great collector of maps.

[4] W. J. Carlton, *Timothe Bright* (1911), esp. pp. 13, 48–49, 111; Sir G. Keynes, *Dr. Timothie Bright, 1550–1615* (1962), pp. 3–5, 9–13. Bright's treatise on shorthand was published in 1588, the year of the Armada. The same printer issued a treatise on book-keeping by double-entry in the same year (Carlton, op. cit., p. 81). Shorthand was one of the discoveries which Hakewill noted (wrongly) to the credit of the Moderns (*Apologie*, p. 298). For Bright see also pp. 69–75 above, 311–12 below.

[5] Berta Siebeck, *Das Bild Sir Philip Sidneys in der englischen Renaissance* (Schriften der Deutschen Shakespeare-Gesellschaft, Neue Folge, Weimar, 1939), pp. 55–56; *D. Nathanaelis Baxteri Colcestrensis quaestiones et responsa in Petri Rami dialecticam* (1585). Baxter (of Colchester, like William Gilbert) was Warden of St. Mary's College, Youghal. In the fifteen-nineties Ralegh rented the Warden's house from the College and lived in it when he visited his Youghal estates.

education of Abraham Fraunce, who became a noted Cambridge Ramist and Puritan. Fraunce dedicated several unpublished Ramist treatises to 'his very good master and patron Mr. Philip Sidney'.[1] William Temple, the most important English Ramist, dedicated his edition of Ramus's *Dialectics* to Sidney in 1584, and in consequence became his secretary.[2] Milton's Preface to the *Art of Logic* cites Sidney for the view (which Milton shared) that Ramus was the best writer on the subject. Sidney, in recommending arithmetic and geometry to his brother Robert in 1580, added that Ciceronianism was the worst abuse of Oxford men, 'qui dum verba sectantur, res ipsas negligunt'.[3] 'All is but lip-wisdom, which wants experience', cried Musidorus in *Arcadia*.[4] And Fulke Greville observed that

> Sciences from Nature should be drawn
> As arts from practice, never out of books.[5]

Sidney's friend Daniel Rogers wrote a poem *In Indignissimum Petri Rami fatum* on Ramus's death in the Massacre of St. Bartholomew.[6] When Bruno visited England in 1582 he found the scholastic atmosphere of Oxford uncongenial: he hastened to London to enjoy the company of Sidney and Greville. Bruno dedicated two of his books to Sidney. 'Why turn to vain fancies', he asked, 'when there is experience itself to teach us?'[7] The

---

[1] Siebeck, op. cit., pp. 182–3; Howell, *Logic and Rhetoric in England, 1500–1700*, pp. 222–3. Fraunce's *Arcadian Rhetorike* (1588) illustrates its Ramist points from Sidney and Spenser. Fraunce later published *The Lawiers Logike*, a Ramist treatise on law. For Fraunce's Puritanism see a comparison of Caiaphas to a prelate in *The Countesse of Pembrokes Emanuell* (1871), p. 49: first published 1591. See also pp. 31–32 above.

[2] Sidney left Temple an annuity of £30. Temple was later secretary to the Earl of Essex, and Provost of Trinity College, Dublin. For Trinity College see p. 277 below.

[3] Sidney, *Works* (ed. A. Feuillerat, 1912–26), iii. 132. Sidney was a friend of Sir Henry Savile, for whose attempts to reform Oxford see p. 54 above.

[4] Quoted by Haydn, *The Counter-Renaissance*, p. 8.

[5] Ed. Bullough, *Poems and Dramas of Fulke Greville*, i. 172. Greville interested himself in the election of at least one Gresham professor (*H.M.C., Salisbury*, xvi. 176).

[6] J. A. van Dorsten, *Poets, Patrons and Professors* (Leiden, 1962), p. 29: see Part I, *passim*, for Rogers.

[7] Buxton, op. cit., p. 160–7; Johnson, *Astronomical Thought*, p. 169; M. H. Carré, *Phases of Thought in England*, pp. 214–16; Van Dorsten, op. cit., pp. 41–42. The influence of Bruno in England has never been properly investigated. But he clearly affected many of the men with whom this book deals. He influenced Sidney (F. A. Yates, *A Study of Love's Labour Lost*, 1936, pp. 111–12; Siebeck, op. cit., pp. 58–62, 182), Bacon, Gilbert, Hariot, Nicholas Hill, Ralegh, Northumberland, and the Ralegh

Sidney group was almost unique in England in welcoming Buchanan's criticisms of the Ancients in his *Rerum Scoticorum Historia*.[1]

Ralegh was a friend of Sidney's, whom he quoted in *The History of the World*, and on whom he wrote a noble epitaph: his cousin and intimate friend, Sir Arthur Gorges, wrote two.[2] Ralegh took over some of Sidney's patronage, notably that of Hakluyt. *The Faerie Queene*, which began under Sidney's patronage, was published with Ralegh's.[3] Michael Lok translated *The Mexican History in Pictures* (1591) for Ralegh, at Hakluyt's instance.[4] Richard Carew, a Cambridge contemporary and friend of Sidney's, dedicated his *Survey of Cornwall* to Ralegh in 1602. When Sidney's father, Sir Henry, died in 1586, Ralegh took over the patronage of John Hooker's *Irish Historie*.[5] Sidney, devout Protestant though he was, was little more backward than Ralegh in plundering the Church.

The Sidney circle shared Ralegh's hostility to Spain and desire for a Dutch alliance, as well as 'that heroical design of invading and possessing America'.[6] Fulke Greville's *Life of Sidney* was one of the most powerful expressions of this policy.[7] Greville attributed to Sidney the view (shared by Ralegh) that the Spanish empire by its cruelty had flouted divine law and so was doomed.[8] Greville, both in his own person and in Sidney's, spoke, like Ralegh, of the importance of freedom for the commercial

group generally (Singer, *Giordano Bruno*, pp. 36–37, 45, 67–68, 72, 181–2; Yates, op. cit., 92–94). Northumberland had Bruno's books in his library and carefully annotated them (J. W. Shirley, 'The Scientific Experiments of Sir Walter Raleigh, the Wizard Earl and the three Magi in the Tower, 1603–17', *Ambix*, iv. 64–66; G. R. Batho, 'The Library of the "Wizard" Earl', *The Library*, 5th Series, xv. 259–60). Alexander Dicson, Bruno's disciple, dedicated his books to Leicester (Singer, op. cit., p. 38). See also G. Bruno, *Cause, Principle and Unity* (trans. J. Lindsay, 1962), pp. 7, 42, 158, for Bruno's influence on Sidney, Spenser, and Ralegh. For Northumberland and the Ralegh group see pp. 141–5 below.

[1] J. E. Phillips, 'George Buchanan and the Sidney Circle', *H L.Q.* xii. 49–55.
[2] Ralegh, *History of the World* (1820), iii. 262; *Poems* (ed. A. M. C. Latham, Muses Lib., 1951), p. 5; *Poems of Sir Arthur Gorges* (ed. H. E. Sandison, 1953), pp. 117–18.
[3] *The Shepheardes Calender* had an introductory sonnet to Leicester.
[4] For Lok and Sidney see p. 133 above.
[5] E. Rosenberg, 'Giacopo Castelvetro', *H.L.Q.* vi. 128–9.
[6] F. Greville, *The Life of Sir Philip Sidney* (1907), p. 77.
[7] Ibid., pp. 110–19, 215, 219–20; cf. p. 156.
[8] Ibid., pp. 116–17. Greville intended to illustrate these divine laws by his tragedies (ibid., p. 221). See p. 185 below.

classes, and especially for free access to the Spanish empire; and
in favour of the yeomanry.[1] Many of Greville's ideas, as has
often been pointed out, anticipate or echo those of his friend
Bacon: but his political speculations are much more daring.[2]
His scepticism compares with that of George Gascoigne and
Ralegh.[3] The *Life of Sidney* was first published in 1652, under
the Commonwealth.

There are links between the political thought of the Sidney
group and Ralegh, as well as in attitudes towards foreign policy.
The Sidney circle admired the political theory of George
Buchanan, and Greville showed lasting traces of his influence,
as well as of that of his friend Duplessis-Mornay.[4] So did Ralegh.
Like Ralegh, Greville accepted the fact of rebellion, though both
were anxious to deny it as a right.[5] There are passages in the
Life of Sidney which are closely parallel to *The Prerogative of
Parliaments*.[6]

Most interesting of all is the literary connexion. The Sidney
group has been described as the workshop of the New Poetry; it
is remarkable how often and how closely Ralegh's name is associated with them. Both in printed and manuscript collections
his poems occur alongside those of Sidney, Greville, and Dyer;[7]

[1] F. Greville, *The Life of Sir Philip Sidney* (1907), pp. 56, 113, 203; 189–90. See
p. 195 below.

[2] H. Schultz, *Milton and Forbidden Knowledge* (New York, 1955), pp. 31–33; R. W.
Gibson, *Supplement to a Bacon Bibliography* (1959), p. 9; Greville's *Poems and Dramas*,
i. 54; cf. pp. 171–2. Even in Charles II's reign Richard Baxter thought Greville's
Inquisition upon fame and honour 'a poem . . . for subjects' liberty, which I greatly
wonder this age would bear' (quoted ibid. i. 27).

[3] Kocher, *Science and Religion in Elizabethan England*, p. 55.

[4] Hotman was also an intimate of the Leicester–Sidney circle (Van Dorsten, op.
cit., p. 84). It has been plausibly argued that there are echoes of Huguenot political
theory in *Arcadia* (W. D. Briggs, 'Political Ideas in Sidney's *Arcadia*', *S.P.* xxviii, and
'Sidney's Political Ideas', ibid., xxix). I am not convinced by Mr. Ribner's criticisms of this thesis in 'Sir Philip Sidney on Civil Insurrection', *J.H.I.* xiii. 259–63.
Professor Zeeveld's argument seems more plausible—that the revised *Arcadia* is more
orthodox and less democratic in its political theory because Sidney was trying to
recover court favour (W. G. Zeeveld, 'The Uprising of the Commons in Sidney's
Arcadia', *M.L.N.* xlviii. 209–17). For *Arcadia* as political allegory see p. 12 above.
Buchanan influenced Milton, and is alleged to have impressed Oliver Cromwell
(G. Burnet, *A History of My own Time*, 1724, i. 76).

[5] J. E. Phillips, 'George Buchanan and the Sidney Circle', pp. 23–56; H. N.
MacLear, 'Fulke Greville, Kingship and Sovereignty', *H.L.Q.* xvi. 239–64. For
Ralegh's political ideas see pp. 149–53 below.

[6] e.g. *Life*, pp. 62, 98, 173–4.

[7] Ed. Latham, *Poems of Sir Walter Ralegh* (1951), p. 96; ed. W. A. Ringler, *The
Poems of Sir Philip Sidney* (1962), pp. 554, 559; Buxton, op. cit., p. 112.

and his name is mentioned together with theirs in the main contemporary works of criticism.[1] Between Spenser and Ralegh the links are obviously close, of ideas as well as in politics. The Preface and Conclusion to Ralegh's *History* seem to echo the Mutability Cantos. And Nature's reply to Mutabilitie in these cantos, it has been argued, anticipates the position which Hakewill took up against Goodman in denying the decay of the world.[2] Change for Spenser is the fate of everything, and this change is both cyclical and not cyclical. All things

> By their change their being do dilate,
> And turning to themselves at length again
> Do work their own perfection so by fate:
> Then over them Change doth not rule and reign,
> But they reign over Change, and do their states maintain.[3]

It is not without reason that Marvell (or whoever wrote *Britannia and Rawleigh*) quoted Spenser as well as Ralegh. .

We first hear of Ralegh as a literary figure when he contributed a laudatory poem to George Gascoigne's *The Steel Glass* in 1576. Gascoigne was a friend and associate of Ralegh's half-brother, Sir Humphrey Gilbert.[4] He was also one of the early translators of the classics who had suffered persecution.[5] In *The Steel Glass* Ralegh no doubt approved of Gascoigne's social attitudes in criticizing officials, soldiers, lawyers, and exalting Piers Plowman: but it is notable too that the poem is written in blank verse, which Gascoigne himself claimed in his preface was a more exalted form, more effective for satire. Now we

---

[1] George Puttenham (1589) and Francis Meres (1598) each name Ralegh between Sidney and Dyer, though their lists are not identical; Gabriel Harvey (1598–1601) linked Ralegh's name closely with Dyer's; Edward Bolton (1618) with Greville's. (All these are conveniently reprinted in Miss Latham's edition of Ralegh's *Poems* pp. lix–lx). Ralegh's name is also associated with Sidney's (and Sir Thomas Smith's) in Ben Jonson's list of eloquent prose writers (G. Williamson, *The Senecan Amble*, 1951, p. 89). For Smith see pp. 270–1 below.

[2] G. Williamson, 'Mutability, Decay and 17th century Melancholy', *Journal of English Literary History*, ii. 126. See pp. 200–2 below.

[3] Spenser, *The Faerie Queene*, Book VII, canto vii, stanza 58.

[4] Gascoigne, a kinsman of Frobisher, wrote an Epistle to the Reader for Gilbert's *Discourse of a Discoverie for a new passage to Cataia* (1576), in which he quoted Dee's Preface to Billingsley's *Euclide*. This Epistle was omitted when Hakluyt reprinted the treatise (ed. D. B. Quinn, *The Voyages and Colonising Enterprises of Sir Humphrey Gilbert*, Hakluyt Soc., 1940, i. 129–33, 166–7).

[5] Conley, *The First English Translators of the Classics*, pp. 97–99. Cf. p. 31 above.

know that Sidney himself in the *Defence of Poesie* opposed 'the tinkling sound of rhyme, barely accompanied with reason'; and it appears to have been a settled conviction of his group, shared by Dyer and the puritanically-minded Thomas Drant.[1]

A line of poets could be traced from Sidney and Spenser through Sylvester and Browne[2] to Wither—not, admittedly, of a rising quality, but of a consistent political attitude. We might find that Milton bore more relation to this group than has been realized. We might also with profit reflect more, as Edward Thompson suggested, on the influence of Ralegh's prose on Milton's writings.[3]

After the deaths of Sidney and Leicester, Ralegh continued their patronage of scientists and navigators. He helped Dee. Ralegh and Humphrey Gilbert planned to found a teaching and research academy in London, which would bring modern and practical subjects to royal wards and other sons of nobles and gentlemen—mathematics, cosmography, astronomy, naval and military training, navigation, shipbuilding, engineering, medicine, cartography, languages, and above all history. The teaching would be in English. The object of the academy was to teach 'matters of action meet for present practice': the doctor of physic would lecture alternately on physic and surgery.[4] Elizabeth, however, was as unwilling to finance this academy as James I was to finance Bacon's schemes. As with many similar projects which lacked the capital backing of a merchant prince like Gresham, nothing came of it. Bacon, however, expected Ralegh's support for a scientific college.[5] Ralegh's relative and ally Sir Arthur Gorges translated Bacon's *De Sapientia Veterum* into English, and his *Essays* into French, both in 1619.

---

[1] Sidney, *An Apologie for Poetrie*, in *Elizabethan Critical Essays* (ed. G. G. Smith, 1904), i. 196. I owe this point to Mr. Leo Miller. Thomas Drant, whose rules for versification Sidney adopted and enlarged, paid tribute to Ramus in 1572 (Howell, *Logic and Rhetoric*, pp. 55–56).

[2] Cf. the reference to Ralegh in *Britannia's Pastorals*, Book I, Song 4, lines 67–82; and Browne's epitaph on 'Sidney's sister, Pembroke's mother'.

[3] E. Thompson, *Sir Walter Ralegh* (1935), pp. 236–7, 239. On Sidney's place in the evolution of plain prose see Williamson, *The Senecan Amble*, p. 89.

[4] D. Stimson, *Scientists and Amateurs* (New York, 1948), pp. 9–10. Another of Ralegh's half-brothers, Adrian Gilbert, was a patron of John Dee, and later had a chemical laboratory in the Countess of Pembroke's house at Wilton (Aubrey, *Brief Lives*, i. 262, 311). The academy derived from an earlier project of Sir Nicholas Bacon, Francis's father.   [5] See p. 99 above.

II

Thomas Hariot, one of the greatest astronomers and mathematicians of his day, is another link between Ralegh and the Sidney circle. Hariot was successively mathematics tutor to Philip Sidney's younger brother Robert, to Ralegh, and to his son. As Viscount Lisle Robert Sidney was Hariot's executor when he died in 1621. Ralegh fully appreciated the importance of mathematics and astronomy for the art of navigation. In his lessons to Sir Walter and his sea-captains Hariot always contrived to 'link theory and practice, not without almost incredible results'. The words are Hakluyt's.[1] Hariot remained a protégé of Ralegh's—some said a deistic or atheistic influence on him.[2] In fact there is no doubt of Hariot's faith, which he told his doctor was threefold—'in God Almighty, in medicine as being ordained by Him', and in 'the doctor as his minister'. 'I have learnt of you', one of Hariot's correspondents told him, 'to settle and submit my desires to the will of God.'[3]

Ralegh, who made each of his voyages a scientific expedition, in 1585 sent Hariot as surveyor to Virginia with Sir Richard Grenville's expedition. Hariot's *Brief and True Report of the New Found Land of Virginia* (1588) was much admired by Hakluyt, who reprinted it.[4] It is one of the earliest examples of a large-scale economic and statistical survey, including 'marketable commodities' as well as a very sympathetic account of native religion and customs. (Hariot learnt the Indians' language and preached to them.) The first edition was illustrated by John White, another of Ralegh's protégés. The edition of 1590 included engravings of Picts, which showed that they had been as savage as the natives of Virginia: a notable contribution to historical imagination, which was used by Vico.[5] Hariot was later an adviser to the Virginia Company.[6] He acted as agent for Ralegh during the latter's absence at sea.[7] He was one of

[1] Ed. D. B. Quinn, *The Roanoke Voyages* (Hakluyt Soc., 1955), i. 36.

[2] Aubrey, *Brief Lives*, i. 287.

[3] H. Stevens, *Thomas Hariot* (1900), pp. 148, 124.

[4] R. Hakluyt, *Virginia Richly Valued* (1609), sig. A 3.

[5] Giambattista Vico, *La Scienza Nuova* (third ed., 1744), Book I, section iii, para. 337. John Speed used four of these engravings to illustrate 'Ancient Britaines' in his *Historie of Great Britanie* (1611) (T. D. Kendrick, *British Antiquity*, 1950, pp. 123–5).

[6] Stevens, op. cit., p. 15; Taylor, *Late Tudor and Early Stuart Geography*, p. 162.

[7] E. Edwards, *Life of Sir Walter Raleigh* (1868), ii. 420; cf. A. L. Rowse, *Ralegh and the Throckmortons* (1962), p. 248.

Ralegh's constant associates during his imprisonment in the Tower, and the 'true and loving friend' of Sir Arthur Gorges.[1]

Hariot was in close and friendly touch with Dee and Hakluyt, knew Gilbert and his work, corresponded with Kepler on optics, and was using the telescope for astronomical purposes at about the same time as Galileo.[2] Hariot produced telescopes for sale in the last twelve years of his life (1609–21). He first observed what we know as Halley's Comet, and is said to have predicted seven of the nine comets he saw.[3] Hariot determined specific gravities by weighing in air and in water, though he did not publish his results.[4] He was also 'one of the founders of algebra as we know the science to-day', and made advances towards its application to geometry.[5] He believed in the existence of a North-Western Passage, and like Briggs wrote a treatise to prove it.[6] He was held in the highest esteem by Briggs and by the early members of the Royal Society.[7] Wallis thought that Hariot laid 'the foundation . . . without which that whole superstructure of Descartes (I doubt) had never been'.[8] Descartes, we now know, had in fact read Hariot's *Artis Analyticae Praxis*, published posthumously in 1631.[9] The Royal Society conducted a diligent but unsuccessful search for Hariot's papers in 1662–3. Some of them have been discovered recently, and historians of mathematics are astonished at the way in which 'deep Hariots mind, In which there is no dross but all's refined'[10] had apparently solved some of the most complicated problems in navigational mathematics a whole generation before Napier, Briggs, and Gunter. But his tables, instruments, and rules for making charts were reserved for the use of Ralegh and his associates.[11]

[1] H. E. Sandison, 'Arthur Gorges, Spenser's Alcyon and Ralegh's friend', *P.M.L.A.* xliii. 669.

[2] S. P. Rigaud, *Supplement to Dr. Bradley's Miscellaneous Works, with an Account of Hariot's Astronomical Papers* (1833), pp. 20, 42–43.

[3] Stevens, op. cit., pp. 113–15, 178–80, 197–8; Aubrey, *Brief Lives*, i. 285.

[4] J. R. Partington, *History of Chemistry*, ii (1961), pp. 397–8.

[5] D. E. Smith, *History of Mathematics* (1923–5), i. 388.

[6] Taylor, op. cit., pp. 236–8; Taylor, 'The Doctrine of Nautical Triangles Compendious', *Journal of the Institute of Navigation*, vi. 137.

[7] Hakewill, op. cit., p. 302; [Seth Ward], *Vindiciae Academiarum*, p. 20; *Petty–Southwell Correspondence*, p. 322.   [8] J. Wallis, *A Treatise of Algebra* (1685), p. 126.

[9] Ed. C. Adam and P. Tannery, *Correspondance de Descartes* (1897–1903), ii. 456–61.

[10] *The Poems of Richard Corbett* (ed. J. A. W. Bennett and H. R. Trevor-Roper, 1955), p. 64.

[11] Waters, *The Art of Navigation*, pp. 194, 359, 373, 546–7, 582–91; Taylor,

Hariot clearly felt constrained by the censorship, felt 'stuck in the mud'.[1] In 1598 his friend George Chapman suggested that Hariot's writings could not be published 'now error's night chokes earth with mists', 'this scornful . . . world . . . her stings and quills darting at worths divine'.[2]

Hariot leads us to consider the connexions between Ralegh and Henry Percy, ninth Earl of Northumberland, 'the wizard Earl'. They had been intimate since at least 1586, and political associates from about 1600. Northumberland, Essex's brother-in-law, protested vigorously against Ralegh's condemnation in 1603. But after Gunpowder Plot the Earl himself was sentenced to a fine of £11,000 and perpetual imprisonment for misprision of treason, on evidence not much stronger than that which had led to Ralegh's conviction. In the early fifteen-nineties, when Ralegh was in disgrace, a number of his followers, including Hariot and Robert Hues, passed from his service to Northumberland's, though Ralegh retained their close friendship.[3] About this time George Peele apostrophized Northumberland

> That artisans and scholars dost embrace
> And clothest Mathesis in rich ornaments,
> That admirable mathematic skill,
> Familiar with the stars and zodiac.[4]

Hariot drew a pension of £80, later £100, from Northumberland from 1589 to 1621. Whilst the Earl was in the Tower, Hariot seems to have acted as supervisor of his affairs and tutor to his children. He was Librarian at Sion, Northumberland's house, and had a laboratory there.[5] It seems to have been Hariot

'Hariot's Instructions for Ralegh's Voyage to Guiana, 1595', *Journal of the Institute of Navigation*,' v. 345; 'The Doctrine of Nautical Triangles Compendious', ibid. vi. pp. 134–5; D. H. Sadler, 'Calculating the Meridional Points', ibid. vi. 147. Hariot also left papers on fortifications (N. L. Williams, *Sir Walter Ralegh*, 1962, pp. 57, 83).   [1] See pp. 32–33 above.

[2] G. Chapman, 'To my admired and soul-loved friend, master of all essential and true knowledge, M. Harriots', in *Poems and Minor Translations* (1875), pp. 53–55.

[3] Rosenberg, 'Giacopo Castelvetro', *H.L.Q.* vi. 139.

[4] Quoted by F. A. Yates, *A Study of 'Love's Labour Lost'*, p. 95. Note the close association of artisans and scholars, typical of the early development of English science (see pp. 86–88 above)—though Peele's 'mathesis' is presumably magic. Cf. Alexander Read's description of Northumberland as 'the favourer of all good learning and Maecenas of learned men' (A. Read, *Works*, 1650, p. 248).

[5] Stevens, op. cit., pp. 93–94, 98–99; ed. G. R. Batho, *The Household Papers of Henry Percy, ninth Earl of Northumberland (1564–1632)* (Camden Soc., 1962), p. 154; Shirley, 'The Scientific Experiments of Sir Walter Ralegh . . .', p. 58.

who first roused the Earl's interest in mathematics and astronomy.[1] Northumberland was also interested in anatomy, medicine, geography, and cosmography: he had books by Napier, William Gilbert, Kepler, Tycho Brahe, Bruno, and Hakluyt in his library, and many others on chemistry, mathematics, and medicine.[2] He advised his son to study—*inter alia*—arithmetic, geometry, the doctrine of motion, optics, astronomy, the doctrines of generation and corruption (alchemy and/or biology?), cosmography, and navigation.[3]

Around Ralegh and Northumberland we can distinguish a literary and scientific group. This consisted of the Earl's 'three Magi'—Hariot, Robert Hues, and Walter Warner—together with the poet, mathematician, and Hermeticist, Matthew Roydon, a former friend of Sidney's, who may have written *Willobie His Avisa* as a defence of the Ralegh group,[4] and George Chapman, who dedicated books to Ralegh and Bacon. Chapman spoke warmly of Hariot and Hues in the Preface to his translation of Homer.[5] Hues had been an undergraduate at Brasenose College and then went to sea. He dedicated the first (Latin) edition of his *Treatise on Globes* to Ralegh in 1592. The dedication attacked the 'great ignorance' of the Ancients, and pleaded for more mathematical knowledge among navigators. Praised by Hakewill, it remained the standard work throughout the seventeenth century. There were thirteen editions before 1663. Hues was one of Ralegh's executors.[6] He also acted as tutor

[1] Yates, op. cit., pp. 138–40, 206–11.

[2] Shirley, op. cit., pp. 63–66; Batho, 'The Library of the "Wizard" Earl', *The Library*, fifth series, xv. 254–60.

[3] Ed. G. B. Harrison, *Advice to His Son by Henry Percy, ninth Earl of Northumberland* (*1609*) (1930), pp. 67–71. But the Earl disparaged alchemy as 'a mere mechanical broiling trade'.

[4] Ed. G. B. Harrison, *Willobie His Avisa* (*1594*) (1926), pp. 184–5, 226–7. Despite its suppression in 1599, there had been six editions of this work by 1635.

[5] Chapman (like Marlowe, who also had associations with Ralegh's circle) was very up to date in his technical meteorological knowledge: he evidently read the almanacs. He used virtually no religious imagery (S. K. Heninger, Jr., *A Handbook of Renaissance Meteorology*, Duke U.P., 1960, pp. 183, 192, 195).

[6] Hakewill, *Apologie*, pp. 311–12. Hues's *Treatise* was reprinted by the Hakluyt Soc. in 1889 (ed. C. R. Markham). It described the globes made by Emery Molyneux, to whom Ralegh and Hakluyt had furnished information (see pp. 42–43 above). The Fifth Part of the *Treatise* was an essay by Hariot on rhumb lines. In the English translation of 1638 the name of Ralegh was omitted from the dedication, together with its opening lines (see Markham's Introduction, *passim*).

to Northumberland's eldest son, the later Parliamentarian,[1] and received a pension of £40 from the Earl.[2] He is said to have had connexions with Gresham College.[3] Warner, pensioner of Northumberland's, friend of Hakluyt and Gorges, continued Briggs's work on logarithms, and claimed to have given Harvey the idea which led to his discovery of the circulation of the blood.[4] He was later alleged to have taught Thomas Hobbes all the mathematics he knew: Hobbes certainly had mathematical manuscripts of Warner's in his possession in 1634.[5]

To these we must add Marlowe until his death in 1593— Marlowe who was once described as Ralegh's 'man', who 'read the atheist lecture to Ralegh and others', whose *Passionate Shepherd* Ralegh answered, whose *Hero and Leander* Chapman completed. Marlowe held discussions on Biblical criticism and comparative religion with Hariot, Warner, and Roydon, of a kind which scandalized the government's informers and helped to create the legend of Ralegh's 'school of atheism'.[6] Marlowe is interesting for our purposes because he was very much aware of the potential political implications of the new science. This is the subject of *Doctor Faustus*: but the theme was also touched upon by Tamburlaine when he said

> Our souls, whose faculties can comprehend
> The wondrous architecture of the world,
> And measure every wandering planet's course,
> Still climbing after knowledge infinite,
> And always moving as the restless spheres,
> Will us to wear ourselves and never rest,
> Until we reach the ripest fruit of all,
> The perfect bliss and sole felicity,
> The sweet fruition of an earthly crown.[7]

[1] Ibid., p. xxxvi. Though a moderate man, the tenth Earl sided with the Independents over the Self-Denying Ordinance and in the crisis of July 1647. His sister was the famous Countess of Carlisle, Pym's friend. For the tenth Earl see also p. 102 above.

[2] Batho, *Household Papers*, p. 155.   [3] See p. 42 above.

[4] A story to this effect was circulating in the early sixteen-forties (Shirley, op. cit., p. 55). Cf. G. Rolleston, *The Harveian Oration* (1873), pp. 50–62. For Gorges see H. E. Sandison, 'Arthur Gorges', *P.M.L.A.* xliii. 645 ff.

[5] Aubrey, *Brief Lives*, ii. 16, 291–3; ed. J. O. Halliwell, *A Collection of Letters Illustrative of the Progress of Science*, pp. 65–69. Warner had been Leicester's protégé.

[6] *Willobie His Avisa*, pp. 206–11; J. Bakeless, *Christopher Marlowe* (1938), pp. 199–202.

[7] C. Marlowe, *Tamburlaine*, Part I, Act II, scene vii.

The very personal individualism of Tamburlaine's conclusion would not be shared by all those who appreciated his statement of the problem created by the new lust for knowledge and power over things. And Marlowe's own interest in the republican Lucan suggests that he too may have had more general ideas.[1]

Giacopo Castelvetro, a radical Italian Protestant refugee, was probably in Northumberland's service from 1597 to 1607: he had previously been a protégé of Ralegh's. He published books on medicine and cryptography, and seems to have helped Hakluyt in his propaganda campaign on behalf of overseas exploration. In Italy Castelvetro was in trouble with the Inquisition as a relapsed Calvinist heretic, who believed in nothing; in England he was regarded as an Arian.[2] Northumberland also gave a pension of £40 to the mathematician and astronomer Nathaniel Torporley (1564–1632), literary executor under Hariot's will.[3] Among the other 'Atlantes of the mathematical world' who frequented Northumberland's household was Thomas Allen of Gloucester Hall, friend of Dee and Hariot, whom the Earl of Leicester had consulted as an astrologer.[4]

In some ways the most interesting member of the group was Nicholas Hill, the first Modern to defend actively the atomic theories of Democritus and Epicurus. Hill was an intimate acquaintance of Ralegh's, and was in Northumberland's service. He helped the Earl with his alchemical and astrological experiments. Although Hill rejected all aristocratic patronage on principle, he dedicated his *Philosophia Epicurea* to the Earl's eldest son.[5] Hariot appears to have considered atomism a plausible hypothesis, basing himself on Gilbert.[6] Hill accepted the idea of a heliocentric and infinite universe, and of a plurality of worlds. He was discussed by Robert Burton, quoted by Wilkins, and looks forward to Hobbes and Locke in his mechanist

[1] See p. 150 below.

[2] S. E. Dimsey, 'Giacopo Castelvetro', *Modern Language Review*, xxiii. 424–31; Rosenberg, 'Giacopo Castelvetro, Italian publisher in London and his Patrons', *H.L.Q*. vi. 122–39; *C.S.P.Ven., 1610–13*, pp. 219–20. See pp. 214–15 below.

[3] Shirley, op. cit., pp. 56, 59; Batho, *Household Papers*, p. 163.

[4] Aubrey, *Brief Lives*, i. 27; Curtis, op. cit., p. 236. See also p. 310 below. The Earl's younger brother, George Percy, led the 1607 expedition to Virginia.

[5] Aubrey, *Brief Lives*, ii. 192; G. McColley, 'Nicholas Hill and the *Philosophia Epicurea*', *Annals of Science*, iv. 392.

[6] Stevens, op. cit., pp. 180–2. Both Hill and Hariot knew and valued the writings of Bruno. Walter Warner was another atomist.

philosophy.[1] Hill is often described as a papist, apparently on the authority of John Aubrey.[2] A Catholic who chose to live much of his life at Rotterdam, and whose books were published at Geneva, must have been something of an oddity. I suspect Hill was no more a Catholic than his patron the Earl of Northumberland.[3] Finally, Richard Lilburne, father of the future Leveller leader, was probably serving in the Earl's household when he married in 1599.[4]

III

Ralegh, 'whose reading made him skilled in all the seas', was praised as early as 1586 as a patron of the sciences connected with navigation and exploration.[5] He had a detailed knowledge of scientific and technological developments as they affected navigation, at a time when such a knowledge was regarded as lower-class and 'mechanical' rather than respectable and 'martial'. He was noted for his own experiments and innovations in shipbuilding, and appreciated the importance of having the most up-to-date style of pump in order to reduce dampness on board ship.[6] He was a pioneer in naval medicine, dietetics, and hygiene. His orders for his voyage of 1617, stressing cleanliness, absence of litter between decks, and the precautions to be taken by landing parties in eating fruit, fish, and hogs, were well ahead of contemporary practice. He tried, though unsuccessfully, to discover from the Guianan Indians their remedy for the wounds made by poisoned arrows.[7] The apothecary John Hester, whose running battle with the surgeons and physicians helped to establish Paracelsanism in England, dedicated *A Hundred and Foureteene Experiments of Paracelsus* to Ralegh in the early fifteen-eighties: in it Hester pleaded for liberty of research.[8]

[1] McColley, op. cit., pp. 390–2, 403–4.   [2] Aubrey, *Brief Lives*, i. 321.
[3] The mistaken idea that Northumberland was a papist has been corrected by Mr. Batho (*Household Papers*, p. xx). For Hill's religion see also pp. 5, 92 above.
[4] P. Gregg, *Freeborn John* (1961), pp. 16, 363.
[5] M. Drayton, *Complete Works* (1876), iii. 12; Rosenberg, 'Giacopo Castelvetro', p. 122.
[6] Ralegh, *Works*, ii. 78; cf. Greville, *Life of Sidney*, p. 71.
[7] J. J. Keevil, *Medicine and the Navy*, i. *1200–1649* (1957), pp. 115–23.
[8] Hester, op. cit. (1596 ed.), sig. A 2, quoted by E. A. Strathmann, *Sir Walter Ralegh: A Study in Elizabethan Scepticism* (Columbia U.P., 1951), pp. 240–1; cf. Kocher, 'John Hester, Paracelsan', *Joseph Quincy Adams Memorial Studies* (Folger Library, 1948), pp. 621–38.

The surgeon John Gerarde dedicated his *Herbal* to Ralegh in
1597. He may have been a subscriber to Ralegh's 1589 scheme
for planting Virginia, as Thomas Hood certainly was.[1]

During his imprisonment in the Tower Ralegh (like Northumberland) conducted chemical and medical experiments
with the aid of the Puritan Lady Apsley, Lucy Hutchinson's
mother. Bacon recorded this activity in his private notebook as
a good omen for the future reception of his own philosophy of
works. Among other things, Ralegh tried to distil fresh from salt
water, to find ways of keeping meat fresh at sea, and to devise
remedies against scurvy. He supplied medicines to many of his
friends.[2] His 'cordial' cured Queen Anne, and was cited in 1664
to prove 'the great advantages that the modern pharmacy carri-
eth legitimately above the ancient, by reason that it is enlightened with the glorious light of chemistry'.[3] It was still used
by Robert Boyle to cure fevers, and in 1712 Swift discussed it with
Stella.[4] Boyle's father, the great Earl of Cork, used to recommend his friend Ralegh's remedy for the spleen and the gravel.[5]

In his *History* Ralegh praised Galileo, as Milton did in *Paradise
Lost*.[6] Ralegh accepted diurnal rotation of the earth, and
owned a copy of Copernicus as well as of Machiavelli.[7] Ralegh's
opposition to the 'verbal doctrine' of Aristotle must have
delighted Bacon, as his refusal to defer to the authority of the

---

[1] Ed. Quinn, *The Roanoke Voyages*, ii. 570. See p. 79 above.

[2] Rowse, *Ralegh and the Throckmortons*, p. 259; cf. p. 332; L. Hutchinson, *Memoirs
of Colonel Hutchinson* (1885), i. 21. Hutchinson was later a regicide.

[3] N. Le Febure, *A Discourse Upon Sir Walter Rawleighs Great Cordial* (1664), pp. 5,
91–102, sig. A 4. Le Febure increases our respect for Ralegh when he tells us that
he had by 'the counsel and approbation of Sir Kenelm Digby and Sir Alexander
Francis, his Majesty's chief physician', added the flesh, heart, and liver of a viper to
the comparatively simple ingredients of the cordial in Ralegh's prescription (ibid.,
p. 14; cf. J. Evelyn, *Diary*, ed. E. S. de Beer, iii. 336). The Paracelsan chemist Le
Febure was author of 'the true ancestor of the modern textbook of practical
chemistry', translated into English in 1663 as *A Compleat Body of Chymistry*, with
dedication to the English apothecaries (M. Boas, *Robert Boyle and 17th century
Chemistry*, 1958, p. 56; R. J. Forbes and E. J. Dijksterhuis, *A History of Science and
Technology*, Penguin Books, 1963, i. 219).

[4] Aubrey, *Brief Lives*, ii. 182; J. Swift, *Works* (1814), iii. 89.

[5] *Reliquiae Wottonianae* (1651), p. 498.

[6] Ralegh, *History*, i. 210.

[7] Ibid. i. 25–27; W. F. Oakeshott, *The Queen and the Poet* (1960), p. 119. I do not
associate myself with the claim that Ralegh anticipated Darwin's theory of the
origin of species because he said that Noah did not need to take into the ark all the
animals that now exist, but only those from which the present species are descended
(J. Bonar, *Theories of Population from Ralegh to Arthur Young*, 1931, p. 21).

early Christian Fathers would delight Milton.[1] Despite occasional professions of belief in the decay of the world, Ralegh normally spoke up for the Moderns against the Ancients. The whole emphasis of the *History*, after a few preliminary genuflections, is on law as against chance.[2] Even Ralegh's interest in magic links up with his interest in chemistry and medicine. Magic is 'the wisdom of Nature'. Referring specifically to 'the chemists', Ralegh said: 'The third kind of magic containeth the whole philosophy of nature; not the brabblings of the Aristoteleans, but that which bringeth to light the inmost virtues, and draweth them out of nature's hidden bosom to human use.'[3] Magic he defined as 'the investigation of those virtues and hidden properties which God hath given to his creatures, and how fitly to apply things that work to things that suffer'. Magic, like science for Bacon, could be used for 'the help and comfort of mankind'.[4] Bacon had thought that there was a core of physical knowledge in alchemy, magic, and astrology, which was worthy of scientific investigation.[5] Sir Thomas Browne also believed that 'traditional magic' proceeded upon 'principles of nature'; 'at first a great part of philosophy was witchcraft'.[6] Boyle later attempted the investigation which Bacon had proposed.[7]

There is as yet no agreement among historians about the exact contribution of alchemy to the origins of scientific thinking. Paracelsus had boasted that natural magic and alchemy were 'firmly based on experience, . . . by which all arts should be proved'.[8] For our purposes it is notable that Recorde, Dee, Thomas Digges, Gilbert, John Woodall, Napier, Matthew Roydon, and Nicholas Hill, as well as Copernicus, Bruno, and Kepler, were interested in magic; and that John Hester, the

[1] Ralegh, *History*, i, p. xli, iii. 205.   [2] See pp. 182–7 below.
[3] Ralegh, *History*, ii. 154–5, 159–60, 165–6, 400–1, 404; Strathmann, *Sir Walter Ralegh*, pp. 175–81; Haydn, *The Counter-Renaissance*, pp. 195, 280, 515–16, 535.
[4] Ralegh, *History*, i, p. xi.
[5] Bacon, *Works*, iii. 289, iv. 34–57, 365–9; cf. J. R. Partington, *History of Chemistry* ii (1961), pp. 389–414.
[6] Sir T. Browne, *Religio Medici* (1642), in *Works* (Bohn ed.), ii. 367.
[7] Mason, *A History of the Sciences*, pp. 188–9; W. Pagel, 'Religious Motives in Medical Biology of the 17th century', *Bulletin of the Institute of the History of Medicine*, iii. 305.
[8] Haydn, op. cit., p. 190. See above p. 89 for the alchemists' hope of getting back behind the Fall: cf. Haydn, op. cit., pp. 191, 464, 516–19; Pagel, loc. cit., *passim*; Mason, 'The Scientific Revolution and the Protestant Reformation', *Annals of Science*, ix. 154–75.

leading English exponent of Paracelsus's doctrine, had links with Ralegh.[1] Dee defined 'archemistrie' as 'scientia experimentalis'.[2] There was certainly an underground alchemical tradition which had long been handed on verbally: Richard Bostock in 1585 argued that Paracelsus was no more the inventor of chemistry than Wyclif, Luther, and Calvin were the inventors of the Gospel when they restored religion to its primitive purity. So long as Scotus and Aquinas were 'maintained, defended and privileged by princes and potentates, it was hard for truth to show his face abroad openly'. A reformation was as necessary in science now as it had formerly been in religion, to overthrow Aristotle, Galen, 'and other heathen and their followers', and allow 'the chemical doctrine agreeing with God's word, experience, and nature' to 'come into the schools and cities', relying on 'due trial by labour and work of fire and other requisite experiments'.[3] Dee's Preface, as Professor Haydn pointed out, was in the Paracelsan alchemical tradition: it looked back as well as forwards. Marlowe's Faustus, the magician *par excellence*, defended Ramus against Aristotle as well as Paracelsus against Galen.[4] In science, as in religion, the sixteenth century saw the break-through to respectability of ideas which had long seethed underground among the craftsmen. It is noteworthy how often the intellectual spokesmen of the plebeian religious radical movements were men with a medical background—from Paracelsus and Servetus to Chamberlen and Culpeper. The combination of chemistry with magic and radical religious convictions was repeated by John Webster in the sixteen-fifties: he quoted Dee's Preface.[5]

We should beware of thinking that, because in the long run science shed alchemy and astrology, therefore every scientist

[1] Haydn, op. cit., pp. 177–8, 193–6, 248; Kocher, 'Paracelsan Medicine in England', pp. 458–73; M. Boas, *The Scientific Renaissance, 1450–1630*, pp. 185, 190. For Woodall see pp. 70–71 above. Bruno, says Mr. Lindsay, used the term 'magic' to cover the scientific effort to grapple with the unknown (*Cause, Principle and Unity*, pp. 10, 34–35).

[2] Dee, Preface to Billingsley's *Euclide*, sig. A ii–iiiv.

[3] R[ichard] B[ostock], *The Difference betwene the auncient . . . and the latter Phisick* (1585), chapter 19.

[4] Haydn, op. cit., pp. 186–9. Ramus was associated with Paracelsus by the future bishop, John Earle (p. 129 above), and by Bishop Goodman; both were defended by Hakewill (*Apologie*, ii. 130, 134).

[5] J. Webster, *Academiarum Examen*, pp. 20, 27, 51–52, 68–69, 105–6, and *passim*; *Metallographia* (1671), pp. 8, 34.

who took these subjects seriously was a charlatan. Recorde, Dee, Digges, Napier, Copernicus, Kepler, Bacon are not so lightly to be dismissed. 'In those dark times', said Aubrey apropos Thomas Allen, 'astrologer, mathematician, and conjurer were accounted the same things.'[1] So cool and level-headed a sceptic as John Selden was at once a supporter of the new astronomy and a great admirer of Robert Fludd the Rosicrucian, who thought chemistry was the search for God. Selden himself used often to dive into the books of alchemists, astrologers, and soothsayers.[2] If Ralegh believed in sympathetic medicines—and the evidence is dubious—so did Bacon and Fellows of the Royal Society, including Sir Kenelm Digby and John Locke, much later in the seventeenth century.[3] What is interesting for us is Ralegh's defence of the alchemical tradition, which, from Paracelsus to Webster, was more than once associated with religious and political radicalism.

IV

'As theory, Ralegh's political writings have no importance whatsoever. He thought of nothing new.'[4] Mr. Stapleton's first sentence does not seem to me to be proved by the second. It is true that Ralegh was not a Bodin, a Hobbes, or a Harrington. It is true that the *Cabinet Council*, the *Maxims of State*, and other works attributed to him are compilations with commentary, not original works. But these very compilations introduced some of the ideas of writers like Machiavelli and Bodin[5] under the respectable shadow of Ralegh's name: and in the *Prerogative*

---

[1] Aubrey, *Brief Lives*, i. 27.

[2] Johnson, *Astronomical Thought*, pp. 253–4; *Reliquiae Hearnianae* (ed. P. Bliss, 1869), ii. 197–8, iii. 181–2. Webster also praised Fludd.

[3] Robert Fludd said in 1631 that Lady Ralegh had told him that her husband 'would suddenly stop the bleeding of any person (albeit he were far and remote from the party) if he had a handkerchief or some other piece of linen dipped in some of the blood of the party sent unto him' (*Doctor Fludds answer unto M. Foster*, 1631, quoted by J. B. Craven, *Dr. Robert Fludd*, 1902, p. 212). Cf. R. T. Petersson, *Sir Kenelm Digby*, pp. 261–74.

[4] L. Stapleton, 'Halifax and Ralegh', *J.H.I.* ii. 211.

[5] Bodin was translated into English in 1606. Machiavelli's *Art of War* had been translated in 1563, the *Florentine History* in 1595. But there was no English version of the *Discorsi* until 1636, of *Il Principe* until 1640. Ralegh himself was called a Machiavellian both in contemporary songs and by Coke at his trial (N. L. Williams, *Sir Walter Ralegh*, pp. 172, 177).

of Parliaments he put forward a programme which opponents of the court in the sixteen-twenties found useful. Without claiming too much for the originality of Ralegh's political ideas, we may see some importance in the fact that they were collected together and systematized by the victim of Spain and James I.

We need not take too seriously the story, which Aubrey repeats, that Ralegh advocated a republic in 1603.[1] But it is significant that during the years 1600–28 three English translations of Lucan—regarded as the republican poet *par excellence*—were published. The first was by Marlowe, a member of Ralegh's circle. The second was by Ralegh's cousin and close associate, Sir Arthur Gorges, with a congratulatory sonnet by Ralegh. The third was by Tom May, the future historian of the Long Parliament and the friend of the republican Henry Marten.[2] Republican opinions were attributed to Ralegh in Marvell's *Britannia and Rawleigh* (if it is Marvell's); in 1683 there was a eulogistic biography of Shaftesbury called *Rawleigh Redivivus*—not Hampden or Pym or Vane or Cromwell, but Ralegh.

Ralegh's political thought ruthlessly emphasizes expediency, utility, in a way that anticipates Hobbes. In civil wars 'all former compacts and agreements for securing of liberty and property are dissolved, and become void: for flying to arms is a state of war, which is the mere state of nature, of men out of community, where all have an equal right to all things: and I shall enjoy my life, my subsistence, or whatever is dear to me no longer than he that has more cunning, or is stronger than I, will give me leave'. 'That any particular government is now *Jure Divino* is hard to affirm, and of no great use to mankind. For let the government of any country where I am a subject be by divine institution or by compact, I am equally bound to observe its laws and endeavour its prosperity.'[3] James would not like that very much. The very title of *The Prerogative of Parliaments* must have sounded like a manifesto to the king who exalted his own royal prerogative, who thought that Parliament's liberties were

---

[1] Aubrey, *Brief Lives*, ii. 186. Cf. Lucy Hutchinson, op. cit., i. 109.

[2] I owe this point to Mr. Charles Hobday. For Gorges see pp. 135, 138, 140, 143 above, 213–19 below. For May see p. 65 above.

[3] Ralegh, *Works*, ii. 50. Compare a fascinating passage in Fulke Greville's *Mustapha* (*Poems and Dramas*, ii. 130–1). Cf. P. Lefranc, 'Un inédit de Ralegh sur la succession', *Études Anglaises*, 1960, pp. 40–46.

derived from him by grace, and who considered that Ralegh's *History* had been 'too saucy in censuring princes'.[1]

But it is difficult to extract a consistent political philosophy from Ralegh's writings. His account in the *History* of the origin of political society appears to derive from Buchanan, Sidney's favourite. Yet Ralegh also declared that the sovereign, the prince, is exempt from human laws;[2] elsewhere he advocates an ultimate right of resistance, 'since no prince can shew a patriarchal right, and a community is under conditions'.[3] In particular 'the common people of England' have often been persuaded to fight 'for such a liberty as their leaders never intended they should have'—hence their reputation abroad for 'a turbulent and disquiet spirit'. But the greatest liberty is good government, and this England has, at least potentially.[4] Ralegh never suggested that monarchy was more acceptable to God. He had no use for theories of paternal government derived from God's grant to Adam of 'dominion over . . . every living thing that moveth upon the earth'. The rule of a king, on the contrary, is the rule of one freeman over others.[5] In the Preface to the *History* Ralegh distinguished between a 'Turk-like' monarchy, such as Philip II tried to establish over the Netherlands, and the absolute monarchies of England and France.[6] Asiatic despotism, with the consequent 'general want of liberty among the people', makes a foreign conquest 'easy and sure'.[7] Whereas it was traditional to regard Nimrod as a subverter of liberty, Ralegh collected authorities who regarded him as a colonizer rather than a tyrant. Nimrod was a *de facto* ruler, elevated for

---

[1] *Letters of John Chamberlain*, i. 568. Cf. the reference to 'the prerogative of the Parliament', in a letter from Richard James to Sir Robert Cotton, quoted in F. S. Fussner, *The Historical Revolution* (1962), p. 138. For James see p. 193 below.

[2] Ralegh, *History*, ii. 342–4. Cf. *The Prerogative of Parliaments*: 'the immortal policy of a state cannot admit any law of privilege whatsoever but in some particular or other, the same is necessarily broken' (*Works*, i. 223; cf. p. 241). What interests Ralegh is *sovereignty*.

[3] *Works*, ii. 51–52. Ralegh only mentions this 'as the utmost the most zealous advocates can urge for the power of the people', which can be exercised only when 'the person or persons possessing the supreme power are incurably defective'. The passage in the *Cabinet Council* urging passive obedience is not Ralegh's (ibid. i. 97–98).

[4] Ibid. ii. 67–68.

[5] *History*, v. 107–12.

[6] Ibid. i. xxvi; cf. Greville, *Life of Sidney*, pp. 62, 98, 173–8, 190–9, 203–5.

[7] *History*, iv. 453–4; *The Prerogative of Parliaments*, *passim*.

sound Hobbist reasons, which Ralegh is at pains to make clear.[1]
With his accustomed slide from first to second causes,[2] Ralegh
argued that God first made men see the necessity of kingship,
which he had ordained by his eternal providence; but '(speaking
humanly), the beginning of empire may be ascribed to reason
and necessity'; laws were soon established 'for direction and
restraint of royal power'.[3]

Ralegh in fact had a very Harringtonian view of the evolution
of the English constitution. He approvingly quoted Bacon for
the view that 'monarchs need not fear any curbing of their
absoluteness by mighty subjects, as long as by wisdom they keep
the hearts of the people. . . . Every sheriff and constable being
sooner able to use the multitude, in the king's behalf, than any
overweening rebel, how mighty soever, can against him.'[4]
Ralegh was still thinking in traditional Tudor terms, of feudal
revolt as the greatest danger, and of the middling sort as the
natural supporters of sovereignty. He had after all helped to
suppress Essex's revolt in 1601. Most of the laws of England,
like Magna Carta, are Acts of Parliament, 'to the obedience of
which all men are therefore bound, because they are acts of
choice and self-desire'.[5]

It is only when we come to *The Prerogative of Parliaments* that
we see how far Ralegh would have limited kingly power. With
an appearance of great objectivity, the Justice in Ralegh's
dialogue makes out a case for political opposition to the crown—
even violent opposition—in every historical instance which the
Councillor brings forward. Ralegh's argument urges the King
to abandon those councillors—including, though he is too wise
even to hint this, the Spanish ambassador—who advise him

[1] *History*, ii. 119–35.
[2] See pp. 181–92 below.
[3] *History*, ii. 107. I do not understand how Mr. A. Williams can see Ralegh as in
the patriarchal royalist tradition which leads from Overall to Filmer (A. Williams,
'Politics and Economics in Renaissance Commentaries on *Genesis*', *H.L.Q.* vii.
213–14). Cf. C. H. and K. George, *The Protestant Mind of the English Reformation,
1570–1640* (Princeton, 1961), p. 204; Milton, *Complete Prose Works* (Yale ed.),
iii. 466 n.
[4] *History*, iii. 219.
[5] *History*, ii. 340–1. Contrast this view of Magna Carta with that expressed by the
Councillor in the *Prerogative of Parliaments* (*Works*, i. 180–2), so often quoted out of
context by Ralegh's opponents. (See p. 212 below.) For Ralegh's own views
see *Works*, i, pp. 179, 183, 240–2.

to dispense with Parliaments.[1] Ralegh's aim is to convince James that Parliament *cannot* be wished out of existence, because those whom it represents cannot be wished out of existence. Therefore the King would be prudent and well advised to co-operate with Parliament. For, Ralegh says in a Carlylean passage, 'that policy hath never yet prevailed (though it hath served for a short season) where the counterfeit hath been sold for the natural, and the outward show and formality for the substance'.[2] 'Shall the head yield to the feet? certainly it ought, when they are grieved', as they are, for example, by monopolies, impositions, arbitrary imprisonment, and refusal of free speech in Parliament.[3] The remedy for the financial difficulties of the Crown 'doth chiefly consist in the love of the people', which 'is lost by nothing more than by the defence of others in wrong-doing—the only motives of mischances that ever came to kings of this land since the Conquest'.[4]

The tone is mild and persuasive, but the implied threat is clear. When the J.P. (who represents Ralegh's point of view in the dialogue) mentioned digging 'out of the dust the long buried memory of the subjects' former contentions with the king', the Councillor asked sharply 'What mean you by that?' 'I will tell your Lordship, when I dare', was the reply. 'To say that his Majesty knows and cares not, that, my Lord, were but to despair all his faithful subjects.'[5] 'It cannot be called a dishonour, for the King is to believe the general Council of the kingdom, and to prefer it before his affection.'[6] James will do himself no good by kicking against the pricks: even kings are subject to historical necessity. This doctrine would not be unacceptable to Parliamentarians who could not counter the traditional royal arguments, but felt that they had a stronger case than they could establish in terms of mere legalism.[7]

V

Ralegh's condemnation in 1603 was, among other things, part of the price paid for the Spanish peace of 1604. For, though

[1] Ralegh always very sharply draws the traditional distinction between the King and his evil councillors (*Works*, i. 200–2, 208–9, 211–13, 216–17, 233–5, 240–8).

[2] Ibid. ii. 318.

[3] It is in the *History* that sale of honours is denounced (ii. 117).

[4] *Works*, i. 175–6.   [5] Ibid. i. 242, 246–7.   [6] Ibid. i. 212.

[7] I discuss Ralegh's 'Harringtonianism' further at pp. 195–9, 203 below.

Ralegh was accused of plotting with Spain, in fact he was leader of the bellicose anti-Spanish party, and many of the judges who condemned him soon accepted Spanish pensions.[1] In 1618, it was generally held, Ralegh was betrayed to execution by the Spanish faction, 'then absolute at court'; he was 'sacrificed to advance the matrimonial treaty' with Spain, said Howell.[2] In this case popular legend was entirely justified, except that it underestimated the complicity of James I, who was personally responsible for betraying to Spain all the details of Ralegh's Guiana expedition of 1617, so ensuring its failure and Ralegh's execution. Of the relation of his execution to James's foreign policy there can be no doubt. Secretary Winwood, Ralegh's backer, whose son supported Parliament in the civil war, died towards the end of 1617; and for the next seven years James pursued a pro-Spanish policy with as much vigour as he was capable of. But, as a contemporary shrewdly observed in 1618, Ralegh's 'death will do more harm to the faction that procured it than ever he did in his life'.[3]

Ralegh's foreign policy was not his private affair, but was the policy of a whole group, whose main publicists were the two Richard Hakluyts. Ralegh was intimately connected with them. The younger Hakluyt's *Discourse of Western Planting* was written in 1584 'at the request and direction of Ralegh', to whom most of Hakluyt's works were dedicated.[4] The policy of the Hakluyts was at once patriotic and imperialist. England had got left behind in the grab for the New World by Spain and Portugal, whose empires were menacingly united in 1580. After a rapid expansion of English cloth exports in the first half of the sixteenth century, relative stagnation followed. Unemployment created social, political, and national dangers, as Ralegh and many other observers noted.[5] But the younger Hakluyt was shrewd

[1] Cf. Bishop Goodman: 'Now suppose King James had intended to continue the wars, how should he then have been able to have given the Scots as much as he did?' (G. Goodman, *The Court of King James I*, 1839. i. 61). Goodman exaggerates: but he only exaggerates what may have seemed to many courtiers a self-evident point.
[2] Osborn, *Traditional Memoirs*, in *Secret History of the Court of King James*, i. 157–64; J. Howell, *Epistolae Ho-Elianae* (Temple Classics), ii. 232: first published 1645–55.
[3] *C.S.P.D.*, *1611–18*, pp. 588–9; cf. pp. 203–11 below.
[4] Ed. E. G. R. Taylor, *The Writings . . . of the two Richard Hakluyts, passim.*
[5] e.g. Robert Hitchcock, *A Politic Plat* (1580), *passim*, written in collaboration with John Dee; cf. Ralegh, *History*, v. 109. Over-population is a major cause of wars, Ralegh thought (*Works*, ii. 26–28).

enough to realize that England's over-population was only relative. The colonization of North America would not only get rid of England's immediate surplus population: it would also provide raw materials for home industries, and so prepare for a long-term solution.[1] The object of economic policy should be to make England self-sufficient, an exporter of highly finished manufactured goods. North America would yield dye-stuffs for the clothing industry, the naval stores for which England was dependent on Baltic supplies, and timber to relieve England's fuel shortage. The reduction of the Indians 'to civility, both in manners and garments' would provide a new market. Given an economically self-sufficient Empire, England need not bother about capturing markets in Europe.[2]

But England's road was blocked by Spain, on whose empire, in Bacon's phrase, 'the sun never sets'.[3] Spain closed the whole American continent to English settlers, English goods, and English religion. So this policy, as Sidney and Hakluyt saw, involved war with Spain.[4] Colonization was thus strategically vital. Occupation of North America could command the New-foundland fishing banks and the Spanish homeward route from the Indies. 'Traffic followeth conquest.'[5] But with this base in the New World, war against Spain could be made to pay for itself: 'we must not look to maintain war upon the revenues of England', Ralegh warned Cecil in 1595.[6] Privateering could enrich individual merchants and gentlemen: gold and silver could be diverted from Spain to England.[7] Such a war had religious as well as patriotic overtones. Foxe had traced the

---

[1] These points were made in a plea for reviving Ralegh's scheme for conquering Guiana, by Col. Thomas Modyford in 1652 (*C.S.P. Col., 1574–60*, pp. 373–4).

[2] R. Hakluyt, *The Principal Navigations, Voyages, Traffiques and Discoveries of the English Nation* (Everyman ed.), vi. 61; cf. Taylor, *Original Writings, passim*: K. G. Davies, *The Royal African Company* (1957), p. 168. The Hakluyts evolved this theory before the export of the New Draperies to European markets began to expand in the early seventeenth century.

[3] Bacon, *Works*, vii. 21.

[4] Cf. F. Greville, *Life of Sidney*, pp. 110–19.

[5] Taylor, *Original Writings*, i. 37.   [6] Edwards, *Life of Raleigh*, ii. 111.

[7] There was from the start considerable potential tension between the merchants who financed and planned the colonizing expeditions, and the gentlemen sea-dogs who could rarely resist combining them with piracy and the hunt for gold (cf. Taylor, *Original Writings*, i. 135). This dichotomy looks forward to the rivalry between the aristocratic planters whom the first two Stuarts encouraged, and the merchants and settlers who strove to outwit them.

sufferings and struggles of God's people down to the Marian martyrs: Hakluyt's book also started with the beginning of the Christian epoch; but his Englishmen have passed over to the offensive against Antichrist, bringing the Gospel to parts of the world which had never yet heard it. If the worst came to the worst—and this illustrates the anxieties still felt by Elizabethan Englishmen, which we are too apt to forget because we know the end of the story—'a place of safety might there be found, if change of religion or civil wars should happen in this realm'[1]

War against Spain was necessary, the Hakluyts thought, not only to preserve England's national independence, but also to bring salvation to millions of American Indians, who had within living memory been subjugated to popery and Spanish cruelty. Puritan ministers, dangerously unemployed and restless at home, could be sent abroad to convert the heathen.[2] 'God hath reserved' North America 'to be reduced unto Christian civility by the English nation'.[3] Because of Spanish cruelty the Indians—'a poor and harmless people created of God'[4] —would offer willing allies against Spain, as Ralegh often found.[5] Ralegh's imperial policy envisaged the export of English arts and English women to Peru, the arming and training of the Indians, who were to be used to establish Peruvian independence of Spain, under allegiance to England.[6] Ralegh's good treatment of the Indians at Trinidad in 1595 was remembered in 1605 and 1626, when they 'did unanimously own the protection of the English' against Spain. In Guiana 'he left so good and so great a name behind him . . . that the English have often been obliged to remember him with honour'.[7] 'Most of

---

[1] Taylor, *Original Writings*, i. 119–20. In a sense the 'revolution by evasion' of the emigration of the sixteen-twenties and thirties was thus foreseen by Hakluyt, though hardly the enemy from whom God's people had to flee. He had hoped indeed, as Ralegh did, that colonization would prevent civil wars (ibid. ii. 457–8; cf. Ralegh, *Works*, i. 26–28). But Hakluyt did realize that 'the English there would aspire to the government of themselves' (Taylor, *Original Writings*, i. 143).

[2] Taylor, op. cit. ii. 217.

[3] Hakluyt, *Principal Navigations* (Everyman ed.), vi. 3.

[4] Ralegh, *The Last Fight of* The Revenge (Hakluyt, op. cit. v. 13). Hakluyt's attitude towards the native population was rather more robust (Taylor, op. cit. ii. 503).

[5] Cf. Ralegh's *Discovery of Guiana* and *Fight about the Islands of Azores, passim.*

[6] N. L. Williams, op. cit., p. 137, quoting *The Discovery of Guiana* (ed. V. T. Harlow, 1928), Appendix C.

[7] Ed. Harlow, *Colonising Expeditions to the West Indies and Guiana, 1623–1667* (Hakluyt Soc., 1925), pp. lxiii, 141. Cf. R. Harcourt, *A Relation of a Voyage to Guiana* (1613), in *Harleian Miscellany* (1744–56), vi. 460.

his contemporaries', Professor Quinn sums up, 'regarded the Spanish empire as something to be robbed: Ralegh thought of it as something to be replaced by an English empire. He therefore considered seriously the problems of English rule over a native population.'[1] This underlines the tragedy that Ralegh could interest James only in robbery.

Hakluyt and Ralegh, then, put forward a national policy which offered something to all sections of the community. From the unemployed to Puritan ministers anxious to extend true religion, from City merchants to discontented younger sons of the landed class, all, it seemed, had something to gain.[2]

In 1596 Ralegh's devoted adherent Lawrence Kemyis, a Balliol geographer and mathematician who like Wright had thrown up his fellowship to go to sea,[3] published a *Relation of the Second Voyage to Guiana*. To this George Chapman, member of Ralegh's circle and friend of Hariot, prefixed a poem. Chapman urged 'patrician spirits', 'that know death lives where power lies unused' no longer to

> be content like horse to hold
> A threadbare beaten way to home affairs.

They should

> scorn to let your bodies choke your souls
> In the rude breath and prison'd life of beasts.
> You that herein renounce the course of earth
> And lift your eyes for guidance to the stars,
> That live not for yourselves, but to possess
> Your honour'd country of a general store;
> In pity of the spoil rude self-love makes
> Of those whose lives and years one aim doth feed,
> One soil doth nourish, and one strength combine;
> You that are blest with sense of all things noble,
> In this attempt your complete worths redouble.

---

[1] D. B. Quinn, *Raleigh and the British Empire* (1947), p. 270.

[2] Cf. Hakluyt, *Principal Navigations*, vii. 393. Sir Thomas Smith's scheme for a joint-stock venture to settle Ulster in 1571, 'the first printed publicity for an English colonial project', remarkably anticipates the Hakluyts and Ralegh. The reasons which Smith gave for overseas expansion included the over-population of England, and the need to provide for the younger sons of the gentry now that the monasteries had been dissolved (D. B. Quinn, 'Sir Thomas Smith (1513–77) and the beginning of English colonial theory', *Proceedings of the American Philosophical Soc.*, lxxxix. 550–2, 560). For Smith see pp. 270–1 below.

[3] Wood, *Athenae Oxonienses*, i. 433; see pp. 304–5 below.

Once Elizabeth blessed

> with her wonted graces
> Th'industrious knight, the soul of this exploit [Ralegh]

she would create

> A golden world in this our iron age. . . .
> A world of savages fall tame before them,
> Storing their theft-free treasuries with gold;
> And there doth plenty crown their wealthy fields,
> There Learning eats no more his thriftless books,
> Nor Valour, estridge-like, his iron arms. . . .
> There makes society adamantine chains,
> And joins their hearts with wealth whom wealth disjoin'd.[1]

Hakluyt and Ralegh, like Bacon, synthesized and gave organized form to the thinking of large numbers of less articulate Englishmen. John Hawkins saw himself as the successor of Foxe's martyrs when he was frustrated in his attempt to sell bootleg negro slaves in Spanish America.[2] Martin Frobisher prayed in 1577 for a safe return to England so that his discoveries 'might redound to the more honour of [God's] holy name, and *consequently* to the advancement of our commonwealth'.[3] Lawrence Kemyis thought it had 'pleased God of his infinite goodness, in his will and purpose to appoint and reserve this empire [of Guiana] for us'.[4] Hakluyt was the spokesman of this newly self-conscious nationalism.

A full-scale policy of imperial conquest could not be carried out without government support, without a powerful navy. In 1577 Ralegh's friend John Dee, who appears to have originated the phrase 'the British Empire', had advocated a standing royal navy to police the seas against pirates, and so protect merchants and the fishing industry.[5] Under James and Charles this became a crying need, when the Algiers pirates mastered

---

[1] G. Chapman, *Poems and Minor Translations* (1875), pp. 50–52; cf. pp. 53–55.
[2] Hakluyt, *Principal Navigations*, vii. 62.
[3] Ibid. v. 210. My italics.
[4] Ibid. vii. 400.
[5] J. Dee, *The Petty Navy Royal*, in *General and Rare Memorials* (1577). There was a vast literature on the importance of encouraging the fishing industry, extending in Ralegh's lifetime from Dee and Hitchcock's *Politic Plat* of 1580 to Tobias Gentleman's *The Way to Wealth* of 1614.

up-to-date techniques of navigation.[1] But, apart from Mansell's abortive expedition of 1620–1, it was not until the sixteen-fifties that Blake's fleet bombarded Algiers and Cromwell's troops captured Jamaica and Dunkirk. For two generations the advocates of the Hakluyt–Ralegh policy laboured to convince governments of its desirability and feasibility: but in vain. Elizabeth 'did all by halves', as Ralegh said.[2] 'Neither James I nor Charles I . . . ever sent a ship across the Atlantic.'[3] There were serious limits to the effectiveness of colonization by private enterprise, as the early colonists found to their cost.

After the defeat of the Armada had first shaken the fixed belief of Englishmen in the omnipotence of Spain, a massive propaganda campaign was undertaken to convince a sufficient number of influential people that England's destiny lay in grandiose exploits across the ocean. The younger Hakluyt decided to embark on his *magnum opus*, a careful collection and publication of facts on Baconian lines, ⌐ few months after the Armada's defeat had opened up dazzling new prospects.[4] Hariot's *Brief and True Report* on Virginia appeared in 1588; Ralegh's *Discovery of Guiana* in 1591;[5] and Hakluyt's *Voyages*, reprinting both of them, rounded off the campaign. In merchant circles, at least, it was very successful. The East India Company supplied as reading matter to its ships the Bible, Foxe's *Acts and Monuments*, Perkins's *Works*, and Hakluyt.[6] The combination is significant. Hakluyt acted as Ralegh's publicity agent in the campaign, and seems deliberately to have worked to get books

---

[1] Waters, *The Art of Navigation*, p. 253. In 1588, as Ralegh pointed out, Spain was buying English guns (M. Lewis, *Armada Guns*, 1961, p. 137). Dee too had protested in *The Petty Navy Royal* against the export of armaments.

[2] Edwards, *Life of Raleigh*, i. 245; Ralegh, *Works*, i. 273–4.

[3] J. A. Williamson, *The English Channel* (1959), p. 243.

[4] Taylor, *Late Tudor and Early Stuart Geography*, p. 14; Parks, *Hakluyt and the English Voyages*, p. 183.

[5] 'I have . . . laboured all my life, both according to my small power and persuasion, to advance all those attempts that might either promise return or profit to ourselves, or at least be a let or impeachment to the quiet course and plentiful trades of the Spanish nation' (*Discovery of Guiana*, To the Reader, printed with Ralegh's *History*, vi. 14). Cf. Hakewill, *Apologie*, pp. 310–14.

[6] L. B. Wright, *Religion and Empire* (North Carolina U.P., 1943), pp. 53, 71, 176; ed. E. Lynam, *Richard Hakluyt and his Successors* (Hakluyt Soc., 1946), p. 39. But the *Principal Navigations* was not used only for light reading. It also did service as a ruttier, and on one occasion saved the Company £20,000 when it helped the ships to make Sierra Leone harbour (Waters, op. cit., p. 236).

dedicated to Ralegh, often dictating the content of the dedication so as to stress Ralegh's international reputation.[1]

Throughout the *History of the World* the over-riding importance of exhorting his readers against Spain is never far from Ralegh's mind. Spanish America would be as easy to conquer as Syria under the sons of Aram.[2] Xerxes reminded Ralegh of Philip II.[3] Alexander's tactics against Bessus led Ralegh to urge future invaders of Guiana or the West Indies always to 'burn down the grass and sedge to the east of them'.[4] The wars between Rome and Carthage gave rise to a long digression on sea power and naval strategy, and to warnings against the dangers of trading with Spain.[5] A discussion of tyranny prompted the improbable reflection that under a king like James 'it is likely, by God's blessing, that a land shall flourish with increase of trade in countries before unknown; that civility and religion shall be propagated into barbarous and heathen countries; and that the happiness of his subjects shall cause the nations far removed to wish him their sovereign'.[6] In the 'Conclusion to the whole work' Ralegh noted that Spanish power was the greatest that had been seen in western Europe since the fall of the Roman Empire; still this power could easily and cheaply be restrained if England, France, and the Netherlands went over to the offensive.[7] 'The obedience even of the Turk is easy and a liberty in respect of the slavery and tyranny of Spain', Ralegh had written in 1591.[8]

For Hakluyt and Ralegh an alliance with the Netherlands was the necessary concomitant of their anti-Spanish policy. For this there were ideological reasons ('after my duty to mine own sovereign', wrote Ralegh, 'and the love of my country, I honour them most').[9] The Netherlands also provided a model

---

[1] Rosenberg, 'Giacopo Castelvetro', *H.L.Q.* vi. 122–32. For dedications to Ralegh see L. Einstein, *The Italian Renaissance in England* (New York, 1902), p. 359; Parks, *Richard Hakluyt and the English Voyages*, pp. 217–18.

[2] Ralegh, *History*, ii. 91–92.

[3] Ibid. iv. 42.

[4] Ibid. iv. 315.

[5] Ibid. v. 37–38, 54–63, 199.

[6] Ibid. v. 111; cf. vi. 242–3—an equally improbable hope that James would prove less mean to military men than Elizabeth had been.

[7] Ibid. vi. 369. Cf. *A Discovery of Guiana*, To the Reader, and *A Discourse touching War with Spain* (*Works*, ii. 1–20), for the decline and poverty of Spain.

[8] *The Last Fight of* The Revenge (Hakluyt, *Principal Navigations*, v. 13).

[9] Ralegh, *Works*, ii. 88. See pp. 167, 206–8, 280–4 below.

of economic behaviour.[1] But a Dutch alliance was also a practical necessity, even if the Dutch proved ungrateful competitors. For 'this long calm' after the peace of 1604 'will shortly break out in some terrible tempest',[2] as it did in the year of Ralegh's execution. Yet Ralegh's interest in the shipping industry led him to advocate its encouragement and something very like a Navigation Act against Dutch competition.[3] Like many English merchants, Ralegh was ambivalent in his attitude towards the Netherlands. Dutch merchants monopolized the carrying trade, and insisted on continuing to trade with Spain even in time of war. Ralegh 'was the first which made public the growth by sea of the Dutch, and the riches they derived from their fishing upon the coasts of England and Scotland, and the consequences which would necessarily follow, not only to the loss of the King's sovereignty of the British seas, but to the trade and navigation of England otherwise'. The cry was taken up by Tobias Gentleman and other pamphleteers, and echoed by Hakewill. But James 'stopped his ears to Sir Walter's advice concerning the Dutch fishing' and only opened them when Ralegh promised him gold from Guiana.[4] To the Dutch alliance Ralegh came to add an alliance with the Palatinate and the maintenance of the Protestant interest in France and Switzerland—an object dear to Oliver Cromwell's heart.[5]

Neither Elizabeth, James, nor Charles had any use for this foreign policy. They regarded the Dutch as rebels and Spain as the greatest monarchy in Christendom, with whom it would be folly for England to engage in war *à l'outrance*. Nor had any of them much sympathy with the commercial or religious ideals which underlay Hakluyt's and Ralegh's schemes. But to many

---

[1] Ibid. ii. 109–36; cf. T. Mun, *Englands Treasure by Forraign Trade*, in *Early English Tracts on Commerce* (ed. J. R. McCulloch, 1856), pp. 193–204. Written probably in the early sixteen-twenties; first published 1664.

[2] Ralegh, *Works*, i. 278, 253, 275–6; ii. 8–9. Among many others who echoed the call for a Dutch alliance was Dr. Alexander Leighton, *Zions Plea against the Prelacie* (1628), p. 163 and *passim*. Probably printed in the Netherlands.

[3] Ralegh, *Works*, ii. 89–90, 130–1. Ralegh made a remarkably accurate prophecy when he observed that whichever of the three powers, England, France, or Spain, secured a permanent Dutch alliance, 'will become the greatest and give the law to the rest' (ibid. i. 276). The prophecy was realized after 1688.

[4] R. Coke, *A Detection of the Court and State of England* (1694), i. 92–93; Hakewill, *Apologie*, ii. 135.

[5] Ralegh, *Works*, i. 264, 273–5.

merchants and ministers, and to a large group in every House of Commons, the policy was very attractive. From 1612 the Virginia Company tried to carry it out. Hakluyt, a founder-member, may have organized the Company's propaganda campaign.[1] Bacon, Coke, Fulke Greville, Viscount Lisle, Hariot, and Briggs were members, together with Theodore Gulston, Thomas Winston, and Sir Oliver Cromwell, uncle of the Protector. All the great London livery companies subscribed.[2]

A list of the motives of the Virginia Adventurers, drafted in 1612, is a summary of Hakluyt's policy: (i) convert the Indians; (ii) export surplus population, 'the rank multitude'; (iii) supply England with naval stores and (iv) minerals; (v) provide a base for Atlantic shipping and (vi) explorations to reveal a north-west passage to the Far East.[3] The Virginia Company was supported by a propaganda campaign conducted by ministers (mainly Puritan). Thus William Crashawe spoke in 1613 of 'a work so honourable to God, our religion, our King and our country; so comfortable to the souls of the poor savages, and so profitable to the Adventurers . . . as the like . . . hath not been attempted in the Christian world these many ages'.[4] Propaganda against Spain and for American colonization was continued by Samuel Purchas, whose *Pilgrimage* ran to four editions between 1613 and 1626, and together with his *Hakluytus Posthumus* had a great influence.[5]

---

[1] Lynam, *Hakluyt and his Successors*, p. 177.

[2] W. F. Craven, *The Virginia Company of London, 1606–24* (1957), p. 18; T. H. O'Brien, 'The London Livery Companies and the Virginia Company', *Virginia Magazine of History and Biography*, lxviii. 148. See pp. 43–45, 61, 78 above, 217 below.

[3] W. Strachey, *For the Colony of Virginia Britannia* (1612), quoted by Taylor, *Late Tudor and Early Stuart Geography*, p. 163. Cf. T. Morton, *The New England Canaan* (1637): 'If our beggars of England should with so much ease as [the Red Indians] furnish themselves with food at all seasons, there would not be so many starved in the streets, neither would so many gaols be stuffed or gallows furnished with poor wretches, as I have seen them' (quoted in Taylor, op. cit.. p. 168). Cf. p. 47 above.

[4] W. Crashawe, *Good Newes from Virginia* (1613), Epistle Dedicatory to Sir Thomas Smith. Crashawe was not attached to Smith's faction in the Company. In his will eight years later he left £105 to some honest merchant of London, 'whom Sir Edwin Sandys shall like', 'to better the stipend of the preachers of St. Antolin's'. Crashawe was a friend of Briggs, Selden, and Thomas James: a protégé of Coke (P. J. Wallis, *William Crashawe*, 1963, *passim*). For more about clerical 'demonstrations of Virginia's role in the scheme of providence', see Perry Miller, *Errand into the Wilderness* (Harvard U.P., 1956), pp. 99–140. Cf. also R. Gray, *A Good Speed to Virginia* (1609), sig. B 2–C: over-population in England necessitates emigration.

[5] Purchas was chaplain to and enjoyed the patronage of Archbishop Abbott, for whom see pp. 19, 71 above. Purchas was helped by Sir Dudley Digges and Sir Thomas

Sir Edwin Sandys, who was Treasurer of the Virginia Company in 1619–20, consciously aimed at carrying out Hakluyt's policy.[1] He was a friend of Selden's and a leading opposition figure in the House of Commons. In the Parliament of 1614 he supported Sir Roger Owen's view that all kings had originally been elected, 'with reciprocal conditions between king and people'. A king by conquest might be forcibly overthrown.[2] Sandys introduced secret balloting at the Company's elections, a procedure which Charles I was to forbid to all companies, but which the Pilgrim Fathers and the Royal Society alike used in elections.[3] In the 1621 Parliament Sandys said 'Let us not palliate with the King, but with the people', and even went so far as to ask 'What is the bill of the Sabbath . . . to a man in want?'[4] In 1620 James intervened to force Sandys's replacement as Treasurer of the Virginia Company: 'Choose the devil if you will, but not Sir Edwin Sandys.'[5] Gondomar asserted that the Company 'was but a seminary to a seditious Parliament'.[6] But Sandys remained a force until the Company was dissolved in 1624. He attacked Gondomar as an enemy of the Company in the 1624 Parliament, where 'there was above one hundred Parliament men that were of the Virginia Company'.[7] Sandys, son of a Marian exile, was a patron of the Pilgrim Fathers. His *Europae Speculum* was often associated with Ralegh's *History* as a source of general information.[8]

Smith (Taylor, *Late Tudor and Early Stuart Geography*, p. 57). Dury recommended the study of Purchas, and according to Hartlib (quoting Haak) Milton in 1648 started the very necessary task of epitomizing Purchas's work (Turnbull, *Hartlib, Dury and Comenius*, p. 40).

[1] Craven, op. cit., pp. 48–49.

[2] *C.J.* i. 493; T. L. Moir. *The Addled Parliament of 1614* (1958), p. 115. For Owen and Ralegh see p. 205 below.

[3] W. Bradford, *History of Plymouth Plantation* (Massachusetts Historical Soc. Collections, 4th Series, iii), p. 266; Sprat, *History of the Royal Society*, p. 93.

[4] N.R.S. ii. 416; v. 190. Sandys advocated the abolition of feudal tenures.

[5] Craven, op. cit., p. 143; ed. S. M. Kingsbury, *Records of the Virginia Company of London* (1906–35), iv. 194.

[6] H. R. Trevor-Roper, *Archbishop Laud* (1940), p. 99.

[7] John Ferrar, in B. Blackstone, *Ferrar Papers* (1938), p. 22.

[8] E. Sandys, *Europae Speculum, or a View of the State of Religion in the Westerne part of the world*. A pirated edition was published in 1605 and suppressed, it is said with the connivance of the author. It was reprinted at The Hague in 1629 and circulated in England, where the first legal edition appeared in 1638. Fra Paolo Sarpi may have helped Sandys to prepare the work, and certainly co-operated in the Italian translation. For Sarpi see pp. 277–8 below.

There is thus clear continuity of the imperial theme in cement-ing the alliance between merchants and a section of the gentry. A paper of 1623, 'Reasons showing the benefit of planting in New England', in addition to the conventional themes of convert-ing the heathen, finding cloth markets, exporting the unem-ployed, providing work for those of the poor who remained in England, added that 'if he be a gentleman, or person of more eminency who hath no great stock to continue his reputation here at home', and if he could raise £100 or £200 capital, by emigrating he would 'not only be able to live without scorn of his maligners but in a plentiful and worthy manner'.[1]

Ralegh's associate, the third Earl of Cumberland, had at-tempted in 1598–9 to capture Porto Rico as a base against Spain.[2] This looks forward to Pym's Providence Island Com-pany and Cromwell's Western Design, linked by the voyages of Captain William Jackson in 1642–5. Jackson, who had the backing both of the Providence Island Company and of Maurice Thompson, later Cromwell's leading financier, seized Jamaica in 1643 and so (Jackson echoes Ralegh's words) 'the veil is now drawn aside, and their weakness detected by a handful of men, furnished and set out upon the expense of one private man'. What could not the English state do?[3] Cromwell soon showed.

For the continuity of policy we have to look from Hakluyt and Ralegh through the Virginia and Providence Island Com-panies and Captain Jackson, on to Hugh Peter, who in 1645 told the Lord Mayor and Aldermen of London, the two Houses of Parliament, and the divines of the Westminster Assembly, that England had a double interest: first the maintenance of the Protestant cause on the Continent; secondly war with Spain for the West Indies.[4] When Cromwell resumed Ralegh's policy, he found that his problem was exactly that which Ralegh had explained to James: 'how to free your people from the Inquisi-tion of Spain, enlarge their trades, and be secured not to have your ships stayed in his ports at his pleasure'.[5] The manifesto

[1] *City of Exeter MSS.* (H.M.C.), pp. 167–9.

[2] G. C. Williamson, *George, Third Earl of Cumberland* (1920), pp. 186, 223.

[3] Ed. V. T. Harlow, 'The Voyages of Captain William Jackson', *Camden Mis-cellany*, xiii, *passim.*

[4] H. Peter, *Gods Doings and Mans Duty* (1646), p. 30.

[5] Ralegh, *Works*, ii. 17. Ralegh thought a Dutch alliance essential for achieving

which Milton drafted in 1655 to justify war on Spain dwelt, as Ralegh would have done, on Spanish ill-treatment of the Indians as crying for retribution.[1] After the Restoration Sprat in his *History of the Royal Society* again echoed Ralegh (and Bacon) when he said: 'the English greatness will never be supported or increased in this age by any other wars but those at sea':[2] though now he spoke from experience, not speculatively.

VI

Ralegh himself made no mean contribution to the future English economy if it is true that he and Hariot introduced potatoes and the fashion of smoking tobacco to these islands. Marlowe and Thomas Allen were early smokers. But more important was Ralegh's contribution to economic theory, or rather to the popularization of theory. In an age when it was still often denounced as morally wrong for men of property to 'do what they would with their own', Ralegh was an early and outspoken exponent of economic liberalism—so much so that Charles Kingsley thought his ideas worthy of the nineteenth century.[3]

Ralegh wanted to repeal the statute of tillage, 'for many poor men are not able to find seed to sow so much as they are bound to plough'. In any case it would be easy for England to import corn, like 'the Hollander, which never soweth corn', yet 'hath by his industry such plenty that they will serve other nations. . . . And therefore I think the best course is to set it at liberty, and leave every man free, which is the desire of a true Englishman.'[4] In the next Parliament Ralegh secured the defeat of a bill 'touching the sowing of hemp'. 'I do not like this constraining of men to manure their grounds at our wills,'

those objectives: the Protectorate was strong enough for this no longer to be vital. But Cromwell still found that to ask for freedom of conscience and freedom of trade in the West Indies for English merchants was to ask for the King of Spain's two eyes.

[1] J. Milton, *Prose Works* (Bohn ed.), ii. 335–6.

[2] T. Sprat, *History of the Royal Society*, p. 404. For the whole of this section see A. P. Newton, *The Colonising Activities of the English Puritans* (Yale U.P., 1914), *passim*.

[3] C. Kingsley, *Plays and Puritans and other Historical Essays* (1879), p. 151.

[4] Sir S. D'Ewes, *Journals of all the Parliaments During the Reign of Queen Elizabeth* (1682), p. 674. Fulke Greville attributed a belief in freedom of trade to Sidney (*Life*, pp. 113, 203).

he said, 'but rather let every man use his ground to that which it is most fit for, and therein use his discretion.'[1] Despite his own practice, he attacked monopolies on more than one occasion.[2] His jurisdiction over the Stannaries under Elizabeth marked an era of reform, and the rules which he laid down continued long in force. He claimed that the tinners' wages doubled.[3] As Governor of Jersey (1600–3) Ralegh adopted a scheme which had been recommended for forty years, but which no one hitherto had bothered to carry out: he established a public register of title for real property, which still survives.[4] Such a land register was to be the nostrum of English legal reformers during and after the Revolution; but Cromwell in this did not emulate Ralegh.

'Take heed that thou love God, thy country, thy prince, and thine own estate, before all others. . . . Be not made an ass to carry the burdens of other men. . . . Money in thy purse will ever be in fashion.'[5] Such conventionally cynical passages occur not only in the *Advice to his Son*: Ralegh interrupted an eloquent passage on vanity in the Preface to his *History* to ask, 'Shall we therefore value honour and riches at nothing, and neglect them as unnecessary and vain?' And he answered, 'Certainly no.' For God had distinguished even the angels by degrees: it would be foolishness to condemn care for worldly goods. Monarchy originated to defend property, Ralegh declared in the *History*, traditionally enough.[6]

Ralegh had backers in the City. William Sanderson, Merchant Adventurer and generous patron of popular science, married Ralegh's niece and acted as his banker, man of business, and

---

[1] H. Townshend, *Historical Collections* (1680), p. 188. Cf. Ralegh, *Works*, ii. 5, on the profit motive. Serjeant Hoskyns, Ralegh's friend, defended liberty to buy and sell in the Parliaments of 1610 and 1614 (L. B. Osborn, *The Life, Letters and Writings of John Hoskyns*, Yale U.P., 1937, p. 37).

[2] Ralegh, *Works*, i. 174–6, 237–41; cf. p. 17.

[3] G. R. Lewis, *The Stannaries* (Harvard U.P.. 1924), p. 217.

[4] A. J. Eagleston, *The Channel Islands under Tudor Government, 1485–1642* (1949), p. 98. Cf. the suggestion that Sir Arthur Gorges's *Publique Register for Generall Commerce* (1611) 'may owe something to the practical mind' of Ralegh, 'reaching out towards the coming era of business and banking' (ed. H. E. Sandison, *The Poems of Sir Arthur Gorges*, 1953, p. xxvi). In its turn, Gorges's scheme may have influenced Hartlib's office of addresses.

[5] Ralegh, *Works*, ii. 343, 351, 353.

[6] Ralegh, *History*, i, pp. xxxiii–xxxiv; cf. p. 67; ii. 134–5; *Works*, i. 125; ii. 319.

go-between.[1] Sir Thomas Smith lent him money.[2] Sir Thomas Myddelton financed some of his voyages.[3] Sir Arthur Ingram was interested in Guiana, though unkindly spoken of by Ralegh.[4] In many ways Ralegh made himself the spokesman of the merchants' interests. Against the still prevalent snobbery of the landed class, he pointed out that 'all the nobility and gentry in Europe trade their grass and corn and cattle, their vines and their fruits. . . . The King of Spain is now the greatest merchant.'[5]

Ralegh noted the absence of a rich nobility in the Netherlands.[6] Dutch merchants 'more fully obtained there their purposes by their convenient privileges and settled constitutions' than in England; and he listed the reforms needed to bring commercial advantages to England—lower customs (which would increase total royal revenue),[7] free access for foreign merchants, stimulus to home manufactures and fishing, ending of the privileges of the Merchant Adventurers, a Navigation Act, taking regular and constant advice from merchants. It is an economic programme which the next two generations carried out.[8] Like Mun, Ralegh praised the low customs and 'great and pleasing privileges' of merchants at Leghorn.[9] He urged the use of state power to protect merchants' interests.[10] Ralegh wanted governments 'to allure and encourage the people for their private gain to be all workers and erectors of a commonwealth'.[11]

Above all Ralegh had grasped the commercial importance of sea power. 'Whosoever commands the sea, commands the

---

[1] D. B. Quinn, 'Ralegh's American Colonies', in Essays in Honour of J. E. Todd, ed. H. A. Cronne, T. W. Moody, and D. B. Quinn (1949), p. 76; Waters, Art of Navigation in England, pp. 190, 197. Sanderson gave financial assistance to Ralegh's protégé Hues, as well as to Robert Hood and Emery Molyneux. See pp. 42–43 above.

[2] Ed. Quinn, The Roanoke Voyages, ii. 544.

[3] E. D. Jones, 'An Account Book of Sir Thomas Myddelton, 1583–1603', National Library of Wales Journal, i. 83; G. M. Griffiths, 'An Account Book of Ralegh's Voyage, 1592', ibid. vii. 352.

[4] A. F. Upton, Sir Arthur Ingram (1961), p. 5; Ralegh, Works, i. 234.

[5] Ibid. i. 276–7.   [6] Ibid. ii. 15.

[7] This point was repeated by Sir John Eliot in the Commons in 1624 (J. Forster, Sir John Eliot, 1865, i. 168–70).

[8] Ralegh, Works, ii. 112–36; cf. pp. 89–90, 317–20.

[9] Ibid. ii. 119; Mun, Englands Treasure by Forraign Trade, in Early English Tracts on Commerce (ed. J. R. McCulloch, 1856), p. 139; cf. Lewes Roberts, The Treasure of Traffike (1641), ibid., pp. 91–92.

[10] Ralegh, Works, ii. 31–32.   [11] Ibid. ii. 135.

trade,' he proclaimed; 'whosoever commands the trade of the world, commands the riches of the world, and consequently the world itself.'[1] 'The very binding cause of amity between all kings, princes, and states is their trade and intercourse of their subjects.'[2] It is not surprising that it was a rich City merchant who after Ralegh's execution said that his head would do better on the shoulders of Secretary Naunton.[3]

On many occasions Ralegh noted passages disapproving of arbitrary taxes.[4] He spoke for a rationalization of the English system of taxation, with its absurd under-assessment of the aristocracy. In 1593 he had opposed a survey of men's taxable wealth, on the characteristic ground that it might damage men's credits.[5] Yet in 1601, when Francis Bacon made a smug reference to the excellence of the English system of taxation, Ralegh retorted 'call you this *par jugum*, when a poor man pays as much as a rich? And peradventure his estate is no better than it is set at, or but little better? When our estates that are three or four pounds in the Queen's book, it is not the hundredth part of our wealth.'[6] On this and other occasions Ralegh made himself the spokesman not only of the merchants, but of the middling sort in general. The criticism of gentlemen sea-captains attributed to him was quoted by Samuel Pepys in 1681.[7]

> Not Caesar's birth made Caesar to survive
> But Caesar's virtues, which are yet alive.[8]

This impeccable Protestant sentiment, rather secularized in the application to Caesar, appears frequently in Ralegh's writings.[9]

---

[1] Ralegh, *Works*, ii. 80. Cf. the very similar opinion expressed by Bacon in his Essay 'Of the True Greatness of Kingdoms and Estates', and in *Considerations touching a War with Spain* (*Works*, xiv. 499–500).   [2] Ralegh, *Works*, i. 263.

[3] *Letters of John Chamberlain*, ii. 178; Osborn, *Traditional Memoirs*, in *Secret History of the Court of James I*, i. 162.

[4] Ralegh, *Works*, i. 232–5, 238–41; cf. pp. 14, 55–56, 71, 96.

[5] D'Ewes, *Journals*, p. 492.

[6] Townshend, *Historical Collections*, p. 204. Cf. Fulke Greville in 1593: 'The poor are grieved by being over-charged; this must be helped by increasing our own burthen; for otherwise the weak feet will complain of too heavy a body: that is to be feared. If the feet knew their strength as well as we know their oppression, they would not bear as they do' (*Parliamentary History of England*, 1806, i. 822).

[7] A. Bryant, *Samuel Pepys: the Years of Peril* (1952), p. 284; Ralegh, *Works*, ii. 92.   [8] Ralegh, *Poems* (ed. A. M. C. Latham), p. 53.

[9] Ralegh, *History*, i, p. xxi; ii. 16–17. Cf. pp. 266–8 below.

Even a poem like *The Lie* embodies an economic attitude which might commend itself to Puritan business men. For Ralegh, in stressing the differences between principles and practice, said

> Tell them that brave it most
> They buy far more by spending.

Men spent large sums in conspicious consumption at court, in the hope of acquiring office or favour. The money might have been more profitably invested, and the apparent glamour surrounding the monarch was a sham:

> Say to the Court it glows
> And shines like rotten wood.

Ralegh often went out of his way to pay tribute to labour.[1] A vagabond is 'a man without protection, and cast out from the favour of God': here Ralegh agreed with William Perkins.[2] With vagabonds are to be contrasted 'the needy and labouring souls' who have Ralegh's sympathy. Ralegh indeed thought poverty a deplorable state, 'a vexation of every worthy spirit'.[3] He urged his son to 'strive . . . to make good thy station in the upper deck; those that live under hatches are ordained to be drudges and slaves'.[4] But he was not without sympathy for 'the meanest sort of people', who formed the rank and file of armies, and 'must either die for 8*d.* wages or if he live with many wounds, perchance beg all his life after'. Ralegh put words into such a man's mouth not unlike those which Winstanley was to use in 1649: 'Let the rich fight for themselves. What have we to do, who lived miserably in peace, and must now also die for those that have [furnished] themselves with plenty?'[5]

Indeed Ralegh had a powerful, if not original, sense of the corrupting power of gold, worthy of Spenser's picture of

---

[1] Ibid. i. 98; *Works*, ii. 319, cf. p. 326.

[2] *History*, i. 154; cf. W. Perkins, *Workes* (1609–13), i. 755, iii. 92, 191, 539; and see my *Puritanism and Revolution*, pp. 227–8.

[3] Ralegh, *Works*, ii. 352–4.

[4] Quoted by A. M. C. Latham, 'Sir Walter Ralegh's *Instructions to his Son*', in *Elizabethan and Jacobean Studies presented to F. P. Wilson* (1959), p. 208.

[5] Pierre Lefranc, 'Un inédit de Ralegh', *Études Anglaises*, viii. 205–6; cf. G. Winstanley, *An Appeale to all Englishmen* (1650), in Sabine, op. cit., p. 414.

Mammon or Timon himself. Spanish gold 'purchaseth intelligence, creepeth into councils, and setteth bound loyalty at
liberty in the greatest monarchies of Europe'.[1] The man who
ruined himself in the search for gold came ultimately to long for

> Heaven's bribeless hall,
> Where no corrupted voices brawl;
> No conscience molten into gold,
> No forged accuser bought and sold.[2]

Despite his cynical advice to his son, Ralegh himself married
for love.

VII

The confusion about Ralegh's 'atheism' has been cleared up
by Professor Strathmann, as it was for Ralegh's contemporaries
by the *History of the World*. But I believe Professor Strathmann
rather overstates the case, as Ralegh himself did.[3] Ralegh was
certainly no atheist: his contemporary reputation as such began
in Jesuit propaganda, seizing on Ralegh's known interest in
science, his anti-Aristoteleanism, his open questioning mind,
his pleasure in shocking the conventionally pious. It is the sort
of smear that was normally put upon daringly original thinkers
like Ralegh and Hariot and Marlowe. In 1595 Ralegh went
'daily to hear sermons',[4] and the Rev. Richard Hakluyt always
assumed that he was a good Christian.[5] He was given a testimony of orthodoxy by the clergyman who attended him in his
last hours. He patronized the Puritan Hugh Broughton.

Ralegh liked to shock parsons. 'But we have principles in

---

[1] Ralegh, *Works*, ii. 149.   [2] Ralegh, *Poems*, p. 50.
[3] Cf. p. 191 below.
[4] *MS. Lord de l'Isle and Dudley* (H.M.C.), ii. 173.
[5] Strathmann, *Sir Walter Ralegh*, pp. 21–26. We do not know how close was
Ralegh's association with Marlowe, of which Miss Bradbrook makes much in *The
School of Night* (1936); nor is there much positive evidence that Marlowe was anything more than a perpetrator of rash phrases to shock the respectable. That
Francis Kett, who may have been Marlowe's tutor, was burnt *on a charge* of atheism
in 1589 hardly convicts Marlowe, still less Ralegh. Fear of atheism seems to have
been at its height in the early fifteen-nineties, when the government's campaign
against the sectaries was under way (see M. Maclure, *The Paul's Cross Sermons*,
Toronto, 1958, pp. 79–80). By 1633 Ralegh himself could be quoted in a sermon at
Paul's Cross (ibid., p. 150).

our mathematics', he snapped at the Rev. Ralph Ironside when the latter became circular in his attempt to prove the existence of God and the soul.[1] Clearly Ralegh had no strong feelings about dogma. In company with Essex he intervened in 1591 to save John Udall, who had been sentenced to death in the government's terror campaign against religious radicals. Udall appealed to Elizabeth for clemency through Ralegh, and received a pardon in 1592. He died in prison a year later, whilst proposals that he should be allowed to go to Syria for the Turkey merchants were being debated.[2] Ralegh's action in this case showed considerable courage, since Udall was no ordinary religious radical: he was believed to be linked with the authors of the seditious Marprelate Tracts. In the Parliament of 1593 Ralegh spoke up for the Brownists, whose numbers he estimated at 20,000. His opposition was to condemning men for their opinions. 'What danger may grow to ourselves if this law pass, it were fit to be considered', he said, especially when a jury 'shall be judges what another man means'.[3] Ralegh likewise opposed 'giving authority to a mere churchwarden to compel men to come to church'.[4]

Ralegh indeed hunted down papists in the fifteen-nineties, but this was for political reasons: he regarded them as agents of his main enemy, Spain. He spent a night amicably discussing theology with at least one Jesuit, and offered to intervene on his behalf; but he prevented the same Jesuit from speaking to the crowd which came to witness his execution.[5] He had at one time a secretary who was a papist.

Ralegh, in short, seems to have had the sort of tolerance born of indifference which finally triumphed in 1689. We may compare Bacon's erastian tolerance. Despite, or because of, Ralegh's own participation in the French religious wars between 1569 and 1575, he abhorred 'war, massacres, and murders for religion', by which 'we are all in effect become comedians in

---

[1] Ed. Harrison, *Willobie His Avisa*, p. 267. All the relevant documents on Ralegh's 'school of atheism' are collected here.

[2] *H.M.C., Second Report, Appendix*, p. 43; Strype, *Life of Whitgift* (1822), ii. 98–102.

[3] D'Ewes, *Journals*, p. 517.

[4] H. Townshend, *Historical Collections* (1680), pp. 320–1.

[5] *Records of the English Province of the Society of Jesus* (1878), iii. 462; Strathmann, *Sir Walter Ralegh*, pp. 35–39. Another example of Ralegh trying to save a priest is in Williams, *Sir Walter Ralegh*, pp. 103–4.

religion'.[1] Allegations that he was an atheist may have been put about in the fifteen-nineties in order to discredit a man who had close connexions with the Puritans.[2] Even in the *History of the World* Ralegh still thought it necessary to rebut the charge that he was a Puritan.[3] He vindicated his orthodoxy against those 'mad dogs' who 'condemn all such in the pride of their zeal, as atheists and infidels, that are not transported with the like intemperate ignorance'. Hardly better were those who, 'when they themselves cannot touch a man in open and generous opposition, will wound him secretly by the malicious virtue of an hypocrite'.[4]

Nevertheless, the fact remains that some of Ralegh's writings —notably the *Instructions to his Son*—are more compatible with deism than Christianity. There are few references to Christ in the *History*.[5] The Ten Commandments define the necessary bonds of society, which would have to be observed for reasons of Hobbist expediency, 'if there were not any religion nor judgement to come'.[6] Ralegh indulged in textual criticism of the Bible, if of rather an elementary kind; and discouraged excessive literalism of interpretation.[7] He condemned the Romish practice of blindly maintaining 'whatsoever they have been formerly known to hold and believe'.[8] Many Catholic practices, like image-worship, had been borrowed from the pagans.[9]

Hariot's and Ralegh's reports of the New World may have done something to stimulate interest in comparative religion, and also primitivist ideas. 'We found the people most gentle, loving, and faithful, void of all guile and treason, and such as live after the manner of the golden age', said Ralegh.[10] Hariot's *Brief and True Report* on Virginia contained a serious account of

[1] Ralegh, *History*, i, pp. xxix–xxx; cf. *Works*, ii. 34, 39, 55. It may have been in France that Ralegh first became acquainted with the daring and fashionable speculations of Pomponazzi's school of atheism (G. T. Buckley, *Atheism in the English Renaissance*, 1932, pp. 151–2).

[2] Strathmann, op. cit., pp. 35–39.

[3] *History*, vi. 97. Cf. Ralegh's criticisms of Familists, Anabaptists, and Brownists, ibid. ii. 352.

[4] Ibid. ii. 505.   [5] Strathmann, op. cit., p. 137.

[6] *History*, ii. 331–4.

[7] Ibid. ii. 63, 75–79, 85–89, 158, 231, 257, &c.

[8] Ibid. ii. 206. Ralegh showed his independence in his attitude to the Geneva Bible, whose versions he sometimes accepted, sometimes rejected (*History*, i. 132, 225; ii. 4, 371).

[9] Ibid. ii. 143.   [10] Hakluyt, *Principal Navigations*, vi. 128.

native religion and customs. We might well follow the example of their healthful moderation in eating. 'They are untroubled by the desire to pile up riches for their children, and live in perfect contentment with each other, sharing all those things which God hath so bountifully provided them. Yet', Hariot continued, not surely entirely innocently, 'they do not render Him the thanks which His providence deserves.' Whether or not their priests use religion as a deliberate instrument of policy, the fact remains that 'the belief in heaven and the fiery pit makes the simple folk give strict obedience to their governors, and behave with great care, so that they may avoid torment after death and enjoy bliss'.[1]

'Certain hellish verses devised by that atheist and traitor Rawley', in the *Bath MSS.*, contain an account of the simultaneous origin of the family, private property, and the state, and of the deliberate invention of religion as

> bugbears to keep the world in fear
> And make them quietly the yoke to bear,
> So that religion of itself a fable
> Was only found to make that peaceable.

There was no life after death.[2] But there is no reason to suppose that the attribution to Ralegh is correct.[3]

VIII

Ralegh illustrates the intimate connexion between early science and historical studies. Dee in 1556 tried to persuade Queen Mary to take action 'to discover and preserve ancient writings and monuments', and to found a national library to house them. He tried again with Cecil in 1574, equally unsuccessfully.[4] Robert Recorde edited Fabyan's *Chronicles* and had a large collection of historical manuscripts; Sir Philip Sidney, Sir Henry Billingsley, Lord Lumley, Sir George Buc, and Edward Brerewood, Gresham Professor of Astronomy, were all

---

[1] Hariot, *A Brief and True Report*, in *The New World* (ed. S. Lorant, 1954), pp. 250, 268.
[2] *Bath MSS.* (H.M.C.), ii. 52–53.
[3] Ralegh, *Poems* (ed. Latham), p. 173.
[4] Ed. J. Crossley, *Autobiographical Tracts of Dr. John Dee* (Chetham Miscellany, i. 1851), pp. 46–49; Fussner, *The Historical Revolution*, p. 90. Dee lived long enough to correspond with Sir Robert Cotton (C. Fell Smith, *John Dee*, 1909, p. 265).

members of the Society of Antiquaries.[1] The Oxford mathematician Thomas Allen was also an antiquary. Sir Henry Savile, founder of chairs of geometry and astronomy at Oxford, translated Tacitus and edited St. John Chrysostom. The combination of scientific and antiquarian interests was repeated in John Hall, would-be scientific reformer of the universities, who wanted to have a library of historical manuscripts created,[2] in Sir Thomas Browne and many of the early Fellows of the Royal Society, like Pepys, Evelyn, and Aubrey. Anthony Wood took lessons in chemistry from a protégé of Boyle's, and gave the title *Britannia Baconica* to his collection of rarities.[3] Sir Edward Coke, the main proponent of Parliamentarian historical theory, had an astonishing number of scientific books in his library—Billingsley's *Euclide*, works by Boorde, Recorde, Dee, Digges, Gilbert, Hues, Blundeville, Bacon, and others.[4] The historical method of Sir Henry Spelman, we are told by the chronicler of *The Historical Revolution*, is that of the natural sciences.[5] Ralegh and Selden[6] were historians keenly interested in science, Bacon one of the greatest of our early historians as well as the prophet of the scientific movement. Shakespeare himself was much possessed by history, and in this as in so many other respects he was typical of his age, or responding to it. One play in five in the two decades after the Armada was drawn from English history: such plays were produced exclusively at the popular theatres.[7] The vogue for books on history seems to have reached a peak in the fifteen-nineties.[8]

There are two main reasons for the importance of history in our period. First, by the early seventeenth century the crisis in intellectual life had penetrated the writing of history. The easy patriotism of the Elizabethans, of Foxe and Holinshed,

---

[1] See pp. 132–8, 18, 78, 62, 51–52 above. For Sidney's friend Daniel Rogers, antiquarian geographer, see p. 134 above.

[2] J. Hall, *An Humble Motion*, p. 36; cf. pp. 88–89, 122–3 above.

[3] Ed. P. Bliss, *Life of Wood* (1848), pp. 134–6; Ornstein, *The Role of Scientific Societies in the 17th century*, p. 42.

[4] Hassall, *Catalogue of the Library of Sir Edward Coke* (Yale Law Library Publications no. 12, 1950), pp. 46–85. Some of these books may have come from Sir Christopher Hatton's library when Coke married his son's widow.

[5] Fussner, op. cit., pp. 100–2, 116, 305–21; cf. pp. 94, 105–6.

[6] For Selden see ibid., Chapter XI, *passim*.

[7] F. Schelling, *Elizabethan Drama, 1558–1642* (New York, 1908), i. 251–2; Harbage, *Shakespeare and the Rival Traditions*, pp. 85, 260.

[8] E. L. Klotz, 'A Subject Analysis of English Imprints for every tenth year 1480–1640', *H.L.Q*. i. 418.

had worn thin. The contrast between the monarch as symbol of the independent English commonwealth, and the actual occupants of the throne, was too marked. Already in Marlowe's *Tamburlaine the Great* and *Edward II*, in Shakespeare's Histories and some of his Tragedies, we note a divergence between the divinity that doth hedge a king and the all too human attributes of some monarchs. Translations of Greek and Roman historians had brought about a shift in readers' assumptions about the nature of the state:[1] the influence of Machiavelli, Guicciardini, and other Italian historians worked in the same direction. Many of the translations from the Italian which Leicester patronized were of historical writings. Leicester himself, we are told, was a devoted reader of history, and relied on historians for help in solving problems of government.[2] By the time of Ralegh and Bacon historians had to meet a new sophistication in their readers, and could no longer afford to shirk fundamental moral problems. The patriotic and theological assumptions of Tudor historians were not openly repudiated; but they were now qualified by sceptical acceptance of the tendency of all government to become corrupt.[3]

Secondly, history was an issue in the universities, where it played a role similar to that of sociology today—popular with most undergraduates and some dons, suspected by the

---

[1] Conley, *The First English Translators of the Classics*, pp. 62–63.

[2] T. Blundeville, *The True order and Methode of writing and reading Hystorie* (1574), sig. A 2, quoted by H. G. Dick, 'Thomas Blundeville's *The True order* . . .', *H.L.Q.* iii. 154–5. Blundeville's book was an adaptation and abridgement of Francesco Patrizzi's *Della Historia Dieci Dialoghi* (Venice, 1560), and of an unpublished work on history presented by Acontius to Leicester (Dick, op. cit., pp. 149–50; see also Einstein, *The Italian Renaissance in England*, pp. 309–13, for the importance of Blundeville's book in the development of English theories of history. It may well have influenced Ralegh). Blundeville (see p. 38 above) was a friend of Acontius, who is of considerable significance in the history of religious toleration in England (W. K. Jordan, *The Development of Religious Toleration in England*, i. 1932, 303–65). Acontius's *Sathanae Stratagemata*, translated into English in 1648 under the auspices of John Goodwin, Hartlib, and Dury, had a good deal of influence on the Independents (B. Gustafsson, *The Five Dissenting Brethren*, Lund, 1955, pp. 103–12). Acontius was a skilled engineer, land drainer, and inventor, as well as an anti-Aristotelean. His thesis of preliminary doubt is interestingly close to the positions of Bacon and Descartes: Patrizzi was 'one of Bacon's forerunners in the method of experimental research' and an opponent of Aristotle (Einstein, op. cit., p. 309).

[3] The above paragraph draws upon ideas contained in W. M. Merchant's 'Lord Herbert of Cherbury and seventeenth century historical writing', *Trans. of the Hon. Soc. of Cymmrodorion*, 1956, pp. 52–55. Cf. Fussner, *The Historical Revolution*, esp. pp. xxii, 17–19, 55–59, 99–100, 213. Mr. Fussner emphasizes especially the new middle-class reading public for history.

established authorities. Sidney recommended the study of history to his brother Robert in 1580.[1] Bacon tried in his will to set up lectureships at Cambridge, but did not leave enough money. His friend Fulke Greville did establish a history lectureship in 1628, and Bacon's influence is clear in the instructions which he drew up. No one in holy orders was to be eligible. No Englishman was thought competent to hold it, and Isaac Dorislaus, a doctor of civil law from Leiden University, was appointed the first lecturer. He at once ran into political trouble for assuming that 'what they hear with applause' in the republican Netherlands 'might as freely be spoken' in England.[2] After Dorislaus's first lecture the course was suppressed by the efforts of the Laudians, because of Dorislaus's alleged hostility to monarchy.[3] Twenty-one years later he was assassinated by royalists for the same reason. In between he had won the friendship of Selden and Lord Wharton as well as of Lord Brooke, had been employed in the diplomatic service of Parliament, was Judge-Advocate of the Earl of Essex's army during the civil war, judge of the Court of Admiralty (1648), and had taken part in the trial of Charles I. Although Clarendon was wrong to say that Dorislaus was a Gresham professor,[4] his son became a Fellow of the Royal Society. Dorislaus's one lecture, and his silencing, seem to have made a strong impression on at least one young Cambridge man—John Milton.[5]

In Oxford the struggles were less exciting. In 1622 Camden endowed a readership. The first reader, at Camden's suggestion, was Degory Wheare, a friend of the third Earl of Pembroke, of Sir Benjamin Rudyerd, and of Francis Rous (later Speaker of the Barebones Parliament) as well as the tutor and friend of John Pym.[6] Wheare, who preferred Ralegh 'before all other

---

[1] Sidney, *Complete Works* (ed. Feuillerat), iii. 130–2.

[2] J. B. Mullinger, *The University of Cambridge from . . . 1626 to the decline of the Platonist Movement* (1911), pp. 88–89.

[3] R. Parr, *Life of . . . Usher*, pp. 393–4. Brooke continued to pay Dorislaus's stipend and clearly hoped that the lectures might one day be resumed.

[4] See p. 59 above.

[5] In Milton's *Fifth Prolusion* a series of historical examples is followed by an attack on suppression of truth; in the *Seventh Prolusion*, by a criticism of 'our bad methods of teaching the arts'. Cf. the *Third Prolusion*.

[6] W. H. Allison, 'The first endowed Professorship of History and its first Incumbent', *American Historical Review*, xxvii. 733–7; H. S. Jones, 'The Foundation and History of the Camden Chair', *Oxoniensia*, vii. 169–79.

historians', was a staunch Calvinist, a supporter of Hakewill, and Principal of Gloucester Hall from 1626 to 1647.[1] Against the wishes of the university, Camden persevered in his original intention that his reader should lecture on civil history: nevertheless there were squabbles about this between Wheare and the university authorities.[2] In view of this and of Cambridge's experience, it is hardly surprising to find the Laudian statutes of 1636 insisting that the history reader is to lecture 'in historians of ancient date and repute'.[3]

History was still a subject in which, as Ralegh ruefully put it, it was dangerous 'to follow truth too near the heels'.[4] Leicester had protected historians, but towards the end of Elizabeth's reign Sir John Hayward got into trouble for his *Life of Henry IV*, and Sir Francis Hubert's verse *Historie of Edward the Second* was 'by supremest authority forbidden to be printed'. From 1599 all English histories had to be authorized by a Privy Councillor: Drayton removed from *Englands Heroicall Epistles* any passages which could have been interpreted to refer to contemporary events.[5] Under James I the Society of Antiquaries fell into disfavour and ceased to meet. Attempts to revive it (under George Hakewill's lawyer brother) were 'misliked' by the King, even though assurances were given that no matters of state or religion would be discussed.[6] Under Charles, Sir Robert Cotton and Sir Edward Coke, as well as Dorislaus, suffered for saying the wrong things about the past. Even Viscount Falkland, Lord Deputy of Ireland, left his

---

[1] Aubrey, *Brief Lives*, ii. 191; Hakewill, *Apologie*, sig. C 1–C 2. The success of Wheare's *Method and Order of Reading History* testifies to public interest in the subject (five Latin editions beteeen 1623 and 1684, three English translations before the end of the century). It was still in use as a textbook at Cambridge at the beginning of the eighteenth century. History, Wheare thought, was 'moral philosophy clothed in examples'. In his lectures he drew parallels between events in Roman history and those of modern times. (Cf. Fussner op. cit., pp. 165, 169–70.) For Wheare and Ralegh see p. 211 below.

[2] Curtis, op. cit., p. 117.

[3] F. Watson, *The Beginnings of the Teaching of Modern Subjects in England*, p. 52.

[4] Ralegh, *History*, i, p. lviii.

[5] Ed. B. Mellor, *The Poems of Sir Francis Hubert* (Hong Kong, 1961), pp. xx–xxi, 301.

[6] Joan Evans, *A History of the Society of Antiquaries* (1956), p. 13; ed. L. Fox, *English Historical Scholarship in the 16th and 17th Centuries* (1956), p. 52. Whether Ralegh was or was not a member of the Society is disputed (Evans, op. cit., p. 10). For William Hakewill see p. 199 below.

History of . . . Edward II, written about 1627, unpublished.[1]
The *History of . . . Richard III*, written by Sir George Buc, friend
of Selden, Camden, and Coke, was published posthumously in
1646.[2] Samuel Daniel, who had been in trouble at the end of
Elizabeth's reign, was wise to profess in 1627 his anxiety to
avoid '*Laesa Majestas*, even against dead princes'.[3]

In a sense the Parliamentary opposition's case against the
first two Stuarts was wholly based on history, even if this history
was not always very accurate. A full consideration of the intellectual origins of the English Revolution could not omit the middle-
class historians patronized by Leicester—Grafton, a printer who
dedicated his *Abridgement of the Chronicles of England* to Leicester
in 1562, and his *Manuell of the Chronicles of England* to the Sta-
tioners' Company in 1565, and Stow, a tailor, who dedicated
his *Summaries of the English Chronicles* (1566) to the Lord Mayor
and Aldermen of London, the Merchant Taylors' Company,
and 'all the commons' of London, and his *Chronicles of England*
(1580) to Leicester. The second edition of Holinshed was dedicated, *inter alios*, to Leicester and Ralegh. Stow had a pension
from the Merchant Taylors; Speed was also a tailor. Fulke
Greville succeeded to Leicester's patronage of Speed and
Camden.[4] Nor could it omit the legal antiquarianism of Sir
Edward Coke.[5] I have tried to discuss one aspect of the historical
approach to politics in the seventeenth century elsewhere.[6]

Leaving the antiquarians aside, we come to an even more
influential book—John Foxe's *Acts and Monuments*. There were
nine editions of this massive work between 1563 and 1641, and
two more before 1684. Three abridgements were published
before 1615, one by Sidney's protégé, the popular scientific
writer Timothy Bright, another dedicated to Archbishop Abbott
and Coke.[7] Though Elizabeth thought Foxe too radical to

[1] It was published in 1680. Falkland's approach suggests the influence of Ralegh.
[2] Eccles, 'Sir George Buc', in *Thomas Lodge and other Elizabethans* (ed. Sisson), pp.
474–5, 505. See pp. 62, 173 above.
[3] C. H. Firth, *Essays, Historical and Literary* (1938), pp. 57, 59.
[4] Rosenberg, *Leicester, Patron of Letters*, pp. 64, 72; cf. pp. 81–92 for other
historical works dedicated to or patronized by Leicester.
[5] Books on history were acquired by Coke more steadily throughout his life than
on any other subject (Hassall, *Catalogue of the Library of Sir Edward Coke*, p. xx).
[6] See *The Norman Yoke* in my *Puritanism and Revolution* pp. 50–122.
[7] Wright, *Middle-Class Culture in Elizabethan England*, pp. 333–4. For Bright see
pp. 69, 75, 133 above. Foxe was a friend of Sir Thomas Gresham.

receive ecclesiastical promotion, she and her archbishops encouraged churches and parsons to buy either the *Acts and Monuments* or Bright's ultra-patriotic abridgement.[1] Foxe did much to form the mythology which saw Englishmen as God's chosen people courageously defending His truth through the centuries. Foxe was extensively used by Hakluyt; and we saw above[2] how Gellibrand suffered for following him. There are plenty of echoes of Foxe in men as different as William Prynne and John Milton.[3] In the sixteenth century Foxe saw Antichrist personified in Spain, and it was the anti-Spanish aspect of his patriotism which was most useful to the officially encouraged legend. The sermons which Houses of Commons in the seventeenth century used to order for 5 November drew on a hatred of Spanish and popish cruelty which Foxe had made familiar to all Englishmen. No wonder Laud disparaged him and refused to allow his works to be reprinted.[4] Yet Foxe's is no narrow patriotism. The English Church was part of the international Church, even though in most other countries that Church was oppressed. Englishmen had international as well as patriotic duties.[5]

In addition to its patriotic appeal, the *Acts and Monuments* had radical overtones. The godly remnant who defended Christ's truth at the cost of their own lives were shown in Foxe's book— as they had been in reality—as mostly springing from the humblest of the people. For Shakespeare the original sin which led to the tribulations of the fifteenth century and the Wars of the Roses was the deposition of Richard II: for Foxe it was the rejection of Wyclif and the Lollards. Yet the story ended happily with the triumph of Protestantism. This point was noted by radical English revolutionaries, and it did much to fortify them. Governor Bradford and Winstanley quoted Foxe.[6] Lilburne, Walwyn, and Overton looked back to Marian martyrs and medieval heretics as their direct ancestors. Cromwell

[1] J. F. Mozley, *John Foxe and his Book* (1940), p. 147; ed. H. R. Wilton Hall, *Records of the Old Archdeaconry of St. Albans* (St. Albans and Herts. Architectural and Archaeological Soc., 1908), p. 72.   [2] See p. 57 above.
[3] W. M. Lamont, *Marginal Prynne*, pp. 16, 31, 47; Milton, *Areopagitica, passim.*
[4] Laud, *Works* (1847–60), iv. 226. Cf. p. 212 below.
[5] W. Haller, *Foxe's Book of Martyrs and the Elect Nation* (1963), *passim.*
[6] W. Bradford, *History of Plymouth Plantation* (Massachusetts Historical Soc. Collections, 4th Series, iii), p. 3; Winstanley, *The Breaking of the Day of God* (1649), p. 133.

at Naseby saw his troops as 'a company of poor ignorant men', but he had 'assurance of victory, because God would by things that are not, bring to nought the things that are'.[1] Cromwell may have got that assurance from his schoolmaster, Doctor Thomas Beard: but Beard's *Theatre of Gods Judgments . . . specially against the most eminent Persons in the World whose exorbitant power had broke through the barres of Divine and Human Law* (1597) was in the Foxe tradition.[2]

The appeal of Beard's book was to a relatively unsophisticated popular audience, and its political lesson was clear and specific. 'If you be mighty, puissant and fearful, know that the Lord is greater than you, for he is almighty, all-terrible, and all-fearful: in what place soever you are, he is always above you, ready to hurl you down and overturn you, to break, quash, and crush you in pieces as pots of earth.'[3] Yet, though it is a much more subtle and sophisticated work, not dissimilar lessons could be drawn from Ralegh's *History of the World*. Ralegh must have known his Foxe well, since the martyrologist tells a story of Sir Walter's mother. Like Foxe and Shakespeare, Ralegh drew lessons from English history: and the severity of his judgements on kings from Henry I to Henry VIII amply justified James I's remark that Ralegh was 'too saucy in censuring princes'.[4]

IX

Yet, though history is for Ralegh too the theatre of God's judgements, it is much more than that. God represents the principle of law in history. Unlike Beard, Ralegh does not show God directly intervening to smite the sinner: he shows the ineluctable working out of cause and effect at the human level, so that evil actions ultimately but inevitably produce evil consequences for the doer. Already in 1591 Ralegh had seen the

[1] W. C. Abbott, *The Writings and Speeches of Oliver Cromwell* (Harvard U.P. 1937–47), i. 365. Cf. Rushworth, 'this poor condemned army', 'this despised army' (ed. H. G. Tibbutt, *The Letter-Books of Sir Samuel Luke, 1644–5*, 1963, pp. 566, 571).

[2] Title-page of the 1648 edition, the fourth since 1597. This edition contains a second part by Thomas Taylor, the Puritan.

[3] Op. cit., p. 412. Cf. pp. 9–10, and Chapter XLIX *passim*, 'How rare and geason good Princes have been at all times'.

[4] *History*, i. viii–xv, xxviii–xxxviii. Though the *History* stops with the second Macedonian War, there is a great deal of medieval history, especially English, in the Preface, in the *Prerogative of Parliaments*, *A Discourse touching a War with Spain*, *A Discourse of the Origin . . . of . . . War* and in the two *Discourses* touching royal marriages.

defeat of the Armada as God's verdict 'against the ambitious and bloody pretences of the Spaniard, who seeking to devour all nations, are themselves devoured'.[1] Bacon separated science from theology by pushing God upstairs after he had established the laws of motion for the universe. In exactly the same way Ralegh's emphasis on law looks forward to the Newtonians: Ralegh even used the metaphor of winding up a clock to describe God's relation to his universe.[2] Ralegh secularized history not by denying God the first cause,[3] but by concentrating his vision on secondary causes *and insisting that they are sufficient in themselves for historical explanation.* 'To say that God was pleased to have it so, were a true but an idle answer (for His secret will is the cause of all things). . . . Wherefore we may boldly look into the second causes', which Ralegh proceeded to do in respect of the development of Jewish history.[4]

The emphasis on second causes was suspect and sometimes led to accusations of atheism—e.g. against doctors who emphasized dirt rather than God's wrath as the explanation of plague; or those who looked for natural causes in illnesses which were more easily diagnosed as diabolic possession. Throughout the period with which we are dealing many members of the medical profession were slowly but perseveringly striving to eject the supernatural from medicine. Lip service still had to be done to the first cause, and may have been meant; but in practice it was second causes that mattered. 'All Christian men must pray to God to be their defence', said William Bullein in listing the remedies against plague; 'then one must make a fire in every chimney within the house.'[5] A Puritan divine,

[1] *The Last fight of* The Revenge, in Hakluyt, *Principal Navigations*, v. 11; cf. Laurence Kemyis, *The Second Voyage of Guiana*, ibid. vii. 388.
[2] Ralegh, *History*, i. 28.
[3] Indeed at the beginning of the *History* he goes out of his way to say the opposite, to the confusion of commentators who have read little further than Book I (ibid., pp. 28–29).
[4] Ibid. ii. 214; cf. p. 587: 'If we seek the material and politic causes. . . .' Cf. i. 33–35, iii. 205–7, 261–7, iv. 343. An early example of the phrase 'second cause' is in Sidney's *Defence of Poesie* (J. C. Maxwell, *Notes and Queries*, June 1962, pp. 218–19. I am indebted to Mr. Maxwell for drawing my attention to this note). Although written about 1580, the *Defence of Poesie* was not published until 1595. For use of the phrase in print in 1580 see next page.
[5] W. Bullein, *The Government of Health* (1595), p. 30v, quoted in Kocher, *Science and Religion in Elizabethan England*, p. 275; cf. pp. 109–13. This paragraph is largely drawn from Professor Kocher's book.

William Fulke, wrote a treatise to demonstrate 'the natural causes of all kind of meteors', so often treated as supernatural events. Thomas Twyne insisted that 'God worketh evermore by second causes unless He worketh miracles which are against the common course of nature'.[1] In 1609 Robert Gray complained that 'amongst us at this day, if any strange accidents do happen, either in the air, or in the earth, or in the waters, . . . we refer them to some material cause or other, being unwilling (as it were) to acknowledge God to have a hand in this'.[2] Yet the battle was by no means won. As late as 1654 an opponent of the new science condemned the 'presumption, if not impiety, in taking men off from [God], the first, to ascribe all or too much to Nature and second causes'.[3] He was, of course, opposing reform of the universities.

As soon as theocentric history is replaced by a history which stresses second causes, consequences follow. It becomes important to ascertain how, at the human level, effects follow causes. Time and experience teach us these lessons, and they are accessible to all. 'The cheese-wife knoweth, as well as the philosopher, that sour rennet doth coagulate her milk into a curd.' Nevertheless, there are 'fundamental laws of human knowledge', and these can be ascertained and tested by reason.[4] Ralegh's emphasis here on the *de facto* knowledge of the practitioners, and the duty of learning from them, is exactly parallel to Bacon's emphasis on the duty of scientists to learn from craftsmen: and when Ralegh claims to be 'not altogether ignorant in the laws of history', he adds that they have been taught by none better than Bacon.[5] In history as in science, the laws which reason discovers may conflict with those traditionally accepted by authority, custom, and precedent. Ralegh attacked Aristotle and his 'verbal doctrine' as vigorously as Bacon did.[6] He was

---

[1] W. Fulke, *A Godly Gallery* (1563, reprinted 1571, 1601, 1602), quoted in Heninger, *A Handbook of Renaissance Meteorology*, p. 21; T. Twyne, *A Shorte Discourse of All Earthquakes in Generall* (1580), quoted by Kocher, op. cit., p. 113. Gabriel Harvey also insisted on the natural origin of earthquakes (Heninger, op. cit., p. 26).

[2] Robert Gray, *An Alarum to England* (1609), sig. C 1, quoted by E. A. Strathmann, 'Ralegh on Natural Philosophy', *Modern Language Quarterly*, i. 53.

[3] Thomas Hall, *Histrio-Mastix* (1654), printed in his *Vindiciae Literarum* (1655), pp. 238-9.   [4] Ralegh, *History*, i, pp. xli-xlii.

[5] *History*, i, p. lvii. Ralegh quotes Bacon on such laws (ibid. iii. 219, v. 354; cf. iv. 353, v. 399-401). Bacon quoted Ralegh in his *Apophthegms*.

[6] *History*, i, pp. xli-xliii, 1.

equally critical of those who preferred 'rather to follow old errors than to examine them', and of 'princes and governors' who do not adapt their policies to changing circumstances.[1] It is 'the end and scope of all history, to teach by example of times past such wisdom as may guide our desires and actions'.[2] 'We may gather out of history a policy no less wise than eternal, by the comparison and application of other men's forepassed miseries, with our own like errors and ill-deservings.'[3] We arrive at useful knowledge by experience, not by scholastic disputation.

Therefore progress and improvement are possible by the use of human reason. Time '(after the Creator of all things) hath by degrees taught all mankind'.[4] Down to Ralegh's time cyclical theories of history had been fashionable: the men of the Renaissance prided themselves on returning to the standards and values of antiquity, the reformers on returning to the primitive church. Foxe breathes an air of optimism, because he saw his century on the upward swing of the cycle. Bodin in 1566 was one of the first to introduce the idea that change might be possible if human beings willed it.[5] But for most of the intellectuals among Ralegh's contemporaries the cyclical theory was a pessimistic one: it put inevitable limits to the possibilities of human advance. (Cyclical theories, Mr. Carr recently suggested, are 'the characteristic ideology of a society in decline'.)[6] Ralegh, like Bacon, was on the side of the Moderns against the Ancients. 'The age of Time hath brought forth stranger and more incredible things than the infancy'—though not all of them were good.[7]

The idea that Ralegh himself held a consistently cyclical theory of history is based on the incorrect attribution to him of *The Cabinet Council*, which in fact consists of extracts from other

---

[1] Ibid. v. 226, vi. 141–2. See pp. 152–3 above.

[2] Quoted by Firth, *Essays Literary and Historical*, p. 41. Up to a point this is traditional Tudor historical doctrine. But 'no one has more abundantly declared the value of history as a teacher of political morals' than Ralegh (L. B. Campbell, 'The Use of Historical Patterns in the Reign of Elizabeth', *H.L.Q.* ii. 138).

[3] *History*, i, p. v. Hakluyt's attitude to history was the same, when he criticized Ralegh's step-brother Sir Humphrey Gilbert for trying to found a colony on a carelessly chosen site and with too little capital behind him. 'Putting all to God and good fortune', 'presuming the cause pretended on God's behalf would carry him to the desired end'. This was an 'intemperate humour' (Hakluyt, *Principal Navigations*, vi. 48).

[4] Ralegh, *History*, iv. 573; cf. v. 63.

[5] Cf. J. B. Bury, *The Idea of Progress* (1920), pp. 39–43.

[6] E. H. Carr, *What is History?* (1961), p. 37.   [7] Ralegh, *History*, v. 572–3.

writers. True, Ralegh thought that in certain respects mankind had deteriorated, and he was shaken by the conclusions of modern astronomy; he shocked Hakewill by some of his remarks; but he also gave that great propagandist for the Moderns against the Ancients many points to quote on the other side,[1] as well as the fact that Ralegh's own historical achievement could be matched against the best of the ancient historians.[2] Ralegh refused to look for a Golden Age in the past. 'He that governs by discourse of former times, shall but take counsel of the dead; for the natures of all things under the sun are subject to change, but the nature of reason only. And it is certain that, in the times of alteration, the wisdom of nature is better than of books.'[3] Humanity may not be able to control the laws which human reason extracts from history. 'God . . . hath given unto man the knowledge of those ways by which kingdoms rise and fall, yet hath left him subject unto the affections which draw on these fatal changes in their times appointed.'[4] But men can, and indeed must (consciously or unconsciously), execute God's sentence, as when L. Aemilius Paulus 'brought the kingdom of Macedon to that end for which God had appointed over it a king so foolish and so cowardly'.[5]

'The judgements of God are for ever unchangeable', Ralegh tells us, and therefore 'those that are wise, or whose wisdom, if it be not great, yet is true and well-grounded, will be able to discern' these laws of history; by the use of a reason not restricted to the 'wise', they will be able consciously to co-operate with them.[6] Milton, Ralegh's great admirer, might have

---

[1] Ralegh, *History*, ii. 113–15, vi. 551; contrast i. 163–6, 176, 204. Hakewill quoted at length Ralegh's rejection of traditional authorities concerning the Flood, and his argument that English soldiers are better than those of Rome or Macedon (*Apologie*, pp. 52, 4, 286, 518; cf. pp. 161, 184, where Ralegh is cited).

[2] In 1648 a royalist newspaper sneered at certain Independent M.P.s as men who despised rhetoric and logic, and preferred Holinshed to Livy. Ralegh would have been a fairer and probably more accurate name to use: but the association of Independents with the Moderns is interesting (*Mercurius Bellicus*, 11–18 April 1648, quoted in J. Frank, *The Beginnings of the English Newspaper*, Harvard U.P., 1961, p. 144).

[3] Ralegh, *Works*, ii. 8; cf. *History*, ii. 113–15, 141, 182, iv. 544–52.

[4] *History*, v. 355.   [5] Ibid. vi. 319.

[6] Ibid. i, pp. vii–viii. Ralegh went on to give other examples drawn from the history of English, Scottish, and other kings. In *The Cabinet Council* the first cause of civil war is destiny, God's providence, about which we can do nothing; but 'touching the second causes of civil war, some remedies may be used', and many

appealed specifically to the example of L. Aemilius Paulus when he said that though it was for God to punish wicked princes, yet God might choose to act through human agents: as He had done on 30 January 1649.[1] Certainly Milton's lines on the endowment of human beings with reason by the Creator— 'And Reason He made right'—are in Ralegh's spirit. Above all, when we contrast Ralegh's attitude with, say, Calvin's, we are conscious of a great advance in historical sense. For Calvin the Jews of the Old Testament do not exist as living individuals: they are characters in an allegorical play which only makes sense because of the morals which the audience reads into it.

This humanization of history was not, of course, original with Ralegh: he found it in Machiavelli, Guicciardini, and many others; he found it in the philosophy of Ramus. Nearer home, Ralegh could have found a plausible atheistic argument based on the independence of second causes elaborated by the wicked Cecropia in Sidney's *Arcadia*.[2] Bacon in 1603 had attacked those who supposed that 'the ignorance of a second cause doth make men more devoutly to depend upon the providence of God, as supposing the effects to come immediately from His hand'. Bacon suggested that the search for final causes had distracted too many scientists away from their real business.[3] Bacon, like Ralegh, admired Machiavelli, and was convinced of the importance of history. 'Knowledges', he wrote, 'are as pyramids, whereof history is the basis.'[4] 'By integrating history into the scientific movement of his day', Professor Fussner writes, 'Bacon lent the weight of his authority to progressive historical practice.'

are then listed (*Works*, ii. 94). Cf. Fulke Greville *Life of Sidney*, pp. 116–17, where the laws of history lead us to expect that England will oust the cruel Spaniards from the New World (and cf. p. 221).

[1] Milton, *Complete Prose Works* (Yale ed.), iii. 211. We may compare Dury's argument in the same year, that the Commonwealth government should be accepted since it had manifestly been God's will that the Parliamentary army should conquer (quoted by P. Zagorin *A History of Political Thought in the English Revolution*, 1954, p. 68). Cf. p. 203 below.

[2] Sidney, *The Countesse of Pembrokes Arcadia* (1590), Book 3, Chapter 10. On second causes cf. F. Greville, *Life of Sidney*, pp. 100, 141.

[3] Bacon, *Works*, iii. 219, 499–503. Cf. William Perkins: God's decree does not jeopardize the 'nature and property of second causes, but only brings them into a certain order; that is, it directeth them to the determinate end' (*A Golden Chaine*, translated by Robert Hill, 1621, p. 31, quoted in H. Baker, *The Wars of Truth*, 1952, p. 22).   [4] Bacon, *Works*, iii. 356.

But he 'contributed to the advancement of history by telling historians what and how they ought to write', rather than by his own practice as an historian.[1] Bacon's attachment to second causes seems more firm than Ralegh's, yet Bacon called in 'the secret providence of God', no less than Ralegh, as soon as he began to write history. Bacon thought that comets, 'out of question', had 'power and effect over the gross and issue of things'. Camden, whom Professor Fussner regards as 'a true Baconian', looked to the conjunction of the stars for historical explanation.[2] Even Clarendon had a belief in the working of divine law in history which was very similar to Ralegh's: 'if God would suffer a lasting union in any notorious wickedness, which He never doth, the world itself would be shaken'.[3]

Ralegh had a knowledge of up-to-date continental sceptical trends, as is shown by his translation of Sextus Empiricus's *The Sceptic*.[4] The distinction between first and second causes was indeed the only way in which Ralegh could keep his fundamental scepticism within bounds. He had a healthy distrust of the evidence he had to use: 'informations are often false, records not always true'; the version that happens to survive may well be one-sided. Even when the facts are well established, motives remain obscure. Historians weary, and lack imagination. The historian then is forced to conjecture; only he must distinguish clearly between conjectures and facts.[5] It could hardly be better put. Ralegh's scepticism of the possibility of arriving at historical truth made him cling to the Biblical certainties. But to put the age of miracles firmly into the past, as Ralegh and so many Protestant historians did, was a great advance: credulity about the past, where one was dependent on authorities, did not

[1] Fussner, *The Historical Revolution*, pp. 263–4; cf. p. 274. See p. 202 below.
[2] Fussner, op. cit., pp. 261–2, 269, 239, 243; Bacon, *Works*, vi. 513. Cf. p. 147 above for Bacon and magic.
[3] Clarendon, *Contemplations and Reflections upon the Psalms of David*, in *A Compleat Collection of Tracts* (1747), pp. 738–9.
[4] On the importance for sixteenth-century thought of Sextus Empiricus, see R. H. Popkin, *The History of Scepticism from Erasmus to Descartes* (Assen, 1960), pp. 17–18, 66, 128. Professor Popkin does not mention Ralegh's translation (see pp. 205–6 below). Fulke Greville was also influenced by Sextus Empiricus (Margaret L. Wiley, *The Subtle Knot: Creative Scepticism in Seventeenth-century England*, 1952, Chapter II, passim).
[5] Ralegh, *History*, iii. 262–7, v. 266–7. Cf. Professor Fussner on Camden's use of conjecture (op. cit., p. 236).

exclude a scientific attitude towards the present, where one trusted one's own experience. Matthew Arnold was quite wrong, for the sixteenth century at least, to say that 'the mental habit of him who imagines that Balaam's ass spoke in no respect differs from the mental habit of him who imagines that a Madonna of wood or stone winked'.[1]

Ralegh thought it was the historian's job 'to illustrate and make good in human reason those things which [Biblical] authority alone, without further circumstance, ought to have confirmed in every man's belief'.[2] But he strained as hard as he dared within the strait-jacket in which historical thought had been strapped for over a thousand years. We can always feel the pull between the old and the new. Whether for prudential reasons or because of genuine unclarity, Ralegh never resolved the tension in the grand theoretical passages of his *History*. But whenever he gets down to detail he has in fact resolved it; and in *The Prerogative of Parliaments* he resolved it in theory too.

What is important for our purposes is Ralegh's freedom within his self-imposed limits, limits which Bacon accepted and which very few indeed crossed in the earlier seventeenth century except Hobbes and Harrington; and Harrington, I shall suggest, with Ralegh's help.[3] Hobbes in effect discarded the first cause altogether, and listed 'ignorance of second causes' as one of the seeds of religion.[4] Yet even Hobbes arrived at such devastating conclusions—in print at all events—very late. In 1629 he defined 'the principal and proper work of history' in words as traditional as any Ralegh ever used—'to instruct and enable men by the knowledge of actions past to bear themselves prudently in the present and providently towards the future'.[5]

Ralegh's importance is that he employed a secular and critical approach to a study of world history which was in very large part a study of Biblical history; and that he did this

---

[1] M. Arnold, *Culture and Anarchy* (the Nelson Library, n.d.), p. 256.
[2] Ralegh, *History*, iii. 266.   [3] See pp. 195-9, 202-3 below.
[4] Hobbes, *De Corpore*, p. 132, quoted by S. I. Mintz, *The Hunting of Leviathan* (1962), p. 66; *Leviathan* (Everyman ed.), pp. 55-56. It was in Charles II's reign that Petty coolly proposed 'to consider only such causes as have visible foundations in nature' (*Economic Writings*, i. 244).
[5] Hobbes, translation of Thucydides, in *English Works* (ed. Sir W. Molesworth, 1839-45), viii, p. vii.

in English, in a work which was a best-seller. So he contributed, perhaps more than has been recognized, to that segregation of the spiritual from the secular which was the achievement of the seventeenth century, and which the radical revolutionaries of the sixteen-forties and fifties carried to its furthest extent. Those wealthy merchants whose wills Professor Jordan has studied with such effect, who prudently and cautiously applied their doubtless ill-gotten wealth to the endowment of scholarships, apprenticeships, almshouses, &c.—what were they doing but looking to second causes for the reconstruction of English society? Their popish predecessors, who had distributed their equally ill-gotten wealth in the form of indiscriminate largesse, left it to God to solve society's problems. The emphasis on second causes stimulates self-help.[1]

'Moses well knew that he went out with a mighty hand, and that God guided his understanding in all his enterprises; so he lay not still in the ditch crying for help, but using the understanding which God had given him, he left nothing unperformed, becoming a wise man, and a valiant and skilful conductor.'[2] We may compare Thomas Hariot's words: 'We must act earnestly, fight strenuously, but in His name, and we shall vanquish.'[3] 'Well we know', Ralegh observed, 'that God worketh all things here amongst us mediately by a secondary means, the which means of our defence and safety (being shipping and sea-forces) are to be esteemed as His gifts, and then only available and beneficial when He withal vouchsafeth His grace to use them aright.'[4] What is 'Trust in God and keep your powder dry' but a recognition of the fact that, at the level of second causes, human action is all-important? 'Fate will be overcome, if thou resist it; if thou neglect, it conquereth.' Such is Ralegh's conclusion to a consideration of the power of the stars over human actions.[5] 'After seeking the advancement of the kingdom of Christ', said the younger Hakluyt in his *Discourse*

[1] Ralegh himself, in his *Instructions to his Son*, condemned indiscriminate charity to vagabonds and beggars (*Works*, ii. 354).

[2] Ralegh, *History*, ii. 262.

[3] H. Stevens, *Thomas Hariot* (1900), p. 148.

[4] Ralegh, *Works*, ii. 107. This work (*Observations concerning the Royal Navy*) is probably not wholly Ralegh's.

[5] Ralegh, *History*, i. 34, quoting a Latin tag which he attributes to Quintilian. Hence, Ralegh adds, the importance of education.

of Western Planting, 'the second chief and principal end of the same is traffic.'[1] The principle was of wide application.

In another respect Ralegh's *History* can be associated with the new science. The great intellectual stimulus of the sixteenth century had been its absorption of the existence of the New World, with all that this implied for relativity of standards. Ralegh brought to bear on the history of the ancient world a lively mind full of the marvels of the New World. He discussed the location of the earthly Paradise in the light of 'those places which I myself have seen, near the line and under it'.[2] He decided that there was nothing beyond the normal course of nature in the Flood, comparing the torrential rainfall of the West Indies.[3] The movements of the ark were in accordance with the laws of navigation, and its capacity was assessed in relation to Ralegh's experience in stocking a ship for a voyage.[4] In addition to his careful examination of the available geographical literature, Ralegh also studied the best botanical writings of his time.[5] His recognition of climatic and geographical influences, of the pressure of population—all this had the effect of reducing (while not denying) the area of divine intervention in history.[6] He knew that Indian communities had 'devised laws without any grounds had from the Scriptures, or from Aristotle's *Politics*, whereby they are governed'. He saw religion (except the true one) as an historical phenomenon. 'The fire,

---

[1] Ed. E. G. R. Taylor, *Original Writings . . . of the. . . Hakluyts*, ii. 274. Cf. 'Mr. Cushman's Reasons and Considerations touching the lawfulness of removing out of England into the parts of America' (1622): 'We must consider whether there be not some ordinary means and course for us to take to convert them, or whether prayer for them be only referred to God's extraordinary work from heaven. Now it seemeth unto me that we ought also to endeavour and use the means to convert them, and the means cannot be used unless we go to them, or they come to us. To us they cannot come, our land is full. To them we may go, their land is empty.' Q.E.D. (G. B. Cheever, *The Pilgrim Fathers*, n.d., p. 79).

[2] Ralegh, *History*, i. 97; cf. pp. 120–1, 138–9, 146. Cf. *The Times* of 29 November 1952 for Ralegh's discussion of Dee's views on the location of Ophir, and for evidence that he worked these problems out for himself.

[3] *History*, i. 223.

[4] Ibid. i. 228, 236; cf. pp. 233–4, 246, 257; ii. 13–16, 56.

[5] Taylor, *Late Tudor and Early Stuart Geography*, pp. 34–35.

[6] Ralegh, *History*, ii. 369; cf. Fussner, op. cit., p. 204. Even Ralegh's notorious account in *The Discovery of Guiana* of 'men whose heads do grow beneath their shoulders' may be rationally explained as an accurate report of the disguises of medicine men (C. Kingsley, *Plays and Puritans*, 1879, pp. 133–4). Ralegh was right about the equally improbable oyster trees and tree-living men.

which the Chaldeans worshipped for a God, is crept into every
man's chimney.'[1] He noted that similar stories recur in different
religions, though he believed 'that Homer had read over all
the books of Moses', and 'by places stolen thence almost word
for word'.[2]

A growing pre-occupation with the problem of time in our
period is very important for our purposes, since it links the
activities of the Copernican scientists (concerned with the
philosophical notion in general) with those of the instrument-
makers (concerned with the accurate measurement of short
intervals, for nautical purposes, among others),[3] and of the
historians, from the future Leiden professor Scaliger's *De
Emendatione Temporum* (1583) to Ussher's chronology of the
Bible. (We may note the basis of these scientific pre-occupations
in clock-making, a typically Protestant industry.)[4] Ralegh oc-
cupies an important position in this sequence. He very carefully
studied the many contemporary experts on chronology (of
whom Hariot was one of the chief) but arrived at his own
conclusions, ones which deservedly won him a considerable
reputation in the seventeenth century.[5] When John Preston
deduced the reliability of Scripture from the fact that its
chronology was corroborated by heathen historians, he might
well have been reading Ralegh.[6]

Scholars who read only the Preface to the *History of the World*
are apt to exaggerate the orthodoxy of Ralegh's outlook. The
Preface has reasonably been described as 'the culminating
document of Renaissance historiography in England', which
did for historiography what Sidney's *Defence of Poesie* did for
literary criticism.[7] Yet when we get into the body of the work,
what impresses is not so much Ralegh's conventional acceptance
of, say, the Biblical story, as his extraordinary freedom within

---

[1] *History*, i. 201; cf. pp. 180–1. Cf. Hariot's use of engravings of Picts to illustrate
the savages of Virginia (p. 139 above).

[2] Ibid. i. 195; cf. pp. 167, 182, 193, 226; iv. 572–3.

[3] Cf. L. Pearsall Smith, *Life and Letters of Sir Henry Wotton* (1907), ii. 396.

[4] A. G. H. Bachrach, *Sir Constantine Huygens and Britain*, i (Leiden, 1962), 37–
38.

[5] Fussner, op. cit., pp. 105, 201–2. Cf. Selden's insistence on the importance of
exact chronology (ibid., p. 292); and see pp. 215–16 below for Lydiat's *Emendatio
Temporum*.

[6] Preston, *Life Eternal* (fourth ed., 1634), p. 55.

[7] L. B. Campbell, *Shakespeare's Histories* (1947), pp. 79–84.

the limits which he accepted.[1] Since one object in writing and publishing the *History* was to rehabilitate himself with James I, and in particular to clear his name of the stigma of atheism, naturally Ralegh emphasized his orthodoxy whenever possible. That he was successful (except with James) is clear if we compare Coke's 'damnable atheist' of 1603 and C. J. Popham's 'the most heathenish and blasphemous opinions' with C. J. Montague's remark in 1618: 'I am resolved you are a good Christian, for *The History of the World*, which is an admirable work, doth testify as much.'[2]

In Jewish history the first cause intervenes regularly: outside it second causes prevail, and Ralegh applied his sceptical-critical method to all human authorities. He turned to writing history only in his old age, and he is alleged (not very reliably) to have had many assistants, including Sir Robert Cotton, Bedwell, and Ben Jonson. As some 660 authors are quoted in the *History*, this would not have been unreasonable for a man in the Tower.[3] He was to a great extent at the mercy of his sources. Yet he could show considerable independence of judgement. 'It behoveth me to give reason for my own opinion', he said once, 'and with so much the greater care and circumspection because I walk aside, in a way apart from the multitude.'[4]

So, though it is right to praise Ralegh for 'realizing the need for geographical study in connexion with history', and for his 'chronological exactness',[5] there is rather more to be said than

[1] Cf. for example the *History*, ii. 222–3: after saying that the text of the Bible must be accepted, Ralegh proceeds to conjecture how it might nevertheless be explained away. Cf. ibid. i. 15: it is 'curiosity' to ask *how* the spirit moved on the waters, and the *manner* of creation: but its results may be critically considered.

[2] Ed. T. B. Howell, Cobbett's *Complete Collection of State Trials*, i. 221, ii. 340. His neglect of the propaganda purposes of Ralegh's *History* seems to me the only serious criticism to be made of E. A. Strathmann's otherwise admirable *Sir Walter Ralegh: A Study in Elizabethan Scepticism*. Professor Strathmann tends to use the *History* as a touchstone by which to test Ralegh's views expressed elsewhere, or views attributed to him. Naturally, given this procedure, he concludes that Ralegh grew more orthodox as he grew older. This comforting conclusion may be true; but it is hardly proven. Cf. p. 170 above.

[3] T. N. Brushfield, 'Sir Walter Ralegh and his *History of the World*', in *Trans. of the Devon Assoc. for the Advancement of Science, Literature and Art*, 1887, p. 399. Ralegh did not quote them all at first hand.

[4] Ralegh, *History*, ii. 187; cf. pp. 103, 130, 182, 222–3, 278–82; iii. 266.

[5] J. W. Thompson, *A History of Historical Writing* (New York, 1942), i. 611.

that. It was through Ralegh that much of the most advanced continental thought was popularized in England—Machiavelli, Bodin, scepticism. The spirit of free inquiry had not yet won the day, even in the restricted area in which Ralegh applied it.[1] His onslaught on Aristotle ('I shall never be persuaded that God hath shut up all light of learning within the lanthorn of Aristotle's brains'),[2] and his insistence on the right of reason to decide when authorities differed, the 'private conjectures' which Ralegh carefully distinguished from what he believed to be facts,[3] his rational-critical approach (as in his rejection of the Brutus legend), all helped the new attitude to triumph, thanks very largely to the popularity of the *History*. 'Every human proposition', said Ralegh, quoting Charron, 'hath equal authority, if reason make not the difference.'[4] Francis Osborn observed gratefully that 'Sir Walter Ralegh was the first (as I have heard) that ventured to tack about and sail aloof from the beaten track of the Schools: who upon the discovery of so apparent an error as a Torrid Zone intended to proceed in an inquisition after more solid truths.' This gave him the reputation of being an atheist, 'though a known asserter of God and providence. A like censure fell to the share of Venerable Bacon and Selden.'[5] 'This is the reward I look for, that my labours may but receive an allowance suspended, until such time as this description of mine be reproved by a better.'[6] It was thanks, among others, to Ralegh that ideas like those expressed in Spelman's *History of Sacrilege* had already become old fashioned when Wentworth appealed to them in 1634, suggesting to Laud that Ralegh had come to a bad end because he 'laid his unhallowed hands' upon Church property; and hoping that the Earl of Cork, who had built upon Ralegh's 'rotten sacrilegious foundation', would similarly fail to prosper.[7]

---

[1] Strathmann, op. cit., p. 238.   [2] Ralegh, *History*, i, p. xlii.   [3] Ibid. iii. 553.

[4] Ibid. i, pp. xli–xlii. Ralegh quoted Charron's *De La Sagesse* (1601) in French, though an English translation by S. Lennard had been published in 1606, reprinted 1612.

[5] F. Osborn, *A Miscellany of sundry Essayes, Paradoxes and Problematicall Discourses, Letters and Characters* (1659), sig. (a) 2. Osborn was writing about Ralegh's reputation under Elizabeth, not about the *History*. One wonders if Milton had read this sentence about Ralegh as an asserter of divine Providence.

[6] Ralegh, *History*, i. 140.

[7] Quoted by T. O. Ranger, 'The Career of Richard Boyle, First Earl of Cork, in Ireland, 1588–1643', Oxford D.Phil. thesis, 1958, p. 292.

X

Turning now to the reasons for and nature of the influence of the *History of the World*, we may note first that Ralegh's patriotism was as burning as that of Foxe or Hakluyt. His boast that the English were better warriors than the Romans or Macedonians is famous.[1] Throughout his writings the anti-Spanish note is also a deeply patriotic note.[2] Like Bacon, Ralegh held out a vision of the future greatness of England which was more novel, more clear-cut, and probably more influential than his theory of history. Insufficient attention has perhaps been paid to the anti-aristocratic overtones of the patriotic motif in Elizabethan literature. Foxe identified Englishmen with the chosen people, but most of his examples came from men and women of humble rank: he intended his book to be of 'utility and profit' to the multitude, to every man.[3] The theory of the Norman Yoke was both a patriotic and a class theory.[4] The sixteenth century was the epoch in which foreign merchants ceased to dominate English trade, in which English craftsmen began to catch up with their foreign rivals.[5] It was the epoch in which the vernacular finally established itself against the Latin of the scholars: Sidney's *Defence of Poesie*,[6] Spenser's *Faerie Queene*, the middle-class historians patronized by Leicester, historical and descriptive poems like *Albion's England*, *Polyolbion*, *Britannia's Pastorals*—all testify to a new pride in England and its civilization.

Thanks to the circumstances in which the Reformation took place, this patriotism at first centred round the monarchy.[7] But as the aspirations of merchants and sea-dogs, Protestants, pirates, and patriots expanded, the monarchy proved incapable of

---

[1] *History*, iv. 544–51. It was referred to, *inter alios*, by Richard James in his *Iter Lancastrense* (Chetham Soc., 1845, p. 3). James was a friend of Cotton, Selden, Eliot, and of Richard Holdsworth, Gresham professor (ibid., p. lii; Sir Simonds D'Ewes, *Autobiography and Correspondence*, 1845, ii. 42).

[2] Ralegh, *History*, vi. 368.

[3] Foxe, *Acts and Monuments*, Preface to the 1563 edition.

[4] See my *Puritanism and Revolution*, pp. 50–122.

[5] H. Kohn, 'The Genesis and Character of English Nationalism', *J.H.I.* i. 73.

[6] Cf. Sidney's own views on history, in a letter to his brother Robert, written on 18 October 1580 (*Complete Works*, iii. 130–2).

[7] Ralegh's *The Last Fight of* The Revenge is a good example (Hakluyt, *Principal Navigations*, v. esp. pp. 13–14).

realizing them. And under James I the monarchy came to be associated with alien favourites—Scots and Gondomar. From Ralegh and Hakluyt onwards the forward-looking party was calling for the use of state power to further the cause of God, profit, and national prestige.[1] In the sixteen-twenties and thirties Puritans and advocates of an aggressive anti-Spanish policy seemed the staunchest patriots. The royal cause was undoubtedly much weakened by the ability of its opponents to draw on this new *popular* nationalism.[2] We may compare the simultaneous development in the constitutional sphere of a distinction between loyalty to the King and loyalty to the Commonwealth.[3] For Spenser and Ralegh Elizabeth symbolized England: few spoke in such terms of James or Charles. Milton saw England as the English people, Cromwell the English as God's chosen people. There is an important silent revolution in this transition.

In Ralegh as in Foxe there is a feeling especially for those of humble station. Ralegh's main indictment of the great princes and conquerors is their senseless cruelty, 'giving in spoil the innocent and labouring soul to the idle and insolent'.[4] In discussing the Eighth Commandment he sharply contrasted 'the poor and miserable souls, whom hunger and extreme necessity enforceth' to steal, with 'those detested thieves who, to maintain themselves lordlike, assault, rob, and wound the merchant, artificer, and labouring man, . . . and spend in bravery, drunkenness, and upon harlots, in one day, what other men sometimes have laboured for all their lives'. These aristocratic ruffians behave in this way only because they rely upon a royal pardon for their offences.[5] Social rank is 'but as the change of garments' in a play. When 'every man wears but his own skin, the players are all alike'.[6] So for Ralegh history is only in appearance an

---

[1] The word 'forward-looking' is not intended to convey moral approval. Nor do I want to imply that all English merchants did support or would have been well advised to support anti-Spanish policies in the earlier seventeenth century, anti-French policies in the later seventeenth and eighteenth centuries. There were of course divergent interests among different groups of merchants. But considerations of colonial expansion played a greater part in the formation of foreign policy as merchants became more influential in the state, after 1640 and especially after 1688. In this merely temporal sense Hakluyt and Ralegh were 'forward-looking' and expressed commercial interests.   [2] Cf. pp. 203–13 below.

[3] I have discussed this point in my *Century of Revolution* (1961), pp. 63–66.

[4] Ralegh, *History*, vi. 368.

[5] Ibid. ii. 328.

[6] Ibid. i, p. xl.

aristocratic subject. 'The marks set on private men are with their bodies cast into the earth.' 'God's judgements upon the greater and greatest have been left to posterity.'[1] Hence the history of the great has a significance for all of us.

In one of his longest digressions Ralegh attacked duelling and the feudal conception of 'honour'.[2] He thought courage a quality not much to be admired, even in Alexander the Great. 'If adventurous natures were to be commended simply, we should confound that virtue with the hardiness of thieves, ruffians, and mastiff dogs.' It is the cause in which courage is shown that determines its quality.[3]

It may well have been from Aristotle that Ralegh learnt that 'that man which prizeth virtue for itself' must 'content himself with . . . a mean and free estate'.[4] But his application of the principle in the *History* is entirely English. 'The husbandman and the yeoman of England are the freest of all the world.' This explains England's military prowess, for 'it is the freeman, and not the slave, that hath courage and the sense of shame deserved by cowardice'. This wholly traditional reflection leads Ralegh on to his famous anticipation of Harrington. The husbandmen and yeomen 'are more free now than ever, and our nobility and gentry more servile; for since the excessive bravery and vain expense of our grandees hath taught them to raise their rents; since the enclosures and dismembering of manors, the court-baron and the court-leet, the principalities of the gentry of England have been dissolved; the tenants having paid unto their lords their rack-rent, owe them now no service at all, and (perchance) as little love'. 'The strength of England doth consist of the people and yeomanry'—as opposed to France, where the peasantry 'have no courage nor arms'.[5]

Ralegh thus foreshadowed Harrington's concept that in England the balance of property, and therefore of military power, had been altered in the decades before he wrote. 'By such maintenance of their dependants, many noblemen, in all forms of government and within every man's memory, have

[1] Ibid. i, p. vi.
[2] Ibid. v. 366–74. Cf. C. L. Barber, *The Idea of Honour in the English Drama, 1591–1700* (Göteborg, 1957), *passim*.
[3] Ralegh, *History*, iv. 344.   [4] Ibid. i. 47; cf. *Works*, i. 9
[5] Ralegh, *History*, iv. 554; *Works*, i. 183. On the yeomanry cf. Greville, *Life of Sidney*, pp. 189–90.

kept themselves in greatness, with little help of any other virtue.'[1] But feudal armies no longer exist. 'The justices of peace in England have opposed the injustices of war in England; the King's writ runs over all, and the Great Seal of England, with that of the next constable, will serve the turn to affront the greatest lords in England that shall move against the King.'[2] Since monastic lands—which might have made the King of England richer than the King of Spain—have been dissipated 'but to make a number of pettifoggers and others gentlemen',[3] this economic change inevitably draws political consequences with it. 'The kings of England, to lessen the power of the nobility, and balance them, have yielded to the growing greatness and privileges of the commons, and what effect that will have time can only show.'[4] His readers can hardly have failed to notice that in the Netherlands, which Ralegh praised so lavishly, 'the States have . . . banished and put from them all their nobility, but a very few poor ones', and shared their property.[5]

'The power of the nobility being now withered, and the power of the people in flower', the King will neglect the latter at his peril. To attempt to reverse the historical trend of a century would be fatal folly. The gentry are now 'the garrisons of good order throughout the realm'.[6] 'The people therefore in these latter ages are no less to be pleased than the peers.' 'It cannot be called a dishonour for the King to believe the general council of the kingdom, and to prefer it before his affection.'[7] Here, in *The Prerogative of Parliaments*, Ralegh is urging on James the lesson of the *History*: history is a law-abiding process. We must remember 'this terrible sentence, that God will not be mocked'. Princes *can* flout God's will; but in the long run it will do them no good. They should not be subjected to force; yet they are subject to historical necessity. Where change has taken place, it is prudent to recognize it. We can see the laws of history becoming almost Hobbist as well as Harringtonian in Ralegh's

[1] Ralegh, *Works*, ii. 28–29.
[2] Cf. Selden, *Table Talk* (1847), pp. 105–6.   [3] Ralegh, *Works*, i. 227–8.
[4] Ibid. ii. 68. Cf. R. H. Tawney, *Harrington's Interpretation of his Age* (1941), *passim*, for Harrington's debt to Ralegh.
[5] Ralegh, *Works*, ii. 15.
[6] Ibid. ii. 320. Ralegh, like everyone else who discussed the subject in the early seventeenth century, excluded 'the rascal and beggarly sort' from 'the people' (ibid. i. 9).   [7] Ibid. ii. 68, i. 212.

insistence that though there can be no *right* of revolution, still if men are pushed too far they will *in fact* revolt. It is this combination of philosophical depth with the conventional attitudes of M.Ps.—though expressed with a systematic rationalism found nowhere else before 1640—that made Ralegh the hero of men like Eliot and Oliver Cromwell.

The alternative to co-operation with Parliament could only be rule through a standing army: on this point Ralegh clearly anticipated what Harrington was to say.[1] Already in the *History* Ralegh had warned 'that these are not dreams; though some Englishmen, perhaps, that were unacquainted with history', might not realize 'how tyranny grows to stand in need of mercenary soldiers'.[2] At the very end of the *History*, when Ralegh is exerting all his eloquence, he sounded the warning note again. 'The greatest oppressors', he wrote, for all their 'wantonness of sovereignty', saying 'I will do what shall please myself', are still subject to divine law. 'For who sees not that a prince, by racking his sovereign authority to the utmost extent', only brings evil on his progeny?[3]

Ralegh's 'Harringtonian' passages suggest an appeal to the middling sort; and he prized virtue more than birth. A younger son himself, he noted that the genealogy of Christ given by St. Matthew ran through 'those whom God had chosen and blessed, without respect of the first-born, who have hereby the prerogative in estates, worldly and transitory only'.[4] God's favours frequently went not to 'the eldest in years but in virtue'.[5] The middling sort, and men who believed themselves to be 'those whom God hath chosen' formed the backbone of Parliament's support in the civil war.

Ralegh's work then helped to establish the rule of law in history, as against the more arbitrarily providential and moralizing chronicles of Foxe and his like; and yet Ralegh also helped

---

[1] Ibid. i. 183; cf. J. Harrington, *Oceana and Other Works* (1737), p. 70.

[2] Ralegh, *History*, v. 93.

[3] Ibid. vi. 356. Lest the reference to James should be too obvious, Ralegh covered himself by quoting the *Trew Law of Free Monarchies* against tyranny.

[4] Ibid. i. 161. Cf. Ralegh's economic analysis of the causes of civil war: 'Where many younger sons of younger brothers have neither lands nor means to uphold themselves; and where many men of trade, or useful professions, know not how to bestow themselves for lack of employ', a revolutionary situation is likely to develop (*Works*, ii. 26).

[5] *History*, ii. 4; cf. p. 200.

to break the merely cyclical theories with which a conception of historical law had hitherto usually been associated. He thus prepared the way for the more modern sociological history of Harrington. As long as history is cyclical, or politics is thought of as a branch of morals, men cannot conceive of political progress or of improving very greatly on the past: for we cannot learn by our fathers' mistakes, as Ralegh realized.[1] But once cyclical assumptions are questioned, and politics is thought of as an art or a science related to changing social and economic circumstances, then politics can be separated from morals. Hence the importance of Ralegh's incipient Harringtonianism, his realization that it will not do just to repeat past specifics in new circumstances. He trembled on the edge of a science of politics, which would be dominated by history. We must study historical change in order to adapt our political ideas. Ralegh never really mastered this idea in the *History*: but it is there clearly enough in *The Prerogative of Parliaments*, and was vital for the *action* of the Parliamentarians. History is *not* just a bran-tub, waiting for us to pick our precedent, nor yet a story of degeneration from a golden past. It is a story of adaptation to change which may be for the better. Thus political skill is not identical with moral virtue: it is knowledge of necessity, and so can be learnt. Even if it is not learnt, necessity will assert itself. So it is important even for those not in the seats of power to study history. It is therefore appropriate that Harrington alluded to Ralegh's *The Prerogative of Parliaments* in the title of his *The Prerogative of Popular Government*, and that he should have been buried next to Ralegh at St. Margaret's, Westminster.

Harrington, like Bacon, like Ralegh, wanted to use history as raw material for human reason to play upon. His economic theories were an attempt to state what Ralegh would have called secondary laws, Bacon axioms of the middle sort. Though Harrington carried the argument a stage further than Ralegh, the principle of applying reason to the assembled phenomena is both Baconian and not inimical to Ralegh's mode of thought. But because of his optimistic Baconian belief in the possibilities of rational science (and because of the changed political circumstances), Harrington abandoned Ralegh's pessimism, as Hakewill had done, and hoped by reason to establish a common-

[1] *History*, i, p. xxviii. Cf. p. 222 below.

wealth which would survive. This further stage, Professor Macpherson and the late Dr. Raab have suggested, relates to Harrington's anxiety (which he shared with Hobbes) to give politics the certainty of natural science. He fused the scientific tradition with Ralegh, in fact.[1]

The pre-Baconian scientists had emphasized experience as against authority. Bacon himself protested against the worship of precedents.[2] Ralegh's *History* taught that precedents were not to be followed simply because they were old, but to be studied and learnt from, as Bacon said all evidence produced by the practitioners should be learnt from. In Bacon's theory, Parliament played the role of practitioner, the King advised by his Council the role of political experts who analysed, diagnosed, and acted.[3] For Ralegh historical evidence was the raw material for political judgement, for adjusting institutions to suit changing circumstances; but Ralegh had a less narrow view of who constituted a political expert.

XI

The three Hakewill brothers are a symbolic trio. The second stayed at home to become Mayor of Exeter.[4] The third, William, was a common lawyer, the moving spirit in the revived Society of Antiquaries which roused James I's wrath in 1607–8. He was a friend of Sir Thomas Bodley and John Hampden, a critical member of Parliament whose speech on Bate's Case in 1610 was reprinted in 1641. George, the eldest, became chaplain to Prince Charles at the age of 34. But his outspoken opposition to the Spanish marriage,[5] and his failure to accept the fashionable Arminianism, prevented his rising higher than the Arch-

[1] C. B. Macpherson, *The Political Theory of Possessive Individualism* (1962), pp. 30, 77–78, 101, and Chapter 4, *passim*; F. Raab, *The English Face of Machiavelli* (1964), Chapter VI. Dr. Raab suggested plausibly that Harrington's scientific method derived from Harvey (op. cit., pp. 198–201, 219). Harrington used evidence from Ralegh's *History* to justify his theory of balance, but criticized Ralegh for not drawing the appropriate conclusions (Harrington, *Oceana and Other Works*, pp. 77, 389).

[2] Bacon, *Works*, v. 66, 71, 93–94.

[3] G. P. Gooch, *Political Thought in England from Bacon to Halifax* (1915), p. 32.

[4] W. T. MacCaffrey, *Exeter, 1540–1640* (Harvard U.P., 1958), p. 262.

[5] Both George and William Hakewill were in trouble in 1622 for this reason (*C.S.P.D., 1619–23*, pp. 279, 284–5, 333; *Letters of John Chamberlain*, ii. 393). It is interesting that the correspondent who told Dudley Carleton about George Hakewill's memorandum against the Spanish match should have called him 'Hakluyt' (*C.S.P.D., 1619–23*, p. 284).

deaconry of Surrey which he obtained in 1617. Only in 1642, in very different political circumstances, was he elected Rector of Exeter College. He resided away from royalist Oxford during the civil war, but returned to co-operate with the Parliamentary Visitors.

George Hakewill, who admired and frequently quoted Ralegh in his panegyric of the Moderns, thought that to establish the law-abidingness of the universe was scarcely less important than to combat the theory of decay.[1] Nature, he held, is governed by constant laws. So far from physical nature having been corrupted by the Fall, it is the corruption in fallen man's mind that leads him to attribute decay to nature. Science can redeem us from this error: Hakewill believed with Bacon that 'the apprehension of [natural] truth helps to repair that image of God' which was partially lost at the Fall.[2] 'Like Spenser Hakewill sees behind mutability a divine order and constancy.'[3] For unless we can expect effects to follow causes in a rational and predictable way, leaving room for human freedom, there is no stimulus to that moral effort to which Hakewill (and the Puritans) attached such importance. 'The first step to enable a man to the achieving of great designs is to be persuaded that by endeavour he is able to achieve it.'[4] Hakewill's was one of the most widely read books of the century, for it combined Baconian optimism with a providential view of history: on both counts it relieved men of the sense of hopelessness. Milton read Hakewill with profit, and within a year of the publication of the *Apologie* reproduced the idea of law in the universe in his undergraduate *Naturam non pati senium*.[5] But Hakewill's major influence, like that of Bacon and Harvey, came after 1640.[6]

[1] Hakewill, *Apologie*, pp. 4, 52, 161, 182, 184, 286, 295–6, 308, 320, 518; ii. 148.
[2] Ibid., p. 17.
[3] D. Bush, *English Literature in the Earlier 17th Century* (1962), p. 294.
[4] Hakewill, op. cit., sig. a3; cf. pp. 20–23, and the remark of Hariot quoted on p. 188 above, Cf. also R. W. Hepburn, 'Hakewill: the Virility of Nature', *J.H.I.* xvi. 150. See p. 291 below.
[5] Cf. H. Baker's valuable *The Wars of Truth*, pp. 84–86. Mr. Baker gives examples of men influenced by Hakewill: to these we might add Francis Osborn and Joseph Glanvill. Comenius also opposed the idea of decay in his *Synopsis Physicae* (English translation 1651) (V. Harris, *All Coherence Gone*, Chicago, 1949, p. 164). Hobbes, Bacon's secretary, naturally supported the Moderns; Izaak Walton, equally naturally, thought he lived in 'this weak and declining age of the world' (*Life of Hooker*, 1655, in I. Walton, *Lives*, World's Classics, p. 220).
[6] See p. 11 above.

Hakewill was in many ways astonishingly modern. He knew better than most of his contemporaries that what most sharply distinguished the age in which he lived was the rapid development of trade and industry.[1] He cited mathematics, navigation, anatomy, chemistry, and medicine among the evidences of human advance. He had no more use than Ralegh for the idea of a golden age in the past. He regarded himself as 'a citizen of the world'.[2] In the concluding section of his book he passed severe strictures on courtiers who allowed themselves to be bought by projectors; on judges who passed sentence for fear or favour; on lords and gentlemen who made merchandise of church livings, who 'strip the backs of the poor, that they may apparel their walls', and 'snatch their meat from their mouths, that they may give it to their hawks and dogs'.[3] Bishop Goodman was careful to point out where the logic, not only of a rather conventional passage like this, but of Hakewill's whole argument, was leading: 'If we be so meanly and basely persuaded of the Ancients, how apt shall we be for innovation, what danger of a mutiny; the country boors may rise in sedition, and not without cause; for by your opinion all things may be improved.'[4]

Hakewill, like Ralegh, did not quite break out of cyclical theories. But he thought that there was no age 'but hath exceeded all others in some respects, and again in other respects hath been exceeded by others'.[5] Like Ralegh, he saw in all things 'a kind of circular progress: they have their birth, their growth, their flourishing, their failing, their fading, and within a while after, their resurrection and reflourishing again'.[6] This reminds us of Harvey's remarks on 'the round which makes the race of common fowl eternal; now pullet, now egg, the series is continued in perpetuity; from frail and perishing individuals an immortal species is engendered. By these, and means like to these, do we see many inferior and terrestrial things brought to emulate the perpetuity of superior or celestial

---

[1] Hakewill, op. cit., pp. 20–25, 163–4, 312, 316–17, 323; ii. 135. Contrast Goodman, who had cited the economic *malaise* of the age (high prices, enclosures, decay of housekeeping and charity) as evidence of decline.

[2] Ibid., Preface.

[3] Ibid., pp. 604–5.

[4] Ibid. ii. 132. Hakewill's defence against this charge is weaker than usual.

[5] Ibid. ii. 192.   [6] Ibid., p. 259.

things.'[1] And both passages recall a famous speech by Pym:
'Time must needs bring some alterations, and every alteration
is a step and a degree towards a dissolution; those things only
are eternal which are constant and uniform: therefore it is observed by the best writers upon this subject, that those commonwealths have been most durable and perpetual which have
often reformed and recomposed themselves according to their
first institution and ordinance; for by this means they repair
the breaches and counterwork the ordinary and natural effects
of time.'[2] Pym, like Ralegh, thought that human beings by
understanding the cycle could perhaps intervene to restore
a desirable state of affairs. This idea, again, was developed by
Harrington.

The seventeenth-century emphasis on history, I suggest,
witnesses to a sense of change, of crisis. Some men looked backwards for solutions—Protestants to the primitive Church, Lilburne to the medieval heretics and the Marian martyrs, lawyers
and politicians to the free Anglo-Saxons. The pre-revolutionary
idea of the historical process, dominated by the dogma of the
Fall of man, was one of degeneration: we could hope to stop
the degeneration only by going back to purer origins. Spenser,
Ralegh, Pym were all struggling to assert the power of humanity
to escape by the use of reason from an ineluctable cyclical
decline. Those who looked most brashly forward were the
Chiliasts, those irrational lower-class optimists-of-desperation
who hoped for the intervention of Christ here and now to bring
about the rule of his Elect, the lowly remnant. Here again we
see the importance of Bacon. He not only made a scientific
philosophy out of the practice of artisans: he also secularized
their age-old chiliastic dreams, and suggested the possibility of
getting back behind the Fall on earth before the millennium.
This made possible a new attitude towards history—progress
without chiliasm, change without apocalypse, reformation without tarrying for the Second Coming. The battle of the Moderns
against the Ancients was a battle of optimism against pessimism.

Ralegh as well as Bacon and Hakewill helped to take arbitrariness out of history, to replace God's direct intervention
by the idea of historical law. When Cromwell asked, 'What are

[1] W. Harvey, *Works* (1847), p. 285.
[2] J. Rushworth, *Historical Collections* (1721), i. 596.

all our histories and other traditions of actions in former times but God manifesting Himself that He hath shaken and tumbled down and trampled upon everything that He hath not planted?'[1] he was expressing Ralegh's view of history. None knew better than Cromwell that in recent years God had acted through human agents. And so Ralegh's and Bacon's view of history, plus the experience of the Revolution, made the idea of *controlled* change conceivable—change that should not be an act of God in the sense either of a disaster or of doomsday. Just as, after the Revolution, Bacon's former secretary Thomas Hobbes could say that politics was a science because men made the state, so Harrington could conceive of history as a science because men could control it. This was the high point of historical thinking in seventeenth-century England, a point not to be surpassed until the Scottish school of a century later. As with chemistry, so with history, the advanced ideas thrown up during the revolutionary decades were not developed until a century later, when their revival coincided with a resurgence of political radicalism.[2]

XII

The only work which Ralegh published legally under James I was the *History of the World*; and James made a determined effort to suppress this.[3] But too many copies had already been distributed for this attempt to do more than advertise the work (there were at least three separate issues of the first edition); and the King compromised by allowing it to appear without Ralegh's name attached to it.[4] Six editions of the massive folio appeared between 1614 and 1634, and at least five more before the end of the century. This is nearly three times as many

[1] Abbot, *Writings and Speeches of Oliver Cromwell*, iii. 590. The divine right of facts, after doing duty for each successive government after 1640, had a final revival to reassure churchmen of the respectability of William and Mary after 1688: anything that happened was God's providence and resistance to it was consequently wrong (G. Straka, 'The Final Phase of Divine Right Theory in England, 1688-1702', *E.H.R.* lxxvii, 638-58). This was poor stuff compared to Ralegh, but it shows the tenacity of the body of ideas which he expressed and transcended.

[2] See p. 298 below.

[3] *Letters of John Chamberlain*, i. 568; Firth, *Essays Historical and Literary*, pp. 53-55; T. N. Brushfield, 'Raleghana IV', *Trans. Devon Assoc. for the Advancement of Science, Literature and Art* (1904), pp. 184-5.

[4] In 1617 Ralegh's name was allowed to appear on the title-page.

editions as Shakespeare's *Works* had. Ralegh's was also the most popular of all histories by an Englishman in seventeenth-century America. An abridgement, a continuation, and a volume of commentary (each by Alexander Ross) all appeared in England in the freedom of the sixteen-fifties; two more abridgements and another continuation in the next sixty years.[1] Two historical works were fathered on to Ralegh in the sixteen-thirties.[2] The popularity of such of his writings as were allowed to be printed is shown by the five editions (at least) of his politically harmless *Instructions to his Son* published between 1632 and 1636.

Ralegh's main political work was *The Prerogative of Parliaments*, written in 1615. This could not be legally published before 1640, though it circulated extensively in manuscript, one copy having been read and carefully annotated by Sir John Eliot.[3] The first edition was stated to be printed at Middelburg in 1628, though this may conceal an illegal English publication. No less than three editions appeared in that year.

As soon as the collapse of royal government set the press free there was an astonishing flow of work attributed to Ralegh. *Maxims of State* was first published in 1642, Toland says by Milton;[4] Ralegh's last letter to his wife in 1644; an extract from Book V of the *History*, dealing with 'the cruel War between the Carthaginians and their own Mercenaries', was published in 1647, presumably as a tract against the New Model Army. *Selected Essays and Observations* appeared in 1650, reprinted 1667. At least ten collections of Ralegh's *Remains* under various titles were published between 1651 and 1681. Two variants of *Observations touching Trade and Commerce with the Hollander* (attributed to Ralegh) were published, and two more before the end of the century. Oldys noted that 'there are several manuscripts of this treatise in the libraries of our nobility and gentry (more ancient than the earliest edition in print)'.[5] *The Cabinet Council* was attributed to Ralegh when it was published by Milton in 1658 (two issues), from a manuscript which he had possessed

---

[1] All this bibliographical information comes from T. N. Brushfield, *A Bibliography of Sir Walter Ralegh* (second ed., 1908), pp. 88–100.

[2] *Tubus Historicus* (1636) and *The Life and Death of Mahomet* (1637).

[3] See pp. 208–9 below.

[4] Ed. Helen Darbishire, *Early Lives of Milton* (1932), p. 188.

[5] W. Oldys, 'Life of Sir Walter Raleigh', in *Works of Sir Walter Raleigh* (1829), i. 442.

for many years; there were new editions in 1661, 1664, 1692, and 1697.

In 1651 a prophecy was fathered on Ralegh which foretold the landing of an English army in France that year, leading to the capture of Rome.[1] Epitaphs on Ralegh began to appear in print from 1640 onwards.[2] There were also a number of ballads and broadsheets at the time of Ralegh's execution, most of which have disappeared. The first printed version of what later became *The Golden Vanity* was about Ralegh's ship *The Sweet Trinity*. Ralegh appears as a character in the two parts of Heywood's play about Sir Thomas Gresham, *If You Know Not Me, You Know Nobody*.

Significant evidence of Ralegh's popularity was the habit of fathering works upon him. (But it is also evidence of Ralegh's industry, since he probably translated, copied out, or summarized most of the works attributed to him.) *The Sceptic* is a translation from the fashionable Sextus Empiricus; *The Causes of the Magnificence and Opulency of Cities* is extracted from Botero; *The Cabinet Council* and *Maxims of State* are compilations from Aristotle, Machiavelli, Francesco Sansovino, Bodin, and Justus Lipsius, though they have been newly synthesized.[3] The *Discourse of Tenures* is copied from an unprinted work by Sir Roger Owen, which was often quoted by opposition M.Ps.[4] The *Breviary of the History of England* is a version of part of Samuel Daniel's *History of England*.[5] *Observations . . . concerning the Royall Navye* appears to be, at least in part, Sir Arthur Gorges's.[6] *Observations touching Trade and Commerce with the Hollander* was also probably not by Ralegh but by John Keymer.[7]

[1] Brushfield, *A Bibliography of Sir Walter Ralegh*, p. 166.
[2] e.g. *Witts Recreations*, in *Musarum Deliciae* (1640–63), ii. 280–2. Cf. also p. 150 above.
[3] L. Stapleton, 'Halifax and Ralegh', *J.H.I.* ii. 213; Strathmann, *Sir Walter Ralegh*, pp. 12, 164–5; N. Kempner, *Raleghs Staatstheoretische Schriften* (Leipzig, 1928). In the *Times Literary Supplement* of 13 April 1956, Professor Strathmann argued that *The Cabinet Council* was not by Ralegh but by 'T. B.', who may be Thomas Bedingfield, the translator of Machiavelli's *History of Florence*.
[4] Strathmann, 'Ralegh's *Discourse of Tenures* and Sir Roger Owen', *H.L.Q.* xx. 223–5.
[5] Ibid., p. 229; R. B. Gottfried, 'The Authorship of *A Breviary of the History of England*', *S.P.* liii.
[6] Ed. P. W. Long, *Essays and Studies in Honor of Carleton Brown* (New York, 1940), p. 242, and *The Mariner's Mirror*, xx. 323, quoted in Gorges, *Poems*, p. xxvii.
[7] Macvey Napier, *Lord Bacon and Sir Walter Raleigh* (1853), p. 230; T. W. Fulton, *The Sovereignty of the Seas* (1911), p. 127, quoted by Sir G. N. Clark, *The Birth of the*

Further evidence of the popularity of Ralegh's name is provided by the existence of no less than four *Ralegh's Ghosts* between 1620 and 1631, either published abroad or circulating in manuscript. One tract called *Sir Walter Rawleighs Ghost* (1626) was by Thomas Scott, whose part in the pre-history of the English Revolution has never been fully studied. He was a Puritan divine, minister successively in the Puritan cities of Norwich and Ipswich, chaplain both to James I and to the anti-Spanish Earl of Pembroke. Compelled to emigrate to the Netherlands, he was a preacher to merchants at Utrecht and to the English garrison at Gorcham. From there he poured forth a spate of anti-Spanish propaganda aimed at securing English intervention in the Thirty Years War. He was assassinated for his pains in 1626. He wrote at least twenty-five pamphlets against James's Spanish policy, some of which went through several editions.[1]

In *Sir Walter Rawleighs Ghost*, as in many of Scott's writings, Ralegh is the victim of Gondomar's intrigues; if Ralegh had not been cut off in time, the Spanish Ambassador boasted, he 'had near made a new conquest of the West Indies'.[2] In *Vox Populi*, of which there were five editions between 1620 and 1623, Scott described the pro-Spanish party in England as consisting of 'divers courtiers who were hungry and gaped for Spanish gold', and most of the great landowners, who rig Parliamentary elections through their control over their tenants. Plain people hated the Spanish match.[3] In 1623 Scott called on ministers and freeholders to take care to get godly men elected to Parliament.[4]

Dutch Republic (Raleigh Lecture, 1946), p. 1. As late as 1696 an economic tract was published as *Select Observations of the Incomparable Sir Walter Raleigh*.

It is surely time we had a full critical edition of Ralegh's works? Since 1829 a great deal has been rejected from the canon, and some items have been added. Yet some of the works whose rejection has been suggested need careful sifting to ascertain how much original matter is contained alongside the wholesale copying. How far did Ralegh act as a channel for transmitting the most advanced continental thought to England? How early was his translation of Sextus Empiricus, for instance? How many people before Ralegh had quoted Charron? (See pp. 186, 192 above.) There has never been a critical edition of *The History of the World*, though Brushfield long ago indicated divergences between the various editions of 1614, one of them of some interest (Brushfield, 'Raleghana IV', p. 189; cf. Adolphe Buff, 'Über drei Ralegh'sche Schriften', *Englische Studien*, ii, Heilbron, 1879, 392–416).

[1] L. B. Wright, 'Propaganda against James I's "Appeasement" of Spain', *H.L.Q.* vi. 160–1.   [2] *Harleian Miscellany* (1744–56), v. 56.

[3] *Vox Populi* (Utrecht, 1624), sig. C.

[4] *The High-Waies of the King* (1623), p. 86.

A year later he declared that the common people cannot be restrained from hostility to Spain, but many influential nobles and gentlemen, for their own ends, will be easily persuaded to betray their country.[1] Prerogative rule without Parliament, Scott argued, is a Spanish policy. So is the silencing of ministers who preached against the Spanish marriage.[2] The King is cut off from his true friends by the guards around him, and cannot be approached except in print.[3] This was a very extreme form of the conventional plea that opposition was only to the King's evil counsellors, not to the King himself, which was to do duty right down to the civil war, and beyond. Scott even suggested that the Prince of Wales could not marry without Parliament's consent.[4] He favoured an alliance with the Netherlands, and held up the Dutch as models of industry and thrift. He wanted to 'raise another England to withstand ... new Spain in America'.[5]

Scott thus both expressed and helped to popularize a class analysis of English politics. *Vox Populi*, Sir Simonds D'Ewes tells us, was 'generally approved of, not only by the meaner sort that were zealous for the cause of religion, but also by all men of judgement that were loyally affected to the truth of the Gospel and the crown'. But the King was 'much incensed'.[6] The Grand Remonstrance with its reference to 'such councillors as for private ends have engaged themselves to further the interests of some foreign princes or states'[7] echoed Scott's line of propaganda; so, more clearly, did the Declaration of the Lords and Commons issued on 9 August 1642, against 'papists, the prelatical clergy, delinquents, and that part of the nobility

---

[1] *The Second Part of Vox Populi* (1624). For confirmation of Scott's allegations see *C.S.P. Ven., 1615–17*, p. 37. The calling of Parliaments, the Venetian ambassador said, was opposed by 'those who are dependent on the Spaniards and receive pensions from them, who are very numerous'. Scott's class analysis was also confirmed by James Howell in a letter from Madrid of December 1622. In England, he said, 'the people are averse to the match, and the nobility with most part of the gentry inclinable' (*Familiar Letters or Epistolae Ho-Elianae*, Temple Classics, i. 168). Cf. R. Dugdale, *A Narrative of the wicked Plots carried on by Seignior Gondamore* (1679), in *Harleian Miscellany* (1744–56), iii. 318–19, 321–2; *Cowper MSS.* (H.M.C.), p. 108.

[2] *Vox Populi*, sig. C 3.

[3] *Vox Regis* (1624), p. 2.

[4] Ibid., p. 14.

[5] *Vox Populi*, sig. B 4–4v.

[6] D'Ewes, *Autobiography*, i. 159.

[7] Ed. S. R. Gardiner, *Constitutional Documents of the Puritan Revolution* (1906), p. 207.

and gentry which either fears reform or seeks preferment by betraying their country'.[1]

Rawleighs Ghost and Scott's other vigorous, illegal, and widely distributed pamphlets reflected and stirred up the patriotic and Protestant feelings of those middling men who wanted an anti-Spanish policy, and carefully fanned their resentment against the court and the allegedly pro-Spanish aristocracy. For Scott Ralegh is the symbol of English patriotism. Yet it seems possible that Scott was converted to approval of Ralegh only by the *History of the World*.[2] This may well have been true of many Puritans; and Ralegh's death would reinforce the new image.

Rushworth, who began his *Collections* with 1618, printed a letter from 'a great minister of state' to the English representative in Spain, stating that Ralegh's death had 'moved the common sort of people to much remorse, who all attributed his death to the desire his Majesty had to satisfy Spain'. The writer of the letter clearly shared this popular assumption.[3] 'It grows very questionable', said the odious Sir Lewis Stukeley in 1618, 'whether this man did more hurt by his life or by his death.'[4] We may compare a letter from Toby Matthew to Bacon in August of the same year, where he speaks of 'Ralegh and the prentices' in one breath as anti-Spanish.[5] But, popular as his stand against Spain was, Ralegh's main influence was with men of the class which sat in Parliament. The fact that he had been a good House of Commons man no doubt helped.

The Parliament of 1624 passed a Bill reversing Ralegh's attainder: James refused his assent. Led by Eliot, the Commons tried again in 1626, and succeeded in 1628, though Charles drove a hard bargain.[6] Eliot, distantly related to Ralegh, was probably on the scaffold at his execution, and was profoundly influenced by that experience. He possessed, read, and carefully annotated a manuscript copy of *The Prerogative of Parliaments*. The tract seems to have been the source of Eliot's tactics in

---

[1] *L.J.* v. 258. For an example of Scott's influence see Jordan, *Social Institutions in Kent, 1480–1660* (Archaeologia Cantiana, 1961), p. 87.
[2] If he was the author of verses sent by Mr. Thomas Scott to Sir Walter Ralegh, printed by Professor Harlow in his edition of *The Discoverie of Guiana* (1928), p. xxiv.   [3] Rushworth, *Historical Collections*, i. 9.
[4] *The Humble Petition and Information of Sir Lewis Stukeley* (1618), in *Harleian Miscellany* (1744–56), iii. 63; cf. p. 154 above.
[5] Bacon, *Works* (1826), vi. 265.   [6] Forster, *Sir John Eliot*, i. 512.

1626, when his aim was to limit the crown's freedom to the ultimate benefit of the crown. All the precedents which Eliot cited in this Parliament, and his comments and recommendations, are to be found in Ralegh's treatise.[1] During his last imprisonment Eliot's mind reverted to the memory of Ralegh, with whom Eliot's *Monarchy of Man* is permeated. Hampden was another who possessed large quantities of Ralegh's manuscript treatises. No less than 3,452 sheets of them, we are told, were transcribed for him at considerable expense 'a little before the wars'.[2] Pym was also probably present at Ralegh's execution, which he recorded in his notebook. We can frequently hear echoes of Ralegh in Pym's majestic historical generalizations.[3] Among other prominent Parliamentary figures we may mention John Hoskyns and Sir Robert Cotton, friends of Ralegh's who probably helped with the *History of the World*;[4] Sir Edward Coke, who had *The Discoveries of Guiana* and two copies of *The History of the World* in his library;[5] John Selden, a friend to whom Ralegh lent manuscripts;[6] Sir Benjamin Rudyerd.[7] The first Earl of Clare was a firm friend of Ralegh's. He tried hard to save Ralegh's life, and wrote after his execution:

> His soul is gone
> To inhabit many, too much for one.[8]

The later political attitude of his son Denzil Holles is sufficient comment.

Most famous of all is Cromwell, who recommended the *History of the World* to his eldest son Richard as a much-needed remedy for 'an unactive vain spirit'. The virtue that Oliver singled out for praise in Ralegh's work was that it comprised

---

[1] J. N. Ball, *The Parliamentary Career of Sir John Eliot, 1624-9* (Cambridge Ph.D. thesis, 1953), pp. 135-40. I am very grateful to Dr. Ball for permission to quote from this valuable work.

[2] D. Lloyd, *State-Worthies* (1766), i. 565. A Sir John Hampden had accompanied Ralegh to Guiana in 1616.

[3] H.M.C., *Tenth Report, Appendix, Part VI*, p. 85; Governor Winthrop's father transcribed into his commonplace book *The Confession and Execution of Sir Walter Raleigh* (ed. R. C. Winthrop, Massachusetts Hist. Soc., 1873).

[4] Forster, *Sir John Eliot*, i. 411. Ralegh certainly used Cotton's library.

[5] Hassall, *A Catalogue of the Library of Sir Edward Coke*, pp. 46, 76.

[6] Oldys, 'Life of Raleigh', in *Works* (1829), i. 453, 456; Aubrey, *Brief Lives*, ii. 192. [7] Aubrey, op. cit., ii. 185.

[8] G. Holles, *Memorials of the Holles Family, 1493-1656* (Camden Soc., 1937), pp. 101-2; Howell, *Epistolae Ho-Elianae*, ii. 231.

'a body of history', and so would 'add much more to your understanding than fragments of story'.[1] It was in his speech to the Barebones Parliament that Cromwell distinguished between 'stories that . . . give you narratives of matters of fact' and 'those things where the life and power of them lay, those strange windings and turnings of Providence'.[2] Cromwell, we recall, was a pupil of Thomas Beard, and may have found the latter's philosophy of history as indistinguishable from that of Ralegh as some historians have done. William Prynne linked Beard and Ralegh together as sources for God's judgements against kings.[3] Lilburne—who seems to have read little except legal writings—quoted Foxe and Ralegh's *History*.[4] Adam Eyre read both writers in 1647.[5] Another Leveller pamphlet, *Vox Plebis*, quoted Ralegh three times.[6] The radical law reformer John Jones cited him against the clergy.[7] John Lewis, protagonist of the Parliamentary cause in Wales, also quoted him.[8]

Robert Greville, Lord Brooke, cited Ralegh with approval alongside Bacon.[9] Milton, in addition to publishing *The Cabinet Council*, made extracts from the *History* in his commonplace book, echoed Ralegh in a sonnet, and showed admiration for him again and again.[10] So we could extend the list—Archbishop Ussher,[11] Joseph Hall,[12] William Drummond,[13] James

[1] Abbot, *Writings and Speeches of Oliver Cromwell*, ii. 236.   [2] Ibid. iii. 53.

[3] Ed. J. Bruce and S. R. Gardiner, *Documents relating to the Proceedings against William Prynne* (Camden Soc., 1877), p. 47: cf. Lamont, *Marginal Prynne*, p. 223.

[4] Ed. W. Haller and G. Davies, *Leveller Manifestoes* (Columbia U.P., 1944), pp. 41, 445.

[5] Ed. H. J. Morehouse, *Diary of Adam Eyre*, in *Yorkshire Diaries and Autobiographies of the 17th and 18th centuries* (Surtees Soc., 1877), pp. 68, 79.

[6] *Vox Plebis* (1646), pp. 63, 65, 68. The pamphlet has been variously assigned to Overton, Lilburne, and Henry Marten. Does the title recall Thomas Scott?

[7] J. Jones, *The New Returna Brevium* (1650), p. 44. For Jones see pp. 261–3 below.

[8] But in his *Some seasonable and modest Thoughts in order to the furtherance and promoting the affaires of Religion and the Gospel especially in Wales* (1656), p. 17; not in his more important *The Parliament explained to Wales* (1646).

[9] Brooke, *The Nature of Truth* (1640), pp. 141–3.

[10] 'Methought I saw my late espoused saint' echoes 'Methought I saw the grave where Laura lay'. The conception of *Paradise Lost*—a universal history—may owe something to Ralegh, who also wanted to 'assert eternal Providence'. Milton's use of Ralegh and the latter's influence on Milton's style would be worth further study (cf. Firth, *Essays*, pp. 51–52; E. Thompson, *Sir Walter Raleigh*, pp. 64, 236–7).

[11] D. Bush, *English Literature in the Earlier 17th Century* (1962), p. 224.

[12] J. Hall, *The Balm of Gilead*, in *Works* (1808), viii. 162.

[13] W. Drummond, *Familiar Letters*, in *The History of Scotland* (second ed. 1680), p. 387.

Harrington,[1] James Howell,[2] Francis Osborn,[3] Nathaniel
Bacon,[4] Captain Baddiley,[5] Andrew Marvell,[6] John Bunyan,[7]
William Penn,[8] the Earl of Shaftesbury,[9] the Marquis of Halifax,[10] John Locke,[11] Ambrose Barnes,[12] Daniel Defoe.[13] Ralegh's
History was cited as a model as early as 1618; it was quoted
in the standard works on geography and history by Nathanael
Carpenter and Degory Wheare.[14] Edward Harley wanted to
buy a copy of the History in 1639; Tom Verney wanted to have
one bought for him in 1654.[15] Dr. Johnson admired Ralegh
as an historian,[16] and Gibbon thought The History of the
World the best which had till that time appeared. He contemplated at one time writing a life of Ralegh.[17]

[1] Aubrey, Brief Lives, ii. 185–93; and see pp. 152–3, 195–9 above.
[2] J. Howell, Epistolae Ho-Elianae, ii. 231–4.
[3] F. Osborn, A Miscellany of Sundry Essays (1659), sig. (a) 2; Traditional Memoirs, in Secret History of the Court of James I (1811), i. 157–64.
[4] Bacon in the Parliament of 1656 quoted the History when arguing against 'the tyranny of a commonwealth', in which 'every man had liberty to find out the richest to destroy for himself'. Bacon also cited Coke. He favoured the Protectorate (ed. J. T. Rutt, Burton's Parliamentary Diary, 1828, iii. 123).
[5] Captain Badeley's Answer unto Captain Middletons Remonstrance (1653), pp. 119–20.
[6] See p. 150 above.   [7] Thompson, op. cit., p. 235.
[8] W. Penn, No Cross, no Crown, Chapter XXI, paragraph 11.
[9] [Anon.], Rawleigh Redivivus (1683). Shaftesbury's grandfather's widow married Ralegh's son Carew (Aubrey, Brief Lives, ii. 195). I am grateful to Professor Haley for drawing my attention to this point.
[10] L. Stapleton, 'Halifax and Ralegh', J.H.I. ii. 211–24.
[11] Locke recommends the History in Some Thoughts Concerning Reading and Study for a Gentleman, in Works (1824), ii. 409.
[12] Ed. W. H. D. Longstaffe, Memoirs of the Life of Mr. Ambrose Barnes (Surtees Soc., 1867), p. 33.
[13] D. Defoe, A System of Magic (1840), p. 140 (published 1728); A Tour of Great Britain (Everyman ed.) i. 223. Cf. also A Historical Account of the Voyages and Adventures of Sir Walter Raleigh (1719), sometimes attributed to Defoe. The author, however, claims to be related to the blood of Ralegh, 'one of the most illustrious commoners that England or perhaps the whole world ever bred' (pp. 4, 8).
[14] T. Gainsford, History of Perkin Warbeck, in Harleian Miscellany, vi. 496; Nathanael Carpenter, Geographie (1625); D. Wheare, De Ratione et Methodi Legendi Historias Dissertatio (1623 and many later editions: that of 1637 first ventured to praise Ralegh as one 'who deserves the first place' among modern historians). Cf. P. Heylyn, Microcosmos (1629), pp. 20, 375, 679: first published 1621, twelve editions by 1657. For Carpenter see p. 305 below, and for Wheare pp. 176–7 above.
[15] Ed. T. T. Lewis, Letters of the Lady Brilliana Harley (Camden Soc., 1854), p. 27; ed. F. P. and M. M. Verney, Memoirs of the Verney Family (1892–9), iii. 163–4. Ralegh was also quoted by John Trapp, Sir Thomas Browne, Abraham Cowley, Samuel Butler, the Duke of Newcastle, the Earl of Derby, Dugdale, Gervase Holles, Evelyn, Stillingfleet.   [16] The Rambler, 18 May 1751.
[17] E. Gibbon, Miscellaneous Works (1796), i. 107–8. We may perhaps regard the ineluctable decline and fall of the Roman Empire, resulting from an initial loss of

Not that Ralegh was read and approved only by Parliamentarians. But it is worth noting those on the other side who read him with a difference. Despite Ralegh's efforts to please him, James I thought he saw himself in Ralegh's portrait of Ninias, the effeminate successor of Queen Semiramis, and rather naturally disliked Sir Walter's writings.[1] It was Princess Elizabeth, the toast of the Puritans, who carried a copy of *The History of the World* with her to Prague.[2] John Donne wrote an early attack on the *History*.[3] Alexander Ross, chaplain to Charles I and protégé of Laud, not only epitomized the *History* but also presumed to correct it—together, significantly, with Hobbes's *Leviathan*.[4] Ross denounced almost every thinker who mattered —Copernicus, Galileo, Bacon, Servetus, Fernel, Harvey, Comenius, Sir Kenelm Digby, Sir Thomas Browne, Wilkins, Hobbes, and Nathanael Carpenter.

Laud read the illegally published *Prerogative of Parliaments*, quoted it in the House of Lords in the year of publication, and wanted to use it again at his trial. But he cited the Councillor's opinion of Magna Carta (it 'had an obscure birth from usurpation, and was . . . fostered and shewed to the world by rebellion'); whereas the J.P. in the dialogue represents Ralegh's point of view.[5] Sir Robert Filmer and Judge Jenkins similarly quoted Ralegh as an authority who will impress their opponents: 'as Sir Walter Raleigh confesseth', 'if we believe Sir Walter Raleigh'. Filmer too cited the Councillor in the *Prerogative of Parliaments* as though he expressed Ralegh's own opinion.[6] Sir John Oglander, who possessed the *History of the World*, thought

---

freedom, as a secularized version of Ralegh's conception of law in history. This conception died hard: see J. A. Froude, *Short Studies on Great Subjects* (ed. D. Ogg, 1963), pp. 34, 39.

[1] 'Though you in this, as in the rest, find me a fool', said Ralegh in a draft letter to James (E. Edwards, *Life of Sir Walter Raleigh*, 1868, ii, p. lxii; Thompson, op. cit., p. 238; *Letters of John Chamberlain*, i. 568).

[2] Captured by the Spaniards in 1620, her copy was recovered by a German when the Swedes recaptured Prague in 1648 (W. B. Rye, *England as seen by Foreigners in the Days of Elizabeth and James I*, 1865, p. 222). Elizabeth also had a copy of Foxe.

[3] Thompson, op. cit., p. 239.

[4] A. Ross, *The Marrow of Historie* (1650); *Som Animadversions and Observations upon Sir Walter Raleighs Historie of the World, wherein his mistakes are noted* (1653). *The Marrow of Historie* contains a poem by Benlowes which was not noticed by H. Jenkins in his *Edward Benlowes, 1602–1676* (1952).

[5] Laud, *Works* (1847–60), vii. 627–8; cf. iv. 375.

[6] Ed. P. Laslett, *Patriarcha and other Political Works of Sir Robert Filmer* (1949). pp. 97, 117, 143, 292; D. Jenkins, *God and the King* (1649), p. 6.

James I's attitude towards Ralegh in 1603 showed that the King was 'exceeding merciful'.[1] Laud's friend, Lord Scudamore, disapproved of Ralegh.[2] Bishop Goodman thought Sir Walter was 'a man of a great but of a dangerous wit', and held him in high esteem, but believed that he had been justly executed.[3] The Tory North family, Aubrey tells us, 'speaks not well of Sir Walter Ralegh, that Sir Walter designed to break with the Spaniard and to make himself popular in England'.[4] Enmity to Spain and a relatively democratic outlook: this adequately sums up the image of Ralegh which remained influential throughout the seventeenth century.

XIII

Ralegh's *History* was written for Prince Henry: so were the *Discourses* on the marriages of the royal children. So, it is said, was the *Discourse on the Invention of Ships*. The *Maxims of State* were probably presented to the Prince.[5] Henry's enthusiastic support for Ralegh, and the high hopes which his favour gave the latter, are well known. Sir Arthur Gorges, Ralegh's ally, Hariot's friend, translator of Lucan and Bacon, held 'a place of right good trust' in the Prince's service, as well as being a copyholder of Henry's manor of Richmond. Gorges dedicated his *Relation of the . . . Island Voyages* to Prince Henry in 1607, as well as the *Observations and Overtures concerning the Royal Navy*, probably written in collaboration with Ralegh, in 1610. The same year also saw Gorges's *Breefe Discourse tending to the wealth and strength of this Kingedome, written to . . . Henry, Prince of Wales*, which criticized court extravagance, the inflation of honours, and neglect of trade. Like all Gorges's writings, this is pervaded with Ralegh's spirit and policies.[6] Gorges wrote two poems on the Prince, and on his death composed not only a sonnet but also a full-dress poem, *The Olympian Catastrophe*, which incorporated lines previously used in Gorges's elegy on

[1] Ed. F. Bamford, *A Royalist's Notebook* (1936), pp. 194, 232.
[2] Aubrey, *Brief Lives*, ii. 188.
[3] G. Goodman, *The Court of King James I* (1839), i. 65, 68–69.
[4] Aubrey, *Brief Lives*, ii. 96.
[5] E. K. Wilson, *Prince Henry and English Literature* (Cornell U.P., 1946), p. 142.
[6] H. E. Sandison, 'Arthur Gorges, Spenser's Alcyon and Ralegh's friend', *P.M.L.A.* xliii. 664–72. The *Relation of the . . . Island Voyages* was reprinted by Purchas.

Sidney.[1] Again there are implicit criticisms of court flattery, faction, and parasitism.[2]

> Arts grew faint when this sweet prince was dead
> That in his life time them with bounty fed.[3]

So Gorges: for Henry had been seen as the new Maecenas of science and the arts.

The Prince's household, its Governor believed, 'was intended by the King for a courtly college or a collegiate court'.[4] It lived up to this aspiration. 'Without offence to either of the famous universities', said John Cleland in 1607, 'for all sorts of good learning I recommend in particular the Academy of our noble prince, . . . the true pantheon of Great Britain.'[5] The household was indeed a very remarkable collection of persons. Sir Thomas Chaloner (1561–1615), Governor of the Household, was the son of a translator of Chrysostom and Erasmus who was also a contributor to *The Mirror for Magistrates* (Sir Thomas Chaloner, 1521–65). The younger Sir Thomas was a naturalist and chemist, whom Bacon thought of as a possible supporter for his scientific schemes.[6] He was the father of a regicide (Thomas Chaloner, 1595–1661). Adam Newton, secretary and tutor to the Prince, had previously studied and taught in Protestant schools in France. Though a layman he was appointed Dean of Durham in 1605, an office which he sold in 1620 to buy a baronetcy. He employed his leisure in translating Paolo Sarpi's *History of the Council of Trent* into Latin, in co-operation with his friend William Bedell.[7] Giacopo Castelvetro, a former protégé of Ralegh and Northumberland, ended his days in Newton's household. In 1614 Castelvetro wrote a treatise to persuade the English to imitate the wholesome Italian habit of eating fruit and vegetables, which he dedicated to Lucy, Countess of Bedford, sister of Prince Henry's most intimate friend, Sir John Harrington of Exton (1592–1614).

---

[1] Ed. Sandison, *Poems of Sir Arthur Gorges* (1953), pp. 128–30, 135–82, 222.

[2] Ibid., pp. 172–3; cf. similar criticisms of James's pacific foreign policy in ibid., p. 133.   [3] Ibid., p. 165.

[4] T. Birch, *The Life of Henry, Prince of Wales* (1760), p. 97.

[5] Wilson, *Prince Henry and English Literature*, pp. 51–53.

[6] Bacon, *Works*, xi. 23. For Chaloner see p. 99 above. The elder Sir Thomas was a friend of Gresham.

[7] Birch, op. cit., pp. 372–3; J. W. Stoye, *English Travellers Abroad, 1604–1667* (1952), pp. 96, 147, 149; cf. pp. 51–52. For Bedell see p. 277 below.

Castelvetro had taught the latter Italian.[1] Sir Charles Cornwallis (d. 1629), Treasurer of Henry's household, was imprisoned for his opposition activities in the 1614 Parliament. He was the father of Sir William Cornwallis, the Baconian essayist. Richard Holdsworth was chaplain to and protégé of Sir Henry Hobart, Henry's Chancellor.[2]

Another of the Prince's tutors was Lord Lumley, a patron of scholars and founder of the Lumleian lectures on anatomy at the College of Physicians. Lumley, who was a Roman Catholic, was a member of the Elizabethan Society of Antiquaries, and had the best library in England, except perhaps for that of Sir Robert Cotton. On Lumley's death in 1609 Henry purchased this library out of his privy purse, and made Edward Wright, another of his tutors, its Librarian.[3] (In 1648 this library is said to have owed its preservation to Hugh Peter. In 1649 the Commonwealth appointed Bulstrode Whitelocke its Librarian, with John Dury as his deputy. Dury's *The Reformed Library Keeper* of 1650 resulted.)[4]

The appointment of Wright, one of the leading scientists of his day, as Henry's tutor, is remarkable enough. Wright caused a large sphere to be made for the Prince, which not only represented the motions of the heavens but likewise the positions of the sun and moon, and demonstrated the possibility of eclipses. Henry could hardly help being a Copernican or having an interest in mathematics, as well as in cosmography and fortifications.[5] Wright dedicated the second edition of his *Certaine Errours* to the Prince. Another of Henry's tutors was William Barlow.[6] Thomas Lydiat, friend and correspondent of Henry Briggs, and friend of the Puritan William Crashawe, was chronographer and cosmographer to the Prince's

[1] K. T. Butler, 'An Italian's Message to England in 1614', *Italian Studies*, ii. 4–16; Harleian MS. 3344, f. 3; E. Rosenberg, 'Giacopo Castelvetro, *H.L.Q.* vi. 122–39. See p. 144 above.

[2] For Hobart see p. 239 below.

[3] Birch, op. cit., pp. 161–3, 453; Wilson, op. cit., pp. 67–68; Taylor, *The Haven-Finding Art*, p. 215. For Lumley see p. 173 above; for Wright, pp. 38–42.

[4] Birch, op. cit., p. 164; Whitelocke, *Memorials of the English Affairs*, 28 July 1649. For Dury see pp. 100–4 above.

[5] Birch, op. cit., p. 389; Wilson, op. cit., pp. 53–55; Sir Charles Cornwallis's *Discourse of the most Illustrious Prince Henry* (1626, published 1641), in *Harleian Miscellany* (1744–56), iv. 323.

[6] Waters, op. cit., pp. 217, 275–6. For Barlow see pp. 38, 65–66 above.

household.[1] Joshua Sylvester, the translator of Du Bartas, was Groom of Henry's Chamber.[2] George Chapman was Sewer-in-Ordinary to the Household.[3] Inigo Jones was Henry's Surveyor of Works, John Bull, Gresham Professor of Music, one of his Musicians.[4] The Household also perhaps included Tom Coryate the traveller, as well as Sir Arthur Gorges in some place of trust.[5] Even Henry's nurse has a place in our story, since she was the mother of Ralph Cudworth and subsequently became the wife of Hartlib's friend John Stoughton.[6] Henry is said to have intended to found an academy for the English nobility and gentry, and especially the King's wards, on the lines of Ralegh's and Gilbert's 'Queen Elizabeth's Academy':[7] particular emphasis would have been laid on mathematics and languages. In the Parliament of 1621 Buckingham brought forward such a plan, attributing it to Henry.[8]

In addition to the scientific atmosphere of Henry's household, there seem to have been powerful influences in the Prince's entourage which favoured Puritanism. Sir John Harington of Kelston (1561–1612), another of Henry's tutors, wrote his

[1] Wilson, op. cit., p. 75; ed. J. O. Halliwell, *A Collection of Letters Illustrative of the Progress of Science in England* (1841), pp. 46–49, 54–55, 63–64. In 1603 Lydiat dedicated his *Emendatio Temporum* to the Prince. For Crashawe see p. 162 above.

[2] Wilson, op. cit., p. 105; P. Sheavyn, 'Patrons and Professional Writers under Elizabeth and James I', *The Library*, New Series, vii. 311. Sylvester dedicated the Fourth Day of the Second Week of Du Bartas to Henry, and wrote a sonnet to him. For Sylvester see pp. 138 above, 280 below.

[3] Wilson, op. cit., pp. 74–75. The *Iliads* and others of Chapman's poems were dedicated to Henry. For Chapman see pp. 141–3 above.

[4] Birch, op. cit., pp. 455–6. Since Henry would have had no one in his household who did not go regularly to Communion, this is an additional piece of evidence to disprove the legend that Inigo Jones was a Catholic (see E. S. de Beer, 'Notes on Inigo Jones', *Notes and Queries*, clxxviii. 292; R. Wittkower, 'Inigo Jones— "Puritanissimo Fiero" ', *Burlington Magazine*, xc. 51).

[5] M. Strachan, *The Life and Adventures of Thomas Coryate* (1962), p. 13. Coryate's *Crudities* was dedicated to the Prince.

[6] J. Tulloch, *Rational Theology in England in the 17th Century* (1874), ii. 194. For Stoughton and Cudworth see p. 101 above.

[7] See p. 138 above.

[8] J. Gutch, *Collectanea Curiosa* (1781), i. 212–15; E. M. Portal, 'The Academ Roial of King James I', *Proceedings of the British Academy*, 1915–16, p. 192. This scheme is often confused with the academy proposed by Edmund Bolton, a much more aristocratic (indeed papist) and less scientific affair. See also W. E. Houghton, 'The English Virtuoso in the 17th century', *J.H.I.* iii. 62; J. Evans, *A History of the Society of Antiquaries* (1956), pp. 17–19.

Briefe View of the State of the Church of England 'for the private use of Prince Henry, upon occasion of that proverb,

> Henry VIII pulled down monks and their cells,
> Henry IX should pull down bishops and their bells'.

It was not published until 1653. Sir Robert Darcy, the Prince's Gentleman Usher (whose widow was later a great patron of Puritan ministers), Lord Harrington of Exton (d. 1613, Governor to the Princess Elizabeth), and James Montague, Bishop of Winchester, brought some remarkable men to the Prince's attention, like Arthur Hildersham, the Puritan divine, and Henry Jacob, later an Independent. They designed John Burges to be Henry's chaplain, until he preached a sermon before James I which was so radical in its Puritanism that Burges had to emigrate to Leiden, where he took a medical degree. They then cast their eyes on Theodore Gulston's friend Thomas Gataker, another Puritan divine: but he proved too modest.[1] Joseph Hall the satirist, whom Bishop Montague denounced as a Puritan, became Henry's chaplain in 1608.[2] Prince Henry's household, in which servants were fined for swearing, thus gives physical confirmation of the congruence of Puritanism and science.[3]

Bacon dedicated his 1612 edition of his *Essays* to the Prince; four years earlier he had hoped to find him a better patron for his scientific projects than James I.[4] William Gilbert dedicated his *Philosophia Nova* to Henry some time before his death in 1603; it was not published until 1651. In 1607 Matthew Gwinne, Gresham Professor of Physic, dedicated his play *Vertumnus* to Henry, before whom it had been performed two years

---

[1] Birch, op. cit., pp. 390–1; Wilson, op. cit., p. 112. On his return to England Burges was neither allowed to preach nor to practise physic in London (despite commendations from Sir Theodore Mayerne) (ed. McClure, *Letters of John Chamberlain*, i. 470). He ultimately obtained a living in Warwickshire, after Lucy, Countess of Bedford, and Bacon had intervened with the King on his behalf. The famous Puritan William Ames married Burges's daughter and succeeded him as chaplain to Sir Horace Vere, commanding English troops in the Netherlands (Bacon, *Works*, xii. 371–2; S. B. Babbage, *Puritanism and Richard Bancroft*, 1962, p. 173; A. G. H. Bachrach, *Sir Constantine Huygens and Britain, 1596–1619*, Leiden, 1962, p. 25).

[2] Quoted by W. M. Lamont, *Marginal Prynne* (1963), p. 22. This is Richard Montague, Bishop of Chichester in 1628.   [3] See pp. 22–27 above.

[4] Bacon, *Works*, xi. 340 Cf. p. 99 above. For an alleged letter from Bacon to Prince Henry discussing the loadstone and magic, see J. W. Gough, *The Superlative Prodigall: a Life of Thomas Bushell* (1932), p. 147. Cf. also Bacon's character of the Prince in *Works*, vi. 319–29.

earlier. George Hakewill presented his treatise against regicide to the Prince. Thomas James dedicated the 1605 catalogue of the Bodleian Library to him.[1] Many other examples could be given.

Henry supported Ralegh's foreign policy, and would gladly have become 'in person the executor of that noble attempt for the West Indies'.[2] He obtained a patent for Robert Harcourt to revive Ralegh's Guiana schemes. The Prince was convinced of the importance of the North-West Passage, and in 1612 sent Thomas Button to discover it.[3] Phineas Pett, who made model ships for Henry, was sworn his servant in 1604, and was supported against Northampton in 1609. (Consistently with his general outlook, the Prince disliked the Howards.) He was also a patron of the East India Company.[4] In 1611 Henry held shares (along with his father and brother) in Simon Sturtevant's patent for smelting iron with coal. This precocious patent was subsequently transferred to a protégé of Henry's, John Rovenzon.[5]

So we can perhaps understand something of the despondency which Henry's premature death in 1612 caused. Elegies were written by William Browne, George Chapman, Donne, Drayton, Drummond, John Davies, Sir Arthur Gorges, Thomas Heywood, Henry Peacham, Ralegh, John Taylor, Cyril Tourneur, John Webster, George Wither, and very many others. Some of these names have figured in our story.[6] But not only men of letters had cause to grieve. Thomas Button's explorations ceased on his return after Henry's death, though Button remained convinced of the existence of the North-West Passage, and confided this belief to Henry Briggs.[7] Thomas Scott looked back in 1624 to Elizabeth and Henry as champions of aggressive Protestantism and a strong navy.[8] Already legends were forming

---

[1] Wilson, op. cit., pp. 33, 37, 111, 142. For Gwinne see p. 51 above; for Hakewill, pp. 199–202; for James, p. 25.

[2] Sir Charles Cornwallis, *Discourse of . . . Prince Henry, Harleian Miscellany*, iv. 322.

[3] Harcourt, *A Relation of a Voyage to Guiana* (1613); Birch, op. cit., p. 264.

[4] Ibid., pp. 96–97, 110–12; Wilson, op. cit., pp. 76–77. Pett's son Peter was a supporter of Parliament during the civil war.

[5] T. S. Ashton, *Iron and Steel in the Industrial Revolution* (1924), p. 10; P. Mantoux, *The Industrial Revolution in the 18th Century* (trans. M. Vernon, 1928), p. 292.

[6] Birch, op. cit., p. 367; Wilson, op. cit., pp. 137–49.

[7] Birch, op. cit., p. 265. Button was a near relation of the St. Johns and so a distant relation of Oliver Cromwell. He was subsequently knighted by his cousin Sir Oliver St. John, Lord Deputy of Ireland.

[8] T. Scott, *Vox Coeli* (1624), quoted by Wilson, op. cit., p. 169. *Vox Coeli* ran to four editions in 1624.

round his name, as they were to form round Ralegh's.

Henry's apparent interest in and patronage of science and Puritanism no doubt derives from the group which surrounded him. Although these men were originally selected by James I, by the time of the Prince's death there was a rivalry between the royal court and that of the Prince of Wales which almost anticipates the eighteenth century: and the nature of Henry's court gave to this personal rivalry political and ideological overtones. We need not exaggerate Henry's precocity if we note (as contemporaries noted) the striking contrast between his personality and interests and those of his younger brother. Whether if Henry had come to the throne he would have realized the high hopes held of him is conjectural, as Sir Arthur Gorges seems delicately to hint.[1] But at the time his death seemed to presage the end of an epoch. There was no more hope henceforth that Baconianism would receive government support than that exploration or a Protestant foreign policy would. Ralegh's cordial rallied the Prince but could not revive him; his grief rings out at the conclusion of the *History* and of its Preface. Ralegh is said to have burnt his notes for the second part of the *History*.[2] Coinciding as it did with real decline, Henry's death in many ways marks a turning-point between the glorious Elizabethan age and the age of melancholy and despair.[3] Many threads of our story lead forward from Henry's court: it is highly appropriate that the Prince's best biographer, Thomas Birch, should have been a Secretary of the Royal Society.

XIV

Finally, Ralegh was not only a sea-dog, a scientist, and an historian: far more important, even for our purposes, he was a great poet, and important figure in the history of English culture. He is supposed to have founded the Mermaid Club at the end of Elizabeth's reign. Chapman, Drayton and Ben Jonson as well as Spenser and Marlowe and perhaps William

[1] Gorges, *Poems*, pp. 172–3.
[2] Aubrey, *Brief Lives*, ii. 191. Sir William Petty referred to this incident in a letter of 1682, an allusion altogether misunderstood by his editor (*The Petty–Southwell Correspondence, 1676–1687*, ed. Lansdowne, 1928, p. 112).
[3] See pp. 8–12 above.

Warner were closely associated with him.[1] Ralegh helped a company of English players to obtain permission to go to Sweden in 1591–2.[2] The frontispiece to his *History of the World* and the explanatory verses attached (probably by Jonson) have their place in the history of emblem literature in England.[3] Set to music by Ferrabosco, Ralegh's 'Like to a hermit poor' was a popular song, very hackneyed by the sixteen-sixties.[4] Ralegh's lines, 'Even such is time', are inscribed on many seventeenth-century tombstones.[5] In his architecture too Ralegh was a forward-looking influence on the gentry: Sherborne Castle was a very early example of the non-courtier type of gentleman's house.[6]

The nature of Ralegh's poetry is relevant. Miss Bradbrook has reminded us of the uniqueness of *Cynthia*, in that the whole of its 500 lines have only one subject—Ralegh's state of mind.[7] Ralegh's place in the history of introspection, of the evolution of poetry from public to personal, of reflective poetry generally, still deserves consideration.[8] *Cynthia*, his longest poem, we are told, 'is the poem of a man blocked, a man conscious of exceptional powers which have been at the service of Cynthia-Elizabeth-England, and which are now wasting for want of use; a proud man, who cannot contemplate his fall, and yet has to'.[9] When we think of Ralegh in conjunction with Bacon and Coke, and indeed with the whole tone of Jacobean literature, we may suggest that the frustration was social as well

---

[1] M. C. Bradbrook, *The School of Night* (1936), pp. 38, 65, and *passim*; E. G. Clark, *Ralegh and Marlowe* (New York, 1941), *passim*. Warner's *Albions England* went through six editions between 1586 and 1612.

[2] Erik Wikland, *Elizabethan Players in Sweden, 1591–2* (Stockholm, 1962), pp. 25–26.

[3] Brushfield, 'Sir Walter Ralegh and his *History of the World*', *Trans. Devon Assoc. for the Advancement of Science, Literature and Art* (1887), p. 410. It is not mentioned in Rosemary Freeman's *English Emblem Books* (1948).

[4] Pepys, *Diary*, 12 February 1667; S. Butler, *Hudibras*, Book I, Canto ii, line 1169, quoted by N. L. Williams, *Sir Walter Ralegh*, p. 80.

[5] *Times Literary Supplement*, 12 and 26 October 1951.

[6] Mercer, *English Art, 1553–1625*, pp. 28–29. See pp. 22 above, 270 below.

[7] Bradbrook, op. cit., p. 87.

[8] Cf. the passage on individuality in the Preface to the *History*: 'Among those . . . whom we see and converse with, every one hath received a several picture of face, and every one a diverse picture of mind. . . . From whence it cometh, that there is found so great diversity of opinions' (*History*, i, p. iii; cf. p. vii). This type of individualism also made its contribution to the evolution of toleration.

[9] Joyce Horner, 'The Large Landscape', *Essays in Criticism*, v. 205.

as individual; and see the concern with law in the *History* as part of Ralegh's attempt to 'assert eternal Providence' and justify the ways of God to man. Here, no less than in his proposals in the sphere of foreign policy, economics, and the constitution, Ralegh had something to say to the pre-revolutionary generation.

Think of the typical lines in which Ralegh expressed 'those inmost and soul-piercing wounds, which are ever aching while uncured':

> And past return are all my dandled days.

> [Love] is won with a world of despair
>   And is lost with a toy.

> The broken monuments of my great desires.

> From fruitful trees I gather withered leaves
> And glean the broken ears with miser's hands,
> Who sometime did enjoy the weighty sheaves
> I seek fair flowers amid the brinish sand.

> Of all which past the sorrow only stays.

> What I possess is but the same I sought;
> My love was false, my labours were deceit.

> The grief remaining of the joy it had.[1]

And in prose the famous apostrophe to Death: 'Thou hast drawn together all the far-stretched greatness, all the pride, cruelty, and ambition of man, and covered it all over with these two narrow words, *Hic jacet*.'[2] 'When you have travailed and wearied your thoughts on all sorts of worldly cogitations,' Ralegh wrote to his wife in 1603, when he was expecting execution, 'you shall sit down by sorrow in the end.'[3] Professor Bush pointed out that nearly all the greatest meditations on death in English literature come from the early seventeenth century—the Bible, Shakespeare, Webster, Donne, Drummond, Bacon, Henry King, Sir Thomas Browne, Jeremy Taylor, Milton, &c.,

---

[1] Ralegh. *History*, i, p. i; *Poems* (ed. Latham), pp. 12, 23, 25–26, 29, 41, 44. Cf. the reply to Marlowe (p. 16) and *A Poem* (p. 21).

[2] *History*, vi. 370.

[3] Edwards, *Sir Walter Raleigh*, ii. 283.

&c.[1] Their concentration in this period would suggest social causes: so would the apparently exaggerated symbolic significance which contemporaries gave to the death of Prince Henry.

Ralegh's writings were as full of paradoxes as his life. He had tremendous vigour, energy, lust for life: 'he can toil terribly' said the deformed Robert Cecil enviously.[2] On the one hand he demanded unlimited human freedom; on the other he expressed a sense of utter impermanence, a lack of confidence in the effectiveness of human actions: 'the sorrow only stays'. 'Even his love-songs could at will supply an epitaph', Miss Latham noted.[3] In a heightened form it is the paradox of all the Jacobeans. The whole framework of the *History* is similarly paradoxical. Ralegh proclaims law in the universe—'this terrible sentence, that God will not be mocked'—and yet 'to what end do we lay before the eyes of the living the fall and fortunes of the dead, seeing the world is the same that it hath been, and the children of the present time will still obey their parents?'[4] Ralegh had at this stage a deep pessimism about the ability of human beings to learn the obvious lessons of history, to adjust their desires to what they know to be reasonable—a difficulty Ralegh himself shared to the full. He stated but did not solve the problem, though in *The Prerogative of Parliaments* he came near to it.

Solutions were, however, at hand, since the problem was not personal to Ralegh. One was the Puritan doctrine of predestination, which combined Ralegh's belief in an historical law with confidence in the ability of the Elect to carry God's historical purposes into effect. Ralegh was a Puritan without a sense of election. He believed in the abstract in the existence of the Elect: he did not feel on his pulses the power, confidence, and optimism which the conviction of salvation gave to many men of lesser intellectual stature. What a tremendous book the *History of the World* must have seemed to Cromwell when he read it after his conversion! The lessons—God's judgements on

[1] D. Bush, 'Science and Literature', in *17th century Science and the Arts* (ed. H. H. Rhys, Princeton, 1961), p. 48; cf. V. de Sola Pinto, *Enthusiast in Wit: a Portrait of John Wilmot, Earl of Rochester* (1962), pp. 189–90.

[2] Quoted by A. Latham, *Poems of Sir Walter Ralegh*, p. xvii.

[3] Ibid., p. 155.

[4] Ralegh, *History*, i, pp. xxviii, xxxv. See perceptive passage in Philip Edwards's *Sir Walter Ralegh* (1953), pp. 164–5.

the pride, ambition, and cruelty of princes—were clear to all; but Cromwell had a confidence in the ability of men like himself to be the agents of God's will on earth. It is a matter of temperament, of inner conviction, not a difference in intellectual outlook. At Naseby Cromwell had assurance of victory with his 'company of poor, ignorant men'. 'And God did it.'[1] To men with that inner spirit, Ralegh's pessimism played its part in undermining what they fought against: they simply did not share his doubts about human ability to build any more lasting mansion. Ralegh's scepticism is perhaps more sympathetic to our generation: but the Puritans got things done.

Another solution, of wider application, was that of Bacon. Separating—like Ralegh—first and second causes, and concentrating almost exclusively on the latter, Bacon virtually excluded God from the universe: the universe thus confronted man as nature. God was still not mocked, but nature was controllable. Man could master his circumstances by amassing and improving knowledge: he could conquer nature by obeying her. If in the past 'the road itself has been mistaken, and men's labour spent on unfit objects, it follows that the difficulty has its rise not in things themselves, which are not in our power, but in the human understanding, and the use and application thereof, which admits of remedy and medicine'.[2] Bacon's thesis is not unlike Ralegh's: he differs in his psychological confidence that enough men could learn the lessons of history, could throw off the frustrating traditions of the past, could sufficiently understand and follow God's and nature's laws to be able to remould the material world to the relief of man's estate: could get back behind the Fall in at least this respect.

'My system levels men's wits', said Bacon. This democratic appeal was an essential part of the Baconian optimism which rang out so sharply in the age when men found themselves stuck in the mud of melancholy and despair. 'I am now therefore to speak touching Hope. . . . And therefore it is fit that I publish and set forth these conjectures of mine which make hope in this matter reasonable; just as Columbus did, before that wonderful voyage of his across the Atlantic: . . . which reasons, though rejected at first, were afterwards made good by experience,

[1] Abbott, *Writings and Speeches of Oliver Cromwell*, i. 365.
[2] Bacon, *Works*, iv. 92.

and were the cause and beginnings of great events.'[1] The call, the challenge, and the promise would not be lost on men brought up in the assumption that God's Elect were always a small remnant, and that they would nevertheless always win.

Bacon and the Puritan Elect lacked the pessimism through which Ralegh and so many of his contemporaries expressed their frustrations, personal and social. Yet Ralegh too helped by his writings to build up the confidence which in the next generation saw George Hakewill fight the battle of the Moderns against the Ancients, and combat the theory of cosmic decay in order to establish the law-abidingness of the universe.

And by his life and death, even more than by his writings, Ralegh helped to brace Englishmen to the effort needed for carrying out the programme which he and Hakluyt had set before them. We must never forget how suddenly the possibilities opened up for England in Ralegh's own lifetime, how tenaciously he had to struggle to overcome the deeply ingrained conviction of Spanish invincibility. He never overcame it in James and his courtiers. But in preaching to the merchants and craftsmen, the sailors, instrument-makers, and scientists who were revolutionizing English navigation, Ralegh was going with the tide. In the end it went faster and further than he had perhaps dared to hope.

Even Ralegh's obsession with death was relevant for the pre-revolutionary generation. The *History* concludes with Death the Avenger, who humbles the proud and insolent. 'O eloquent, just and mighty Death! whom none could advise, thou hast persuaded; what none hath dared, thou hast done; and whom all the world hath flattered, thou only hast cast out of the world and despised.'[2] Did no one apply those words to the first two Stuarts, whom none could advise and whom all the world flattered? What none had dared, the men of 1649 did; and called in Death the Leveller to cast kingship out of the world.[3]

[1] Bacon, *Works*, iv. 91.

[2] Ralegh, *History*, vi. 370; cf. i. 60–61. Cf. Marlowe, *Tamburlaine*, Part II, Act IV, scene i.

[3] In 1649 Abiezer Coppe did in fact refer to God as a Leveller in the political sense (*A Fiery Flying Roll*, in N. Cohn, *The Pursuit of the Millennium*, 1957, p. 360). Winstanley said that Jesus Christ was the head Leveller (Sabine, op. cit., pp. 360–1).

V

SIR EDWARD COKE—MYTH-MAKER

These two movements—science and law reform—were at
the centre of the seventeenth-century revolution.

B. S. MANNING, 'The Nobles, the People and the Constitution',
P. and P., No. 9, p. 53.

To the grave and learned writers of histories my advice
is, that they meddle not with any point or secret of any
art or science, especially with the laws of this realm,
before they confer with some learned in that profession.

SIR EDWARD COKE, *3 Reports*, sig. D 2.

I

SIR EDWARD COKE was born in 1552. Throughout Elizabeth's reign he throve as a lawyer, steadily out-distancing
his great rival Bacon, and rising to be Speaker of the House
of Commons and Attorney-General. His famous *Law Reports*
began to appear in 1600. Eleven volumes were published during
his lifetime, two posthumously. Under James, Coke became
Lord Chief Justice, a position in which he distinguished himself
by defending the rights and privileges of the common law even
against the wishes of the King, until finally he was dismissed in
1616. In the twenties he was a leading critic in the House of
Commons, and has a large place in English history for the
constitutional theories and myths which he uttered there and in
the four volumes of his *Institutes*. Coke the constitutional lawyer
is a familiar figure. I shall be more concerned with the contribution of his legal ideas to the origins of the English Revolution.

Sir Edward was not a wholly attractive character. When he
died in 1634 his widow looked back over the ups and downs of
thirty-six years of married life. She said, 'We shall never see his
like again—praises be to God.'[1] Bacon had been Coke's rival

[1] Quoted by S. E. Thorne, *Sir Edward Coke, 1552–1952* (Selden Soc. Lecture,
1952, published 1957), p. 4.

for the lady's hand, as for so many other things. The Viscountess St. Albans left no equally memorable tribute to her husband —except that she married her gentleman usher within three weeks of Bacon's death. Coke made a fortune at the bar which James I regarded as too great for a subject,[1] and he had the reputation of being mean and a harsh landlord.[2] He was 'neither civil, nor affable, nor magnificent' said James, puzzled to account for his great influence.[3] As Attorney-General Coke behaved atrociously to Ralegh at his trial for treason, and no doubt to many lesser men of whom no record has survived.[4] Yet the bully was also a coward. When King James threatened him with clenched fist, Lord Chief Justice Coke literally grovelled and 'fell flat on all four'.[5] When he himself had broken the law three times over in his haste to marry Lady Hatton before Bacon could get her, and was had up in the Church courts, the greatest legal expert in the country pleaded ignorance of the law, made humble submission—and got off.[6]

After Coke's fall from royal favour in 1616, he hoped to reingratiate himself by marrying his daughter Frances to Sir John Villiers, brother of the royal favourite. When the lady refused, the ex-Lord Chief Justice seized her from her mother's protection in an armed raid and (according to one account) tied her to the bedpost and flogged her until she agreed.[7] The marriage was not an unqualified success. Her husband soon became subject to fits of melancholic depression, and was alleged to be impotent. Understandably, his wife soon left him, and had an illegitimate son amidst a blaze of high-society scandal.[8] In the week of the marriage Coke was restored to his

[1] C. W. Johnson, *Life of Sir Edward Coke* (1837), i. 25.

[2] See a letter wrongly attributed to Bacon in Bacon, *Works* (1826), v. 402. For an example of Coke's sharp dealing see *The Poems of Sir Francis Hubert* (ed. B. Mellor, Hong Kong, 1961), pp. xxxiii–xxxiv.

[3] Bacon, *Works*, xiii. 95.

[4] Ralegh's case is conspicuously not referred to in the *Third Part* of Coke's *Institutes*, which deals with high treason.

[5] Quoted in Sir W. Holdsworth, *History of English Law* (1922–50), v. 431.

[6] Strype, *Life of Whitgift* (1822), ii. 376, 401. The marriage was solemnized without banns or licence, in a private house, and at an illegal hour. Lady Hatton at least repented at leisure.

[7] L. Nosworthy, *The Lady of Bleeding Heart Yard* (1935), p. 62.

[8] *Letters of John Chamberlain*, ii. 88–89, 601. The son subsequently married the daughter of Sir John Danvers, a regicide, and changed his name to Danvers out of hatred to that of Villiers (Johnson, *Life of Coke*, ii. 80).

place on the Privy Council, but his fortunes at court were not permanently retrieved.

Coke can hardly be left out of an inquiry into the intellectual origins of the English Revolution, yet he presents difficulties. He was a lawyer, not an intellectual. The confusion and self-contradiction in his writings are so great that one is apt to dismiss them as of no significance for our purposes. Yet the legal historians have no doubt of his importance. 'A second father of the law, behind whose writings it was not necessary to go', said Sir James Fitzjames Stephen.[1] His books are 'the great dividing line' between medieval and modern, said Maitland. 'Though his work confounds the legal historian, its value can hardly be overestimated', adds Professor Thorne.[2]

To grasp Coke's significance we must recall what had been happening to English law. During the Tudor century decisive changes were taking place in society. The Church was completely subordinated to the secular power; the House of Commons rose to a position of new importance; there were sweeping economic changes. Peace and internal order, the end of feudal violence, the dissolution of the monasteries, and increased prosperity—I follow Hakewill's analysis—had 'set lawyers a-work'.[3] 'Peace is the mother of plenty—and plenty the nurse of suits', wrote Coke himself.[4] The common law had evolved in an agrarian society: it was the law of the land in both senses. In the early sixteenth century it seemed as though Chancery and the prerogative courts would secure jurisdiction over commercial cases with which the procedures of the common law were ill-adapted to cope. But the common law, in ways that are still obscure, made a remarkable comeback. Many leading lawyers were themselves men of property with growing commercial interests; and by a series of judicial decisions the common law began to be modernized and liberalized. But the process had not gone very far by the end of the sixteenth century. The resulting confusion, as many observers agreed, created a paradise for the dishonest lawyer.[5]

---

[1] Sir J. Fitzjames Stephen, *History of the Criminal Law of England* (1883), ii. 205.
[2] S. E. Thorne, op. cit., pp. 5, 13.
[3] Hakewill, *Apologie*, p. 548.
[4] Coke, *IV Institutes*, p. 76.
[5] Hakewill, loc. cit.; W. Carey, *The Present State of England* (1627), in *Harleian Miscellany* (1744–56), iii. 201–4. Carey gave excessive suits in law as one of three

So there was every reason for clarification and codification of the law, to define and systematize its adaptation to the needs of the new business society, to weed out the obsolete, to define relations between Church, prerogative, and common-law courts. Archbishop Bancroft's Canons of 1604 and the unpublished Canons of 1606 tried to codify the law of the Church.[1] A protégé of Bancroft's, Dr. Cowell, attempted in his *Interpreter* (1607) to codify secular laws in the interest of the prerogative. Parliament in 1606–7 and 1610 attacked the 1604 Canons as 'contrariant to the . . . great charter and other laws, statutes, liberties and free customs of this realm' and called for the abrogation of twenty-three of them.[2] The same Parliament, possibly at Coke's instigation, attacked Cowell.[3] The controversies over the billeting of troops and martial law, leading up to the Petition of Right, may be seen as two rival attempts to redefine the law.[4] It has been suggested that Charles I's Book of Orders of 1631 amounted to 'a most unambiguous abridgment of the law, both procedural and substantive, covering nearly the whole field of local government'.[5]

That the law was out of date, uncertain, and in need of refashioning was agreed on all sides. The laws of England, Barclay said in 1614, 'are few and very ambiguous. Much dependeth upon custom and the opinion of judges.'[6] There was, Ralegh suggested, 'none other difference between the judge and the thief, than in the manner of performing of their exploits; as if the whole being of justice consisted in point of formality'.

reasons why 'our fathers were very rich with little, and we poor with much'. Cf. also Wither:

> So costly be their wild interpretations
> Of laws and customs; and such variations
> Are found in their opinions, that few know
> When they uprightly or in safety go.

(*Brittans Remembrancer*, Spenser Soc. reprint, 1880, ii. 374–9: first published 1628.

[1] The former were accepted as binding by common-law judges until 1640 (R. G. Usher, *The Reconstruction of the English Church*, 1910, ii. 117).

[2] F. Thompson, *Magna Carta: its Role in the Making of the English Constitution, 1300 1629* (Minnesota U.P., 1948), p. 258.

[3] S. R. Gardiner, *History of England, 1603–42* (1883–4), ii. 66–67.

[4] L. Boynton, 'Martial Law and the Petition of Right', *E.H.R.* lxxix. 255–84.

[5] T. G. Barnes, *Somerset 1625–40* (1961), p. 179.,

[6] J. Barclay, *The Mirrour of Mindes* (Englished by T. May, 1631), p. 115. Hakewill agreed on the necessity for codifying and rationalizing the law (*Apologie*, p. 548).

This excessive formalism of English law permitted the corruption of justice 'by reward, hatred, favour'.[1] In 1603 Ralegh assumed that the commissioners for his trial would agree that the law was old fashioned and barbarous. 'You will know that the law of England hath need of a merciful prince', he said.[2] That this was not merely an *ad hoc* argument is shown by the passage in the *History* which stresses the royal prerogative of mercy, 'the law, in his own nature, being no other than a deaf tyrant'.[3] Bacon agreed that the penal laws should not be enforced too rigorously, or they would be 'a shower of snares upon the people'.[4]

From this confusion in the state of the law, Bacon tells us, followed multiplicity and length of suits; advantage to the litigious; excessive power to judges; and insecurity to property.[5] Coke agreed that the survival from an earlier age of 'unnecessary statutes unfit for this time' created new problems in a period of rapid changes in economic practice. 'Swarms of informers' were enabled to blackmail and penalize men whose economic activities had become necessary to the community.[6]

---

[1] Ralegh, *Works*, ii. 29–30, Ralegh hinted delicately that only fear of being punished for *scandalum magnatum* prevented louder outcry in England.

[2] Edwards, *Life of Ralegh*, ii. 271–3; cf. *Harleian Miscellany* (1744–56), iii. 248. Ralegh in his trial in fact came up against two of the major abuses of the English law of treason that the seventeenth century was to see amended—the possibility that a man might be condemned on the evidence of a single witness (which rested on a precedent from Mary's reign, and against which John Lilburne had to fight) and use of hearsay evidence, not excluded until near the end of the century (Holdsworth, *History of English Law*, ix. 214). Ralegh rejected hearsay as 'of no authority nor credit'. 'Common bruit is so infamous a historian' (*History*, i. 257; cf. also his speech about the Brownists in 1593, p. 171 above). He has been stigmatized as an uncritical historian; but his standards in regard to evidence were higher than those of Sir Edward Coke. Coke argued at Bacon's trial that only one witness was necessary in a charge of bribery. The need for two witnesses in treason trials was statutorily established in 1661. Sir J. F. Stephen cynically but plausibly observed that this was because members of the ruling class were more likely to be accused of treason than of other offences (*History of the Criminal Law*, i. 226, quoted by J. H. Wigmore, 'The Required Number of Witnesses', *Harvard Law Review*, xv. 91, 101).

[3] Ralegh, *History*, i. 36; cf. *Works*, i. 349. Coke also agreed in regretting the number of executions in England, though he did not think the law was to blame (*III Institutes*, Epilogue).

[4] Bacon, 'Essay of Judicature', *Works*, vi. 507.

[5] Bacon, *Works*, xiii. 64. Cf. E. W. Ives, 'The Reputation of Common Lawyers in English Society, 1450–1550', *Birmingham Historical Journal*, vii. 130–1: 'Lawyers and lawsuits were numerous because of the position which the law occupied in society.'

[6] Coke, *III Institutes*, pp. 191–4; cf. M. G. Davies, *The Enforcement of English Apprenticeship, 1563–1642* (Harvard U.P., 1956), *passim*; M. W. Beresford, 'The

Above all, insecurity to property. Yet it was 'the law which protects our property', a Gresham professor told his City audience in 1598.[1] 'The law of *meum* and *tuum*', Ralegh agreed, marked 'the difference between subjection and slavery.'[2] These definitions would have been accepted equally by Lord Burleigh, Sir John Eliot, John Pym, William Prynne, Henry Ireton, and John Lilburne. A legally protected absolute right of property was challenged only by extremists like Cowell and Roger Mainwaring—and, Pym said in 1641, by Strafford.[3] But James I was suspected covertly to favour Cowell: Charles and Laud made no secret of their support for Mainwaring and Strafford. Coke declared that his object in printing his *Reports* was 'the common good . . . in quieting and establishing the possessions of many'.[4] 'I did not love to have a king armed with book law against me for my life and estate', Sir Roger Twysden confided to his Journal in the agonizing days of choice at the beginning of the civil war.[5] He referred especially to the antiquarian exploits of Noy and his like.

In the Parliaments of 1593 and 1597 law reform in the interest of brevity and certainty had been proposed. In response to this discussion, young Francis Bacon tried his hand at reform by drafting 300 legal maxims, 25 of which he presented to Elizabeth as an aperitif. These maxims were generalizations from existing statutes and cases, drawn from several different fields of law. Books, Bacon told James I, 'must follow sciences, and not sciences books'.[6] But Bacon's maxims also aimed to state 'the general dictates of reason which run through the different matters of law and act as its ballast'. Hence when applied back as a criticism of existing laws they would—Bacon hoped—serve to promote consistency within and between them. So they

Common Informer, the Penal Statutes and Economic Regulation', *Econ. H.R.*, 2nd Series, x. 221–38; P. J. Bowden, *The Wool Trade in Tudor and Stuart England* (1962), Chapters V–VII.

[1] Ward, *Lives of the Gresham Professors*, p. 117. 'Fortunas quae tueatur jurisprudentia': the words are Matthew Gwinne's in his inaugural lecture as Professor of Physic.

[2] Ralegh, *Works*, i. 179.

[3] J. Rushworth, *The Tryal of Thomas, Earl of Strafford* (1680), pp. 662, 669–70.

[4] Coke, *1 Reports*, Preface to the Reader. On property and common law cf. M. A. Judson, *The Crisis of the Constitution* (Rutgers U.P., 1949), pp. 34–38, 335–8.

[5] Quoted in *Certaine Considerations upon the Government of England* (ed. J. M. Kemble, Camden Soc., 1849), p. lxxi.   [6] Bacon, *Works*, xiii. 67.

would help to remedy 'the uncertainty of law, which is the principal and most just challenge that is made to the law of our nation at this time'.[1] As later when he came to deal with natural science, Bacon wanted to draw upon the experience of the practitioners—the lawyers—but to give coherence and predictability to their practice by devising a general theory.[2]

We traditionally think of Bacon and Coke so much as rivals and political opposites that it is worth recalling that they agreed on the necessity for systematization of the law. 'It is a miserable bondage and slavery,' Coke observed, 'when the law is wandering or uncertain.'[3] 'Certainty is the mother of quietness and repose.'[4] Coke wrote in his presentation copy of the *Novum Organum*: 'You propose to reconstruct the teaching of wise men of old. Reconstruct first our laws and justice'[5]—which does not suggest hostility to law reform. Bacon himself was in favour of 'pruning and grafting the law', not 'ploughing it up and planting it again'. He praised Coke's *Reports*, which 'contain infinite good decisions and rulings over cases', side by side with errors and dogmatism. Bacon saw that they were the nearest that England had so far come to a codification of the law.[6] He wanted such reports to be published regularly.[7] Yet Bacon hoped that 'when Sir Edward Coke's *Reports* and my rules and discussions shall come to posterity, there will be (whatsoever is now thought) question who was the greatest

---

[1] Ibid. vii. 319.

[2] Bacon's legal maxims are interesting as his first use of aphorisms. They anticipate his later 'middle axioms' in philosophy, which Bacon always described as the most fruitful for works ('middle' because they stand between the lesser axioms derived from the particulars of sense on the one hand, and on the other those solid, properly defined propositions which Nature herself 'would acknowledge'—Anderson, *The Philosophy of Francis Bacon*, pp. 187-8). Maxims were a commonplace in legal thinking before Bacon, especially in the civil law. But Bacon—in law as in science—claimed that he kept closer to particulars than his predecessors. (For the whole of the above paragraph, cf. Kocher, 'Francis Bacon on Jurisprudence', *J.H.I.* xviii. 3-13.) Coke perhaps meant something similar when he defined a maxim as 'a sure foundation or ground of art and a conclusion of reason' (*I Institutes*, pp. 10b-11a).

[3] Coke, *6 Reports*, p. 42.

[4] Coke, *I Institutes*, p. 212a.

[5]   Instaurare paras veterum documenta sophorum;
        Instaura leges justitiamque prius.

(J. M. Gest, 'Writings of Sir Edward Coke', *Yale Law Journal*, xviii. 514.)

[6] Bacon, *Works*, xiii. 66-71.

[7] Ibid. xii. 86; cf. v. 104.

lawyer'.[1] Bacon's failure to achieve an agreed modernization of the law—the failure of the old régime—was Coke's opportunity.

In the thirteen volumes of his *Reports* Coke undertook the drudgery which Bacon preferred to leave to others. On this basis he could then attempt, in the four Parts of the *Institutes*, his own form of synthesis, very different from that which Bacon had tried to reach by the short cut of axioms.[2] To grasp Coke's achievement we must recall that there had been no Year Books since 1535. When Ben Jonson's Fungoso said, 'There's a parcel of law books . . .—Plowden, Dyer, Brooke and Fitzherbert, such as I must have ere long',[3] he named the only collections of reports (Plowden, 1571, Dyer, 1585) and the two abridgements (Fitzherbert, 1516, Brooke, 1574) published in the sixteenth century. There had been no systematic treatises at all since the fifteenth century.[4] In particular there was a complete absence of *recent* cases, reporting those decisions by which the law was being modernized.[5] This was the gap which Coke so successfully filled. And his method differed from that of his predecessors. Unlike them, he was mainly concerned with the 'resolutions' of the judges, their statements of general principle, whether these formed the basis of their verdict or were *dicta* by the way. ('Setting down sudden opinions of the judges for resolutions', an unfriendly critic called it.)[6] Coke wanted to reduce all to 'the fittest and clearest method', for 'the right understanding of the true reason and causes of the judgement and resolution in the case in question'.[7] His ultimate object was to draw together bodies of principle from a whole series of cases.[8] This is what a contemporary called 'scattering and sowing his own conceits

[1] Bacon, *Works*, xiii. 70.

[2] The *Institutes* partially corresponded to one of the three *desiderata* for the law which Bacon had laid down in *Works*, xiii. 69–70.

[3] Jonson, *Every Man out of His Humour*, Act ii, scene i.

[4] Coke, *3 Reports*, sig. C 2b; *10 Reports*, sig. d v–vi; cf. Van Vechten Veeder, 'The English Reports', *Harvard Law Review*, xv. 1–25; H. A. Hollond, 'English Legal Authors before 1700', *Cambridge Law Journal*, ix. 303–13; T. F. T. Plucknett, 'The Genesis of Coke's Reports', *Cornell Law Quarterly*, xxvii. 194–6.

[5] Cf. Bacon, 'The cases of modern experience . . . are fled from those that were adjudged and ruled in former times', quoted by Thorne, op. cit., p. 6.

[6] *The Lord Egerton's Observations on the Lord Coke's Reports* (n.d., ?1710), pp. 1–2. There is no adequate evidence for attributing these *Observations* to Egerton, but they may be by a clerk in his office.

[7] *8 Reports*, p. 49, quoted by Van Vechten Veeder, op. cit., p. 10.

[8] Plucknett, op. cit., pp. 196–201, 212–13.

almost in every case'.[1] Coke completed the task of collation that Bacon had called for; he applied reason to the work of synthesis with a view to ending the uncertainty of the law. In the application of reason, Coke had his presuppositions, as Bacon or anyone else would have had; but they were different from Bacon's.

II

A generation ago, in a pioneering article, Mr. D. O. Wagner suggested that Coke had a bias in favour of economic liberalism. Where the past offered no rule, as in the case of monopolies, Coke produced one for which his authorities gave no warrant, and declared that monopolies infringed Chapters 29 and 30 of Magna Carta.[2] He carried it off with *dicta* like 'all trades . . . which prevent idleness . . . are profitable for the commonwealth, and therefore the grant [of a monopoly] is against the common law, and the benefit and liberty of the subject'. When faced with a rule he did not like, such as the right of gilds to govern their trades, Coke quietly ignored the precedents, or turned them with another *dictum*—'at the common law no man could be prohibited from working at any lawful trade, for the law abhors idleness . . . especially in young men'.[3] He rejected gild privileges supported by royal charter, on the ground that only Parliament could interfere with the Englishman's right to engage in a lawful trade. And even 'Acts of Parliament that are made against the freedom of trades . . . [and] handicrafts . . . never live long'. He argued, in *laissez-faire* style, that the workings of the market would suffice to eliminate unskilled workmen.[4]

Mr. Wagner based his conclusions on an analysis of all the relevant cases in the *Reports* and *Institutes*, though he discussed

[1] Egerton's *Observations*, p. 2; cf. p. 20.

[2] Cf. *II Institutes*, p. 47: 'Generally all monopolies are against this Great Charter because they are against the liberty and freedom of the subject and against the law of the land.'

[3] *11 Reports*, Cases of Monopolies and of Ipswich Tailors; cf. *II Institutes*, pp. 47, 322, and J. U. Nef, *Industry and Government in France and England, 1540–1640* (American Philosophical Soc., 1940), p. 42. In 1621 the wharfingers of London quoted Magna Carta in a petition against the monopoly of the woodmongers (N.R.S. vii. 99).

[4] D. O. Wagner, 'Coke and the Rise of Economic Liberalism', *Econ. H.R.* vi. 30–44. All quotations from Coke in this paragraph, unless otherwise indicated, are from Mr. Wagner's article. Cf. p. 253 below.

only two of the 600 in any detail. He concluded that Coke sometimes deviated from precedents and stretched the meaning of statutes and Magna Carta. He unwarrantably weakened the statutes against engrossing and usury in the interests of individual enterprise. He accepted the customs of London, even where they were 'against common right and the rule of the common law'. 'There appears in Coke's writings a certain amount of what can only be described as propaganda against control.'[1] Mr. Wagner insisted that Coke merely summed up and consolidated a process that had begun before him; this was a crucial period in which legal decisions contributed very substantially to preventing the Crown establishing a control over the economic life of the country similar to that which the French monarchy enjoyed.[2] And Mr. Wagner was careful to say that his own conclusions were only tentative. They have not, so far as I am aware, been followed up by legal historians: but I have not seen them challenged, and they are accepted at least by Professor Thorne.[3] There is room for further research here, especially into the many cases in the later volumes of the *Reports* which deal with business matters. Although parts I–III are concerned mainly with land law, property and conveyancing, cases dealing with debts occur in ten of the last twelve volumes (2–9, 11–12); with bargain and sale in four (2, 5–7); with the customs of London in three (5, 8, 12); with municipal government (4, 11) and monopolies (11–12) in two; and deeds and agreements (2), bankruptcy (2), fraud (3), house property (4), perjury (5), usury (5), port customs (12), and forgery (13) all at least once.

It may be worth collecting one or two other facts which seem to support Mr. Wagner's thesis. Coke was a member of the Virginia Company, and believed that trade and traffic were the life of every commonwealth. A merchant was 'the good bailiff of the realm'.[4] 'Freedom of trade', Coke told the Commons of 1621, in words that recall Ralegh, 'is the cause that the Low Countries so prosper. They are not burdened with

---

[1] Wagner, op. cit., pp. 32–34, 42–44.

[2] Nef, op. cit., *passim*.

[3] S. E. Thorne, *Sir Edward Coke*, pp. 10–12. But see p. 265 below.

[4] Quoted in F. Thompson, *Magna Carta: its Role in the Making of the English Constitution*, p. 359; Coke, *2 Reports*, p. 79. Cf. N.R.S. ii. 76; Coke, *II Institutes*, pp. 41–42.

impositions to burden trade, nor monopolies to restrain it. In all acts of Parliament freedom of trade is held the life of trade.'[1] Coke wanted market tolls to be reduced.[2] He criticized clerks of the market, whose duties he felt should be taken over by J.P.s—as they were after 1640.[3] He pursued with implacable hatred monopolists and patentees, saltpetre men, informers, purveyors, and those who robbed Church and commonwealth 'by colour of pestilential patents of thievish concealments'.[4] On the other hand he did his utmost to weaken the Statute of Apprentices[5] and the prohibition on forestalling.[6] 'Those two great pronouns, *meum* and *tuum*' were never far from his thoughts.[7]

His digressions are sometimes illuminating. Cap. xi of the Statute of Gloucester was made the occasion for advocacy of an expansion of English exports, as well as of conservation of English timber.[8] A gloss on socage tenure was used to denounce idleness, 'the ground and beginning of all mischiefs'.[9] Coke warmly advocated houses of correction for sturdy beggars.[10] A debate on subsidies in 1625 was used to recommend employing tradesmen rather than aristocrats in the Admiralty and Ordnance departments, and taking steps to improve waste grounds and forests.[11] Coke wanted to see feudal tenures abolished.[12] In 1628 he attacked arbitrary imprisonment as 'a badge of a villein'; 'this imprisoning destroys all endeavours', makes a man 'tenant at will for liberty', and 'a tenant at will

[1] N.R.S. v. 93.   [2] *II Institutes*, pp. 221–2.

[3] *IV Institutes*, pp. 273–5; cf. *The Lord Coke His Speech and Charge* (1607), sig. G 4. Coke denied the authenticity of this pamphlet (7 *Reports*, Preface), but it appears to represent his views on this matter.

[4] *10 Reports*, sig. d, and Arthur Legat's Case; *12 Reports*, Case of the King's Prerogative in Saltpetre; *II Institutes*, pp. 224, 543–6; *III Institutes*, pp. 83–84, 181–5; *IV Institutes*, p. 76; *Speech and Charge*, sig. G 4–H 1b. Cf. Bacon, *Works*, xi. 97–101.

[5] *13 Reports*, pp. 12–13; cf. M. G. Davies, *The Enforcement of English Apprenticeship, 1563–1642*, pp. 241–3, and E. Heckscher, *Mercantilism* (trans. M. Schapiro, 1935), i. 292–3, on Tolley's Case, in which Coke is reported to have gratuitously exempted several unskilled occupations from the Statute of Apprentices.

[6] N.R.S., v. 93.   [7] *III Institutes*, Proeme, sig. B 2.

[8] *II Institutes*, pp. 323, 307.

[9] *I Institutes*, p. 85b; cf. *III Institutes*, Epilogue.   [10] *II Institutes*, p. 734.

[11] Ed. S. R. Gardiner, *Debates in the House of Commons, 1625* (Camden Soc., 1873), pp. 85–87, 131–3.

[12] F. Pollock, *The Land Laws* (1887), p. 127. Cf. J. Hurstfield, *The Queen's Wards* (1958), pp. 166–8; Sir T. Smith, *De Republica Anglorum* (ed. L. Alston, 1906), Book 3, Chapter 5.

never keeps anything in reparation'.[1] One of Coke's most quoted passages of eloquence about the common law being the best birthright of the subject comes in a section discussing the landlord's right to distrain for unpaid rent.[2] In the Case of Corporations Coke strongly favoured the development towards oligarchical rule in municipal government.[3] In Tyringham's Case he went out of his way to advocate *laissez-faire*. 'Make what statutes you please, if the ploughman have not a competent profit for his excessive labour and great charge, he will not employ his labour and charge without a reasonable gain to support himself and his poor family.'[4]

In Bonham's Case (1608–10), Coke denied the power of the College of Physicians to fine and imprison unlicensed physicians practising within seven miles of London. For this would make the Censors of the College at once judges and parties, which was unjust, and so this clause in the act was void. Lawyers and political theorists have perhaps made too heavy weather of this case. We need not read into it issues affecting fundamental law or the sovereignty of statute.[5] Coke was faced with a monopoly which denied the right of men to sell their skills on the open market, and which made the monopolists at once prosecutors, judges, and beneficiaries from the fine. The procedure which the College adopted was sufficiently like that of Church and prerogative courts to strike Coke as 'against common right and reason'. Nor should we over-emphasize the confusion and contradiction which we can see in his attitude to statute and fundamental law. Sir Edward's theory of sovereignty was that of Bodin, not that of Hobbes. Coke's unspoken assumption that men have a right to do what they will with their own persons and skills represents the thread of continuity running through all

---

[1] *Lords' Journals*, iii. 761.

[2] *I Institutes*, p. 142.   [3] *4 Reports*.

[4] *4 Reports*, p. 39. Cf. Coke's pleasure at the assimilation of copyholders to the position of freeholders (*The Complete Copyholder*, para. 9).

[5] Bonham's Case first became of political and constitutional importance when it was quoted against Parliamentary sovereignty—by Judge Jenkins in 1647, and by Lilburne in his *Legall Fundamentall Liberties* (1649). See J. W. Gough, *Fundamental Law in English History* (1955), pp. 30, 64–65, 111; cf. Judson, *The Crisis of the Constitution*, pp. 100–3; S. E. Thorne, 'Dr. Bonham's Case', *L.Q.R.* liv. 543–52. Coke's attitude in Bonham's Case seems to override the judgement in Read *v.* Jenkins (1595), and the other three judges were against him; but Hobart adopted Coke's position later (J. Bell and T. Redwood, *A Historical Sketch of the Progress of Pharmacy in Great Britain*, 1880, p. 5; Gough, op. cit., p. 38).

his decisions.[1] It explains his campaign for economic liberalism. In 1607 Coke is found protecting apothecaries against physiciains: 'to be an apothecary and then a physician is no disparagement, but a mean to prove the better physician, as an attorney or clerk may after prove the better judge'. As a result provincial apothecaries won the right to practise as physicians.[2]

Just as Magna Carta had been transformed from a baronial charter of privileges into a declaration of the rights of all free Englishmen: so Coke gave a new significance to a highly feudal principle when he argued that 'the house of an Englishman is to him as his castle'.[3] For in the sixteenth and seventeenth centuries more and more Englishmen whose houses were also workshops became rich enough to be able to wage law; and at the same time governments strove more and more to enforce a regulation of industry and agriculture which could only be made effective by extending inspection into private houses. And when it came to billeting, as it did in the sixteen-twenties, Coke's phrase acquired an almost revolutionary significance.

Two other examples may illustrate Mr. Wagner's point that Coke was merely summing up a process initiated by other judges. First, the transference of commercial causes from the Court of the Admiralty (as well as from gilds) to the common-law courts. In about 1570 Elizabeth complained that the Lord Mayor and Sheriffs of London were taking on themselves to try cases of contracts arising upon and beyond the seas, which properly belong to 'Our Court of Admiralty', feigning the same to have been done within some parish or ward of London.[4] The complaint was repeated in very similar terms in 1598 and in 8 James I.

Merchants disliked the Admiralty Court, in whose jurisdiction they had no part, and whose personnel and procedure were closely linked with those of the Church courts.[5] One of the

---

[1] Cf. C. B. Macpherson, *The Political Theory of Possessive Individualism* (1962), Chapter III. See also p. 253 below.

[2] Roberts, op. cit., p. 374. Yet Coke—consistently—opposed the patent granted to the Apothecaries by the royal prerogative. See p. 80 above.

[3] *5 Reports*, p. 91b; *11 Reports*, p. 82b; cf. *2 Reports*, p. 32a, *7 Reports*, p. 6a, *8 Reports*, p. 126a; *III Institutes*, p. 162.

[4] A. T. Carter, 'Early History of the Law Merchant in England', *L.Q.R.* xvii. 244; cf. F. C. D. Tudsbery, 'Law Merchant at Common Law', ibid. xxxiv. 398–9; Blackstone, *Commentaries on the Laws of England* (twelfth ed., 1794), iii. 105–8.

[5] J. S. Purvis, *The Records of the Admiralty Court of York* (St. Anthony's Hall Papers,

main functions of the court was the collection of the Lord Admiral's perquisites.[1] (Cf. Ralegh's reference to the loss which merchants might suffer from 'some prowling Vice-Admiral'.)[2] The Privy Council took great interest in the Admiralty's proceedings, and frequently interfered with its judicial functions.[3] But merchants liked the common-law courts little better, since these were slower and unable to order positive action. Gradually, however, the common lawyers began to recognize the existence of a 'law merchant', a separate body of customs accepted by merchants. In the last three decades of Elizabeth's reign there were complaints that the Admiralty's business was falling off, because of common-law prohibitions, and of the right of the Spanish Company to hear and determine suits in which its members were involved.[4] A transitional stage in weaning commercial cases from the Admiralty Court, which shows the active participation of merchants in the process, was the statute 43 Eliz. cap. 12, setting up a Court of Policies and Assurance. The Commissioners of this court were the Recorder of London, two doctors of the civil law, two common lawyers and 'eight grave and discreet merchants'. We do not know how effectively the court functioned: Lewes Roberts in 1641 complained of 'delays and hindrances that happen by tedious suits in adventures at sea among merchants'.[5] In any case the court's activity was confined to London, and no provision was made for excluding either the Admiralty or the common-law courts from its sphere. It seems to have faded out before or during the Interregnum.[6]

In 1622 Gerard Malynes failed to mention the Admiralty in

No. 22, 1962), p. 4; cf. pp. 14–15 for a list of the types of business which the York Court regarded as appertaining to it.

  [1] 'Throughout the sixteenth and seventeenth centuries the Admiralty was looked upon mainly as a source of profit', R. G. Marsden, 'The Vice-Admirals of the Coasts', *E.H.R.* xxii. 477.

  [2] Ralegh, *Works*, ii. 30.

  [3] Ed. Marsden, *Documents Relating to the Law and Custom of the Sea*, i, *1205–1648* (Navy Records Soc., 1915). Mr. Mardsen refers especially to the fifteen-nineties. Cf. *English Privateering Voyages to the West Indies, 1588–95* (ed K. R. Andrews, Hakluyt Soc., 1959), pp. 3–4.

  [4] Ed. Marsden, *Select Pleas in the Court of Admiralty*, ii, *1547–1602* (Selden Soc., 1899), pp. xii–xv, xliii–lvii, lxxix. Cf. R. Zouch, *The Jurisdiction of the Admiralty of England Asserted against Sir Edward Coke* (1663), pp. 143–5.

  [5] L. Roberts, *The Treasure of Traffike* (1641), in *Early English Tracts on Commerce* (ed. J. R. McCulloch, 1856), pp. 81, 85.

  [6] *IV Institutes*, p. 250; F. D. MacKinnon, 'The Origins of Commercial Law',

discussing *Lex Mercatoria*. He argued that matters of account should be tried in Chancery, 'leaving all other cases triable by the common law', though the procedure in all courts should be accelerated. What was really needed was to make the common law 'an art or science' by codification and taking away 'all ambiguities and dark sentences'.[1] In fact, by the time this treatise was written, the common lawyers were well on the way to recognizing law merchant as 'part of the laws of this realm'.[2] In the year which saw the publication of *Lex Mercatoria* C. J. Hobart could state that 'the custom of merchants is part of the common law of this kingdom, of which the judges ought to take notice; and if any doubt arise to them about their custom they may send for the merchants to know their custom, as they may send for civilians to know their law'.[3]

Under Coke the common-law courts were beginning to claim sole jurisdiction over contracts made beyond sea for doing any action or paying any money in England. The Admiralty, which recognized law merchant and had hitherto enjoyed jurisdiction, was declared to be no court of record, and so unable to take recognizances: rivers, ports, and creeks were part of England, and so exempt from Admiralty jurisdiction. Forty-five prohibitions were issued to the Admiralty in the first eight years of James I.[4] Coke vigorously supported this campaign for extending the common law's jurisdiction. His view of the limits of Admiralty jurisdiction conflicts with that of the judges of Queen's Bench in 1575, with Bacon's in 1616, and with the resolutions which Charles I got all the judges to agree to in 1633.[5] Coke had intended to print Thomlinson's Case— the decisive case—in his *7 Reports* in 1608, but the King forbade

L.Q.R. lii. 37; Holdsworth, *History of English Law*, viii. 289; F. Martin, *The History of Lloyds* (1876), p. 50, quoted in W. J. Jones, 'English Marine Insurance', *Journal of Business History*, ii. 63–66.

[1] G. Malynes, *Consuetudo, vel Lex Mercatoria* (1626), sig. A 5, pp. 306–15: first published 1622.

[2] *I Institutes*, p. 182a; cf. 172a.

[3] *Reports of . . . Sir Humphrey Winch* (1657), pp. 24–25, quoted (inaccurately) by MacKinnon, op. cit., p. 33. Hobart was Chancellor to Prince Henry and Holdsworth's patron (see p. 215 above).

[4] *6 Reports*, Dowdale's Case; *12 Reports*, pp. 78–79, 104; *13 Reports*, pp. 51–54; *I Institutes*, p. 261b; *IV Institutes*, pp. 134–6, 141–2. Cf. Holdsworth, *History of English Law*, i. 554; MacKinnon, op. cit., p. 34.

[5] Bacon, *Works*, xiii. 91; Zouch, *The Jurisdiction of the Admiralty*, pp. 47, 120–3; H. J. Crump, *Colonial Admiralty Jurisdiction in the 17th Century* (1931), pp. 18–23.

it. It was not published until 1658.[1] But by then the monarchy had fallen and Coke's battle had been won.

In conducting this squabble, Coke and the other judges may have been motivated mainly by reasons of prestige and profit. But the important underlying factor was the growing corruption of the Admiralty under the Howards and Buckingham, and its use for political purposes. If the common law was to be made (in C. J. Holt's phrase) 'the overriding jurisdiction of the realm', it must subsume law merchant.[2] In fact the Admiralty survived the crisis of 1641, together with Chancery, experience of which in 1624 had made Chamberlain speak of the law as 'one of the greatest grievances of the commonwealth.'[3] In April 1648 Admiralty jurisdiction was limited, and the court brought under Parliament's control. It survived only because the common lawyers, on the defensive against radical reformers, were disinclined to sacrifice *any* existing institution. Yet after 1660 the Admiralty, without a Lord Admiral, dealt with little but prize cases; its commercial jurisdiction went to the common-law courts. The full process was not completed till the eighteenth century; but it was Coke who 'secured for the common law control over the development of the commercial law'.[4]

A similar story can be told about the Commissioners of Sewers. These traditional and inoffensively named bodies were composed of the principal county landowners, nominated by the government. They performed functions which were subtly changing in the sixteenth century with the development of large-scale land reclamation. In the early seventeenth century the Privy Council supported the Earl of Bedford and other great landowners in schemes for draining the Fens which were bitterly opposed by the commoners in the Isle of Ely, led first by Oliver Cromwell's uncle and then by Cromwell himself

[1] *12 Reports*, p. 104.

[2] Sir W. Holdsworth, *Some Makers of English Law* (1938), p. 130.

[3] Chamberlain, *Letters*, ii. 564, 598–9; cf. *III Institutes*, 123–8, *IV Institutes*, p. 86. In 1650 a radical law reformer remarked sardonically that Bacon was the only Lord Chancellor who had died poor (J. Jones, *The New Returna Brevium*, 1650, p. 28). For the greater likelihood that the Admiralty would find for the Crown (in cases of prize and smuggling) than the common-law courts, see G. L. Beer, *The Old Colonial System, 1660–1668* (New York, 1912), i. 294–308.

[4] Holdsworth, *Some Makers*, pp. 130, 159; *History of English Law*, i. 556–8; Purvis, op. cit., pp. 5, 31–33; [Anon.], *Reasons for Settling Admiralty Jurisdiction* (1690), in *Harleian Miscellany* (1744–56), viii. 359–64.

after he had inherited his uncle's land. In backing up the drainers against 'riots, insolencies and disturbances' the Commissioners had departed from their traditional medieval functions of preventing rivers and drainage channels from over-flowing, and keeping them free from obstruction. The Commis-sioners' activities might be of advantage to the commonwealth, though there were two views about that, but they were not merely enforcing traditional common-law obligations.[1] In 1610 Rowland Vaughan alleged that the Commissioners of Sewers arbitrarily overrode both the common law and local opinion to maintain weirs on the river Wye in which some of the Commissioners had vested interests; to the hindrance of river navigation, and so of local trade, and of salmon-fishing, which 'gave sustenance' to many thousands in five or six shires. The opponents of the Commissioners, significantly for our purposes, asked only for the law of the land.[2]

The Commissioners of Sewers had very wide powers: they could fine and imprison without limit, and could decide for themselves what constituted 'contempt' for their authority.[3] The City of London thought it worth while to get a special Act of Parliament (3 Jac. I, cap. 14) removing London watercourses from their jurisdiction,[4] which suggests that there were grounds for apprehension. There were disputes at the beginning of James's reign about the powers of Commissioners of Sewers to make new channels as well as maintaining the old ones.[5] In Rooke's Case (1610) the judges decided that the proceedings of Commissioners of Sewers 'ought to be limited and bound within

[1] L. L. Jaffe and E. G. Henderson, 'Judicial Review in the Rule of Law', *L.Q.R.* lxii. 350–5.

[2] Ed. E. B. Wood, *Rowland Vaughan His Booke* (1897), pp. 50–62. There was a similar quarrel in Kent in 1600. Here the Commissioners ordered weirs to be re-moved, but did nothing to remove mills which obstructed navigation. In 1610 landowners in Devon and Cornwall, in the interests of their weirs, mills, and fish-ponds, tried to stop the use of rivers to float wood down to the coast (Taylor, *Late Tudor and early Stuart Geography*, pp. 120–1).

[3] S. and B. Webb, *English Local Government: Statutory Authorities for Special Purposes* (1922), p. 24, and *passim*. Cf. Robert Callis, *The Reading . . . Upon the Statute of 23 Hen. VIII Cap. 5, of Sewers* (1647: delivered at Gray's Inn 1622), *passim*; [Anon.], *Instructions to Jurymen on the Commission of Sewers* (1664); [Anon.], *The Laws of Sewers* (1732), pp. 35 ff.; [Anon.], *Of the Laws and Commissions of Sewers* (n.d. ? early eighteenth century), esp. pp. 6–9.

[4] *IV Institutes*, pp. 275–7. The Lord Mayor of London was responsible for the conservation of the Thames as far as Staines.

[5] H. C. Darby, *The Draining of the Fens* (second ed., 1956), p. 31.

the rules of reason and law', and refused to support the administration's policy even when pressed to do so. In particular they regarded it as illegal to tax the subject to pay for new drainage schemes which those taxed did not approve of. This was one of the points on which Coke was questioned by the Privy Council in 1616. 'Sometimes when the public good is pretended', said Sir Edward sardonically, 'a private benefit is intended; and if any such new invention is in truth (*quod raro aut nunquam fit*) good for the commonwealth, and yet no consent can be obtained for the making of it, then there is no remedy but to complain in Parliament.'[1] But the Privy Council backed up the drainers, and Coke's dismissal in 1616 led to a temporary defeat of the attempt to prevent Sewers Commissioners acting as agents of royal policy. The Council decided that Commissioners of Sewers could not only make new works, but could lay the charges on the towns and hundreds which would benefit by them, without even waiting for a survey in case of necessity.[2] Court pressure on local Commissioners of Sewers, and resistance to it, continued.[3]

But meanwhile the gentry had fought back. Oliver Cromwell 'was especially made choice of by those who ever endeavoured the undermining of regal authority' to be their spokesman to the Commissioners of Sewers at Huntingdon, 'in opposition to His Majesty's most commendable design' of backing the Fen drainers.[4] When the Long Parliament was preparing the Grand Remonstrance, its summary of Charles I's misdemeanours, Cromwell was added to a committee to 'explain the Commission of Sewers'.[5] The resultant paragraph 32 of the Remonstrance may safely be attributed to him. 'Large quantities of common and several grounds', it said, 'hath been taken from the subject by colour of the Statute of Improvement, and by abuse of the Commission of Sewers, without their consent and against it.' After the abolition of the prerogative courts, com-

---

[1] *5 Reports*, Rooke's Case; *10 Reports*, Case of the Isle of Ely. Such complaint, Coke added with grim satisfaction, had been utterly rejected in 3 Jac. I.

[2] Sir W. Dugdale, *A History of Imbanking and Drayning* (1662), pp. 371–2.

[3] L. E. Harris, *Vermuyden and the Fens* (1953), *passim*.

[4] Dugdale, *A Short View of the Late Troubles in England* (1681), p. 460; cf. Sir Philip Warwick, *Memoirs of the Reign of King Charles I* (1813), pp. 217–18. For the profits which the beneficiaries hoped to gain, see H. Mirrlees, *A Fly in Amber* (1962), pp. 316–22.   [5] *C.J.* ii. 309.

missioners were no longer liable to government pressure on behalf of high-placed individuals, and the common-law courts reasserted their authority. The local Commissions of Sewers seem more and more to have merged with quarter sessions.[1] Thus in yet another sphere the right of the propertied not to be taxed without their own consent was asserted, and an incipient system of administrative law was checked, all the more noxious in that early Stuart administrators were never above suspicion. Coke again seems to have been the decisive figure, though the Lord of the Fens may have made the victory of Coke's interpretation of the law possible.

III

Part of the difficulty in assessing Coke's originality stems from his success. In the Parliament of 1621 he took the lead in proposing a whole programme of law reform. He introduced a Bill against monopolies which failed to pass. But 'good Bills in Parliament seldom die':[2] its passage in 1624 put Coke's interpretation of the law on the statute book.[3] Coke, described as 'the Hercules and pillar of the House',[4] also supported in 1621 a Bill against informers and promoters, which became law in 1624.[5] In 1621 he proposed a Bill to subordinate Chancery to the common-law judges.[6] In the same Parliament William Hakewill was one of the members of a committee to review and rationalize the laws.[7] A number of Bills were proposed, for abolishing the death sentence for small offences, for reforming the law of debt,[8] and many others whose object was to reform the law.[9]

In four important respects Coke anticipated legal reforms which were to be partially realized during the Interregnum,

---

[1] L. L. Jaffe and E. G. Henderson, 'Judicial Review in the Rule of Law', *L.Q.R.* lxii. 355; cf. Barnes, *Somerset, 1625–1640*, pp. 148–52.

[2] *IV Institutes*, pp. 32, 83.

[3] N.R.S. v. 289–90; cf. *II Institutes*, p. 96, *III Institutes*, pp. 181–95; E. R. Foster, 'The Procedure of the House of Commons against Patents and Monopolies, 1621–4', in *Conflict in Stuart England: Essays in Honour of Wallace Notestein*, ed. W. A. Aiken and B. D. Henning (1960), pp. 59–85.

[4] N.R.S. v. 284.

[5] 21 Jac. I, cap. 4; cf. Davies, *Enforcement of English Apprenticeship*, pp. 73–74.

[6] N.R.S. ii. 265, 223; iii. 98; vii. 586.   [7] Ibid. iv. 47–48.

[8] *H.M.C., Third Report, Appendix*, pp. 17, 26.   [9] N.R.S. vii. 300–7.

though two of them not finally until the nineteenth century. First, Coke opposed the sale of legal offices 'for they that buy dear must sell dear';[1] this at a time when a M.P. could say 'the price of a serjeant is as known as the price of a calf.'[2] The actual occasion of Coke's dismissal in November 1616 was his refusal to allow Buckingham to pocket the revenues of the office of chief clerk of pleas in the King's Bench, the incumbent of which was resigning for the purpose. Coke said that the money should go to increase the judges' inadequate salaries.[3] For secondly—and this is a corollary of opposition to sale of office—Coke wanted fees to be replaced by steady and adequate salaries.[4] Thirdly, he opposed torture, which he declared was not warranted by the common law,[5] though as Attorney-General he had (on royal insistence) authorized its application as part of the preliminary examination of a suspect.[6] Fourthly, Coke objected to the traditional practice whereby the government took extra-judicial opinions from the judges, or ordered a stay of judgement until the royal pleasure was known. His new principle was established by the end of the seventeenth century. The collapse of the old régime and the victory of Coke's law led to a permanent separation between judicial and administrative functions and so to the elimination of torture from English judicial proceedings.

James I and his Privy Council in 1616 thought that Coke's *Reports* contained 'many exorbitant and extravagant opinions', and had tried vainly to make him expurgate them.[7] In 1621, when Coke was committed to the Tower, his manuscripts were seized, and three of them were never recovered.[8] Ten years later, when it was reported that Coke was 'about a book

---

[1] *I Institutes*, p. 234; *II Institutes*, p. 566; *III Institutes*, p. 154. The example given is Sir Arthur Ingram's purchase of the office of Cofferer of the Household; so Coke stretched the conception of legal office far into the civil service.

[2] Sir Francis Seymour, in *Debates of the House of Commons in 1625* (ed. Gardiner), p. 111.

[3] C. W. Johnson, *Life of Sir Edward Coke* (1837), i. 329–31. Coke's successor (Montague) had to sign an agreement to Buckingham's proposal before being appointed. Coke also declared that judicial offices could not be granted in reversion (*11 Reports*, Auditor Curle's Case and sig. A 6).

[4] *II Institutes*, p. 210. Cf. R. Robinson, 'Anticipations under the Commonwealth of Changes in the Law', *Select Essays in Anglo-American Legal History*, i (1907), p. 478.

[5] *III Institutes*, p. 35.   [6] Bacon, *Works*, xii. 93, xiv. 78–79.

[7] Bacon, *Works*, xii. 399; G. Goodman, *The Court of King James I*, ii. 161–3.

[8] C. W. James, *Chief Justice Coke, his family and descendants at Holkham* (1929), p. 40.

concerning Magna Carta',[1] Charles I prohibited its publication, fearing 'somewhat may be in prejudice of his prerogative, for Sir Edward is held too great an oracle amongst the people, and they may be misled by anything that carries such an authority as all things do that he either speaks or writes'.[2] When Coke lay dying in 1634 his house was ransacked, and fifty-odd manuscripts were taken away, including the last three Parts of the *Institutes*.[3] The old régime was well aware of the danger and of the appeal of Coke's views, and effectively silenced him. The Long Parliament had hardly sat for a month when it appointed a committee to recover Coke's confiscated writings, and in 1641, on the same day as it voted the execution of Strafford, ordered the remaining three Parts of the *Institutes* to be published.[4] *12* and *13 Reports* appeared in the fifties. Henceforth the *Reports* and the *Institutes* were accepted as the law of the land. Such modernization and codification as English law received it received through Coke's writings.[5] When the compilers of the Massachusetts Code of 1648 were at work, they ordered copies of Coke's *Institutes, Reports, New Terms of the Law*, and *Book of Entries*, as well as Dalton's *Country Justice*. The law of Massachusetts had already proscribed all feudal incidents and monopolies, together with imprisonment for debt, and had simplified procedure by eliminating technicalities. Coke was naturally the main inspiration of those who drew up the first modern code of the western world.[6]

So James and Charles were right enough, from their point of view, to dislike the direction in which Coke was modifying the law. 'He hath made himself popular by . . . pulling down government', said James I.[7] 'Throughout his *Institutes*', Hobbes

---

[1] *H.M.C.*, *Seventh Report, Appendix*, i. 548.

[2] *C.S.P.D., 1629-31*, p. 490. James had been told in 1616 that Coke 'would be accounted the martyr of the commonwealth' if punished (*Letters of John Chamberlain*, ii. 11).

[3] Roger Coke, *Detection of the Court and State of England*, i. 309.

[4] *II Institutes*, p. 746; C. V. Wedgwood, *The King's Peace* (1955), p. 430.

[5] Mr. B. S. Manning suggests that C. J. Rolle's *Abridgment* (published posthumously in 1668) 'came near to being a digest of the whole law' (Manning, 'The Nobles, the People and the Constitution', *P. and P.*, No. 9, p. 55). Rolle was a vocal M.P. from the sixteen-twenties, and a Parliamentarian in the civil war. He was a member of the Council of State after the execution of Charles I.

[6] G. L. Haskins, *Law and Authority in Early Massachussetts* (New York, 1960), pp. 120–35.

[7] Bacon, *Works*, xili. 95.

observed of Coke, 'he endeavours . . . to diminish . . . the King's authority.'[1] There could be no political neutrality in these matters. An attack on monopolies and royal charters to gilds was an attack on the prerogative: this was another point on which Coke was asked to explain himself to the Privy Council in 1616. 'The King has no prerogative', said Coke flatly, 'but that which the law of the land allows him.' He distinguished between 'prerogative disputable and indisputable', what the legal historians call ordinary and absolute prerogative. For Coke prerogative was indisputable in affairs of state, like the right to make war or peace; prerogative disputable concerned property: '*Meum et tuum*, bounded by law.' 'The common law hath so admeasured the prerogative of the King that he cannot take or prejudice the inheritance of any.'[2] Naturally such passages—e.g. the condemnation of the decision in Bate's Case—could not be published under the old régime: but they had been uttered in the Parliament of 1628, when Coke added proudly 'It is not I, Edward Coke, that speaks it, but the records that speak it.' So when Coke said, 'Magna Carta is such a fellow that he will have no sovereign',[3] he really was striking a blow against the royal prerogative. Wentworth wanted to set Charles I's 'power and greatness . . . above the expositions of Sir Edward Coke and his Year Books'.[4]

One way of modernizing the law was by proclamation. When in 1610 Coke challenged the King's right to make new offences by proclamation, Lord Chancellor Ellesmere said that in cases where there is no authority or precedent it should be left to the King to decide: for otherwise the King would be no more than the Doge of Venice. Coke's stand was formally conservative: there must be great consideration before anything of novelty is established, to provide that it is not against the law of the land.[5] But he points the direction in which history was to advance.

[1] Hobbes, *English Works*, vi. 62. Cf. Coke's hope, in 1628, that he would not have 'to live under the law of convenience and discretion' (Judson, *Crisis of the Constitution*, p. 242).

[2] N.R.S. iv. 79; *L.J.* iii. 762; *II Institutes*, pp. 36, 63. Cf. Ralegh's distinction between a 'Turk-like' and an absolute monarchy (see p. 151 above).

[3] Rushworth, *Historical Collections*, i. 562. Coke may have said 'will have no saving' [of sovereign power]. It comes to the same thing, *12* and *13 Reports*, published during the Interregnum, deal largely with questions of royal prerogative.

[4] C. V. Wedgwood, *Thomas Wentworth, Earl of Strafford* (1961), p. 402.

[5] Holdsworth, *History of English Law*, v. 433.

IV

Coke's 'perpetual turbulent carriage' towards courts other than those of the common law[1] was no doubt partly selfish in its motivation. Nevertheless, a desire to restrict their competence goes naturally with his wish to rationalize and systematize the law. Coke held that the Court of Requests was no legal court, though since it existed it would be work worthy of a Parliament to legalize it.[2] He similarly questioned the right to jurisdiction of the Council of the North and the Council in Wales.[3] In the 1621 Parliament he attacked the Chancellor for protecting insolvent debtors: he wanted to subordinate Chancery to the common law.[4] He held that the law of the forests was bounded in England by the common law, and not, as in other countries, *ad principis placitum*.[5] In relation to Church courts there is an even greater logic in Coke's position. (Indeed it is wrong to personalize the dispute too much. Bancroft was already complaining of the issue of prohibitions in 1605, before Coke became Chief Justice of Common Pleas. As in so many other respects, Coke made himself the eloquent and courageous spokesman of a trend already in existence.)[6]

Before the Reformation Church courts had been part of an international organization: now they were part of a national system of justice. Though held in the bishop's name, they were just as much the King's courts as a court leet held in the name of a lord of a manor.[7] Coke of course had to say that Church courts always had been subordinated to the royal authority: but his argument rests in fact on that consolidation of national authority which had been the achievement of the Tudor century. His argument in the discussion of Cawdrey's Case was that there must be a single national system of justice. The danger in the argument, from the point of view of the royal supremacy, was that the Reformation had been enacted *by*

[1] Bacon, *Works*, xiii. 95; cf. pp. 90–91.   [2] *IV Institutes*, pp. 97–98.
[3] Ibid., cap. XLVIII–XLIX; *12 Reports*, pp. 50–56.
[4] *II Institutes*, pp. 582–3; *IV Institutes*, pp. 245–6; *12 Reports*, pp. 50–56. But Coke defended the legality and utility of Star Chamber (*IV Institutes*, pp. 62–63). We have seen how he criticized the Court of Admiralty and the Commissioners for Sewers. Cf. also *II Institutes*, p. 280—against the Commission for Defective Titles.
[5] *IV Institutes*, pp. 290, 319–20.
[6] *II Institutes*, pp. 601–18.
[7] *5 Reports*, Of the Kings Ecclesiasticall law, *passim*; *IV Institutes*, pp. 321–45.

statute; and 'expounding of statutes that concern the ecclesiastical government or proceedings . . . belongeth unto the temporal
judges'.[1] Coke's case against the High Commission was that
it had exceeded its statutory powers. Since the Act of 1559 had
merely restored traditional rights, it could not have given an
ecclesiastical court powers which had not previously been
enjoyed by such courts. The powers which the bishops claimed
for the High Commission would have given them jurisdiction
over lay property (legacies, tithes) without known limitation of
possible sentence and without appeal.[2] Precedents for the High
Commission's actions 'may be many, especially against the
weaker sort', who did not take legal advice. But they had no
validity.[3] (Lest I should seem to be idealizing Coke's and
Parliament's opposition to the Church courts, let us recall that
the result of their stripping alimony cases from the High
Commission was, in Bacon's words, to leave wives 'wholly
to the tyranny of their husbands'.[4] Coke thought burning
Wightman for heresy in 1612 was illegal—but not wrong.)[5]

James said Coke was hostile to 'the liberties of his church and
the state ecclesiastical'.[6] Coke would have replied that there
was 'general complaint against the multiplicity of ecclesiastical
courts', and that he was only defending the liberties of the
subject against ecclesiastical encroachments.[7] In fact his resolute
stand against the oath *ex officio* led to the proclamation of the
splendid individualist principle that a free man should be
accused only of actual words or deeds. 'The ecclesiastical judge
cannot examine any man upon his oath, upon the intention and
thought of his heart. No man may be punished for his thoughts.
For . . . thought is free.' 'An oath in a man's own cause is the
device of the Devil to throw the souls of poor men into hell.'

[1] *II Institutes*, p. 614.

[2] See my *Society and Puritanism*, p. 351, and references there cited.

[3] *IV Institutes*, pp. 324–35; *12 Reports*, pp. 20, 49–50, 59–62, 69, 84–86, 88–89;
cf. Bacon, *Works* (1826), vi. 439–40.

[4] Bacon to James I, 11 November, 1615 (*Works*, xiii. 90). Cf. G. W. Prothero,
Select Statutes and . . . Documents, 1558–1625 (1906), pp. 431–3 for the Commission, and
p. 305 for the Commons' petition on behalf of husbands.

[5] Gardiner, *History of England*, ii. 129.

[6] Bacon, *Works*, xiii. 95. Coke 'as it were purposely laboured to derogate much
from the rights of the Church and dignity of churchmen' (*Egerton's Observations*,
pp. 1–2).

[7] *The Lord Coke His Speech and Charge*, sig. G 2v; *II Institutes*, pp. 599–638.

Oaths should be demanded of laymen only in matrimonial and testamentary causes where no discredit could ensue (a notable restriction!), 'for laymen for the most part are unlettered, wherefore they may easily be inveigled and entrapped, and principally in heresy and matters of faith'. Accordingly between 1608 and 1616 Coke granted prohibitions to men and women whom the ecclesiastical courts were questioning about their opinions, thus overthrowing, he was told, what had been the practice of the High Commission for sixty years.[1] Prohibitions were similarly used to check Bancroft's attempt to increase tithe payments to the Church.[2]

Coke is quoted as saying, 'If no bishops, then no laws, if no laws, no kings'. He denied the accuracy of the pamphlet in which this is quoted, so we should not attach too much importance to it.[3] But since it is the most friendly remark attributed to him about the Church we should note its constitutional implications. Bishops are recognized legislators: to abolish them would be to change the structure of Parliament, and so of the monarchy. Hyde and Waller were to say similar things in 1641;[4] but it was hardly what James meant by 'No bishop, no king'. We should observe too that the same report attributes to Coke very harsh remarks about papists and Church courts, and only a very mild rebuke to Puritans.[5] A more realistic appraisal perhaps was that of Sir Henry Marten (an ecclesiastical lawyer who knew Coke well). He said that Sir Edward's will was 'a monument to his continued malice against the jurisdiction of the Church in testamentary causes', 'a precedent to both men and women how to out the Church of all power . . . in their real and personal estates'.[6] Coke was one of those who took notes at the lectures which Walter Travers, Hooker's Puritan rival, gave at

---

[1] *13 Reports*, p. 10; M. H. Maguire, 'The Attack of the Common Lawyers on the Oath *ex officio*', in *Essays . . . in Honor of C. H. McIlwain* (Harvard U.P., 1936), pp. 222–7, and references there cited. On prohibitions see *II Institutes*, pp. 601–18.

[2] *II Institutes*, pp. 364, 490, 639–64. Cf. my *Economic Problems of the Church* (1956), esp. pp. 127–8, 246–8. See also *II Institutes*, p. 491 (mortuaries) and pp. 625–7 (non-residence).

[3] *The Lord Coke His Speech and Charge*, sig. G; *7 Reports*, Preface.

[4] Clarendon, *History of the Rebellion* (1888), v. 512; *Life* (1759), i. 81, 138–9; *Old Parliamentary History* (1763), ix. 388–9.

[5] *The Lord Coke His Speech and Charge, passim*, esp. sig. G 2.

[6] I owe this quotation from an unpublished fragment in Henry Marten's papers in the Brotherton Library, Leeds, to the kindness of Professor C. M. Williams. Coke's will was seized by the government in 1634 and has never been seen since.

the Temple in the early fifteen-nineties.[1] Sir Edward held the
high Puritan view—or so he told Bacon—that it was sinful
'for a man to go against his own conscience, though erroneous,
except his conscience be first informed and satisfied'.[2] Coke was
guardian to Roger Williams, a man not unlearned in the law.
Williams regarded Coke as a 'blessed man', who would have
sympathized with his emigration to New England.[3] So there
was some affinity between Coke and those Puritans who,
Sibthorpe complained, 'make the law above the King'.[4]

V

When we look at Coke's attitude to the law he praised so
much, what at once impresses us are the apparent contradictions
in his methods.[5] He changed his view on a number of subjects
during his career—on the proper sphere of royal proclamations,
on the validity of benevolences and impositions, on the legality
of commitment by Council, of asking judges for extra-judicial
opinions upon pending cases. It would be easy to make him out
an inconsistent and opportunist politician:[6] easy, but irrelevant.
Nevertheless his ideas are difficult to reconcile one with another.
'The common law', Coke said, 'is the absolute perfection of
reason.'[7] Hence nothing that is contrary to reason is consonant
to law.[8] The common law, 'refined and perfected by all the
wisest men in former succession of ages, . . . cannot without great
hazard and danger be altered or changed'.[9] Yet in fact there
have been 'many changes and alterations of the common law',[10]
and there are today 'variety of opinions'.[11] Coke's object was
'to reconcile doubts . . . arising either upon diversity of opinions
or questions moved and left undecided'.[12] He agreed with Bacon
that peace and plenty had led to increased litigiousness.[13] Coke
attributed the confusion in the law to laymen making 'con-
veyances, assurances, instruments, and wills' without proper

---

[1] Fuller, *Church History* (1842), iii. 128. For Travers and science see p. 277 below.
[2] Bacon, *Works*, xiii. 77.
[3] Morison, *Builders of the Bay Colony*, p. 223.
[4] Quoted by Lamont, *Marginal Prynne*, p. 15.   [5] See pp. 236–7 above.
[6] Holdsworth, *History of English Law*, v. 427–9.   [7] *II Institutes*, p. 179.
[8] *I Institutes*, p. 56b; *4 Reports*, p. 72.
[9] Ibid., sig. B iib; *I Institutes*, p. 97b.   [10] *I Institutes*, p. 395.
[11] *1 Reports*, Preface to the Reader.   [11] *3 Reports*, sig. D 3b.
[13] *IV Institutes*, p. 76; cf. Bacon, *Works*, xiii. 64.

legal advice, and to Acts of Parliament being drafted by lay-men.[1] 'The supposed variety of opinions and rules in our books', and 'the uncertainty' of the law is *'hominis vitium* and not *professionis'*.[2] Nevertheless the fact remained that 'divers doubts and questions of law remained undetermined'. Even judges themselves disagreed.[3] There was a 'multitude of suits in personal actions . . . to the intolerable charge and vexation of the subject'. Often there were many suits in the same case, and different verdicts.[4] 'The learned' had to 'perplex their heads to make atonement and peace by construction of law between insensible and disagreeing words, sentences and provisos.'[5]

An interpreter thus was needed. 'It is the best manner of expounding, so to interpret the laws that they may agree with one another.'[6] 'The best interpreter of the law is custom',[7] which sometimes 'overcometh or mastereth the common law'.[8] Yet custom is not to be followed blindly. 'The custom of any place or country is not be be alleged in things which of common right to all men are granted and allowed.'[9] Failing custom as a guide, 'such an interpretation ought always to be made, that absurdity and inconvenience be avoided'.[10] For 'the law of England cannot abide an absurd thing'.[11] These platitudes gave judges, fettered by no doctrine of binding precedent, a pretty free hand to make what they pleased of the law.[12] If a judge did not like a previous judgement, he could dismiss it as 'a sudden opinion'.[13] Or he could find a later precedent, 'fitter for the modern practice of the law'.[14] If he did not like a statute, he could appeal to custom or 'common right and reason' against

---

[1] *2 Reports*, To the Learned Reader; *4 Reports*, sig. B v.

[2] *9 Reports*, sig. C vi.   [3] *4 Reports*, sig. B v.

[4] *8 Reports*, sig. A iib.   [5] *2 Reports*, To the Learned Reader.

[6] *8 Reports*, p. 169. (Interpretari et concordare leges legibus est optimus inter-pretandi modus.)

[7] *2 Reports*, p. 81; *10 Reports*, p. 70. (Optimus legum interpretes consuetudo.)

[8] *4 Reports*, p. 21. (Consuetudo vincit communem legem.)

[9] *11 Reports*, p. 85. (In hiis, quae de jure communi omnibus conceduntur con-suetudo alicuius patriae vel loci non est alleganda—except apparently that of London—see p. 234 above.)

[10] *1 Reports*, p. 51.

[11] *9 Reports*, p. 22. (Lex Angliae non patitur absurdum.)

[12] C. K. Allen, *Law in the Making* (1951), pp. 192–223; cf. Sir T. Wilson, *The State of England (1600)* (ed. F. J. Fisher, Camden Miscellany, xvi, 1936), p. 37.

[13] *1 Institutes*, p. 148.

[14] Coke, *A Book of Entries* (1614), sig. a ix.

it;[1] or—vaguer still—he could construe it by 'the rule and reason of the common law'.[2] This mysterious process involved bringing 'the reason of the law so to our own reason, that we perfectly understand it as our own, and then, and never before, we have such an excellent and inseparable propriety and ownership therein, as we can neither lose it nor any man take it from us'. 'The law is unknown to him that knoweth not the reason thereof.'[3] 'Reasonableness in these cases belongeth to the knowledge of the law.'[4] Luther had said rather similar things about the grace of God, an equally mystical and personal concept.

Another name for reason was discretion. 'Law and discretion should be concomitant'—not 'every man's discretion that sitteth on the seat of justice', but 'that discretion that ariseth upon the right discerning and due consideration of the true and necessary circumstances of the matter'.[5] Rarely can so many questions have been begged in so few words. In different mood, the judge might adopt an attitude of historical relativism: 'the times being distinguished, the laws will be reconciled'.[6] Or he could apply a legal maxim out of its full context.[7] Or he could appeal to the spirit of the law against its inconvenient letter: 'whilst the property of the words is attended to, we often miss the true sense'.[8] 'The law of England respecteth the effect and substance of the matter, and not every nicety of form or circumstance.'[9] The remarkable *dictum* in *III Institutes*, that it is not lawful to predict the date of the end of the world, or even to announce that it is at hand, appears to be supported only by Biblical texts.[10] Finally, if all else fails, 'necessity has often

---

[1] See T. F. T. Plucknett, 'Bonham's Case and Judicial Review', *Harvard Law Quarterly*, xl. 35–36.

[2] *I Institutes*, p. 272b. 'The rules of the common law' are 'true touchstones to sever the pure gold from the dross and sophistications of novelties and new inventions' (ibid., p. 379b).

[3] Ibid., pp. 394–5; cf. 7 *Reports*, sig. A vi.   [4] *I Institutes*, p. 56b.

[5] Coke, *A Little Treatise of Baile and Mainprize* (second ed., 1635), p. 31.

[6] 9 *Reports*, p. 16. (Distinguenda sunt tempora, et concordabis leges.) Bacon had also advocated an historical approach (*Works*, v. 104).

[7] For an example see Maguire, 'The Attack of the Common Lawyers on the Oath *ex officio*', p. 223.

[8] 9 *Reports*, p. 110. (Plerumque dum proprietas verborum attenditur, sensus veritatis amittitur.)

[9] *I Institutes*, pp. 283; cf. p. 381b, and 5 *Reports*, part ii, p. 4; *11 Reports*, p. 34.

[10] *III Institutes*, pp. 120–9.

overcome the common law, and that which is necessary is lawful'.[1] There were, I am sorry to say, 'malevolent persons' who thought Coke gave himself a further resource by devising precedents 'of his own head'. In the 1621 Parliament he had to produce a manuscript to convince these cavillers.[2] In at least one case Coke reported the exact opposite of the actual decision, and in others the authors he cites do not support his conclusions.[3]

There is a further muddle in Coke's thought, in that he elevated both the common law and Parliament. Sometimes he spoke as though the courts had the right to sit in judgement on statutes: 'in many cases the common law shall control Acts of Parliament, and sometimes shall adjudge them to be utterly void'—e.g. when 'against common right and reason'.[4] Acts of Parliament, 'being part of the laws of the realm', are 'to be expounded . . . by the judges of the law'.[5] Sometimes he spoke as though Magna Carta was a fundamental law, though he admitted that parts of it had been altered by subsequent statutes. At other times he seemed to think Parliament was supreme: 'The power and jurisdiction of the Parliament . . . is so transcendent and absolute, as it cannot be confined either for causes or persons within any bounds.'[6] Clearly the alliance between common lawyers of his type and Parliament was so close that the possibility of a clash between the two did not occur to him, just as Laud never faced the possibility of conflict between the royal supremacy and divine right episcopacy. It was the Levellers who used Magna Carta and the supremacy of law, which Coke had trained on the prerogative, against the sovereignty of Parliament.[7]

So although Coke piously declared that 'no man out of his own private reason ought to be wiser than the law, which is the

[1] 5 Reports, part II, p. 40. (Saepenumero necessitas vincit communem legem, et quod necessarium est, licitum est.)

[2] N.R.S. v. 36.

[3] Plucknett, 'Bonham's Case and Judicial Review', p. 51; Van Vechten Veeder, 'The English Reports, 1292–1865', Harvard Law Quarterly, xv. 11.

[4] Coke's reply on Bonham's Case, in Bacon's Works (1826), vi. 441.

[5] 9 Reports, sig. C iiib. The judicial review which Coke claimed for the common-law courts in Bagg's Case (1615) developed after the abolition of Star Chamber (Jaffe and Henderson, op. cit., p. 359).

[6] IV Institutes, p. 36.

[7] See pp. 260–3 below.

perfection of reason',[1] the object of a legal education is to convey 'the secrets of the law'.[2] When James spoke of determining disputed points of law by his reason, Coke explained that 'Causes which concern the life or inheritance of his subjects . . . are not to be decided by natural reason, but by the artificial reason and judgement of the law, which . . . requires long study and experience.'[3] Similarly, when the House of Commons spoke reason to James in May 1621, the King replied that 'reason was so variable according to several humours that it were hard to know where to fix it'. 'Reason is too large. Find me a precedent and I will accept it.'[4]

  It has been a thesis of this book that there was no longer universal agreement on what was 'reasonable'.[5] Rationality is a social concept, and social divisions in England (and elsewhere) were producing conceptions of what was 'rational' which were so different that in the last resort only force could decide between them. The 'reasonableness' of the sanctity of private property was imposed by the New Model Army's pikes and confirmed by Dutch William's mercenaries. Nor, protest as they might, were either King or Commons really prepared to be bound by precedents they did not like. When in 1621 Coke obeyed James and brought him a precedent, the King retorted that he wished 'that he would bring precedents of good kings' times'.[6] On the other side, Peter Wentworth had distinguished in 1575 between 'good' and 'evil' precedents, and William Prynne rejected some (though of course not all) precedents from 'popish Parliaments in time of ignorance'.[7] Precedents were as interpretable as the Bible. The question that mattered, as Hobbes saw, was Who is to interpret?

  Coke then conveyed a great deal when he described the judge as 'a law speaking'.[8] 'A new judgment doth not give or make a new law, but declares the old; . . . by a judgment, the law is

---

[1] *I Institutes*, p. 97b.

[2] Ibid., p. 395: the phrase recurs.   [3] *12 Reports*, p. 65.

[4] N.R.S. iii. 156; F. Thompson, *Magna Carta: its Role in the Making of the English Constitution*, p. 319; *Letters of John Chamberlain*, ii. 372.

[5] Cf. pp. 122, 185 above, 259, 262, 294 below.

[6] Ed. Lady de Villiers, *The Hastings Journal of 1621* (Camden Miscellany, xx, 1953), pp. 27–28, 31.

[7] D'Ewes, *Journals*, pp. 241–4; Lamont, *Marginal Prynne*, p. 89.

[8] *7 Reports*, p. 4 (Judex est lex loquens); *I Institutes*, p. 130a.

newly revealed, that of long time hath been covered.'[1] 'Without question the law is sprung up from a divine mind, and this admirable unity and consent in such diversity of things proceeds from God, the fountain and founder of all good laws and constitutions.'[2] Coke no doubt saw himself and his fellow judges as God's agents in this work of reconciliation. 'The judges', observed Lord Chancellor Ellesmere, who watched this development with a critical eye, 'themselves do play the Chancellor's parts upon statutes, making construction of them according to equity and enlarging them *pro bono publico* against the letter and intention of the makers, whereof our books have many hundreds of cases.'[3]

Where Ralegh urged James to see that he must adapt himself to social change and co-operate with Parliament, Coke—possibly more realistically—wished this constitutional revolution to be mediated through judges and to be confirmed by statute. Judges did not turn to the legal record with absolutely open minds to find out what past practice really had been: if they had done so they would have found hopelessly conflicting answers. As practical men, facing urgent practical problems, they took what they wanted from the available records of the past, as theologians took what texts they wanted from the vast arsenal of the Bible. The judges were perfectly prepared to prohibit the publication of some statutes whose popular dissemination they thought might be dangerous.[4] Coke himself did his best to suppress any precedents that he did not like, taking care that 'such only as (in my opinion) should hereafter be leading cases for the public quiet might be imprinted and published'.[5] He was very successful: his successors rarely went behind Coke to see what medieval precedents really were. Coke's works, Blackstone said, have 'an intrinsic authority in courts of justice, and do not entirely depend on the strength of their quotations from older authorities'. C. J. Best put it more

---

[1] *10 Reports*, p. 42. (Novum judicium non dat jus novum, sed declarat antiquum; . . . per juditium jus est noviter revelatum, quod diu fuit velatum.)

[2] *3 Reports*, sig. C. 2. (Lex orta est cum mente divina.)

[3] Gough, *Fundamental Law in English History*, p. 38: for examples of the common law overruling statute in the interests of economic liberalism see G. L. Beer, *The Old Colonial System, 1660–1688* (New York, 1912), i. 91.

[4] Thompson, *Magna Carta*, p. 235; cf. *3 Reports*, sig. E, and *IV Institutes*, p. 3.

[5] *9 Reports*, sig. vib; cf. p. 253 above.

bluntly early last century when he said, 'We should get rid of a great deal of what is considered law in Westminster Hall if what Lord Coke says without authority is not law.'[1]

In this work of selection the judges, drawn from a homogeneous social group and with similar ideas of what was right and proper, could work out a roughly agreed line of advance from precedent to precedent. Coke was not a dictator: he summed up and made sense of the groping rationalizations of his predecessors. But because of his tremendous learning, and because the law had not yet been made available in comprehensible form to laymen, Coke was able to acquire a position of authority in interpreting the law such as no Protestant theologian had in interpreting Scripture. Most gentlemen had a legal education of some sort, and thought of politics in legal terms. Exactly half of the 'local governors' of Somerset between 1625 and 1640 had attended one of the Inns of Court (54 out of 108); only 15 of these were called to the bar.[2] No less than 22 of the regicides had been at Gray's Inn.[3]

VI

This then is Coke's importance for our purposes. First, he systematized English law and in the process continued and extended the process of liberalizing it, of adapting it to the needs of a commercial society. In so doing he had to challenge everything that impeded the development of a world in which men of property could do what they would with their own: monopolies and gild privileges, arbitrary taxation and arbitrary arrest, paternal control over the economic life of the country. This brought the common law into conflict with the prerogative and its courts, the Church and its courts; it was natural and inevitable that Coke should turn to the House of Commons for support as soon as he had failed to achieve his aims within the government. In doing so, he contributed his share—it is not for me to say how great a share—to the evolution of a doctrine of fundamental law based on natural reason:[4] the doctrine

---

[1] Quoted in Van Vechten Veeder, 'The English Reports, 1292–1865', *Harvard Law Review*, xv. 12.

[2] T. G. Barnes, *Somerset, 1625–60* (1961), p. 31.

[3] Abbott, *Writings and Speeches of Oliver Cromwell*, i. 34.

[4] See Gough, *Fundamental Law in English History*, *passim*, esp. Chapter III.

which was to be used by Coke's pupil Oliver St. John against Strafford,[1] and later against Charles I; a doctrine which played its part in the political thinking of, for example, Lord Brooke, Henry Parker, John Lilburne. Characteristically, Coke himself in 1628 rejected the idea of fundamental law, 'a word I understand not'. He wanted property and personal liberty to be protected by definite and known common and statute law principles.[2]

Coke's second great contribution was more directly political, but it followed naturally from the liberalization of the common law. His tremendous labours achieved what Camden, Stow, Speed, and Ralegh had failed to do: they gave Englishmen an historical myth of the English constitution parallel to Foxe's myth of English religion.[3] In primitive times Englishmen had had good laws (as they had had a pure Church): the continuous enjoyment of those laws had been broken by William the Conqueror (with the support of the Pope) and by many of his successors. But Englishmen had fought back, as the heretics had fought back, and with greater success. Magna Carta and the Parliamentary statutes which Coke interpreted so lovingly and so inaccurately were monuments to the eternal vigilance with which God's Englishmen had defended their liberties. It was at this point, where liberty and property coincided, that Coke was most eloquent and most urgent. As early as 1605 he used words which are normally quoted only in part:

No subject of this realm, but being truly instructed by the good and plain evidence of his ancient and undoubted patrimony and birth-right (though he hath for some time by ignorance, false persuasion, or vague fear been deceived or dispossessed) but will consult with learned and faithful councillors for the recovery of the same. The ancient and excellent laws of England are the birth-right and

---

[1] J. Rushworth, *The Tryal of Thomas, Earl of Strafford* (1680), p. 703. John Thurloe in his turn was a pupil of St. John.

[2] Judson, *Crisis of the Constitution*, pp. 247–8.

[3] 'Beware of chronicle law reported in our annals', Coke warned his readers, 'for that will undoubtedly lead thee to error.' Monkish annalists were of course especially suspect. Chronicles should be trusted 'in those things they have published concerning the antiquity and honour of the common laws'—for instance in associating them with Brutus and asserting that the laws of the ancient Britons were written and spoken in Greek (*3 Reports*, sig. C 3–D 3; cf. *8 Reports*, To the Reader). Coke thought that Parliament existed before King Arthur, and that there were sheriffs before the Saxon invasions (*9 Reports*, sig. C–C ivb.)

the most ancient and best inheritance that the subjects of this realm have, for by them he enjoyeth not only his inheritance and goods in peace and quietness, but his life and his most dear country in safety. (I fear that many want true knowledge of this ancient birth-right.)[1]

Again and again in the *Institutes* Coke reminds his readers that this vigilance is now more necessary than ever. So the struggle of common lawyers and Parliamentarians was given historical significance and dignity, the prestige of a thousand-years-old tradition. And Coke's interpretation had staying power: Professor Butterfield has called him the first Whig historian.[2] Yet to his contemporaries Coke must have seemed no more an innovator than Luther had been: both merely led men back to purer origins.

We speak of Coke's history (like Foxe's) as mythology. Yet (unlike Foxe) Coke met with no serious challenge to his interpretation in his lifetime, except on political grounds: governments silenced him because they could not answer him. Coke did not, as is often said, invent Magna Carta: the Pilgrims of Grace, the Marian clergy, Cartwright, Penry, and many other Puritan ministers had appealed to it.[3] But he does seem to have invented Magna Carta as a bulwark of economic liberty. And in his speeches to Parliament in the sixteen-twenties he placed this Magna Carta in history and made it the possession of every propertied Englishman. Eliot in 1628 echoed Coke when he complained that 'what Magna Carta itself decides to be *meum et tuum* is now no *meum [et] tuum*'.[4] Coke moreover, who wanted books to sell cheaply, wrote the Prefaces to the *Reports*, and the text of the *Institutes*, in English, unlike all his legal predecessors, who adhered to Law French or Latin. This too was part of the patriotic myth. 'Our English language . . . is as copious and significant, and as able to

[1] 5 *Reports*, sig. A vb–A vi.
[2] H. Butterfield, *The Englishman and his History* (1944), pp. 40, 47–68. For Coke's genuine belief in the importance of historical research for an understanding of the English constitution, see a letter of 1605 to Robert Cecil, quoted in Fussner, *The Historical Revolution*, p. 84.
[3] Ed. L. Fox, *English Historical Scholarship in the 16th and 17th centuries* (1956), pp. 57–58; ed. E. Cardwell, *Synodalia* (1842), ii. 435; F. Thompson, *Magna Carta*, pp. 198, 209, 221, 227, 279; *Examinations of Henry Barrowe, John Greenwood and John Penrie* (1593), sig. Dv.
[4] Stowe MS. 367, f. 9v, quoted by J. N. Ball, *The Parliamentary Career of Sir John Eliot* (Cambridge Ph.D. thesis, 1953), pp. 226–7.

express any thing in as few and apt words, as any other native language that is spoken at this day. And (to speak what we think) we would derive from the Conqueror as little as we could.'[1] It was as natural for Coke to write in English as for Luther to write in German; as natural as it was for him to be so aggressively anti-Spanish that men believed Gondomar was responsible for his imprisonment in the Tower in 1621;[2] or for him to believe that if only government controls were removed an English liberal society could solve all its own problems.

I compared Coke to Luther, and that comparison can be carried further. Luther's translation of the Bible started a movement which he could not control. Coke, more fortunate than Luther, did not live to see the fruits of his labours. From the time of More and Starkey there had been those who described the common law as a conspiracy among the rich to keep the poor in due subjection;[3] the Levellers and Winstanley in the sixteen-forties showed that this tradition had not died, and Cromwell himself said that 'the law, as it is now constituted, serves only to maintain the lawyers and to encourage the rich to oppress the poor'.[4] But there was another legal tradition—that of the communal manor courts. In these 'little Commonwealths', as Coke called them,[5] litigation was cheap; and, where the authority of the lord of the manor was not in question, it may have been fair enough.[6] But part of the rationalization of the common law that we have been describing concerned precisely the position of copyholders and courts leet. The 'reasonableness' of copyhold customs were being tried at common law; and what seemed reasonable to a propertied judge might seem the rankest injustice to a copyholder.[7] In

---

[1] *II Institutes*, p. 745; *III Institutes*, Proeme, sig. B 2v.
[2] *Letters of John Chamberlain*, ii. 419.
[3] Sir Thomas More, *Utopia* (Everyman ed.), p. 112; ed. K. M. Burton, *Starkey's Dialogue between Pole and Thomas Lupset* (1948), p. 174.
[4] Ed. C. H. Firth, *Memoirs of Edmund Ludlow* (1894), i. 246.
[5] Coke, *Compleat Copyholder* (1644), p. 203: first published 1630.
[6] J. C. Dawson, *A History of Lay Judges* (Harvard, 1960), pp. 232–3, 255–6.
[7] R. H. Tawney, *The Agrarian Problem in the 16th Century* (1912), pp. 124–5. To take an example from a different field, it was only in the year 1649 that the journeymen weavers had any chance of establishing it as 'unreasonable' 'that such a number of men as 16 or more should have liberty to exercise a power over as many thousands without, nay against, their wills, consent, or election' (A. E. Bland, P. A. Brown, and R. H. Tawney, *English Economic History: Select Documents*, 1914, p. 309).

1604 William Stoughton argued that the steward was only the chairman of a court leet, and had no authority to hear, examine, or judge 'but by common voice and consent of all the homagers and suitors to the court'.[1] Yet Coke in his *Compleat Copyholder* said that the lord (and presumably his steward as well) 'is not tied to the strict forms of the common law, for he is a chancellor in his court'.[2] The conflicts of the mid- and later seventeenth century over whether juries were judges of law as well as of fact were conflicts about the right of the humbler classes in society to have their say in the administration of justice: as were the Levellers' proposals for leaving far more business to local courts; and their insistence on lay assessors.[3]

Coke's writings, for many on the Parliamentary side, marked the beginning, not the end, of reform. 'What is it that you chiefly aim at in this war?' the troops were asked in *The Souldiers Catechism* of 1644; and the reply was, after reforming religion and bringing the enemies of Church and state to justice: 'At the regulating of our courts of justice, which have been made the seats of iniquity and unrighteousness.'[4] The course of fighting the propaganda and military battles of the civil war brought home to many Parliamentarians that their actions could not all be based on precedent; but the Levellers carried their rejection of the past furthest, and read into Coke's writings conclusions as remarkable as those which Coke himself had read into Magna Carta.[5]

Just as Luther's appeal to individual conscience could be used against Luther, so the contradictory principles to which Coke had appealed in modernizing the common law—reason, natural justice, the spirit of the law, necessity—could be used against Coke himself. Above all, just as Luther taught laymen to criticize priestly mumbo-jumbo and they turned the criticisms against Lutheran ministers; so Coke taught laymen to interpret the law, and the radicals used this against the

[1] W. Stoughton, *An Assertion for true and Christian Church-Policie* (Middelburg, 1604), pp. 368–9. Stoughton was one of the very few people before 1640 to defend the use of the word 'democracy', and to apply it to juries. He was in favour of handing all the business of the Church courts over to the common-law courts (ibid., pp. 90–103). This treatise was reprinted in 1642.

[2] *The Compleat Copyholder*, section 43.

[3] M. James, *Social Policy during the Puritan Revolution* (1930), p. 328.

[4] *The Souldiers Catechism, Composed for the Parliaments Army* (1644), p. 9.

[5] See my *Puritanism and Revolution*, esp. pp. 75–87.

mumbo-jumbo of the lawyers. As early as 1628 George Wither thought that lawyers should

> ... be disposed of, as now they see
> The priories and monasteries be.[1]

Twenty-five years later it was common form to lump together 'the corrupt interests of the lawyers and the clergy' as the main obstacles to reform. Just as some of the sectaries would have abolished a separate priesthood, so Winstanley thought that in the free commonwealth there would be no need of lawyers, 'for there is to be no buying and selling'.[2]

'Do not they [the judges] assume the sole guiding, learning, interpreting, examining, and over-ruling of the law to themselves?' asked John Jones in 1650. 'How can that law be called common to all which they . . . monopolize, ingross, and appropriate to themselves?' The lawyers were worse than the bishops whom Parliament had just abolished.[3] Jones quoted Coke to argue that 'the laws (if published to the people as they ought) would be sufficient to guide them all in all the right ways of justice'. But the judges keep them in French and Latin, so that they can 'devise for themselves to mend where they list, which happeneth sometimes for the rich, but rare or never for the poor'.[4] He wanted to wrest the law 'out of the hands of those false interpreters at Westminster'. The civil war had been fought, he argued, to get the laws reformed against the lawyers.[5] Lilburne infuriated the lawyers by holding adult education classes in the law (whilst he was in Newgate jail) as much as the translators of medical textbooks had infuriated the doctors in Elizabeth's reign.[6]

For the radicals generally, from Hugh Peter through the Levellers and Diggers to John Warr and William Cole, Coke's restatement of the law to safeguard property and preserve its

---

[1] Wither, *Brittans Remembrancer*, pp. 215–16.
[2] Winstanley, *Works* (ed. Sabine), p. 512.
[3] John Jones, *The Judges Judged out of their own Mouths* (1650), pp. 55–56, 115–16.
[4] Jones, *The New Returna Brevium* (1650), p. 15; cf. pp. 32–33. This pamphlet was dedicated to Oliver Cromwell. Cf. Jones, *The Jurors Judges of Law and Fact* (1650), pp. 14, 24–25, where Coke is cited for the argument that corrupt and mercenary lawyers cause civil wars and that jurors ought to be judges. Cf. also William Cole, *A Rod for the Lawyers* (1659), p. 11.
[5] Jones, *The Judges Judged*, title-page and pp. 93–94.
[6] Gregg, *Freeborn John*, p. 124. Cf. pp. 28–30, 75 above.

freedom of action seemed far too conservative. The demand for codification under the Commonwealth came from men who were conservatives only in so far as they wanted to give legal validity to popular customs which the propertied judges were trying to abolish as 'unreasonable'.[1] The reformers came to regard 'the profession of our laws as epidemically evil'[2] and wanted root-and-branch reform of the premises on which law rested, a break with the precedents of the past rather than their adaptation. They bore the same relation to Coke as the radical sects of the same period did to Luther.

We must beware of dismissing the call for further reform and codification as coming from a 'lunatic fringe', if there was such a thing. It started, as we have seen, in the House of Commons. It was supported by the Lord Mayor of London in 1649;[3] by a Committee appointed by the Rump of the Long Parliament, of which the distinguished lawyer Sir Matthew Hale was chairman;[4] by Bulstrode Whitelocke;[5] and by Major-General Fleetwood in 1655.[6] 'There is one general grievance in the nation', the Lord Protector told Parliament in September 1656. 'It is the law.'[7] The cry for the laws in English was an old one. Robert Burton had echoed it.[8] A medical reformer said in 1659 that Edward Noy had agitated for translation. Hering wanted lawyers, like physicians, to be paid by the state and to charge no fees. He hoped to see all books of law and physic translated into English.[9] Inability to understand legal processes without paying for a lawyer was an especial grievance for the middle and lower classes, among whom 'the general and inbred

[1] Cf. Overton, *An Appeale*, in D. M. Wolfe, *Leveller Manifestoes* (New York, 1944), esp. pp. 190–2. For Lilburne's use of 'that most excellent of English lawyers, Sir Edward Cook', see *Legall Fundamental Liberties*, in Haller and Davies, *Leveller Tracts*, p. 406, and D. B. Robertson, *The Religious Foundations of Leveller Democracy* (New York, 1951), pp. 129–30. For Wildman see A. S. P. Woodhouse, *Puritanism and Liberty* (1938), p. 371.

[2] *The Laws Discovery* (1653), in *Harleian Miscellany* (1744–56), ii. 555.

[3] G. B. Nourse, 'Law Reform under the Commonwealth and Protectorate', *L.Q.R.* lxxv. 525.

[4] *Several Draughts of Acts*, in *Somers' Tracts* (1809–15), vi. 177–245.

[5] R. H. Whitelocke, *Memoirs Biographical and Historical of Bulstrode Whitelocke* (1860), p. 455.   [6] Ed. T. Birch, *Thurloe State Papers* (1742), iii. 697.

[7] Abbot, *Writings and Speeches of Oliver Cromwell*, iv. 274.

[8] Burton, *Anatomy of Melancholy* (Everyman ed.), i. 102.

[9] Preface by R. W. (?W. Ryves, Culpeper's quondam servant) to *Culpepers School of Physic* (1659), sig. A 7 (R. W. was arguing in favour of translating medical texts); Nickolls, *Original Letters*, pp. 100–1. See p. 120 above.

hatred . . . against both our laws and lawyers' was particularly keenly felt.[1]

As the civil war and the New Model Army drew the common people more and more into politics, so the demand for legal reform had become a demand for social reform, for protection of the middling and poorer sort. Imprisonment for debt was against Magna Carta and the Petition of Right, said John Jones: he might have added that it had been abolished in Massachusetts.[2] Jurors should be judges both of law and fact, said Jones, Lilburne, and many others: 'mechanics, bred up . . . to handicrafts' could judge as well as the self-appointed experts of gentle extraction, just as they could preach as well as university-trained divines.[3] It was this that closed the ranks of the conservatives around 'the corrupt interest of the lawyers and the clergy', and made any codification other than that in Coke's works out of the question.

In short, the antiquarianism of the House of Commons before 1640 had been functional: it did not exist for its own sake. In the sixteen-thirties Noy demonstrated that Coke's techniques could be devoted to proving opposite conclusions to his. Charles I's personal rule was 'the only period of English history when the policy of the government has actually been based on historical research'.[4] Men were interested in the constitution in order to do things with it, not for its own sake: not even Parliament was sacred. Cromwell's objection to 'arbitrary Parliaments' was that, like arbitrary kings, they might interfere with property.[5]

Here we must return for a moment to Bacon. He thought that the general principles of law should not (as hitherto) be discussed only by practising lawyers or armchair philosophers. For the end of law is 'the happiness of the citizens', and the test of laws is practice. Hence law was a matter for statesmen, 'who

---

[1] J. Hare, *Englands Proper and onely way to an Establishment in Honour, Freedom, Peace and Happinesse* (1648), p. 6; cf. *Some Advertisements for the new Election of Burgesses* (1645), *Somers Tracts* (1748–51), i. 32–38.

[2] J. Jones, *The Crie of Bloud* (1651), sig. A 5v, Epistle Dedicatory to Oliver Cromwell. For Massachusetts see p. 245 above.

[3] Jones, *The Jurors Judges of Law and Fact*, pp. 49–75. 'Writing is but a handicraft taught a lawyer' (ibid., pp. 60–61).

[4] P. Styles, 'Politics and Historical Research', in *English Historical Scholarship in the 16th and 17th centuries* (ed. Fox), p. 70.

[5] Abbott, *Writings and Speeches of Oliver Cromwell*, iv. 487.

best understand the conditions of civil society, welfare of the people, natural equity, customs of nations, and different forms of government, and who may therefore determine laws by the rules and principles both of natural equity and policy'.[1] That sounds admirable—until we reflect on the 'statesmen' who surrounded the first two Stuart kings. The Commons, like Coke, could no more trust the royal reason than he could trust theirs. Coke and the property-owners preferred the existing state of affairs (administered by them and their like, with no control of judges from above) to a codification which, however desirable in Baconian theory, could have been absolutist in Jacobean practice. The apparently excessive vigilance with which the Commons pounced on Dr. Cowell for one or two unfortunate definitions shows how near the surface their anxieties were. In 1610 Coke approved of James's proposal that some penal statutes should be repealed, which 'remain but as snares to entangle the subjects withal'; and that 'one plain and per-spicuous law' should be made, 'so as every subject may know what acts be in force, what repealed, . . . what enlarged . . .; so as each man may clearly know what and how much is of them in force; and how to obey them'. But he was doubtful about 'bringing the common laws into a better method', and insisted that this could be done only by Parliament, with the advice of the judges.[2] Bacon's own condemnation for bribery in 1621, however factiously motivated, helped to set new standards of conduct for judges, as Bacon himself saw.[3]

'We cannot mention the reformation of the law', said Crom-well in 1650, 'but they presently cry out, we design to destroy property.'[4] The common lawyers, the men of property, the House of Commons, came to prefer that the *status quo* should be modified by judge-made precedent, rather than rationalized by the royal government,[5] or later by Leveller or Fifth Monarchy radicals. Just in the same way J.P.s wanted to be left alone by the central government,[6] whether that of Laud or of the Major-

---

[1] Bacon, *Works*, v. 88.

[2] *4 Reports*, sig. B iii; cf. *III Institutes*, Epilogue.

[3] Bacon, *Works*, xiv. 242.   [4] Ludlow, *Memoirs*, i. 246.

[5] 'Judges ought to remember', Bacon had told them, 'that their office is . . . to interpret law, and not to make law' (*Works*, vi. 506).

[6] Coke in the 1621 Parliament supported their protests against the interference of the commissioners for licensing ale-houses (N.R.S. iii. 43, vi. 54.)

Generals. When Laud tried to reform admitted economic abuses in the Church, his attempt brought on the government even more opprobrium than the existence of the abuses had done.[1] So with the law, *both* the need for reform *and* the government's attempt to provide it harmed the *ancien régime*. Once Star Chamber had been abolished and the Privy Council lost its teeth, judges became lions under the mace rather than under the throne. Hobbist sovereignty was never popular with most of the men of property. The muddles of Coke suited them better. Illogical though 'the balanced constitution' was, it met their needs—once kings had been taught their lesson. It is not without its symbolism that Coke should have died on Oliver Cromwell's day of victories—September 3.

[1] See my *Economic Problems of the Church*, esp. Part III.

Postscript. In an interesting article, 'The "Economic Liberalism" of Sir Edward Coke' (*Yale Law Journal*, Vol. 76, 1967), Barbara Malament criticized historians who ascribe to Coke 'an anticipation of *laissez-faire*', and appears to include me among them. The careful reader will agree that I do not adopt 'the *laissez-faire* thesis', or attribute to Coke anything so unhistorical as 'modern notions of competition' or 'full employment' (Malament, p. 1350). Coke was a protectionist who had no objection to regulation *by Parliament*. Ms. Malament seems to me to take a rather unhistorical view of the common law's inherent 'bias' against restraint of trade (p. 1345) and to ignore the climate of opinion in which attitudes towards gilds, towards 'reason', 'the public interest' and 'the rights of Englishmen', were changing (pp. 1341–3, 1358). To suggest that economic and social change produced stresses and strains of which lawyers had to take account is not the same as attributing to Coke a conscious wish 'to destroy the system itself' (p. 1357). What mattered was the later use that others made of Coke's ideas. But it is good to have lawyers at last discussing Wagner's tentative suggestions.

VI

CONCLUSION

> This is the age wherein all men's souls are in a kind of fermentation, and the spirit of wisdom and learning begins to mount and free itself from those drossy and terrene impediments wherewith it has been so long clogged, and from the insipid phlegm and *caput mortuum* of useless notions in which it has endured so violent and long a fixation. . . . Methinks I see how all the old rubbish must be thrown away, and the rotten buildings be overthrown and carried away with so powerful an inundation. These are the days that must lay a new foundation of a more magnificent philosophy never to be overthrown.
>
> HENRY POWER, *Experimental Philosophy* (1664), p. 192.
> Power, yet another Halifax man, began writing this book in 1653.

> No man can rightly and successfully investigate the nature of anything in the thing itself; let him vary his experiments as laboriously as he will, he never comes to a resting-place, but still finds something to seek beyond.
>
> BACON, *Works*, iv. 17.

I

IT is absurd to try to discuss the intellectual origins of the English Revolution in relation only to Bacon, Ralegh, and Coke, even though I have tried to emphasize the extent of the interests and influence of all three. A full discussion would have to deal with far more topics than those I have here picked out. We should have to consider the way in which the Renaissance concept that true aristocracy consisted in virtue, not birth—a doctrine designed by the humanists to civilize the landed class—slowly merged into the Puritan concept of the oligarchy of the godly, which in the civil war period was used to justify the maintenance of revolutionary dictatorship by a minority *against* the mass of the gentry.[1] In the entourage of Thomas Cromwell a few daring spirits subverted the doctrine

[1] Cf. F. Caspari, *Humanism and the Social Order in Tudor England* (1954), pp. 14–15.

of degree by preaching the equality of man and advocating a
career open to the talents.[1] In the entourage of Oliver Cromwell
these doctrines were put into practice. We find various intervening stages of the doctrine not only in the writings of a
religious radical like John Ponet, who thought that aristocracy
originated in *popular* appreciation of the virtuous, and whose
works were reprinted in 1642;[2] but also in *The Mirror for
Magistrates*, and works of men like Ralegh himself and his
friends Spenser, Marlowe,[3] and Chapman.

> Virtue makes honour, as the soul doth sense,
> And merit far exceeds inheritance,

Chapman wrote in 1595, in a poem dedicated to Matthew
Roydon.[4] The Puritan in *An Humerous Dayes Mirth* (1599) said
that in religion there was no difference between estates.[5] But it
was an admirable character in *The Gentleman Usher* (1602) who
drew political conclusions:

> Had all been virtuous men
> There never had been princes upon earth,
> And so no subject; all men had been princes.
> A virtuous man is subject to no prince,
> But to his soul and honour.[6]

The point was not usually so clearly made, at least until the
virtuous were free to organize themselves in the New Model
Army. But in the English society where aristocracy still ruled,
the disturbing doctrine of the superiority of virtue to birth had
meanwhile often been expressed—among others by Robert
Greene,[7] Ben Jonson,[8] John Webster,[9] Robert Burton,[10] George

---

[1] W. G. Zeeveld, *Foundations of Tudor Policy* (1948), esp. pp. 160, 194, 209–11.
[2] 'The people of a great and thankful mind gave them that estimation and honour;
... the respect only of their virtue and love to their country brought them thereto'
(J. Ponet, *A Shorte Treatise of Politike Power*, 1556, sig. [G. vii-vii⁴], quoted in Zeeveld,
op. cit., p. 258). Ponet was also a scientist and a mathematician.
[3] Spenser, esp. *The Faerie Queene*, Book VI; *Teares of the Muses*; Marlowe, *Tamburlaine*, *passim*. For Ralegh see pp. 168, 197 above.
[4] G. Chapman, *Works: Poems and Minor Translations* (1875), p. 34; cf. p. 116—
a poem dedicated to Prince Henry.
[5] Chapman, *Dramatic Works* (1873), i. 58.   [6] Ibid., p. 331.
[7] R. Greene, *Plays and Poems* (1905), ii. 196.
[8] Jonson, *Cynthia's Revels*, Act v, scene i.
[9] Webster, *Complete Works* (1927), ii. 238.
[10] Burton, *Anatomy of Melancholy* (Everyman ed.), ii. 137–44.

Wither,[1] and John Milton.[2] It was stressed by Puritans like
William Perkins[3] and Arthur Dent,[4] by Sir John Eliot writing
in the Tower,[5] by George Hakewill,[6] by Thomas Beedome
apropos Captain James,[7] and by the Presbyterian Samuel
Rutherford.[8] Sprat in his *History of the Royal Society* declared that
'traffic and commerce have given mankind a higher degree
than any title of nobility'.[9] Only in 1688 did the Tory dramatist
Johnny Crowne put the sentiment into the mouth of a traitor.[10]

That is one line of thought which it would be interesting to
work out. Another, perhaps of no less significance, is the
influencing of feudal doctrines of contract by new commercial
and legal ideas. The change was mediated in part by the Puritan
contract theology of the Cambridge and City preachers, the
Ramists Dudley Fenner and Perkins, Preston, Ames, Sibbes—
and of John Dury. This came very near to suggesting that a
bargain could be struck with God, and that He could be held
to the letter of His bond: 'as a rich man oppresseth a poor man,
and gets out of him all that he is worth, he leaves him nothing,
he plays the extortioner with him'.[11] If God could be held to his
promises, it was not as seditious as James thought to dispute the
omnipotence of kings.[12] Part of God's covenant, Hakewill tells
us, is the orderly and perpetual working of the universe.[13] The
exact processes by which the all-pervading contractualism of
seventeenth-century thought evolved still await their historian.
It has frequently been suggested that the covenants which

---

[1] Wither, *Juvenilia* (Spenser Soc. reprint), i. 254–5, 372–4, 383–6, 428–9; ii. 50–
52; *Hymns and Songs of the Church* (1856), p. 231: first published 1623.

[2] Milton, *Complete Prose ·Works* (Yale ed.), i. 471–3.

[3] Perkins, *Workes* (1609–13), i. 119; ii. 293.

[4] Dent, *The Plain Mans Pathway to Heaven*, quoted in A. West, *The Mountain in the Sunlight* (1958), p. 18.   [5] Eliot, *The Monarchie of Man* (1879), ii. 179–81.

[6] Hakewill, *An Apologie*, pp. 604–5.

[7] T. Beedome, *Select Poems* (1928), p. 29; cf. p. 37. First published 1641.

[8] 'A marquis's or a king's word, when you stand before Christ's tribunal, shall be lighter than the wind'—letter of 8 June 1637, in *Letters of Samuel Rutherford* (ed. A. A. Brown, 1894), pp. 327–8.   [9] Sprat, *History of the Royal Society*, p. 408.

[10] J. Crowne, *Darius, King of Persia*, in *Dramatic Works* (1874), iii. 435.

[11] J. Preston, *The New Covenant* (fifth ed., 1630), pp. 477–8; J. M. Batten, *John Dury* (Chicago U.P., 1944), pp. 107–10; P. Miller, *The New England Mind: the 17th century* (New York, 1939), pp. 365–97; J. G. Møller, 'The Beginnings of Puritan Contract Theology', *Journal of Ecclesiastical History*, xiv. 46–67. Cf. Hakewill, *Apologie*, p. 601, and my *Puritanism and Revolution*, pp. 245–9. For Preston's influence on Prynne, see Lamont, *Marginal Prynne*, p. 91.

[12] James I, *Workes* (1616), p. 531.   [13] Hakewill, *Apologie*, ii. 147.

members of sectarian congregations signed between themselves and with their minister influenced the evolution of social contract ideas in political theory.[1] Men like Roger Williams and John Cotton emphasized the parallels between a congregational church and a City company.[2] But ideas drawn from the law of property may have been equally relevant, and at an earlier date. Thus in 1593 we find Horatio Palavicino explaining to his patron the Earl of Shrewsbury that a contract overrode his loyalty to 'an honourable personage whom I greatly reverence'.[3] So feudal principles were undermined. Hobbes was soon to define justice as the keeping of covenants—and no more: where there was no covenant there could be no injustice.

A third relevant idea was that the end of the world was at hand. Fifth Monarchists in the sixteen-fifties found this a stimulus to direct revolutionary action, just as throughout the Middle Ages the poorer classes in the towns had always been ready to embrace the idea when preached to them in time of crisis. But in the century of crisis before the civil war the imminence of doomsday had been announced by many perfectly respectable thinkers, including Fulke Greville, Beard, and Ralegh:[4] it had been popularized by innumerable ballads. An extreme conservative like Bishop Goodman, whose book on the corruption of nature was the occasion for George Hakewill's defence of the Moderns, was so upset by the geographical discoveries, the new astronomy, and the new morality that he thought they could only presage the destruction of the world. Men as different from Goodman as Joseph Meade ('a curious florist, an accurate herbalist thoroughly versed in the book of Nature, a keen student of anatomy'), Napier (the inventor of logarithms), and Francis Potter (later Fellow of the Royal

---

[1] Notably by C. Bourgeaud, *The Rise of Modern Democracy in Old and New England* (transl. B. Hill, 1894), *passim*, and by Lord Lindsay; see for instance his *The Modern Democratic State*, i (1943), p. 119.

[2] R. Williams, *The Bloudy Tenent* (1848), p. 46 (first published 1644); J. Cotton, *Covenant of Gods Free Grace* (1645), quoted by P. Miller, *Errand into the Wilderness* (Harvard U.P., 1956), p. 85. The comparison seems first to have been made, interestingly enough, by the Jesuit Robert Persons. See *A Catholicke Devyse* (1606), sig. oo 4. Cf. also my *Economic Problems of the Church*, pp. 346–8.

[3] L. Stone, *An Elizabethan: Sir Horatio Palavicino* (1956), p. 40.

[4] Greville, *Poems and Dramas*, i. 224–5; Beard, *Theatre of Gods Judgments*, p. 3. Ralegh thought that 'the long day of mankind' was 'drawing fast towards an evening and the world's tragedy and time near at an end' (*History*, i. 204; cf. ii. 65).

Society) occupied themselves in setting a date for it.[1] Lord Brooke and Milton[2] expected Christ's coming in the near future. So did those simpler souls in the Parliamentary Army who in 1643 thought that He would come to destroy King Charles and that the Earl of Essex was John the Baptist;[3] or those who followed Venner the wine-cooper in 1657 and 1661.

A full account of the intellectual origins of the English Revolution would have to discuss the 'liberal' constitutional ideas which descend from Fortescue through Christopher St. Germain, Thomas Starkey, and Sir Thomas Smith. The latter touches our story at many points. The son of a protestant sheep farmer, he himself purchased monastic lands, and disliked 'conjurors and mass-mongers'. At Cambridge he won a reputation as a mathematician: he later got Walsingham to send him medical books and mathematical instruments from Paris. Smith was interested in astronomy, having Copernicus in his library, and making globes with his own hands; and also in astrology, navigation, alchemy, medicine, economics. He had a laboratory in his house, and conducted chemical experiments together with Sidney's mother. He met and discussed with Ramus, and had his works in his library.[4] Smith, like Dee, wanted England to adopt the new Gregorian calendar. He was a defender of the use of the vernacular, and himself (Ben Jonson thought) had a prose style comparable to those of Ralegh and Bacon. Like Ralegh, Smith was a proponent of religious toleration, an admirer of the yeomanry, an advocate of colonization, as well as setting new architectural fashions.[5] Like Bacon, Smith favoured a career open to the talents. Like Coke, he disliked wardship and torture. There were eleven editions of his

[1] J. Meade, *Clavis Apocalyptica* (1627); C. E. Raven, *Synthetic Philosophy in the 17th century* (1945), p. 22; Francis Potter, *An Interpretation of the Number 666* (1642). There are said to have been eighty such treatises published in England before 1649. See my *Puritanism and Revolution*, p. 325. Meade was a friend of Hartlib.

[2] Brooke 'did often say, He should live to see the millenary fools' paradise begin in his life' (Wood, *Athenae Oxonienses*, ed. P. Bliss, 1813–20, ii. 434); Milton, *Complete Prose Works* (Yale ed.), i. 707; iii. 256.

[3] Sir S. Luke, *Journal* (ed. I. G. Philip, Oxfordshire Record Soc., 1950), p. 76.

[4] Strype, *Life of . . . Sir Thomas Smith* (1820), pp. 2, 15, 89, 93, 100–5, 118, 146, 161, 166, 279; Mary Dewar, *Sir Thomas Smith* (1964), *passim*.

[5] B. Farrington, *Francis Bacon*, p. 12; G. Williamson. *The Senecan Amble* (1951), p. 89; E. Mercer, *English Art, 1553–1625* (1962), pp. 63–65. Smith combined a modern outlook with a precociously learned classical taste in architecture: cf. ibid., pp. 133–5, and pp. 22, 220 above. For Smith as colonizer see p. 157 above.

Commonwealth of England between 1583 and 1640: Sir John Eliot possessed a manuscript copy, and it was paraphrased by Milton in *The Tenure of Kings and Magistrates*.[1] Smith founded two mathematics readerships at Queens' College, Cambridge: his instructions anticipate Gresham College's criticism of contemporary lecturing practice. Smith links the radicalism of the reign of Edward VI with the radicalism of the Revolution.

A fifth trend is very difficult to assess because it runs underground. In 1645-6 the Leveller Richard Overton published pamphlets which refer to, and expect his readers to be aware of, the Marprelate pamphlets which had a wide popularity in 1588-9.[2] The latter were suppressed, and those believed to be the authors were hunted down and executed. It may well be that Marprelate's irreverent wit appealed to an erastian anticlerical public which· was not in the usual sense of the word 'Puritan', but which shared Puritanism's enemies: the public which had enjoyed Simon Fish and Bishop Bale. If one wanted to look for links between Marprelate and Overton, one might find them in the pamphlets of Thomas Scott and John Bastwick, which had to be published abroad and smuggled into England. Even the posthumous *Table Talk* of the sophisticated Selden has something of the same robust and brutal anti-clericalism. The general effects of early Stuart censorship also deserve more serious consideration. The generation brought up by Foxe to think of printing as a divine invention for scattering darkness and spreading light was encouraged by Bacon to see printing as an example of the superiority of the industrial craftsman over the academic scholar.[3] How would such men regard censorship? It was not only because of their suppression of lecturers that the bishops were believed to want to bring in darkness 'that they may the easier·sow their tares while it was night'.[4] Laud was alleged to have suppressed Foxe's *Acts and Monuments* and Lewis Bayley's *Practice of Piety*.[5] Many were the complaints of

[1] Sir T. Smith, *De Republica Anglorum: A Discourse on the Commonwealth of England* (ed. L. Alston, 1906), pp. 40–45, 105, 120–1; Milton, *Complete Prose Works* (Yale ed.) iii. 221; Dewar, op. cit., pp. 15–16.

[2] Cf. H. N. Brailsford, *The Levellers and the English Revolution* (1961), pp. 53–54.

[3] J. Foxe, *Acts and Monuments* (ed. J. Pratt, n.d.), iii. 718–22; iv. 252–3; Bacon, *Works* (1826), ii. 118–21; *Works*, iv. 129. Foxe was a friend and protégé of Bale's.

[4] J. A. R. Marriott, *The Life and Times of Lucius Cary, Viscount Falkland* (1907), pp. 182–3.

[5] J. Rushworth, *Historical Collections*, ii. 450; Laud, *Works*, iv. 226.

'tyrannical duncery' in the sixteen-thirties; many mute inglorious *Areopagiticas* appeared at about the same time as Milton's.[1]

I might, again, have said more about the rise of economic theory, starting with Gresham's Law. Thomas Mun knew that private vices might be public benefits, and advanced at least one iron law: 'So much treasure only will be brought in or carried out of a commonwealth as the foreign trade doth over-or underbalance in value.' He advocated a Navigation Act, in common with Ralegh and many M.P.s in the 1621 Parliament.[2] Other merchants, like Wheeler, Malynes, and Misselden discussed economic theory in their practical treatises. Sir Thomas Smith and Sir Henry Spelman seem to have understood the nature of inflation.[3] Bacon, Ralegh, and Coke advocated free trade, and the two former contributed to the idea of law in the social sciences. Only the intellectual stimulus of the Revolution was needed to create a new science. Many reasons led Marx, the Bacon of sociology, to call Petty 'the father of English political economy'.[4] Petty shared his labour theory of value with Winstanley and Hobbes, his economic approach to politics with Winstanley and Harrington.[5] But his emphasis on division of labour and his use of statistics were more original, as was his assertion of the principle that 'making civil positive laws against the laws of nature' was vain and fruitless.[6] Petty and John Graunt, the founders of statistics, were Parliamentarians as well as Baconians and Fellows of the Royal Society: Graunt's method derived from the 'mathematics of . . . shop-arithmetic', from London science, as well as from Bacon.[7]

[1] W. K. Jordan, *The Development of Religious Toleration in England*, iv (1940), p. 210 and *passim*.   [2] McCulloch, op. cit., pp. 208–9; cf. p. 129.

[3] See my *Economic Problems of the Church* (1956), p. 99 for Smith and Spelman.

[4] K. Marx, *A Contribution to the Critique of Political Economy* (1904), p. 60.

[5] Ed. Sabine, *Works of Gerrard Winstanley*, p. 511; T. Hobbes, *Leviathan* (Everyman ed.), pp. 44, 130. The former passage was quoted by Marx in *Value, Price and Profit* (1865), printed in *Selected Works* (Moscow, 1935), i. 313.

[6] Petty, *A Treatise of Taxes and Contributions* (1662), in *The Economic Writings of Sir William Petty*, i. 48; cf. pp. 57, 60; ii. 473. Petty had been Hobbes's amanuensis, as Hobbes had been Bacon's (G. N. Clark, *Science and Social Welfare in the Age of Newton*, 1937, p. 135).

[7] Graunt, *Observations upon the Bills of Mortality*, in Petty, *Economic Writings*, ii. 323; cf. S. Matsukawa, 'The 300th Anniversary of John Graunt's *Observations*', *Hitotsubashi Journal of Economics*, iii. 49–60. Graunt was a protégé of Sir Benjamin Rudyerd and brother-in-law to the Cromwellian Major-General, Thomas Kelsey. He died a Catholic. See now J. O. Appleby, *Economic Thought and Ideology in Seventeenth Century England* (Princeton U.P., 1978).

The controversies concerning the position of women, which raged before and during the civil war, would also be relevant to our discussion. The economic processes which gave a new social significance to small merchants and artisans increased the number of wives who shared in control of the household productive unit. Spinsters too benefited: it is during the lives of Bacon, Ralegh, and Coke that the word ceases to be restricted to female spinners and comes to mean any unmarried woman, so obvious was it that such a woman could find employment in the clothing industry.[1] Professor Jordan in his study of charity during this period concluded that women possessed far more 'disposable wealth and certainly far greater independence of judgement than has commonly been supposed'. In London the proportion of women benefactors increased rapidly between 1621 and 1650.[2]

One consequence of these economic developments was the Puritan doctrine of marriage, emphasizing the wife as helpmeet and partner in the family joint-stock, whilst insisting on children's right to choose whom they would marry. The guides to godliness, of which so many were published during our period, as well as the writings of Spenser, Shakespeare, and Milton, did much to popularize the ideal of monogamous wedded love.[3] Another consequence was a revival of traditional complaints about London citizens' wives dressing above their station, which this time gave rise to a pro- and anti-feminist literature. The drama of the time reflects this interest in the position of women. The playwright who wrote *The Taming of the Shrew* also created Benedick and Beatrice. The popular theatre for which Shakespeare wrote was in general in favour of the improvement in women's status which had taken place. It was the coterie theatre, the haunt of courtiers and Inns of Court men, that had a cynical and contemptuous attitude towards women.[4]

There were many female translators and authors, including Bacon's mother, Sidney's sister and niece. Some of the dates are

---

[1] *The Oxford English Dictionary* has 'spinster' used to describe a wife in 1580; by 1617 a dictionary definition gives the modern meaning.

[2] W. K. Jordan, *Philanthropy in England, 1480–1660* (1958), p. 354; *The Charities of London, 1480–1660* (1960), p. 29.

[3] W. and M. Haller, 'The Puritan Art of Love', *H.L.Q.* v, *passim*; L. L. Schücking, *Die Familie im Puritanismus* (Leipzig, 1929), *passim*.

[4] A. Harbage, *Shakespeare and the Rival Traditions* (New York, 1952), *passim*.

interesting. *Jane Anger her protection for women* appeared in 1589. *Willobie his Avisa* was published in 1594, ostensibly a poem in praise of middle-class women and of bourgeois and Puritan virtue, contrasting the behaviour of aristocratic and court ladies. Some think this book was an allegory written by a member of Ralegh's circle, possibly Matthew Roydon.[1] In 1609 an Oxford don, William Heale, attacked the practice of wife-beating in *An Apologie for Women*, and made a reasoned plea for women's rights, frequently quoting Sidney's *Arcadia* in doing so. He was expelled from his fellowship at Exeter College next year. One hopes that the reason alleged, absenteeism, was the true one. In 1620 appeared *Haec Vir*, a comprehensive reply to those who would have condemned women of all classes to dress in the way traditionally held appropriate to their rank. It broadened out into a fervent plea for freedom from the petty bondage of foolish custom. 'Custom is an idiot', said the author in words that curiously anticipate Tom Paine; 'and whosoever dependeth wholly upon him, without the discourse of reason, will ... become a slave indeed to contempt and censure.' On lines reminiscent of Spenser and Ralegh, the pamphlet argued from the mutability of all nature that a right to change is essential for social progress. This '*Areopagitica* of the London woman', as Professor L. B. Wright called it, proclaimed that women 'are as free born as men, have as free election and as free spirits'.[2]

Professor Wright, from whose admirable *Middle-Class Culture in Elizabethan England* I have taken many of these facts, comments that the feminist writers of 1616–20 present the problem with a clarity of logic and a modernity hitherto unknown. There was, he suggests, a serious undercurrent of intelligent thinking upon women's status in a new commercial age. And this inevitably had political implications. Many bourgeois writers, Professor Wright says, vigorously defended women against the cynicism of the coterie dramatists and cavalier poets.[3] It was a Howard, the Earl of Northampton, who advised his son not to educate his daughters.[4] Comenius favoured the equal education of boys

[1] See pp. 142–3 above.
[2] Wright, *Middle-Class Culture in Elizabethan England*, pp. 495–7.
[3] Ibid., pp. 465, 503, 506–7.
[4] E. H. Miller, *The Professional Writer in Elizabethan England* (Harvard U.P., 1959), p. 60.

and girls: in Bacon's *New Atlantis* women as well as men acted as technical assistants to the philosophers. Professor Notestein has testified to the rapid increase of literacy among women in this period:[1] their share in opinion-forming should not be discounted.

There is a connexion between women and radicalism, as there always had been between women and sectarianism. Women were far more determinedly secular in their charity than men.[2] Many of the religious sects allowed women to participate in church government. In the *émigré* congregation in Rotterdam, to which Hugh Peter was called in 1633, both sexes voted.[3] Mr. Thomas has shown the importance of this for England in the revolutionary decades, when women preachers were succeeded by women petitioners and women demonstrators.[4] As early as 1605 Joseph Hall had depicted the imaginary commonwealth of Viraginia or She-Land as a sort of democracy, ruled by majority vote and perpetual sovereign Parliaments.[5] Fifty years later, after experiencing just such horrors, the author of *The Whole Duty of Man* said that many men had been led into 'schism and sedition' by the same wiles as had induced Adam to eat the apple.[6]

The Revolution did a great deal for women. Civil marriage was—briefly—established; the Quakers gave women equality in practice as well as in theory; the Muggletonians held out the prospect that we shall all be males in heaven. The first professional women painters, and the first women to publish music, date from the Interregnum, as do the first poetesses of any significance: the first professional actresses and women of letters from just after it. And when the first woman novelist, Mrs. Aphra Behn, wrote her masterpiece, *Oroonoko*, about Ralegh's Guiana, the only white colonist whom she praised was Colonel Marten, brother of the republican and regicide Henry Marten.

---

[1] W. Notestein, 'The English Woman, 1580–1650', in *Studies in Social History: A Tribute to G. M. Trevelyan* (ed. J. H. Plumb, 1955), pp. 102–3, 106.

[2] Jordan, *Philanthropy in England*, p. 355.

[3] R. P. Stearns, *The Strenuous Puritan* (Illinois U.P., 1954), p. 77.

[4] K. V. Thomas, 'Women and the Civil War Sects', *P. and P.*, No. 13.

[5] J. Hall, *Mundus Alter et Idem* (1605), English translation by J. H[ealey], *The Discovery of a New World* (1608).

[6] *The Causes of the Decay of Christian Piety*, in *The Works of the ... Author of the Whole Duty of Man* (1704), p. 360.

II

But these are imponderables. Easier to estimate is the intellectual stimulus which Englishmen received from outside. The
translation of the classics into the vernacular, at which so many
men laboured in Elizabeth's and James's reigns and which the
Earl of Leicester patronized, put the republican ideas of Greece
and Rome into the hands of the middle and lower classes, excluded from political influence. Hobbes was not the only one to
think that 'the allowing of such books to be publicly read' was
of scarcely less revolutionary significance than the translation of
the Bible.[1] Professor Fink has demonstrated the influence of
Venice on political and constitutional thought, from the
fifteen-thirties when Thomas Starkey suggested that there might
be advantages in reducing the English king's power to that of
the Venetian Doge[2] down to the poem *Britannia and Rawleigh*
(*c.* 1675), attributed to Marvell. In the late sixteenth and early
seventeenth centuries a large number of books were published
on the Venetian constitution.[3] Sir Thomas Smith, anticipating
Bacon and Ralegh in this too, admired Venice, though he
recognized that the English monarchy was 'far more absolute
than . . . the dukedom of Venice'.[4] Sir Philip Sidney thought
highly of the Venetian constitution,[5] and Bacon regarded
Venice as 'the wisest state of Europe'.[6] Lord Chancellor Ellesmere, on the other hand, declared that James I would become
a mere Doge if he could not determine in cases where there was
no authority or precedent.[7] In 1644 several M.P.s asked the
Venetian Ambassador for an account of his country's constitution; in 1647 George Wither recommended its adoption.[8]

[1] Hobbes, *Leviathan* (Everyman ed.), p. 174; *Behemoth* (1679), in *English Works*
(1840), vi. 190–1; Conley, *The First English Translators of the Classics, passim.* See
pp. 28–30 above.

[2] Starkey, *Dialogue between Pole and Lupset* (ed. K. M. Burton, 1948), pp. 163–7.

[3] Z. S. Fink, *The Classical Republicans* (Northwestern U.P., 1945), *passim,* esp. pp.
41–51; J. W. Stoye, *English Travellers Abroad, 1604–1667* (1952), p. 150.

[4] Smith, *De Republica Anglorum,* p. 59.   [5] Sidney, *Complete Works,* iii. 127.

[6] *Cabala* (1654), i. 8. Venice and Padua were the only places in Italy about
which Shakespeare was well informed (Einstein, *The Italian Renaissance in England,*
p. 370). Cf. Burton, *Anatomy of Melancholy* (Everyman ed.), i. 103.

[7] See p. 246 above.

[8] G. P. Gooch, *The History of English Democratic Ideas in the 17th Century* (1898),
p. 125; Wither, *Miscellaneous Works* (Spencer Soc.), I, no. viii, p. 9, no. xii, p. 15;
III, pp. 48–52. Cf. Henry Parker on the supremacy of law in Venice (*The Cordiall
of Mr. David Jenkins . . . answered,* 1647, p. 28).

But Venice was influential in other spheres as well as the constitutional. On Venetian territory foreign Protestants could live unmolested by the Inquisition. Venice's erastianism was praised by Selden, its tolerance by D'Ewes.[1] The republic's controversy with the Papacy made it popular in England. 'All the world knows they [the Venetians] care not threepence for the Pope', said Selden.[2] The writings of Paolo Sarpi were translated into English and widely read: Coke had one of them in his library.[3] The Calvinist William Bedell, an Emmanuel man, was intimate with Sarpi.[4] Sir Edwin Sandys, leader of Parliamentary opposition under James I, may have written his *Europae Speculum* at Venice, with Sarpi's help.[5] The Puritan Thomas Goodwin spoke of Venice with approval.[6] John Wheeler in 1601 commended the Venetian nobility for not disdaining to take part in trade.[7] Forty years later Lewes Roberts held up Venice as an example of economic liberalism to the Long Parliament.[8]

The Venetian republic was also a centre of scientific influence since it contained the University of Padua, the most liberal in Europe (there were no religious tests) and the one which contributed most to the rise of modern science. Both

---

[1] Selden, *Table Talk*, s.v. 'Religion'; Sir Simonds D'Ewes, *The primitive practice for preserving truth* (1645), quoted by W. K. Jordan, *The Development of Religious Toleration in England*, iv (1940), p. 22. For Venetian tolerance, and the limits to it, see A. Stella, 'Ricerche sul Socinianesimo', *Bolletino dell'Istituto . . . di Storia dello Stato veneziano*, iii. 77–120. [2] Selden, loc. cit.

[3] Fink, op. cit., pp. 44–45; Hassall, *A Catalogue of the Library of Sir Edward Coke*, p. 50. The book was *A full and satisfactorie answer to the late unadvised bull against Venice* (1606).

[4] Ed. E. S. Shuckburgh, *Two Biographies of William Bedell* (1902), *passim*; articles by G. Cozzi in *Bolletino dell'Istituto . . . veneziano*, i. Bedell was subsequently Provost of Trinity College, Dublin, the majority of whose heads, like those of Emmanuel, seem to have combined Calvinism with an interest in science. Bedell was preceded by Walter Travers, who possessed globes and compasses, and whose library contained books on medicine and alchemy (S. J. Knox, *Walter Travers*, 1962, p. 147), by the Puritan Henry Alvey and by the Ramist William Temple (see p. 134 above; for Emmanuel see pp. 311–14 below). Although there were no doctrinal tests, the atmosphere of Trinity College was strictly Calvinist. We may compare Calvinist Edinburgh, where chairs of mathematics and natural philosophy were endowed in 1583, forty years before Oxford. [5] See p. 163 above.

[6] T. Goodwin, *Works* (1862), iv. 252. Goodwin, however, thought it going too far when some men tended to convert God into a Doge of Venice (ibid. vi. 507).

[7] J. Wheeler, *A Treatise of Commerce* (1601), p. 7.

[8] L. Roberts, *The Treasure of Trafficke* (1641), dedicated to the High Court of Parliament; in J. R. McCulloch, *Early English Tracts on Commerce* (1856), pp. 101–2.

Vesalius and Galileo had been safe in their unorthodoxy so long as they remained at Padua.[1] Sarpi corresponded with Bacon and Gilbert, and may have influenced Harvey.[2] Sir Thomas Smith studied law at Padua, Sir Philip Sidney astronomy and mathematics. Sir Francis Walsingham studied there during his Marian exile. English medical students of more than ordinary ability went to Padua to get the training that Oxford and Cambridge could not give them. The number of Paduan degrees among those on the roll of the College of Physicians began to diminish only after 1665. Lawrence Wright, later Cromwell's physician, studied there.[3] Robert Child, one of the early New England scientists, a friend of Hartlib and associate of the founders of the Royal Society, took his doctorate of medicine at Padua.[4] So it is hardly surprising that high-flying royalists, from Bancroft to Filmer, anathematized Venice;[5] that Sir Henry Savile visited and studied the republic in 1582;[6] that Milton spent a month there in 1639; and that Dury recommended for imitation the encouragement of science and inventions by 'the wise state of Venice, the most ancient and best settled republican society of the world'.[7] There is a good book to be written on the overall influence of Venice and Padua on pre-revolutionary England.

Even more important as an intellectual influence than the honorary Protestants of Venice were the fighting Protestants of France and the Netherlands. Whether or not Davila's *History of the Civil Wars of France* really was Mr. Hampden's vademecum, we can find in it many ideas which were to be influential in England, from Sir John Eliot onwards.[8] Davila's

---

[1] J. H. Randall, *The School of Padua and the Emergence of Modern Science* (Padua, 1961), *passim*; A. P. Cawadias, 'Harvey in Padua', in *Circulation: Proceedings of the Harvey Tercentenary Congress* (ed. J. McMichael, 1958), pp. 48–49.

[2] S. P. Thompson, *Notes on the* De Magnete *of Dr. William Gilbert* (1901), p. 17; *William Gilbert and Terrestrial Magnetism in the time of Queen Elizabeth* (n.d., ?1903), pp. 6–7; A. Robertson, *Fra Paolo Sarpi* (1911), pp. 67–71, 78–79.

[3] Stoye, op. cit., p. 143. So did the younger Peter Chamberlen.

[4] S. E. Morison, *Builders of the Bay Colony*, pp. 245, 266–7.

[5] R. Bancroft, *A Survay of the Pretended Holy Discipline* (1593), pp. 7–8; ed. P. Laslett, *Patriarcha and other Political Works of Sir Robert Filmer* (1949), pp. 207–8, 220–2.

[6] J. R. L. Highfield, 'An Autograph Manuscript Commonplace Book of Sir Henry Savile', *Bodleian Library Record*, vii. 75–80.

[7] *A Seasonable Discourse Written by Mr. John Dury* (1649), sig. Dv.

[8] J. Forster, *Sir John Eliot* (1865), ii. 451–2.

view of history, like Ralegh's, was providential.[1] Hampden was
accused of using the pretence of religion to justify Parliament's
cause because 'the people would not be drawn to assist us'
otherwise.[2] So, Davila said, did Coligny; so, Davila tells us,
Henry of Navarre thought the Ligueurs did.[3] The Huguenots
were careful to attack evil councillors only, not the king himself.[4] Sir Philip Warwick said that 'our new statesmen, . . .
well acquainted with the history of D'Avila', learnt from him
how to manufacture or at least encourage plots against themselves.[5] The Huguenots too had realized the importance of
making their enemies appear the aggressors, relying on
popular rumours and panic to support them in their ostensibly
defensive position.[6] They were skilful in their use of preachers
as propagandists, and of the printing press.[7] They financed their
war by selling Church property.[8] The Catholic Ligueurs
used the name 'Cavalier';[9] Marlowe made the Guise family
apply the word 'Puritan' to the Huguenots.[10] Cromwell in 1657
might have been copying the dilatory tactics of Henry IV in
1590.[11]

If the politicians studied Davila, Fairfax much admired the
Huguenot D'Aubigné's *Histoire Universelle*;[12] and many other
books on the French wars, including one attributed to Ramus,[13]
helped to form English opinion before and during the Revolution.[14] One of these, Arthur Golding's translation of Duplessis-

[1] H. C. D'Avila, *The History of the Civil Wars of France* (English trans., 1678),
p. 406. When Charles I read the first edition of this translation (1647), he regretted
that he had not earlier studied 'this original' of 'the Grand Contrivers'.

[2] [Anon.], *Persecutio Undecima* (1648), p. 6; *The Regall Apology* (1648), quoted by
D. W. Petegorsky, *Left-Wing Democracy in the English Civil War* (1940), p. 49.

[3] D'Avila, op. cit., pp. 19, 277.

[4] Ibid., p. 271; cf. R. M. Kingdon, *Geneva and the Coming of the Wars of Religion in
France, 1555-63* (Geneva, 1956), p. 107.

[5] Sir Philip Warwick, *Memoirs of the Reign of King Charles I* (1813), p. 198.

[6] D'Avila, op. cit., p. 281.   [7] Ibid., pp. 378, 359.

[8] Ibid., p. 137.   [9] Ibid., p. 408.

[10] C. Marlowe, *The Massacre at Paris, passim*.   [11] D'Avila, op. cit., p. 456.

[12] J. H. M. Salmon, *The French Religious Wars in English Political Thought* (1959),
p. 27.

[13] *The Three Partes of Commentaries, Containing the whole and perfect discoverie of the
Civill warres of France*, trans. Thomas Timms (1574).

[14] Salmon, op. cit., p. 122. Ralegh in his *History* has a passage drawing on his own
experience in the French wars, which he uses to warn against royal treachery (v. 7).
Milton, Dugdale and many others compared the English Revolution to the French
wars of religion (Milton, *Complete Prose Works*, Yale ed., iii. 176-7; Salmon, op.
cit., p. 142).

Mornay's *A Woorke concerning the Trewnesse of the Christian Religion* (1587), was alleged to have been started by Sir Philip Sidney; the first edition was dedicated to the Earl of Leicester, that of 1604 to Prince Henry.[1] Sidney also translated part of the Biblical epic of the Huguenot Du Bartas. The full translation by Joshua Sylvester, Groom of the Chamber to Prince Henry, entitled *Devine Weekes and Workes* (1605), was a best-seller which contained many political allusions as well as a good deal of popular science.[2] Wentworth, on the other hand, learnt the lessons of the French wars from Matthieu's *Derniers Troubles*, a work which favoured absolutism.[3]

The most obvious source of intellectual influence came from the Revolt of the Netherlands. Under Leicester's patronage *A Tragicall Historie of the troubles and Civile Warres of the lowe Countries* was translated in 1583 by Thomas Stocker, as propaganda for English intervention on the Dutch side.[4] The cause of the rebels seemed to many Englishmen to be their own cause.[5] Henry Robinson observed in 1644 that when men were asked in what country they would choose to be born if not their own, they replied 'in Holland'.[6] Ralegh and Bacon expressed warm admiration for Dutch political and economic organization, and especially for the concentration of wealth there in the hands of the industrious classes rather than of the nobility and gentry.[7] Coke also praised the economic liberalism of the Netherlands.[8]

Citizens of London and East Anglia visited the middle-class republic of the Netherlands,[9] as their betters went on the grand tour. Sir Thomas Gresham had been an enthusiast for the

[1] Rosenberg, *Leicester, Patron of Letters*, pp. 272–4. There were four editions of this translation before 1640.

[2] Sylvester's work ran to twenty editions or summaries. See also p. 216 above.

[3] Stoye, op. cit., p. 65.   [4] Rosenberg, op. cit., pp. 104–7.

[5] See p. 160 above; cf. D'Ewes, *Autobiography*, i. 93–94.

[6] H. Robinson, *John the Baptist* (1644), p. 85, quoted in Jordan, *Development of Religious Toleration in England*, iv. 163–4.

[7] See pp. 97, 167 above. This point was elaborated by Francis Osborn in his *Traditional Memoirs* (*Secret History of the Court of James I*, 1811, i. 84). Cf. Drayton's reference in *Polyolbion* to cheap Dutch labour (M. Drayton, *Complete Works*, 1876, iii. 16).   [8] N.R.S. v. 93.

[9] Osborn, loc. cit.; Stoye, op. cit., pp. 241, 267–72. Cf. a letter of 1605 from Sir Charles Cornwallis to Secretary Cranbourne expressing anxiety at Dutch strength and wealth 'in a people of their condition'. It would not have mattered if the Netherlands had been a monarchy (*Winwood State Papers*, 1725, ii. 76).

Dutch rebel cause.[1] The Puritans, Nashe observed in 1592, 'care not if all the ancient houses were rooted out, so that, like the burgomasters of the Low Countries, they might share the government amongst them as states'.[2] Hobbes, three generations later, in discussing the origins of the civil war, said that the citizens of London and other great trading towns envied the Dutch their prosperity, and 'were inclined to think that the like change of government would to them produce the like prosperity'.[3] Thomas Scott had said in 1622 that the best of what Plato and More 'fancied might be' existed in the Netherlands, 'after a most exact and corrected copy'.[4] Use of the word 'patriot' to describe someone opposed to court and courtiers seems to derive from Dutch examples.[5]

Men could have learnt from the Dutch Revolt the tactic of professing loyalty to a king whilst attacking his ministers, of distinguishing between King and commonwealth,[6] of undermining a government by withholding taxation,[7] the use of theories of natural law and contract.[8] It was because Dorislaus vindicated the Dutch for 'retaining their liberties against the violence of Spain' that Matthew Wren complained of his history lectures at Cambridge.[9] Dr. Alexander Leighton, in a work probably published in the Netherlands, pointed out to the Parliament of 1628 that the Dutch had got rid of bishops and prospered;[10] Robert Burton noted that they excluded the aristocracy 'and will admit none to bear office but such as are learned'. He praised Dutch industry and held it out as a model for Englishmen.[11] John Goodwin in 1649 said that 'a people . . . formerly governed by kings may very lawfully turn these

---

[1] Gresham helped to secure asylum in England for protestant refugees from the southern Netherlands. We should not underestimate the political influence of these refugees. Almost by definition they would have radical views.

[2] T. Nashe, Pierce Penilesse his Supplication to the Divell (1592), in Works (ed. R. B. McKerrow, 1958), i. 212–13. I owe this reference to Mr. Charles Hobday.

[3] Hobbes, Behemoth, in English Works, vi. 168.

[4] T. Scott, The Belgic Pismire (1622), p. 90.

[5] E. H. Kossmann, In Praise of the Dutch Republic (1963), pp. 8–11; The Diary of Sir Henry Slingsby (ed. D. Parsons, 1836), p. 57.

[6] J. L. Motley, The Rise of the Dutch Republic (1892), ii. 178–9, 240–2, 358, 566.

[7] Ibid. ii. 337, 366.   [8] Ibid. iii. 500.

[9] Parr, Life of . . . James Usher, ii. 393–4. See p. 176 above.

[10] [Leighton], An Appeal to the Parliament, or Sions Plea against the Prelacie (1628), pp. 221–2.

[11] Burton, Anatomy of Melancholy (Everyman ed.), i. 86–89, ii. 139–40.

servants of theirs out of doors; as . . . the Hollanders of late have done'.[1] In consequence of having 'revolted from their master', Henry Parker added, the Netherlands 'prosper and flourish beyond all in Europe'.[2] Philip Hunton (Provost of Durham College), the Levellers, Milton, and William Dell all quoted the Dutch Revolt as an example establishing the right of resistance in the name of nature and reason.[3]

M.P.s in 1604 and many others noted with approval what they took to be the economic and social consequences of the Revolt;[4] men praised Dutch practice, whether in fishing or farming, or in their low rate of customs.[5] M.P.s observed enviously in 1610 that when taxes were raised in the Netherlands 'they pay to themselves'.[6] Their religious toleration was widely acclaimed as soon as men could write freely on such a subject; the economic advantages of toleration were not least stressed.[7] For Hugh Peter, William Petty, William Cole, and many others, the Dutch offered models of social and legal reform.[8] Dutch styles in art began to become influential in

---

[1] J. Goodwin, *The Obstructours of Justice* (1649), quoted by P. Zagorin, *A History of Political Thought in the English Revolution* (1954), p. 84.

[2] [H. Parker], *The Cordiall of Mr. David Jenkins . . . answered*, p. 30; cf. W. Cole, *A Rod for the Lawyers* (1659), p. 14.

[3] Hunton, *A Treatise of Monarchie* (1643), p. 10; [Anon.], *The Hunting of the Foxes* (1649), in *Somers Tracts* (1809–15), vi. 47; D. M. Wolfe, *Leveller Manifestoes* (New York, 1944), pp. 356–7; Milton, *Complete Prose Works* (Yale ed.), iii. 49, 226; J. Needham, *Time: the Refreshing River* (1943), p. 100. Cf. G. Griffiths, 'Democratic Ideas in the Revolt of the Netherlands', *Archiv für Reformationsgeschichte*, l–li. 50–63.

[4] Ralegh, *Works*, ii. 109–36 (the fact that this tract is probably not by Ralegh is irrelevant here); W. K. Jordan, *Men of Substance* (Chicago U.P., 1942), pp. 186, 214–15, 225, 238; cf. J. Hall, *An Humble Motion*, p. 31.

[5] E. S., *Britains Buss* (1615); Richard Whitehorne, *A Discourse . . . for the advancement of . . . the New-Found-Land* (1622), p. 22; G. E. Fussell. 'Low Countries' Influence on English Farming', *E.H.R.* lxxiv. 611–14; L. Roberts, in McCulloch, op. cit., p. 101. Eliot assured M.P.s in 1624 that the low rate of customs at Amsterdam led to a greater total yield than in England (Forster, *Sir John Eliot*, i. 169).

[6] Ed. S. R. Gardiner, *Parliamentary Debates in 1610* (Camden Soc., 1862), p. 114.

[7] Among others by Lord Brooke, *A Discourse opening the Nature of . . . Episcopacie*, in Haller, *Tracts on Liberty, 1638–47*, ii. 135; R. Overton *A Remonstrance* (ibid. iii. 366); H. Robinson (Jordan, *Men of Substance, passim*); Roger Williams, *The Bloudy Tenent* (1848), p. 245; George Fox, *Concerning the Jews* (1660), in *Gospel Truth Demonstrated* (1706), p. 244; Marchamont Nedham, *The Case of the Commonwealth* (1650), pp. 90–91; and many others, including Roman Catholics under the Protectorate (Jordan, *Development of Religious Toleration*, iv. 335, 444, 457).

[8] H. Peter, *Good Work for a Good Magistrate* (1651); *A Word for the Armie* (1647); B. Whitelocke, *Memorials of the English Affairs* (1853), iii. 388; Petty, *Economic Writings*, i. 260–1, ii. 653; ed. Lansdowne, *Petty Papers* (1927), i. 77–90, ii. 185–6; Cole, *A Rod for the Lawyers*, p. 14. Cf. Kossman, op. cit., pp. 14, 19.

England from the early seventeenth century.[1] Again the
enemies of Dutch principles and practice are predictable:
James I, Charles I, Sir Robert Filmer, Sir Thomas Aston.[2]

No one, I believe, has so far properly investigated the extent
to which Englishmen dissatisfied with Oxford and Cambridge
sent their sons to Leiden University, or what Leiden's influence
on English thought was. The first student in Leiden's Faculty of
Medicine, and the first English graduate of the university, was
John James, Leicester's physician. Later students included
Geoffrey Whitney the poet, John Robinson, John Burges,
Sir William Paddy, Dury, Haak, Ames, Petty, William Bridge,
Francis Rous, Theodore Diodati, John Bastwick, Robert Child,
Sir Thomas Browne, Samuel Collins.[3] Leiden soon came to
share first place with Padua as a centre for students wanting a
more modern medical education than they could get in
England.[4] Astronomy, botany, and chemistry were also better
taught there than anywhere in Great Britain.[5] Sir Philip Sidney
corresponded with Charles de l'Escluse, Leiden Professor of
Botany.[6] Dorislaus was a Leiden doctor of civil law before he
came to Cambridge. Vossius, who had been Brooke's first
preference for the lectureship, was also of Leiden.

But Leiden, where Cartwright was offered a chair of divinity
in 1580, also attracted theological malcontents: hence James I's
interest in the heresies of Vorstius in 1612. If this Arminian was
not dismissed, James threatened, 'we shall be enforced strictly
to inhibit the youth of our dominions from repairing to so
infected a place as is the University of Leiden'.[7] It would have
been a difficult threat to carry out. Between 1575 and 1600
110 Englishmen matriculated at Leiden; 105 between 1600 and

---

[1] M. Whinney and O. Millar, *English Art, 1625–1714* (1957), pp. 8, 60.

[2] Laslett, op. cit., pp. 207–8, 220–2; Aston, *A Survey of Presbytery* (1641).

[3] J. A. van Dorsten, *Poets, Patrons and Professors* (Leiden, 1962), pp. 59, 107,
123–7; A. G. H. Bachrach, *Sir Constantine Huygens and Britain*, i. *1596–1619* (Leiden,
1962), pp. 13, 25, 286; D. C. Dorian, *The English Diodatis* (Rutgers U.P., 1950),
pp. 26, 32–33, 79–80; Morison, *Builders of Bay Colony*, p. 245. Daniel Whistler's
Leiden dissertations on rickets was the first book printed on the subject.

[4] C. Goodall, *The College of Physicians Vindicated* (1676), pp. 57–64.

[5] Bachrach, op. cit., pp. 13–15. Sir William Brereton, future Parliamentarian
general, visited the Botanic Garden and the Anatomy School at Leiden in 1628
(Stoye, op. cit., p. 244). [6] Van Dorsten, op. cit., pp. 30, 93.

[7] G. N. Clark, *The Colonial Conferences between England and the Netherlands in 1613
and 1615*, Part 2 (Bibliotheca Visseriana Dissertationum Jus Internationale Illustran-
tium, xvii, 1951), p. 12. Leiden was the last European refuge of the Pilgrim Fathers.

1619; 95 in the ensuing decade, 145 between 1630 and 1639 and
300 in the decade of civil war. After the purge of Oxford and
Cambridge the number fell sharply to 70 between 1650 and
1659, rising again to 85 in the decade after the Restoration.[1]

III

As well as the specific influences of the French religious wars
and the Revolt of the Netherlands, we should note the more
general effect of Calvinist political theory. From the start there
had been an unresolved contradiction in Protestant political
thinking. The ultimate logic of Luther's 'priesthood of all
believers' when applied to politics was an individualist anarchy.
Luther himself backed away from this logic when confronted
with the Peasants' Revolt of 1525, but he never arrived at a
satisfactory formulation for a state church which could contain
consciences saying 'Here I stand so help me God I can no other'.
Secular authority, Luther said, must 'be held in respect by
good people, although they do not require its services'.[2] This
begged every possible question: who are the good people, how
can they be known, is there no limit to the respect they must
show for the state? Calvin's political theory is little less ambiguous; but he made an essential distinction, which his successors elaborated into a theory of resistance. Revolt is never
justified except when led by people who are themselves
magistrates—i.e. responsible citizens, men of property with a
stake in the country, whether they be princes of the blood in
France, the States-General in the Netherlands or Parliament in
England. 'Private men' should never take the law into their
own hands, but should tarry for the magistrate.[3] This theory
neatly ruled out revolt by the many-headed monster or by
Anabaptists: and yet preserved society and the Church from

---

[1] Stoye, op. cit., p. 295; cf. Clark, op. cit., pp. 10–14. For the radical political
atmosphere at Leiden in 1627 see *The Oxinden Letters, 1607–42* (ed. D. Gardiner,
1933), p. 33. Comenius was warmly welcomed there in 1642 (J. W. Ashley Smith,
The Birth of Modern Education, 1954, p. 64).

[2] M. Luther, *Preface to the Epistle to the Romans*, in *Reformation Writings* (ed. B. L.
Woolf, 1952–6), ii. 298. But cf. R. Bainton, *Here I Stand* (New York, 1950), for
Luther's anticipation of Calvin's political doctrine in the period before Lutheranism
won legal recognition.

[3] J. Calvin, *Institutes of the Christian Religion* (trans. H. Beveridge, 1949), ii.
674–5.

the absolute subordination to the secular power which had been Lutheranism's fate after the Peasants' Revolt.

England was not exempt from the dualism of Protestant thought, or from fear of the many-headed monster. From Tyndale to Filmer there is a continuous trend of political thought which stresses the need for a strong central authority to curb the individualist anarchy which the priesthood of all believers might appear to foster. The Pilgrimage of Grace taught Henry VIII's government the dangers of egalitarian social theories: *The Homily on Wilful Disobedience* no less than Filmer saw monarchy, the saviour of social order, in perpetual danger of being crucified between two thieves, the Pope and the people.[1] But Mary's reign demonstrated the risks of concentrating power in the hands of a prince who might not be godly enough; and from the time of Ponet, Goodman, and Knox onwards Calvinist theories began to have their attractions for Protestant but propertied Englishmen. These theories gave substance to the alliance which formed in Elizabeth's reign between Puritans and Parliament. But, as Archbishop Whitgift darkly informed the Presbyterian Cartwright, 'the people are commonly bent to novelties and to factions, and most ready to receive that doctrine that seemeth to be contrary to the present state, and that inclineth to liberty'.[2] We must always emphasize the dual function of Calvinist political theory. When Robert Browne threatened to appeal to the many-headed monster by his slogan of 'reformation without tarrying for any' he was directly attacking the body of orthodox Puritan thought which wished to tarry for the magistrate, to wait for agreement between Queen and Parliament.[3] Similarly when John Field said 'it is the multitude and people that must bring the discipline to pass which we desire', he was on the eve of losing the support of moderate men.[4]

But men had to tarry a long time for Elizabeth; and James showed no signs of abandoning her position. Meanwhile the tightly knit Calvinist organization, cemented by the Calvinist

---

[1] Filmer, *The Anarchy of a Mixed Monarchy* (1648), in Laslett, op. cit., p. 277.

[2] Whitgift, *Works* (Parker Soc., 1851–3), i. 466.

[3] Ed. A. Peel and L. H. Carlson, *The Writings of Robert Harrison and Robert Browne* (1953), pp. 150–70.

[4] A. F. Scott Pearson, *Thomas Cartwright and Elizabethan Puritanism* (1925), pp. 252–3.

discipline, produced an admirably effective revolutionary force.[1] Successful Calvinist-led revolt in Scotland and the Netherlands, and the long-drawn-out struggles first in France and then in Bohemia and the Palatinate, increased the international prestige of Calvinist theories of revolt. Buchanan and the Huguenot political thinkers had a considerable influence on the Sidney group, Ralegh, and many others down to Rutherford and Milton.[2] In 1648 the *Vindiciae Contra Tyrannos* was published in an English translation. Paraeus had followers in Oxford, where Laud took the lead in opposing him, for once in complete harmony with James I. Milton used Paraeus in *The Reason of Church Government* and in *The Tenure of Kings and Magistrates*.[3] John Lilburne studied the works of Beza.[4]

Those who equated Calvinist political theory with republicanism—from the hostile Bancroft to the friendly Calibute Downing—were pushing logic further than the Puritans themselves would.[5] Yet in the sixteen-forties a cool secularist like Henry Parker has very close affinities with Calvinist political ideas. A right of revolution if authorized by the lesser magistrates was written into the coronation oath proposed by the Isle of Wight terms offered to Charles I in 1648.[6] Milton reminded Presbyterian critics of the execution of Charles I that the Independents had only acted on the principles of Calvin, Buchanan, and Paraeus.[7] Henry Nevile, Harringtonian republican, who was so little of a Puritan that in 1659 the House of Commons debated at length a charge against him of atheism

[1] Cf. H. G. Koenigsberger, 'The Organization of Revolutionary Parties in France and the Netherlands during the 16th century', *Journal of Modern History*, xxvii. 335–51.

[2] Ed. H. J. Laski, *A Defence of Liberty against Tyrants* (1924), pp. 48–54; S. Rutherford, *Lex Rex* (1644), esp. pp. 140–2, 229, 257. Cf. P. Heylyn, *The History of the Presbyterians* (1670), pp. 79–80, 194–6; Salmon, op. cit., p. 81. See pp. 136, 151 above for Sidney and Ralegh.

[3] Heylyn, *History of the Presbyterians*, pp. 90–91, 430; M. Y. Hughes, 'Milton's Treatment of Reformation History', in R. F. Jones, *The Seventeenth Century*, pp. 260–2; G. W. Whiting, 'Paraeus, the Stuarts, Laud and Milton', *S.P.* l. 221–9. Paraeus's *Irenicon* (1614) urged reunion of Protestants on the lines for which Dury and Comenius were soon to work.   [4] P. Gregg, *Freeborn John*, p. 220.

[5] R. Bancroft, *Dangerous Positions* (1593) and *A Survay of the pretended Holy Discipline* (1593), *passim*; C. Downing, *A Discourse of the State Ecclesiasticall* (second ed., 1634), pp. 13–20.

[6] 'The Form of a Bill for a new Coronation-Oath pursuant to the Treaty in the Isle of Wight', in E. Ludlow, *Memoirs* (1699), iii. 350–1.

[7] Milton, *Complete Prose Works* (Yale ed.), iii. 46, 59, 123–4.

and blasphemy, nevertheless recalled with cheerful condescension that it was 'honest John Calvin' who 'taught some of us to deliver ourselves from the tyrannical yoke'.[1] Nevile wanted to *épater* the godly; but his point was historically accurate. The revolution of 1688 was a secular Calvinist revolution, led by the magistrate, in which no organized group emerged to express the discontent of the lower orders.

IV

If we look at the lives of Ralegh, Bacon, and Coke, they have curiously much in common. All tried to make careers in the royal service, all three obtained knighthoods, Bacon a peerage. Bacon and Coke were Privy Councillors. Yet under James all failed. Ralegh was condemned as a traitor in 1604, executed in 1618. Coke was dismissed from office in 1616. Bacon—who held on longest, since he could not conceive of his programme being implemented except by royal favour—was perhaps the one whose ideas made least impact on the government he served; he was thrown to the wolves in the 1621 Parliament. Their disgrace, and the censorship exercised against Ralegh and Coke, no doubt added to their prestige: it certainly gave them leisure to write some of their most significant books. Their attempts to work with the government may testify to ambition, or to miscalculation, or both, on their part; but we must also see them as reacting to that *crise de conscience* of the early seventeenth century which I discussed above.[2] Each in his different way shows something of the 'double heart' which is so familiar in the literature of the time: Bacon, 'the wisest, brightest, meanest of mankind'; Coke, the brutal persecutor of Ralegh and the courageous defender of liberty; Ralegh, a bundle of paradoxes, monopolist defender of free trade, courtier and philosopher, royal favourite and constitutionalist, a man who is himself the most conspicuous example of the failure to master passion by reason which he so bewailed in history.

Before we condemn any of them for subordinating ideals to ambition (or in the case of Coke, for discovering ideals after ambition had been thwarted), we should recall that the governments of the old régime were far from monolithic. Prince

[1] [H. Nevile], *Plato Redivivus* (1681), p. 93; ed. J. T. Rutt, *Parliamentary Diary of Thomas Burton* (1828), iii. 296–305.   [2] See pp. 7–13 above.

Henry (and in 1624 Buckingham and Prince Charles) played the part of leader of the opposition which in the eighteenth century was to become traditional for the heir to the throne. Henry and Secretary Winwood were Ralegh's friends, and Winwood stood by Coke in 1616;[1] Coke went in and out of the Privy Council from 1616 to 1625, even after he had in the 1621 Parliament led the opposition as a Privy Councillor. Cranfield failed to give the government unity of purpose and action: Laud and Strafford came too late, and anyway never succeeded in overcoming faction. This disunity was an important factor in delaying the evolution of revolutionary ideas. Men genuinely believed, down to 1629 and even later, that only evil councillors stood between the King and an acceptable policy. So there was no republican political theory, at least that we know of; there were none who said that sovereignty should reside in Parliament to the exclusion of the King.[2] Very few before 1640 even differentiated between King and commonwealth. For most of the sixteenth century the only alternatives *in fact* to the sovereignty of the Tudors had been feudal anarchy or civil war or foreign conquest. When under the Stuarts other possibilities arose, there was a time-lag in political thinking before the theory of Parliamentary sovereignty was formulated. 'The truth is,' said George Lawson, 'they were not unanimously resolved what they should build up, though they were agreed well enough in pulling down.'[3] Only after civil war had broken out did men turn from the King to the sovereignty first of Parliament and then of the people: from the Laudian state Church first to an erastian establishment and then to the sects.

Our search for intellectual origins has revealed no Rousseau or Karl Marx; but it has perhaps suggested ways in which minds were being prepared for new courses, by men whose proferred services the old régime was unable to use. Once Laud's power had gone, Parliament ordered the publication of Coke's suppressed works: private enterprise saw to it that Bacon's and Ralegh's books were printed in ever-increasing numbers.

---

[1] *Letters of John Chamberlain*, ii. 7.

[2] J. W. Allen, *English Political Thought, 1603–44* (1938), pp. 386–412; J. H. Hexter, *The Reign of King Pym* (Harvard U.P., 1942), pp. 175–82; cf. my *Century of Revolution*, pp. 62–66.

[3] G. Lawson, *Politica Sacra et Civilis*, First Part (1660), p. 105. Lawson might be paraphrasing the words of Cromwell, cited on p. 111 above.

None of our three was a wholly original thinker, not even Bacon: their function was to state clearly what other men were groping towards, which is the definition of an historical great man. Ralegh, the most sensitive of the three, in his poetry expresses Hamlet's sense that the time is out of joint. The frustration, the sense of great potentialities and small achievements, was only in part personal and temperamental; it was also an expression of the spirit of Ralegh's age, for whom Death was the Leveller. Ralegh faces both ways: together with this poignant sense of transitoriness, and of the dead weight of the past, there is his conception of historical law, the optimism and forward look of his belief in private enterprise, in empire, in Parliament.[1] Bacon similarly summed up one of the ways in which traditional authority was being undermined. He caught the optimism of the merchants and craftsmen, confident in their new-found ability to control their environment, including the social and political environment: and their contempt for the old scholasticism. Coke too contributed to the confidence of the men of property in themselves and in private enterprise; and in the years of national disgrace he revived and dignified the patriotic legend. All three provided ideas for the men who hitherto had existed only to be ruled, but who in the sixteen-forties would help to take over the government. Together with the Puritan sense of destiny and emphasis on self-help, they prepared men for revolution. 'Not to try', Bacon said, 'is a greater hazard than to fail.'[2]

Bacon, Ralegh, and Coke shared common enemies with the Puritans—the dissolute, shallow, increasingly pro-papist court, the pro-Spanish and bribed section of the aristocracy; lack of government interest in or support for educational projects or for overseas expansion; use of historical research to free the government from Parliament and common law; interference with private enterprise; prelatical duncery. Literary historians are becoming conscious of a divergence of attitudes in the early seventeenth century. On the one hand, Puritanism, the new science, optimistic belief in progress, and Parliamentarianism; on the other, neo-popery, traditional medieval theology, sceptical

---

[1] Contrast, for example, the conclusion to Beaumont and Fletcher's *The Tryal of Valentinian* (1611), in which revolt is regarded as mere anarchy: murder or suicide are the only possibilities facing tyranny's victims.   [2] Bacon, *Works*, iii. 617.

pessimism, and royalism. Iconoclasm, austerity, introspection, and insular patriotism, plus an internationalism of Protestant peoples on the one hand; sensuousness, courtly magnificence, rhetorical drama, and an internationalism of counter-reformation monarchies on the other.[1] Of course the lines were never clear-cut: but the tendencies can be traced. The attitudes which each individual adopted, in every sphere, would depend on all sorts of private and psychological considerations. A man like Nashe, bitterly jealous of the 'many base men, that wanted those parts which I had', and yet 'had wealth at command', asked himself, 'Have I more wit than all these? . . . Am I better born? am I better brought up? . . . And yet am I a beggar?' He threw himself into the controversies against the new men and their ideas, whether Puritan, Ramistic, or scientific.[2]

On the other side, the men whose economic and philanthropic activities were transforming their society—from the merchant prince who founded the Royal Exchange and Gresham College to the smaller men who endowed scholarships, almshouses, apprenticeships, and marriage portions for virtuous spinsters—such men might enjoy seeing doubt cast on the usefulness of mere scholars and mere courtiers. The ideas we have been examining offered points of intellectual contact for those dissatisfied with the old ways, just as the Royal Exchange and Gresham College, 'a kind of Exchange for scholars',[3] gave them physical points of contact.

These ideas also had political implications. Government patronage of science, called for by Hakluyt, Bacon, and so many others, was essential if the best use was to be made of the resources of the country: if England was to become a major power. The Royal Society, though not living up to Bacon's hopes, gave science a recognized position in the state: and Newton was its triumphant product. Similarly the policy of colonial expansion, which Sidney, Hakluyt, Briggs, Ralegh, and Coke lauded, became government policy during the Interregnum, and continued after 1660. Science and sea power,

[1] P. Cruttwell, *The Shakespearean Moment* (1954), pp. 249–56; cf. H. Haydn, *The Counter-Renaissance, passim.*

[2] Nashe, *Pierce Penilesse*, in *Works* (1958), i. 158; cf. Jonson's Macilente in *Every Man out of his Humour*. This social discontent is the theme of the three *Parnassus Plays.*

[3] T. Fuller, *The History of the Worthies of England* (1840), ii. 465.

empire and trade, religion and the destiny of God's Englishmen, all went together, with Ralegh as their symbol.[1] The English historical myth, created by Foxe, was elaborated by Hakluyt, Ralegh, Bacon, and Coke till it became a force we have all had to struggle against. Coke's attitude to the law, and Ralegh's constitutional theories, raised political problems even in their own lifetime, problems to be solved by the abolition of prerogative courts in 1641 and by the establishment of the supremacy of common law and statute in the later seventeenth century. The ideas we have been considering not only created scepticism about the attitudes and values of the old régime; they specifically if indirectly forced men to think about state power.

I do not want to claim too much: Jericho was not overthrown by trumpet blasts. But Bacon, Ralegh, Coke, together with the many lesser figures whom we have studied in this book, helped to undermine men's traditional belief in the eternity of the old order in Church and state, and this was an immense task, without the successful accomplishment of which there could have been no political revolution. A man like George Hakewill, son of an Exeter merchant, brother of a Parliamentarian lawyer, rejected the traditional doctrine of the sinfulness and helplessness of man as much because it hamstrings human effort as for historical reasons. His tacit moral assumptions, that effort is good and despair is bad, are those of the activists, of the sea-dogs, of Professor Jordan's men of charity, of the New Model Army. Hakewill's emphasis is Baconian: but it is also Puritan. Like the covenant theology, it finds room for human effort. For Hakewill as for Bacon the starting-point is activity, mankind's endeavour to discover the world in order to change it.

V

Finally, there is no end to the pedigree of ideas. I have arbitrarily chosen three men who themselves summed up the thought of many others. But even in this brief summary one can see tracks leading further back. Behind Ralegh stands Sir Philip Sidney, who anticipated him in so many ways: behind Sidney stands Ramus, advocate of reason rather than authority,

[1] In the reign of George III John Langhorne apotheosized Ralegh as a hero of liberty, of anti-Spanish patriotism, and of empire, associating him with Sidney and Milton (*The Poetical Works of John Langhorne*, 1798, pp. 50, 59–60).

proponent of what has been called 'the common man's logic'. It
was utilitarian, practical; like the Baconian method, it 'levelled
men's wits'.[1] The Duke of Guise, in Marlowe's *Massacre at Paris*,
ordered Ramus to be killed because of 'that peasant's' dis-
respect for authority. 'Ne'er was there collier's son so full of
pride', Anjou agreed. Abraham Fraunce made his Aristotelean
say that Ramus profaned and prostituted logic, 'and made
common to all, which before was proper to schoolmen and only
consecrated to philosophers'. Fraunce replied, 'Cobblers be
men, why therefore not logicians? And carters have reason, why
therefore not logic?'[2] Ramus himself had sought to democratize
the Huguenot churches in Paris by placing in the entire congregation those powers which had resided in the elders.[3] This was
later to be a crucial issue between Presbyterians and sectaries.
In Sweden it was the Ramist Johan Skytte who in the sixteen-
thirties advocated a career open to the talents.[4] Ramus had
opposed the idea of the decay of nature, and Hakewill spoke
approvingly of his logic.[5]

Behind Bacon stands not only the Ramistic Cambridge of
his youth,[6] but also the body of London craftsmen and scien-
tists, which included so many Ramists and translators of Ramus
—Hood, Briggs, Wootton, Bedwell. Behind Ramus again stands
Calvin, who distinguished sharply between first and second
causes, and who thought that nature should be studied that
God might be glorified.[7] Most of the great English Puritans
were followers of Ramus, martyred for his Protestantism in the
Massacre of St. Bartholomew: we need mention only Perkins,
Chaderton, George Downham,[8] Gouge, Ames, Hugh Peter,

[1] Cf. P. Miller, *The New England Mind: the 17th century*, pp. 151–2; H. Craig, *The Enchanted Glass* (1950), pp. 145–51, 182.
[2] Fraunce, *The Lawiers Logike* (1588), Sig. ¶¶ 2v–¶¶ 3, quoted by Howell, *Logic and Rhetoric*, p. 225.
[3] R. P. Stearns, *The Strenuous Puritan*, p. 19
[4] N. Runeby, *Monarchia Mixta* (Stockholm, 1962), pp. 553–4, 558.
[5] Haydn, op. cit., p. 531; Hakewill, *Apologie*, pp. 297–9, ii. 135.
[6] T. Granger's Ramistic treatise on preaching, *Syntagma Logicum or the Divine Logike* (1620), was dedicated to Bacon. Bacon was, however, very critical of Ramus.
[7] Calvin, *Institutes*, i. 57, 104, 122, 144, 483–6, 501; cf. P. Miller, op. cit., pp. 31, 47–48, 173.
[8] Downham published his *Commentarius in Rami Dialecticam* at Frankfort in 1610. He was so Puritan that he could only obtain an Irish bishopric, though he came of an episcopal family. In 1631 he was in trouble with Laud for publishing an attack on Arminianism.

and Milton.[1] Comenius too was a Ramist.[2] Leiden was a
Ramist university. Ramus's critics include Hooker and
Bishops Goodman, Richard Montague, and Earle.[3] Among our
other intellectual influences, the political theory of Huguenot,
Scottish, and Dutch rebels was Calvinist; the new ideas of
contract and covenant, of an aristocracy of merit: none of these
could be discussed without mentioning Calvin.

So though I started by saying I would not discuss Puritanism,
here it is coming back again. I tried above to define what I
mean by the word 'Puritan'.[4] Very few of the so-called 'Puritans'
were 'Puritanical' in the nineteenth-century sense of that word,
obsessed by sex and opposed to fun: 'Puritanism' of this sort
was largely a post-Restoration creation. The body of ideas
which has to be called 'Puritan', for want of a better word,
was a philosophy of life, an attitude to the universe, which by
no means excluded secular interests. Professor Frank, after an
intensive study of newspapers between 1640 and 1660, emphasized the fact that the 'Puritan Revolution' was 'secular rather
than religious. . . . The press of that day was more revolutionary
than Puritan.'[5] 'Puritanism' in the seventeenth century was not
in the narrow sense restricted to religion and morals, any more
than science or history were narrowly 'secular' subjects.

Calvinism was primarily an urban phenomenon, with the
clothing and commercial city of Geneva as its source of origin,
Amsterdam, La Rochelle, and London as its secondary centres.
Without entering into controversies about the nature of the
connexions between Calvinism and capitalism, we can agree
that some correlation exists. Early science is in England, as
it is elsewhere, intimately associated with the towns, with

[1] Howell, *Logic and Rhetoric, passim*; P. Miller, op. cit., Chapter V and Appendix
A, *passim*.
[2] See also J. Wilkins, *Mathematical Magic* (fourth ed., 1691), Sig. A 4–5 (first
published 1648). Hobbes's rendition of Aristotle's rhetoric was bound up with
Dudley Fenner's version of Ramus, under the general title *A Compendium of Logick
and Rhetorick in the English Tongue* (1651). The latter was for long attributed to
Hobbes himself (Howell, op. cit., pp. 276–9). Fenner renounced his Anglican
orders in the Netherlands (cf. p. 31 above).
[3] Hooker, *Of the Laws of Ecclesiastical Polity* (Everyman ed.), i. 167–8; Hakewill,
Apologie, ii. 134; Howell, op. cit., pp. 200–2. Montague's criticism came as part of
his attack on Selden.   [4] See p. 26 above.
[5] J. Frank, *The Beginnings of the English Newspaper, 1620–1660* (Harvard U.P.,
1961), pp. 271–2.

merchants and craftsmen. The two trends are not identical: some scientists were Roman Catholics, but very few in England; some Puritans opposed science, but fewer than we are often led to believe;[1] the scientific movement owed much to the independent Paduan tradition. But the intellectual ferment of the Reformation, the reformers' sceptical attitude towards miracles and images, and some of Calvin's attitudes in particular, contributed to the development of science.[2] The very idea of a reformation which was a return to first principles, and the conception of the progressive revelation of truth, ultimately led to a belief in progress.[3] Scientific utilitarianism and radical Protestantism grew up side by side in the urban centres,[4] with support from some gentlemen but deeply rooted in the middle and lower middle class.

In the sixteenth century the individualist revolt of Luther, together with the scientific and geographical discoveries, had shattered the old universe, the old certainties. The truth which jesting Pilate's generation was seeking was being slowly reconstructed by experiment and by religious experience. Truth could no longer be imposed from above, by authority: it had to be rebuilt from below, on individual conviction. Many of the ideas which we have been looking at can be linked by the emphasis on experience, experiment, rather than authority; on things rather than words, on the test of the senses and the heart as against intellectual exercises divorced from practice, on thinking as against the learning by rote which had been necessary before the invention of printing; on reason against precedent, but on experience against 'reasonings vain'. 'Their whole knowledge of learning without the book', said Ascham, 'was tied only to their tongue and lips, and never ascended to the brain and head, and therefore was soon spit out of the mouth again.'[5]

Sir Thomas Smith, to quote another of the Edwardian forerunners, prided himself that he did not write about 'vain imaginations, fantasies of philosophers to occupy the time and to

---

[1] See pp. 111–12 above.
[2] See pp. 22–33 above.
[3] For a good example of this see R. Greenham, *Workes* (1612), pp. 824–5.
[4] Cf. Haydn, *The Counter-Renaissance*, pp. 245–6, and references there cited.
[5] R. Ascham, *The Scholemaster* (ed. Arber, 1870), p. 88: first published 1570. See also pp. 112–15 above.

exercise their wits'. He described England as he knew it, 'so that whether I writ true or not, it is easy to be seen with eyes (as a man would say) and felt with hands'. 'Thus you see what experience doth', wrote Thomas Wotton, introducing William Lambarde's *Perambulation of Kent* in 1576; 'and thus you see where other folks' experience is to be had: . . . —from the history of England.'[1] Even a relatively credulous man like William Harrison appealed to his own experience against 'talking philosophers, void of all experience', just as William Harvey was to do.[2] 'This I knew experimentally', George Fox was saying of his spiritual experiences two years after the scientists and Comenians began to foregather at Gresham College. When Gilbert Burnet was trying to convert the Earl of Rochester—who had no doubt imbibed the scientific spirit during his two years' stay at Wadham (1660–1)—he endeavoured to show that religious experience was something that could be demonstrated by experiment, something as real as physical experience. It was no use appealing to authority.[3] Similarly Baxter spoke of 'soul-experiments', 'heart-operations'.[4]

Reliance on experience and experiment thus links history, religion, and science. We may compare the shift in legal procedure, beginning in our period, from reliance on gossip of neighbours, extorted confessions, torture, and rhetoric to the scientific use of evidence.[5] There is in literature a parallel emphasis on the all-importance of individual experience. 'Fool, said my muse to me, look in thy heart and write.'[6] Fulke Greville too contrasted traditionally accepted authority with the truth of the heart when he made his priests say:

> Yet when each of us in his own heart looks,
> He finds the God there far unlike his books.[7]

Ralegh, as we have seen, played a part in the evolution of the poetry of introspection.[8]

---

[1] Smith, *De Republica Anglorum* (1906), p. 142; Lambarde, op. cit., Sig. ¶¶.

[2] W. Harrison, *Description of England*, in R. Holinshed, *Chronicles* (1587), p. 236. For Harvey see p. 114 above.

[3] Quoted by G. F. Nuttall, *The Holy Spirit in Puritan Faith and Experience* (1946), p. 8; cf. pp. 35, 39; V. de Sola Pinto, *Enthusiast in Wit* (1962), pp. 6–8, 198–9.

[4] *Reliquiae Baxterianae*, i. 124.

[5] Cf. Howell, *Logic and Rhetoric*, p. 376.   [6] Sidney, *Poems* (1962), p. 165.

[7] Greville, *Poems and Dramas*, ii. 137; cf. *Life of Sidney*, p. 135. In French *expérience* means both experience and experiment.

[8] See p. 220 above.

If we could 'lay aside foolish questions', said Greville's heir in 1641, and 'seek into our hearts . . . we might have our Heaven here'.[1] It is difficult for us to realize how great a revolution lay in this reliance on *one's own* senses, *one's own* conscience, even against traditional authority. We have got so used to regarding originality as a virtue that wins scholarships that we forget the time, not so long ago, when it was regarded as an intellectual offence.[2] In *Ignatius his Conclave* Copernicus, Paracelsus, Machiavelli, and Loyola disputed 'the principal place, next to Lucifer's own throne', which was reserved for those 'which had so attempted any innovation in this life, that they gave an affront to all antiquity, and induced doubts and anxieties and scruples, and after, a liberty of believing what they would; at length established opinions directly contrary to all established before'.[3] The right to believe what one would was an extension to the realm of ideas of the right to do what one would with one's own, which underlay the economic and legal revolutions of this period.[4] Those who in the seventeenth century thought there was a connexion between freedom of thought and freedom of economic activity were quite right.

Confidence in the new attitude was built up very slowly. In 1547 Andrew Boorde, Thomas Cromwell's protégé and an early popularizer, said cautiously: 'Whereas Galen with other ancient and approbate doctors doth praise pork, I dare not say the contrary against them; but this I am sure of, I did never love it.'[5] But Paracelsanism and acquaintance with new drugs in the East and West Indies caused greater flexibility of attitude. Similarly on oceanic voyages men observed facts which contradicted Aristotle and Ptolemy; slow absorption of these transformed men's ideas about the universe and their attitudes to authority. In 1605 the Catholic Richard Verstegan still felt it necessary to apologize for putting forward a geographical theory based on observation and not to be found in ancient

[1] Lord Brooke, *The Nature of Truth* (1640), p. 169.
[2] Cf. Hakewill, *Apologie*, ii. 132.
[3] J. Donne, *Ignatius his Conclave* in *Complete Poetry and Selected Prose* (1929), p. 361: first published 1611. Donne's Loyola was able to defeat the claims of the others to have made innovations equal to his.
[4] See pp. 233-7, 272 above.
[5] A. Boorde, *A Compendyous Regiment* (1547), quoted by R. F. Jones, *Ancients and Moderns*, p. 3. Cf. p. 49 above.

books.[1] But in 1633 when Captain James, friend of Briggs and Gunter, found that his observations on latitude and longitude were different from what traditional mathematical calculations had led him to expect, he had no hesitation in saying flatly: 'but thus we found it by practice'.[2] Nor must we leave out of account experiences linking religion and science, which seem less real to us but which were for contemporaries as conclusive as laboratory experiments. Richard Hakluyt was brought to cosmography by reading the 107th Psalm.[3] Descartes, Pascal, and Lord Herbert of Cherbury had visions no less than Gerrard Winstanley, George Fox, and John Bunyan. The evidence of the heart was for all these men no less real than sense data.

I have argued elsewhere that the Protestant religion of the heart facilitates change in response to social pressures more than the Roman Catholic and Laudian religions of authority.[4] The whole of Coke's work was an exercise in adapting the common law to meet the needs of a changing society: hence its triumphant success. In science the victory of the experimental method over the authority of the Ancients made even more obviously for change. All these fitted the pragmatic attitudes of our merchants and craftsmen. The experimental method led to improvements in science and industry, in surveying and navigation; individual consciences studying the Bible found there new and equally welcome truths. Some consciences found an even greater liberation. The Bible, said Milton in 1641, 'ought to be so in proportion as may be wielded and managed by the life of man, without penning him up from the duties of human society'.[5] 'When we are treating of worldly affairs', Henry Parker agreed, 'we ought to be very tender how we seek to reconcile that to God's law which we cannot reconcile to men's equity: or how we make God the author of that constitution which man reaps inconvenience from.'[6] Already Christianity was ceasing to be

[1] Verstegan, *The Restitution of Decayed Intelligence* (1605), quoted by Taylor, *Late Tudor and Early Stuart Geography*, p. 86. Verstegan was a friend of Gresham.
[2] W. W., *The Strange and Dangerous Voyages of Captain Thomas James* (1633), p. 9, quoted by Jones, op. cit., p. 75. For James see pp. 46–47 above.
[3] Taylor, *Original Writings . . . of the . . . Hakluyts*, ii. 396–7.
[4] 'Protestantism and the Rise of Capitalism', in *Essays . . . in Honour of R. H. Tawney* (ed. F. J. Fisher, 1961), pp. 15–39.
[5] Milton, *Complete Prose Works* (Yale ed.), i. 699. The liberating effects of this approach can be seen in *Areopagitica*.
[6] H. Parker, *Jus Populi* (1644), p. 57.

mysterious: God, like the King, was being subordinated to man-made laws. Never before the sixteen-forties could men have said in print that the Bible should be interpreted with reference to social needs.

Many of the ideas which Puritanism embraced had been prevalent among lower and middle class heretics in the Middle Ages, just as the alchemists had anticipated something of the experimental method and look forward to Boyle. The difference in our period is that the Third Estate, the industrious classes, have risen in social and therefore political importance. Hence industry, thrift, and the bourgeois virtues play so large a part in Protestant ideology; hence the traditional Protestant emphasis on the godly artisan;[1] hence Bacon, 'the philosopher of industrial science', set himself to learn from the craftsmen, to restore contact between the men of theory and the men of practice. The radicals (Webster, Biggs), from whom the most violent attack on the universities came, inherited the craftsmen's alchemical tradition and the doctors' astrological tradition. Mathematicians and astronomers like Wallis and Ward could more easily fit themselves into the universities once they were purged. Bacon had wanted alchemy and astrology to be carefully sifted, and Boyle started. But the radical associations of alchemists, emphasized during the Revolution, were too close. When the political and intellectual reaction came, Boyle worked hard to purge science of subversiveness and irreligion. Newton completed the revolution in mathematics and physics: the chemical revolution had to wait for the 'dual revolution' of the late eighteenth century before it was completed by the political radicals Priestley and Lavoisier.[2] Similarly the intellectual advance of Levellers, Diggers, and Ranters to a rational materialism was picked up by the French Encyclopaedists and late-eighteenth-century English radicals. Marvell's intuitive sense of the interrelation of freedom and destiny, and Harrington's more elaborately scientific approach to history, look forward to the Scottish school. In political economy Adam Smith started from where Petty left off.[3]

---

[1] See my *Society and Puritanism in Pre-Revolutionary England*, Chapter 4, *passim*.

[2] S. F. Mason, *A History of the Sciences* (1953), chapters 25–26. For the 'dual revolution' see E. Hobsbawm, *The Age of Revolution* (1962), *passim*.

[3] See my *Puritanism and Revolution*, pp. 353–66, and p. 203 above. See now J. R. Jacob, *Robert Boyle and the English Revolution* (New York, 1977).

So after the excitement of the revolutionary decades, the pace of intellectual development slowed down for the next hundred years. When the republican Moses Wall, friend of Milton and admirer of Menasseh ben Israel,[1] tried to explain to the former in 1659 the reasons for 'the non-progressency of the nation, and ... its retrograde motion of late, in liberty and spiritual truths', his diagnosis was Bacon's in reverse: men remained fallen because science and industry, and the Third Estate generally, were inadequately developed. 'Whilst the people are not free, but straitened in accommodation for life, their spirits will be dejected and servile.' If liberty and spiritual truths are to be recovered, 'there should be an improving of our native commodities as our manufactures, our fishery, our fens, forests, and commons, and our trade at sea, &c.', plus the abolition of copyhold and tithes: 'which would give the body of the nation a comfortable subsistence'.[2] It is an analysis applicable to many so-called under-developed countries today. Spiritual truths are easier to grasp if one is not hungry.

So my conclusion is the banal and eternal one, that history is all very mixed up. But wisdom lies, I think, in recognizing the complicated interconnexions and not allowing ourselves to be unduly influenced by the categories of analysis which we invent for our own convenience. I should like to end by quoting again from Hiram Haydn's invaluable book, *The Counter-Renaissance*:

Nothing more clearly demonstrates that it is one movement, infecting alike theology, natural science, and the social and political sciences, than the parallel phenomena of the early Reformation's premium on the faith of the lowly and humble, the empirical scientists' concern with the value of the artisans' and practitioners' work, and the emergent democratic principles apparent in the writings of the political and social thinkers of the sixteenth century who scoffed at the established hierarchy of 'professions', 'vocations' and traditional castes. . . . They are utterly alike in their rejection of a middleman of received authoritarian truth—whether a scientific pundit of long standing, the Roman Catholic Church, or a traditionally accepted authority on the nature of the state and the nature of man.[3]

[1] In 1650 Wall had translated Menasseh ben Israel's *The Hope of Israel* (L. Wolf, *Menasseh ben Israel's Mission to Oliver Cromwell*, pp. xxvii, 56–62).
[2] Quoted by Masson, *Life of Milton*, v. 602–3.
[3] Haydn, *The Counter-Renaissance*, pp. xiv–xv; cf. p. 85.

Professor Haydn was arguing against departmentalization of history, the separate analysis of religious, political, and economic 'factors', as Comenius in 1642 argued against the departmentalization of knowledge: 'Can any man be a good naturalist, that is not seen in the metaphysics? Or a good moralist, who is not a naturalist? Or a logician, who is ignorant of real sciences?'[1] Although I left Puritanism out of my analysis of the intellectual origins of the English Revolution, a discussion of science, history, law, repeatedly brought us back to it. The conflicts in all these spheres seem to me to relate to the social and political conflicts in the society which gave them birth, and so to be different aspects of a single revolution.

[1] Comenius, *A Reformation of Schooles* (1642), quoted by J. Needham, *Time: the Refreshing River*, p. 26.

APPENDIX

A NOTE ON THE UNIVERSITIES

I

Since my view on the position, or absence, of science in Oxford and Cambridge before the civil war is closer to that traditionally held than to the view recently put forward by Mr. Curtis (*Oxford and Cambridge in Transition, 1558–1642*, 1959), I should state my reasons for disagreeing with Mr. Curtis. For his book as a whole I have great admiration: he has used new material to draw attention to many interesting points about the universities previously overlooked. He is quite right to insist that historians' descriptions of Oxford and Cambridge have been too lightly based on contemporary criticisms, which from the nature of the case were one-sided. These descriptions often embody a 'Whig' attitude, condemning the past for not being the present. But I feel that in his enthusiasm to correct what he believes to be mistaken views, Mr. Curtis has himself sometimes been guilty of over-statement, straining the evidence, and special pleading. His conclusion that 'the universities, despite their statutes, were teaching the results of recent findings in mathematics and science' seems to me too sweeping if, as appears from the context, this remark is intended to apply to the period before the Parliamentarian purge of Oxford and Cambridge.[1]

The function of the universities during Mr. Curtis's period was twofold: to produce clerics for the state Church, and to give a veneer of polite learning to young gentlemen, few of whom had any intention of taking a degree.[2] Their function, Mr. Curtis rightly insists, was not thought to include research or the pursuit of new truths.[3] One or two dons, and some of the abler undergraduates, might have a spare-time interest in mathematics or science. But such studies were not the reason for coming to Oxford or Cambridge. In 1654, when Seth Ward claimed that 'since the universities came into those hands where now it is', they offered training in scientific subjects, he asked, 'Which of the nobility and gentry desire when they send

---

[1] Curtis, op. cit., pp. 249–50. See other criticisms of Mr. Curtis by Mrs. Simon, 'The Social Origins of Cambridge Students, 1603–1640' (*P. and P.*, no. 26, pp. 58–67).
[2] Of those Somerset men who matriculated at Oxford or Cambridge without intending to pursue a clerical career, only one in five took a degree (T. G. Barnes, *Somerset, 1625–1640*, 1961, p. 31).   [3] Curtis, op. cit., pp. 227–31, 259–60.

their sons hither that they should be set to chemistry or agriculture or mechanics? Their removal is from hence commonly in two or three years, to the Inns of Court, and the desire of their friends is not that they be engaged in those experimental things, but that their reason, fancy and carriage be improved by lighter institutions and exercises, that they may become rational and graceful speakers, and be of an acceptable behaviour in their counties.'[1]

The Church after the fifteen-eighties was becoming increasingly conservative, and increasingly linked to the royal government: so we should expect its influence to work against a serious interest in science.[2] But all that Church and government had to do, in order to prevent change in the universities, was to refrain from encouraging it themselves. As Mr. Costello has convincingly shown, the universities were enmeshed in a centuries-old scholastic synthesis. The schoolmen had been discredited since the Reformation: but this if anything increased the solitary eminence of Aristotle. 'The realm of knowledge', says Mr. Costello, 'was divided into four provinces (each province concerned with some phase of being): metaphysics (being in general), physics (being as qualified), mathematics (being as quantified), and cosmography (the being of this geographical world). The very neatness of such an arrangement concealed an intransigence, and seemed to excuse Cambridge dons, and too many other scholastic masters, from any obligation to rethink the old curriculum in terms of the busy findings of the new mathematics and the New Sciences.'[3] 'The seventeenth-century mind was heir to a system so over-systematized that its only escape was either to attempt a new synthesis by incorporating the new discoveries, to give up the struggle, or to branch off in a new direction. Some, like Suarez, did attempt restatement, but the result was only further bickering and confounded confusion. Others simply gave up and allowed scholasticism to become an empty form. A few branched out in new directions and found themselves in the modern world.'[4]

It would therefore have needed a major philosophical revolution to change the system, a revolution which would have been opposed by the hierarchy of the Church, and by the government. By its very failure to change, the system became more and more intransigent. The time, moreover, was ripe for new syntheses: Oxford and Cambridge, as John Hall pointed out, were lagging behind 'the

---

[1] [Seth Ward], *Vindiciae Academiarum* (1654), pp. 30, 49-50.

[2] See pp. 32-33 above.

[3] W. J. Costello, *The Scholastic Curriculum at early 17th century Cambridge* (Harvard U.P., 1958), p. 148. For Mr. Curtis's view of this work, which appeared too late for him to use, see his review in *Isis*, li. 112-13.

[4] Costello, op. cit., p. 11.

Jesuit Colleges and many transmarine universities'.[1] Leiden and Franeker in the republican Netherlands had shown the possibilities; Padua in republican Venice had moved with the times. But as the Laudian rulers of the Church and the rulers of the Stuart state felt more and more insecure, they became more and more suspicious of change of any sort. And they exercised effective control over the universities.

If we re-examine the evidence in the light of Mr. Costello's thesis, we may see things rather differently from Mr. Curtis. For the contemporary criticisms of Oxford and Cambridge all point in one direction. This is not a matter only of the well-known and possibly prejudiced strictures of Bacon, Hobbes, Milton, and Wallis. In 1583 Giordano Bruno thought Oxford was 'the widow of good learning in philosophy and pure mathematics'. Its doctors were doctors of grammar only.[2] 'Arithmetic, . . . geometry and astronomy . . . are now smally regarded in either' university, William Harrison said in 1587.[3] George Hakewill in 1627 noted the backwardness of Oxford in anatomy, botany, history, and Arabic.[4] Robert Burton said that degrees were awarded to those who 'have spent the usual number of years in chopping logic'.[5] A character in Davenant's *The Platonic Lovers* (1636) asked:

> Is there yet nothing new, to render benefit
> For human life? . . .
> Why do we build you Colleges?

Ever since Aristotle's death academics had done nothing but write comments on his works.[6]

William Oughtred, who went up to Cambridge in 1592, had to teach himself mathematics in his spare time.[7] For Hobbes (Oxford 1603–7) his scientific interests were a pleasing diversion from his academic studies.[8] Hobbes's contemporary, George Wither, learnt nothing from his Oxford tutor, and goes out of his way to tell us that when he acquired an interest in natural science he had to satisfy it for himself. The dons 'heap up a great multitude of words and

[1] J. Hall, *An Humble Motion* (1953), p. 28.
[2] Quoted by F. A. Yates, 'Giordano Bruno's Conflict with Oxford', *Journal of the Warburg and Courtauld Institutes*, ii. 232; cf. G. Bruno, *Cause, Principle and Unity* (translated by Jack Lindsay, 1962), p. 6. Cf. Sidney, quoted on p. 134 above.
[3] W. Harrison, *Description of England*, in R. Holinshed, *Chronicles* (1587), p. 150.
[4] Hakewill, *Apologie*, p. 275. Arabic was of use to mathematicians and scientists, as well as to Levant traders. Cf. p. 44 above.
[5] R. Burton, *Anatomy of Melancholy* (Everyman ed.), i. 327.
[6] Sir W. Davenant, *Dramatic Works* (1872), ii. 56.
[7] W. O[ughtred], *An Apologeticall Epistle*, Sig. A 4v, in *The Circles of Perfection*, translated by W. Forster (1632).   [8] See p. 310 below.

sayings', but do not 'with knowledge into practice go'.[1] William
Gascoigne (1612–44) told Oughtred in 1640 that he left Oxford
without knowing what a proposition in geometry meant.[2] Francis
Gardiner, writing to his son's Cambridge tutor in 1646, assumed
that geometry and arithmetic would be spare-time occupations
('his fancy turning that way', the father rather apologetically said):
he did not mention tutorial help with these subjects, though giving
specific instructions about logic, philosophy, Greek, and Hebrew.[3]
Matthew Robinson, who came up to Cambridge about the same
time, also had to pursue his interests in anatomy, astronomy,
meteorology, and natural history on his own and in his spare time.[4]

In the case of the few men of genius produced by pre-revolutionary Oxford and Cambridge, Osborn tells us, 'the least part of this
excellency came from their mother'. The practice of ordinary tutors,
he says, was to 'throw to their pupils the dry bones, and not the
marrow, of erudition'.[5] As an example of what Osborn meant,
Richard Hakluyt did not learn his cosmography at Oxford but from
his cousin the lawyer; though he lectured on the subject (probably
only to his own college) till 1582 or 1583, after he left it apparently
ceased to be taught until the Savilian chair of Astronomy was
founded in 1619.[6] Bishop Williams in 1638 noted the absence of
public encouragement for mathematics in Oxford or Cambridge.[7]
In fact Dee, William Gilbert, Wright, Hariot, Oughtred, Wallis,
Pell, as well as Harvey and Petty, all left the universities. To study
medicine, Mr. Curtis admits, men went to London or overseas.[8]
Licences to beg were issued in far greater numbers by late sixteenth-
century Oxford than licences in surgery.[9]

'Towardly and capable souls', said John Hall, 'staid men, of tried
and known abilities in their profession' were not 'allured . . . to stay
in the universities.' Their places were filled by 'drones'.[10] Edward
Wright threw up his fellowship at Caius in 1589, Lawrence Kemyis

---

[1] G. Wither, *Juvenilia* (Spenser Soc. reprint), i, pp. x–xiv, 189–90, 345–6. Mr.
Curtis quotes similar criticisms by Sir Humphrey Gilbert, the Earl of Essex, Lord
Herbert of Cherbury (op. cit., pp. 68, 127–8).

[2] Taylor, *Mathematical Practitioners*, p. 81.

[3] H. Cary, *Memorials of the Great Civil War in England* (1842), i. 152.

[4] Ed. J. E. B. Mayor, *Autobiography of Matthew Robinson* (1856), pp. 21, 26; cf.
p. 97.   [5] Osborn, *Miscellaneous Works* (1722), ii. 275–6.

[6] R. B. Parks, *Richard Hakluyt and the English Voyages*, pp. 61–62; J. N. L. Baker,
The History of Geography (1963), p. 120; contrast Curtis, op. cit., pp. 234–5.

[7] See pp. 53–54 above. The founders of English economics were also non-university men (W. Letwin, *The Origins of Scientific Econonomics*, 1963, pp. 83–86).

[8] Curtis, op. cit., pp. 153–4, 163; cf. *V.C.H. Cambridgeshire*, iii. 208.

[9] C. E. Mallet, *History of the University of Oxford*, ii (1924), p. 133.

[10] J. Hall, *An Humble Motion*. pp. 16–17, 28.

his at Balliol in 1582: the latter either because 'he discovered that the demand for mathematical tutors was slight, or else his adventurous soul grew weary of the interminable theological debates of his colleagues'.[1] Hall's point could also be illustrated from the career of Nathanael Carpenter (1589–1628), a Fellow of Exeter whom it is at first sight surprising that Mr. Curtis does not mention as a favourer of the new learning in Oxford. For Carpenter was an anti-Aristotelean exponent of the new astronomy, who wrote the 'one work of outstanding merit' on geography which came from Oxford in the seventeenth or eighteenth century. He was a proponent of navigation and sea-voyages as necessary for 'the promotion of religion and sciences'; an admirer of Ralegh; an early advocate of freedom of scientific investigation and discussion, favourably quoted by Hakewill; a keen Saxonist. A friend of Briggs and Hues, Carpenter studied not only their works but also those of Leonard Digges, Arthur Hopton, Sir Humphrey and William Gilbert, Wright, Blundeville, Brerewood, Verstegan, and Purchas. He almost personifies one theme of this book. Yet Carpenter would not have fitted into Mr. Curtis's picture. For he complained that he was not advanced by Oxford, and he left to become chaplain to Ussher in Ireland. This was no doubt because of Carpenter's religious and political views. He was so fierce a Calvinist that his *Achitophel, or the Picture of a Wicked Politician* (1629) was called in and the anti-Arminian passages were suppressed. In 1627 he had preached three sermons, very critical of kings, which 'were very much applauded by all the scholars that heard them, and were by them most eagerly desired to be printed'.[2]

Hall's own criticism of the universities is familiar: 'Where have we anything to do with mechanic chemistry? . . . Where is there an examination and consecution of experiments? . . . Where have we constant reading from either quick or dead anatomies, or any ocular demonstration of herbs?'[3] John Webster, who also advocated the teaching of chemistry, might equally be cited; or any number of other Interregnum critics.[4] Gerrard Winstanley was not being

[1] H. W. C. Davis, *A History of Balliol College* (revised ed., 1963), p. 85.

[2] N. Carpenter, *Geographie* (1625), esp. pp. 75–115; Hakewill, *An Apologie*, p. 310; A. Wood, *Athenae Oxoniensis*, ii. 422; Foster Watson, *The Beginning of the Teaching of Modern Subjects in England*, pp. 117–22, 136–7, 261, 283; Taylor, *Late Tudor and Early Stuart Geography*, pp. 136–7; R. F. Jones, *Ancients and Moderns*, pp. 68–69; P. Miller, *The New England Mind: the 17th Century*, p. 500; Judson, *The Crisis of the Constitution*, pp. 313–14, 322–3; Baker, op. cit., pp. 1–14. In December 1649 Roger Williams was trying to borrow John Winthrop's copy of Carpenter's *Geographie* (*Massachusetts Historical Society Collections*, New Series, vii. 277). See also pp. 54, 66 above.

[3] J. Hall, *An Humble Motion*, p. 27.

[4] See pp. 119–23 above.

exceptionally radical when he said that 'the secrets of the creation have been locked up under the traditional, parrot-like speaking from the universities'.[1] Thomas Hall's reply to Webster hardly supports Mr. Curtis's view that science was widely taught at Oxford and Cambridge. For this defender of the universities thought that Webster's advice to scholars 'to leave their libraries and fall to laboratories, putting their hands to the coals and furnace' was a 'short cut to bring men to the Devil'.[2]

Isaac Barrow, who came up to Cambridge in 1647, spoke of mathematics then as 'neglected by all and unknown, even on the outward surface, by most'.[3] He first introduced the new philosophy into Cambridge as a Fellow of Trinity after 1649: before 1645 Wallis had never heard of the new philosophy.[4] Unkindest of all, even Godfrey Goodman, the near-papist Bishop of Gloucester who had been Hakewill's opponent, wrote in 1653 of Cambridge that 'whereas before your studying of philosophy did only serve for your disputations and your keeping of acts for your degrees; now I could wish that they might tend to some practice whereby they might be more useful'. So he proposed to give the university his collection of mathematical instruments, optic glasses, herbals 'and some things which belong to chemistry'.[5]

I have said nothing of the descriptions of undergraduate boorishness and ignorance made by Burleigh, William Harrison, Bruno, Travers, Sir Thomas Knyvett, Robert Burton, John Earle, Henry Peacham, and Sir Simonds D'Ewes;[6] nor of the descriptions of the drunkenness, idleness, or other inadequacies of dons by Wither, John Winthrop, and Lady Harley.[7] This is the sort of generalizing gossip of which Mr. Curtis is sceptical. Arthur Wilson, who said he had never drunk so much in his life as at Oxford in the sixteen-thirties, 'with some of the greatest bachelors of divinity there', is not

---

[1] Ed. Sabine, *The Works of Gerrard Winstanley*, p. 271; cf. pp. 214, 238, 474-5.

[2] T. Hall, *Histrio-Mastix* (1655), quoted by Taylor, *Mathematical Practitioners*, p. 96.

[3] P. H. Osmond, *Isaac Barrow* (1944), pp. 38-39.

[4] S. E. Morison, *The Founding of Harvard College* (Harvard University Press, 1935), p. 77. Cf. Sir William Temple, quoted on p. 117 above.

[5] G. Goodman, *The Two Great Mysteries of Christian Religion* (1653), Sig. a 2.

[6] Strype, *Annals of the Reformation* (1824), III, part i, pp. 709-10; Holinshed, *Chronicles* (1587), pp. 149-50; J. B. Mullinger, *The University of Cambridge, 1535-1625* (1884), pp. 263-4, 394-5; ed. B. Schofield, *The Knyvett Letters (1620-1644)* (1949), p. 20; Burton, *Anatomy of Melancholy* (Everyman ed.), i. pp. 327-30; J. Earle, *Microcosmographie* (1628), 'A Young Gentleman of the University'; D'Ewes, *Autobiography*, i. 141-2; cf. *V.C.H. Cambridgeshire*, iii. 440.

[7] Wither, *Juvenilia*, i. 186-7; H. C. Porter, *Reformation and Reaction in Tudor Cambridge* (1958), p. 255; *Letters of Lady Brilliana Harley*, pp. 54-55.

the most reliable witness.[1] But perhaps we should pay more attention to the parent who in a private letter of 1646 to William Sancroft assumed that 'most tutors' at Cambridge were idle.[2] More too might be said about the purchase and sale of scholarships, degrees, and fellowships, and the possibility of obtaining places by court favour,[3] which must have had an effect on academic standards which can hardly be over-emphasized. This at least is suggested by the numerous efforts of Parliament to check such abuses.[4]

II

In establishing his new view of the universities in the early seventeenth-century, Mr. Curtis cites the 'Directions for a Student' attributed to Richard Holdsworth. The attribution is not absolutely certain, and the manuscript presents difficulties for Mr. Curtis's thesis. Books published in 1646 and 1647 are recommended in the 'Directions', though Holdsworth had no connexion with Cambridge after 1643. He ceased indeed to be a college tutor in 1626, and may have ceased to reside two years earlier, when he was appointed to a living in London.[5] No scientific books published before 1638 are included in the list of extra-curricular reading which the document gives.[6] It should therefore be used with caution as evidence for teaching methods in Cambridge before the civil war.

[1] F. Peck, *Desiderata Curiosa* (1779), p. 470. Cf. *Memoirs of the Family of Guise* (ed. G. Davies, Camden Soc., 1917), pp. 116–17, and further references there, for excessive drinking at Oxford.

[2] Cary, *Memorials of the Great Civil War*, i. 151–3, 385.

[3] Holinshed, *Chronicles*, p. 149; Strype, *Life of Whitgift* (1822), i. 149–50, 610–11; Strype, *Annals*, III, part ii, pp. 199, 299; Burton, *Anatomy*, i. 327–8; (Anon.) *The Curates Conference* (1641), in *Harleian Miscellany* (1744–56), i. 481; J. Webster, *Complete Works* (ed. F. L. Lucas, 1927), ii. 244; Peck, *Desiderata Curiosa*, pp. 82–83, 170–1; G. B. Tatham, *The Puritans in Power* (1913), pp. 97–100; G. Soden, *Godfrey Goodman, Bishop of Gloucester* (1953), pp. 56, 388; Mullinger and Mallet, *passim*.

[4] Mullinger, op. cit., pp. 268–9 (Bill of 1576–7, vetoed by Elizabeth; passed in 1589); *Cambridge Characteristics in the 17th Century* (1867), pp. 36–37 (unsuccessful petition in 1625); *The University of Cambridge from . . . 1626 to the decline of the Platonist Movement* (1911), pp. 98–99 (unsuccessful Bill in 1629). Cf. Curtis, op. cit., p. 53.

[5] Holdsworth dated letters from Gresham College on 11 February and 16 June 1631 (information kindly supplied by Mr. F. P. White, Keeper of the Records, St. John's College, Cambridge) and again on 11 May and 8 June 1632 (Add. MSS. 6193, ff. 157–9).

[6] Curtis, op. cit., p. 133. The 'Directions' are printed in H. F. Fletcher's *The Intellectual Development of John Milton* (Illinois U.P.), ii (1961), pp. 623–4, and discussed at length in the text. Unfortunately this volume came to my notice too late for me to be able to make full use of it. The 'Directions' were treated much more cautiously by S. E. Morison, who first drew attention to them in 1935 (*The Founding of Harvard College*, esp. 62–77). He noted the absence of even the most elementary mathematical or scientific studies, apart from Aristotelean physics.

Nor is this all. Even if the document could be used for this period, we must ask, How typical was Holdsworth? First and foremost, although Mr. Curtis does not mention the fact, he was a Gresham Professor from 1629 to 1637. It is hardly surprising that he should have carried some Gresham methods back with him to Cambridge, and should have thought it necessary to apologize for the emphasis on Aristotle which the curriculum forced on him.[1] The books by Comenius and Bacon must have been added to his reading-list after he had ceased to be a tutor. Secondly, despite his adherence to the King in the civil war, Holdsworth (son and brother-in-law of Puritans) had been radical enough in the thirties to co-operate with three future Independents, Thomas Goodwin, Philip Nye, and Henry Burton, in puffing John Dury.[2] Holdsworth protested against one of the canons of 1640, and as late as December 1640 the Scots still thought of him as a possible supporter of Presbyterianism.[3] He refused a bishopric in 1641, and was enough of a Puritan to be nominated to the Westminster Assembly of Divines. So Holdsworth is very far from typical of Oxford and Cambridge tutors. There is a striking contrast between the Instructions alleged to be his and those drawn up by James Duport. The latter are exactly what the traditional view of pre-civil war Oxford and Cambridge would lead us to expect, though in fact they may well date from the sixteen-fifties.[4]

The example of Holdsworth cannot therefore be given the significance which Mr. Curtis seeks to attach to it. His other evidence, interesting though it is, tells us nothing new about scientific teaching in the universities. There were Ramists in Cambridge in the late sixteenth century: Mr. Curtis's examples show how many of them were Puritans, like William Gouge and (at Oxford) John Rainolds. Individual fellows of colleges became eminent in the scientific world, usually after resigning their fellowships, like Hakluyt and Edward Wright. Others like Richard Madox had social contacts with London scientists.[5] Some college libraries had some scientific books. Then as now undergraduates were more up to date in their interests than most tutors. The notebooks of Brian Twyne, active Fellow of Corpus Christi College, Oxford, from 1605 to 1623, 'show that he kept abreast of current developments in mathematics,

[1] Curtis, op. cit., p. 112.

[2] G. Westin, *Negotiations about Church Unity, 1629-34* (Uppsala Universitets Årsskrift, Band i, 1932), p. 207. Other signatories, all Puritans, included Richard Sibbes, Daniel Featley, Stephen Marshall, John Davenport, John White, Samuel Ward, Thomas Taylor, Cornelius Burges. See also pp. 56, 58 above.

[3] Ward, *Lives of the Gresham Professors*, p. 58; R. Baillie, *Letters and Journals* (1775), i, 220. Baillie thought Holdsworth 'famous for learning'.

[4] Curtis, op. cit., pp. 113-14.

[5] Ibid., pp. 118-19, 251, 234-5, 243-5, 237-9.

astronomy, cosmography, and navigation'. (Twyne's interest in science may be due to the fact that his father was a physician.) But Mr. Curtis's suggestion that these notes were 'prepared for use in tutoring' is pure conjecture. 'The most conclusive bit of evidence' for the conjecture, in Mr. Curtis's opinion, is a note by Twyne that he lent a multiplication and division table 'to Mr. Elyott', and the fact that there was a Benjamin Elliott at Corpus during Twyne's 18 years as active fellow there.[1]

On evidence like this—one tutor's notes (ignoring for the moment the problem of dating), the social contacts of some others, the books owned by and the subsequent interests of a few dons and undergraduates—it would be easy to argue that Marxism was being taught to undergraduates at Oxford and Cambridge in the nineteen-thirties. Mr. Curtis quotes via Professor Johnson some interesting subjects for disputations at Oxford between 1576 and 1611, which at least recognize the existence of Copernicus and Gilbert.[2] But do these prove any more than the presence of questions on Marxism in Oxford schools papers today? (It is noteworthy, moreover, that no examples are cited after 1611.) Such teaching of modern subjects as there was in Oxford resulted not from the university's action, but from the chairs endowed by Sir Henry Savile and staffed by professors from Gresham College; from the lectureship in natural philosophy founded by Sir William Sedley, and that in anatomy founded by the Londoner Richard Tomlins. Similarly Camden and Lord Brooke forced history upon the two universities. The first Camden Professor at Oxford had quarrels with the authorities about the scope of his subject; the holder of Brooke's chair at Cambridge was hounded out by the Laudians. When Briggs came to Oxford as Savilian Professor he realized that he was the thin end of a wedge which he hoped to drive in further; and that similar influences were needed at Cambridge.[3]

The next blow on the wedge came from the Parliamentary Commissioners. Mr. Curtis seems to me to miss the significance of their activities in opening a door to science in Oxford. Indeed, he regards the Parliamentary visitations of the universities as 'a crippling blow', which 'enforced rigid conformity to the religious systems then in favour'.[4] This (in my opinion) mistaken belief may explain, though it can hardly excuse, his use of evidence drawn from the sixteen-fifties to illustrate the state of science in Oxford and Cambridge before the civil war.[5] Sprat's remarks

[1] Ibid., pp. 121–2, 230.   [2] Ibid., p. 233.
[3] Ibid., pp. 117–18—contrast p. 246, where Mr. Curtis seems to me to miss Briggs's point.
[4] Ibid., p. 277.   [5] Ibid., Chapter IX, *passim*, and pp. 274–5.

about the universities' contribution to science relate, though the future bishop was too tactful to mention this, to the Parliamentarian epoch.[1] His failure to appreciate this makes Mr. Curtis miss the significance of the controversies of the sixteen-fifties about university education, and makes him less than fair to John Webster.[2] It is true that 'Oxford had become by the 1650's a centre of scientific research', but it had become this very recently indeed. It is true of the fifties that 'the universities, despite their statutes, were teaching the results of recent findings in mathematics and science'.[3] But the statement is not true of the period before the end of the civil war, or at least its truth has not been demonstrated, and the mass of contemporary evidence seems to be against it.

Mr. Curtis's failure (as I see it) to appreciate the significance of the Parliamentarian purge is connected with his interpretation of the preceding period. The century between Reformation and Revolution saw constitutional changes in the universities which are linked with the rise in importance of the colleges. The strength of medieval Oxford, says its historian, had lain in the halls, 'self-governed, un-endowed, and unincorporated'.[4] They were relatively democratic; the colleges, which catered especially for the sons of the gentry, were at first small and privileged communities. Many of the halls were Puritan centres in the sixteenth and seventeenth centuries. They were also more hospitable to intellectual innovation than most colleges. At Gloucester Hall the Principal from 1626 to 1647 was the Calvinist Degory Wheare, first Camden Reader in History and John Pym's friend. Wheare's appointment as Reader seems to have been due to Thomas Allen, Oxford's solitary mathematician of eminence until the arrival of Briggs. Allen had resigned a fellowship at Trinity to transfer to the more congenial atmosphere of Gloucester Hall. He was a protégé first of Leicester, then of Northumberland, a friend of Hariot (formerly of St. Mary's Hall), with whom he corresponded about the comet of 1618, and (like Wheare) a supporter of Hakewill.[5] Thomas Hobbes was an undergraduate of Magdalen Hall, where he indulged in extra-curricular reading of astronomy and cosmography.[6] But the Hall drew its undergraduates especially from Buckinghamshire, a radical county since the days of the

[1] Curtis, op. cit., pp. 227–8, 248–9, 257–8.

[2] Ibid., pp. 232, 246, 274, See pp. 115–25 above.

[3] Ibid., pp. 260, 249–50.

[4] Mallet, op. cit., ii. 287.

[5] Aubrey, *Brief Lives*, i. 26–27; Stephens, *Thomas Hariot*, p. 138; Hakewill, *Apologie*, Sig. c 2. For Wheare, see pp. 176–7 above; for Allen, p. 144. Sir Kenelm Digby was at Gloucester Hall.

[6] T. Hobbes, *The Life of Mr. Thomas Hobbes of Malmesbury* (1680), pp. 33–34, quoted by S. I. Mintz, *The Hunting of Leviathan* (1962), pp. 2–3.

Lollards. It may have been his experience of this 'nest of Puritans'[1] that made the sage of Malmesbury think that the universities turned out too many seditious Puritans: Christopher Guise's tutor there was 'disaffected to the present government' in the sixteen-thirties.[2]

The revisions of the statutes of Oxford and Cambridge, from Cardinal Pole and Whitgift to Laud, restricted university democracy by curtailing the power of proctors and fellows, bringing the Halls under control, and concentrating authority, both in the university and in the colleges themselves, in the heads of houses. The latter were often themselves royal nominees—'those little living idols or monuments of monarchy', a Harringtonian Fellow of Durham College was to call them.[3] This constitutional change had intellectual consequences. The best that even the kindly Fuller could find to say of 'a good Master of a College' was that 'his learning, if beneath eminency, is far above contempt'. Fuller took it for granted that the Head of a House would be expected to make 'a worthless man Fellow' if urged to do so by the court. 'Oftentimes' Masters 'make only dunces Fellows', without even the excuse of royal pressure.[4] The author of *The History of the University of Cambridge*, though disappointed of a fellowship himself,[5] was hardly a prejudiced enemy of the universities.

In the brief radical interlude of Edward VI's reign the royal commission of 1549 tried to stimulate medical education at Cambridge, and made mathematics the subject of the first year of the arts course, relegating grammar to schools. But Edward's reign was as exceptional in intellectual as in religious history. The first Elizabethan revision of the Edwardian statutes reinstated an arts course of rhetoric, logic, and philosophy; Whitgift's statutes of 1570 made no mention of mathematics at all. At Oxford the statutes of 1565 and 1586 reimposed the old subjects and authorities. The Laudian statutes summed up this conservative trend. The bishops in 1584 opposed the making of any provision for research in the universities.[6] It is to the actions of their enemies that we must look for intellectual innovations.

Emmanuel College was founded by a Puritan for Puritans: from the start it had strong scientific leanings. Timothy Bright, medical writer, inventor of shorthand, protégé of Sidney and Walsingham,

[1] F. P. Verney, *Memoirs of the Verney Family during the Civil War*, i (1892), pp. 118–19. Ralph Verney was taught astronomy, chronology, and geography by his Magdalen Hall tutor in the late sixteen-thirties. Walter Charleton and Thomas Sydenham were at Magdalen Hall. So was John Bidle, the Socinian.
[2] Ed. G. Davies, *Memoirs of the Family of Guise* (Camden Soc., 1917), p. 116.
[3] W. Sprigge, *A Modest Plea for an Equal Commonwealth* (1659), p. 45.
[4] T. Fuller, *The Holy State* (1841), pp. 93–95.
[5] I owe this point to Mr. Curtis.
[6] Mullinger, *The University of Cambridge, 1535–1625*, pp. 306–9.

was a witness to its foundation statutes. His brother was a Fellow.[1] Its
first Master was Lawrence Chaderton, the earliest exponent of
Ramus's logic at Cambridge.[2] Chaderton was a keen botanist as
well as a member of the Puritan delegation at the Hampton Court
Conference. Preston, Chaderton's successor, had originally con-
templated a medical career, and scientific images and metaphors
abound in his sermons.[3] The fourth Master was Richard Holds-
worth, who helped John Wallis to find his way to mathematics.
The Cambridge Platonists, of whom all but Henry More were
Emmanuel men, neatly illustrate the fusion of Puritanism, Par-
liamentarianism, and science. Emmanuel men in our story include
Jeremiah Horrocks, the younger Peter Chamberlen, Phineas Pett,
John Bainbridge, William Bedell, Samuel Ward, Anthony Burges,
John Stoughton, Ralph Cudworth, and John Bastwick: though
Bastwick left for Padua to study medicine. Of the university members of the group which began to meet at Gresham College in 1645,
four came from Oxford halls (Wilkins and Goddard from Magdalen
Hall, Merrett and Haak from Gloucester Hall); Wallis and Foster
were Emmanuel men, Ent from Puritan Sidney Sussex. The only
other college represented was Gresham's old college, Caius, with its
strong medical tradition.[4]

So before 1642 there was a cleavage within the academic ranks.
The university establishment was solidly conservative. The university Parliamentary seats became pocket boroughs for Charles I.[5]
There was probably less support for Parliament during the civil
war from dons than from any other section of the population, except
the paid officers of the Church courts.[6] But at Oxford the halls, and to
a lesser extent Wadham,[7] were more forward-looking; at Cambridge

[1] W. J. Carlton, *Timothe Bright*, pp. 41–43; for Bright see pp. 69, 133 above.
[2] Howell, *Logic and Rhetoric in England, 1500–1700*, pp. 179, 222.
[3] See my *Puritanism and Revolution* (1958), p. 239.
[4] D. Stimson, 'Comenius and the Invisible College', *Isis*, xxiii. 378. Contrast
Curtis, op. cit., pp. 248–9. Emmanuel became the largest Cambridge college under
Preston. Its entry was not to be so high again until 1890 (J. A. Venn, *The Entries
in the Colleges of the University of Cambridge, 1544–1906*, 1908).
[5] M. B. Rex, *University Representation in England, 1604–1690* (1954), pp. 57, 97.
[6] Cf. T. May, *History of the Parliament of England* (1647), iii. 79; S. Fisher, *The
Rusticks Alarme to the Rabbies* (1660), in *The Testimony of Truth Exalted* (1679), pp.
579–80; Hobbes, *Behemoth*, in *English Works*, vi. 347–8; L. Hutchinson, *Memoirs of
the Life of Colonel Hutchinson* (ed. C. H. Firth, 1885), i. 114–15; Clarendon, *History of the
Rebellion and Civil Wars in England* (1888), ii. 469.
[7] Wadham drew its undergraduates from the west-country clothing areas. One
of its original statutes begins 'in all matters of education nothing is better than
practice'. The Fellows were not compelled to take orders; they were subject to a
year's probation on appointment, and to a limit of years on their tenure.

Puritan Emmanuel and Sidney Sussex and to a lesser extent Caius and perhaps Puritan Christ's.[1] There were a few tutors in other colleges with advanced ideas, mostly Puritans, who no doubt tried to introduce new methods and subjects into their teaching; there were no doubt many undergraduates who responded. But only after the civil war, and with outside support, did the hitherto repressed minority triumph. All the members of the Oxford halls acknowledged Parliament's authority at the Visitation, whereas more than half the Fellows of colleges were expelled for refusing to submit. At Cambridge eleven of the new heads of houses under the Commonwealth came from Emmanuel.[2]

'Mathematics, which had before been a pleasing diversion, was now to be my serious study.' The words which Wallis applied to his appointment to the Savilian chair of Geometry fit the universities as a whole during the Interregnum.[3] The Commissioners at Oxford put an end to the requirement of celibacy in heads of houses, and introduced lay heads. They tried to reduce the power of the oligarchy, even after they had introduced their own nominees to controlling positions. (A petition from 'divers' of Oxford had complained to the Long Parliament in 1642 that the Laudian statutes illegally took away the liberty of Convocation and Congregation, whilst increasing the power of the Chancellor and heads of houses.)[4] The Commissioners proposed the institution of fellowships terminable (as at Wadham) at stated periods, in order to prevent men becoming 'drones'. College electors were sworn to nominate none to fellowships who were suspected of bribery.[5] Wallis, the Long Parliament's cryptographer, who had given evidence against Laud at his trial,[6] became a professor; Wilkins, later Cromwell's brother-in-law, became Warden of Wadham, with Sydenham and Sprat among his Fellows. Goddard, Cromwell's physician, became Warden of Merton. Petty was Professor of Anatomy and Vice-Principal of Brasenose. Seth Ward as Professor of Astronomy after 1649 revived the reputation of the subject: his chair and that of Physic received handsome augmentations. The whole intellectual atmosphere

[1] Professor Morison plausibly attributes the exceptional interest in astronomy and perspective shown in the 1634 regulations of Sidney Sussex College to its Puritan Master, Samuel Ward (*The Founding of Harvard College*, p. 76; cf. Curtis, op. cit., pp. 243–4). Books in Sidney Sussex library first interested Seth Ward in mathematics (W. Pope, *Life of Seth Ward*, 1697, p. 27). The isolated defender of the circulation of the blood in Oxford was a Sidney Sussex man. (I owe this information to Mr. N. Tyacke.)

[2] Ed. M. Burrows, *The Register of the Visitors of the University of Oxford* (Camden Soc., 1881), pp. 564–71; Mullinger, *The University of Cambridge, 1535–1625*, p. 314.

[3] P. Allen, 'Scientific Studies in the English Universities of the 17th century' *J.H.I.* x. 231 and *passim*.   [4] *Leybourne-Popham MSS.* (H.M.C.), pp. 4–5.

[5] Mallet, op. cit., ii. 372, 387, 393–4.   [6] Prynne, *Canterburies Doome*, p. 73.

changed. By 1654 Ward could claim that, though Oxford respected Aristotle, it did not insist that he should be studied.[1]

Contemporaries believed that equally important changes took place in the social composition of undergraduates. Balliol admitted far fewer Fellow-Commoners between 1640 and 1670. Many men from poorer and socially less distinguished families managed to get to the universities, thanks to newly endowed scholarships. Oxford 'flourished in number, but few nobility, gentry also': they were replaced by 'the sons of upstart gentlemen', and by 'men very mean and poor at their first coming'. Yet royalists like Wood and Clarendon had to admit that Interregnum Oxford 'yielded a harvest of extraordinary good and sound knowledge of all parts of learning'.[2] And to a lesser extent the same was true of Cambridge, though the changes there were less radical than at Oxford since they were made in the period of Presbyterian supremacy.[3] But the Restoration brought back the nobility and gentry, the ruling oligarchies and gowns.[4] By the end of the century 'the best days of the Halls had passed away' at Oxford.[5]

It seems to me, therefore, quite illegitimate to illustrate the condition of Oxford and Cambridge before the civil war by evidence from the fifties, 'since the universities came into those hands where now it is'. It also seems to me mistaken to deny the close connexion between Puritans and the foward-looking minority inside the universities (Carpenter, Holdsworth, Emmanuel, the halls).[6] It seems to me wrong to underestimate the powerful forces within the universities which opposed fundamental changes. These forces used government support to check Puritanism and self-government, and to prevent any modernization of the curriculum. The ideas which mobilized men for revolution came largely from Puritans, with useful support from the scientists; they were directed against (among other things) the 'inquisitorious and tyrannical duncery' of the bishops and consequent intellectual frustration. This struggle had its counterpart inside Oxford and Cambridge: only the Puritans and scientists could never have won there without support from outside.

[1] Pope, op. cit., p. 23; [Ward], *Vindiciae Academiarum*, pp. 32, 58–60.

[2] Davis, op. cit., p. 101; A. Wood, *Life and Times*, i. 149, 299, 301; Tatham, op. cit., p. 194; Clarendon, *History of the Rebellion*, iv. 259; cf. Sprat, *History of the Royal Society*, p. 53; R. H. Latham, *Life of Sydenham*, prefixed to Greenhill's translation of Sydenham's *Works* (1848), i, pp. xxi–xxii.

[3] *V.C.H. Cambridgeshire*, iii. 201, 440, 467. Mr. Curtis agrees that 'the situation improved even at Cambridge' 'shortly after' the sixteen-thirties; but he does not give the credit for the improvement to the Parliamentarians (op. cit., p. 246).

[4] Hair, which Laud had kept cut short, was worn long in Roundhead Oxford.

[5] Mallet, op. cit., ii. 299.

[6] Curtis, op. cit., pp. 248, 287–8.

INDEX